Judicial Power and the Charter

Judicial Power and the Charter:

Canada and the Paradox of Liberal Constitutionalism

Christopher P. Manfredi

University of Oklahoma Press : Norman and London

Published by the University of Oklahoma Press, Norman, Publishing Division of the University, by arrangement with McClelland & Stewart Inc., Toronto. First printing of the University of Oklahoma Press edition, 1993.

Library of Congress Cataloging-in-Publication Data

Manfredi, Christopher P.
   Judicial power and the charter: Canada and the paradox of liberal constitutionalism / by Christopher P. Manfredi.
   p.   cm.
Includes index.
ISBN 0-8061-2527-6

1. Judicial power – Canada.   2. Judicial review – Canada.   3. Canada – Constututional law – Interpretation and construction.   4. Judicial power – United States.   5. Judicial review – United States.   6. United States – Constitutional law – Interpretation and construction.   I. Title.

KE4775.M36 1993
347.73'12 – dc20
[347.30712]   92-50725
                                                                                    CIP

Typesetting by M&S

Printed and bound in Canada

CONTENTS

ACKNOWLEDGEMENTS

Like all books, the present volume could not have been completed without the assistance of others. I owe my initial debt to Ralph A. Rossum, who first introduced me to the study of law and politics at the Claremont Graduate School. The ideas developed in the book also found inspiration in conversations with several friends and colleagues, particularly Rainer Knopff and Ted Morton. Peter McCormick, Jennifer Smith, and Rob Vipond assessed the manuscript for McClelland & Stewart, and their constructive criticism contributed to a much better book. Finally, Michael Harrison, Richard Tallman, and Peter Buck ably guided the manuscript through the editing and production process at McClelland & Stewart.

Much of the work on this book was undertaken while I was supported by the Canada Research Fellowship program of the Social Sciences and Humanities Research Council of Canada. I was also fortunate to receive a small grant from the Council's pilot program on Law and Social Issues in Canada, as well as a grant from the Faculty of Graduate Studies and Research at McGill University. The research funds made available by these grants allowed me to employ several able research assistants: Heather Hanson, Robin Fitzgerald, Laila Wolfish, Susan Dalton, Gayle Noble, and Natalie Amar. Without their help, this book would have been much more difficult to complete. Finally, Michael Lusztig read and commented on the entire manuscript. Naturally, I remain solely responsible for the book's content.

Some of my previously published work has been adapted for use in this book. I gratefully acknowledge permission to incorporate material from the following publications: "*Re Lavigne and Ontario Public Service Employees Union*: Public Administration and Remedial Decree Litigation Under the Charter of Rights and Freedoms," *Canadian Public Administration,* 34 (1991), pp. 395-416; "Fundamental Justice in the Supreme Court of Canada: Decisions Under S.7 of the *Charter of Rights and Freedoms*," *American Journal of Comparative Law,* 38 (1990), pp. 653-82; "The Use of United States Decisions By The Supreme Court of Canada Under the Charter of Rights and Freedoms," *Canadian Journal of Political Science,* 23, 3 (1990), pp. 499-518; "Adjudication, Policy-making and the Supreme Court of Canada: Lessons From The Experience of the United States," *Canadian Journal of Political Science,* 22, 2 (1989), pp. 313-35.

INTRODUCTION

This book concerns the relationship between judicial power and liberal constitutionalism. In particular, it concerns one of the more problematic aspects of that relationship: the use of judicial power to review and to nullify or modify the policies enacted by democratically accountable decision-makers. Judicial power in this form is problematic because of the ambiguity surrounding its legitimacy within liberal democratic theory. On the one hand, judicial review is a positive element of liberal democracy, since it allows courts to perform the important counter-majoritarian function of safeguarding individual rights and liberties by enforcing constitutional limits on legislative and executive power. In this sense, judicial review is one of those "auxiliary precautions" that James Madison (probably the single most important framer of the U.S. Constitution) argued are necessary to ensure that liberal democracy does not degenerate into tyranny.[1] On the other hand, judicial review taken too far can become an anti-democratic power, wielded by courts to alter the fundamental character of a nation's constitution without significant popular participation or even public awareness. Left unchecked, judicial power poses the same threat to liberal democracy as do other forms and uses of political power.

The examination undertaken in this book of this relationship between judicial power and liberal constitutionalism focuses on the Supreme Court of Canada's interpretation and application of the Canadian Charter of Rights and Freedoms. The Charter's impact has been so noticeable, and has occurred in such a compressed period of time, that it clearly illuminates the tension between judicial review and liberal constitutionalism which serves as the subject of this study. To some degree, of course, the issues and themes explored in this book are familiar ones. In *The Supreme Court and Constitutional Democracy* (1984), for example, John Agresto argued on the basis of the American experience that modern judicial power poses a special threat to constitutional democracy when it becomes "active and unchecked in its ability to be the creator, the designer, of new social policy."[2] According to Agresto, the proactive use of judicial power creates an "imperial" judiciary that is exceedingly dangerous to liberal democracy. One of this book's objectives is to determine the extent to which the 1982 enactment of the Charter of Rights and Freedoms carries with it the same danger.

The argument of this book is also offered as an alternative to two perspectives that dominate contemporary discussions of constitutional rights and judicial review in Canada, each of which is in its own way hostile to liberal constitutionalism. The first of these perspectives, which is associated with both communitarian political thought and the Critical Legal Studies movement, argues that the

9

predominantly individualistic nature of liberal democratic "rights," as well as the conservative character of judges, means that judicial enforcement of the Charter will inevitably constitute a serious impediment to progressive social change. Among Canadian commentators, this view is shared to varying degrees by Patrick Monahan, Andrew Petter, Allan Hutchinson, and Michael Mandel.[3] In his book-length treatment of the Charter, for example, Mandel argues that the "legalized politics" created by the Charter is "a defence mechanism developed to preserve the status quo of social power from the threats posed to it by . . . the expansion of the suffrage, the deep involvement of the state in the economy, and the increasing tendency to malfunction of Western industrial economies."[4] Legalized politics, according to Mandel, provides "abstract legitimation for a social system whose concrete benefits are diminishing." In Mandel's view, the principal political task of the post-Charter era is to make legalized politics "wither away" by challenging the authority of courts and by strengthening democracy as he understands it.[5]

In contrast to Mandel's denigration of legalized politics, the second prominent perspective found in post-Charter discussions of judicial power in Canada celebrates rights-based judicial review and is profoundly sceptical about the capacity of popularly controlled institutions and decision-making processes to produce just and progressive policy outcomes. The political process inadequately performs this task, according to this view, because it systematically excludes certain groups and because political decision-makers are inevitably myopic. One of the leading Canadian proponents of this view claims that constitutional review of legislation by courts provides a "means by which individuals and groups, who traditionally have not had much influence in the process of politics, can now make their voices heard."[6] As Dale Gibson argues, the "shifting winds of social, political, and technological change" create an important demand for legal and political reform. Legislators have only a limited capacity to meet this demand because of time constraints, the absence of adequate incentives, and a lack of legal expertise. Moreover, asserts Gibson, legislators have no role to play in the development of constitutional law, which has become the principal vehicle for meeting these demands for change. "The demanding task of putting legal flesh on the Charter's bones," writes Gibson, "is the sole responsibility of judicial law-makers."[7] Consequently, this perspective enthusiastically embraces judicial social engineering and seeks to elaborate theories of constitutional interpretation that can justify using the Charter to achieve particular social policy goals. Perhaps the best example of an attempt to put this theory of judicial power into practice has been the strategy adopted by the Canadian women's movement to use constitutional litigation to advance its policy agenda.[8]

Of these two views of judicial power, the results-oriented jurisprudence of the judicial social engineering school poses perhaps the greatest threat to liberal constitutional democracy. Indeed, to the extent that the Critical Legal Studies movement debunks the myth of judicial infallibility, it serves as an uncommon ally for critiques of judicial power grounded in an entirely different political philosophy. The problem with judicial social engineering, in either its politically conservative or liberal forms, is that the attempt to correct the policy errors of democratic institutions through litigation and adjudication risks undermining the capacity for self-government on which liberal democracy ultimately depends. "The strongest argument against judicial review as an undemocratic power," argues the distinguished American constitutional historian Leonard Levy, is that to

> resolv[e] issues, in the judicial arena, even those issues concerning minority rights or personal liberty, is to lull the people into apathy on matters that are fundamentally their concern. Comforted by the notion that courts will take care of personal and minority rights, the people are effectively deprived of the inestimable benefit of vindicating self-government by taking sober second thought.[9]

As Peter Russell warned in 1982, any significant shift in "policy-making authority . . . to the courts" can produce "a further flight from politics, a deepening disillusionment with the procedures of representative government and government by discussion as means of resolving fundamental questions of political justice."[10] Too great a reliance on the private processes of litigation can both exacerbate social conflict and enervate public discussion of important political questions. It is with problems such as these in mind that this book is written.

Liberal Constitutionalism and the Birth of the Charter

Liberal constitutionalism emerged in response to what has been described as the "Madisonian dilemma."[11] This dilemma results from the impossibility of permanently reconciling two competing constitutional principles: energetic self-government and individual liberty. The first principle leads to majority rule, while the second limits the extent to which majorities can interfere with the rights of individuals. The dilemma is that each principle can frustrate the objectives of the other: energetic self-government based on majority rule can erode the sphere of individual liberty, while individual claims of liberty from majority rule can frustrate the pursuit of the common good. Writing in *The Federalist Papers,* James Madison argued that these principles could at least be accommodated through a constitutional structure that divided legislative authority federally and limited the powers of the national government, that relied on representative (rather than direct) democracy, and that separated the legislative, executive, and judicial powers of government. In an extended, commercial republic, Madison asserted, majority tyranny would be impossible because actual power would be exercised by constantly changing coalitions of minorities whose self-interest would lead to political moderation. Together, these provisions would provide a "republican remedy for the diseases most incident to republican government."[12] Soon after the ratification of the 1787 Constitution, Madison would shepherd an additional safeguard through the U.S. Congress – the Bill of Rights – despite his initial conviction that it was unnecessary to include such a document in the Constitution to protect individual liberty.

Although not faced with the burdensome task of devising completely new constitutional arrangements, the Canadian Fathers of Confederation confronted the same tension between self-government and individual liberty as did their U.S. counterparts. For the most part, the Canadian constitutional draftsmen sought to resolve this tension through the parliamentary institutions of a "Constitution similar in Principle to that of the United Kingdom." Parliamentary government, and the doctrine of parliamentary supremacy in particular, relied on majority rule as the principal solution to the problem of executive tyranny. The Constitution Act, 1867 (formerly the British North America Act) addressed the remaining elements of the Madisonian dilemma largely through federalism and the division of powers. By allocating to the provinces legislative authority over such subjects as property and civil rights, the administration of justice, and education, the constitution ensured that provincial political communities could exercise self-government over important matters through local majorities. At the same time, by reserving matters such as judicial appointments, criminal law, and criminal procedure for the federal government, and by including provisions such as the federal disallowance power over provincial legislation, the constitution provided a means by which national majorities could protect provincial minorities. In addition, the Constitution Act, 1867 provided express protection for certain minority language and education rights.[13]

Given the absence of constitutionally entrenched bills of rights in the original constitutional design of both the United States and Canada, it should be apparent that such documents were not considered necessary for the implementation of liberal constitutionalism. The U.S. Bill of Rights came into existence at the insistence of the Anti-Federalists, who opposed the constitutional plan adopted in Philadelphia in 1787. According to these opponents of the Constitution, the document did not adequately protect local self-government from the tyranny of national majorities; consequently, they insisted on a statement of rights that would bind the national government and prevent it from violating the liberties of state citizens. In its origins, the Bill of Rights did not apply to majority rule *per se*, but only to majority rule as exercised through the institutions of national government. Indeed, the U.S. Supreme Court did not consistently enforce the Bill of Rights against the states until 1925.

One finds in both the origins and structure of the Canadian Charter of Rights and Freedoms a similarly ambiguous connection to the protection of individual liberty against majority rule.[14] Although political pressure to entrench individual rights in the Canadian constitution has existed since at least the 1940s (and achieved some success with the 1960 Bill of Rights discussed below), the immediate origins of the current Charter can be traced to 1968, when then Justice Minister Pierre Trudeau tabled a policy paper entitled "A Canadian Charter of Human Rights." The idea of an entrenched declaration of rights thus became an important component of constitutional discussions, and in 1971 the provincial premiers and Prime Minister Trudeau reached an agreement at a meeting in Victoria to patriate the constitution and to entrench a charter of rights. This agreement ultimately failed, however, because of important objections later raised by both Quebec and Alberta. In Quebec, Premier Robert Bourassa returned from Victoria to face opposition from his cabinet, which attacked the accord for not providing Quebec with sufficient guarantees of cultural sovereignty. The reason for Alberta's opposition was a change in government, with newly elected Premier Peter Lougheed objecting to the veto over future constitutional amendments granted to Quebec and Ontario.

The Victoria plan's failure pushed constitutional reform off centre stage until 1976, when the election of a separatist government in Quebec provoked additional demands for constitutional renewal. In 1978, the federal government under Pierre Trudeau responded to this pressure to resolve "the crisis threatening the stability, unity, and prosperity of the country" by introducing Bill C-60, which contained a proposed Constitution of Canada Act and a charter of rights.[15] Although this charter would not immediately have constitutional status, the federal government saw it as the first step toward overcoming provincial opposition to the constitutional entrenchment of rights and freedoms. This reform effort temporarily stalled in 1979, when the Progressive Conservative Party under the leadership of Joe Clark defeated Trudeau's Liberal Party in a national election. Trudeau returned to power in 1980, however, in time to lead the campaign against Quebec's referendum on sovereignty-association. During the course of this campaign, Trudeau again promised Quebecers and Canadians a renewed federalism. After winning the referendum, Trudeau took the first step toward keeping this promise in September, 1980, when he presented a package of constitutional reforms, including patriation and a charter of rights, to a first ministers' conference.

The vision of renewed federalism contained in this package proved almost universally unpopular to the provincial leaders, however. Failing to secure broad provincial acceptance of this plan for constitutional renewal, Trudeau announced that the federal government would implement it unilaterally. This produced a hostile reaction from almost all of the provinces, who moved politically and legally to block the plan. After acrimonious negotiations, punctuated by hearings before a special joint parliamentary committee and a crucial Supreme Court decision, the governments of Canada and nine provinces agreed in November, 1981, to patriate the constitution and include within it a domestic amending formula and an entrenched Charter of Rights and Freedoms.[16] The product of this agreement, which Quebec continued to refuse to accept, was the Constitution Act, 1982. The Charter of Rights and Freedoms constitutes the first thirty-four sections of the Act and contains provisions governing fundamental freedoms, democratic rights, mobility rights, legal rights, equality rights, language rights, and minority-language education rights. The Charter also contains several interpretive clauses, as well as an enforcement provision (s. 24) that sets forth a qualified exclusionary rule and permits courts "of competent jurisdiction" to remedy infringements of rights in any manner they consider "appropriate and just in the circumstances." Section 52(1) of the Act further provides that "[t]he Constitution of Canada is the supreme law of Canada, and any law that is inconsistent with the provisions of the Constitution is, to the extent of the inconsistency, of no force or effect." As a whole, section 24 of the Charter and section 52(1) of the Constitution Act, 1982 push Canada further away from the tradition of parliamentary supremacy inherited from Britain toward a regime of constitutional supremacy enforced by judicial review.

The impetus for this constitutional change was only partly to provide better security for individual rights and freedoms in Canada. Of equal or even greater importance in the Charter's creation was the federal government's concern with national unity. The federal government expected the Charter to contribute to this objective in two ways: first, by shifting national political debate away from regional concerns toward universal questions of human rights; and second, by subordinating provincial legislation to a document ultimately enforced by a predominantly *national* institution (the Supreme Court). This, the federal government thought, would establish a "unifying counter to decentralizing provincial demands in the Canadian constitutional debate."[17]

In view of this federal strategy, it is hardly surprising that only two provinces (Ontario and New Brunswick) initially supported the patriation project. What eventually convinced seven of the remaining eight provinces to agree to the project was Prime Minister Trudeau's willingness to include a legislative override provision in the Charter. Section 33 of the Charter allows the federal Parliament or any provincial legislature to declare for renewable five-year periods that statutes "shall operate notwithstanding a provision included in section 2 [fundamental freedoms] or sections 7 to 15 [legal and equality rights] of this Charter." This so-called "notwithstanding clause" saved the November, 1981, first ministers' conference from a complete deadlock.

Although the Charter resembles the U.S. Bill of Rights in many ways, it is in other important respects a politically indigenous document. The Charter protects some uniquely Canadian rights, such as general language rights and minority-language education rights. It also contains an explicit limitations clause (section 1), as well as a potentially more effective check on judicial power (section 33) than the provisions listed in Article III of the U.S. Constitution (which sets out the powers, jurisdiction, and structure of the U.S. federal judiciary). Moreover, the Charter does not expressly protect private property rights, nor does it contain anything resembling the "takings" clause of the Fifth Amendment to the U.S. Constitution.[18] Nevertheless, the adoption of the Charter generated considerable interest among Canadian and American commentators in the potential impact of American civil rights jurisprudence on Charter adjudication.[19]

Indeed, the evolution of the Charter suggests a conscious effort by its drafters to allow for the incorporation of some elements of U.S. civil rights jurisprudence into Charter adjudication, while avoiding the more problematic details of the American experience. On the positive side, the Charter's architects removed the reference to "a parliamentary system of government" from section 1 to ensure that Canadian courts would not completely ignore American constitutional jurisprudence when adjudicating Charter issues.[20] At the same time, however, provincial concerns about the interpretation given to the phrase "due process" by American courts led to its replacement by "principles of fundamental justice" in section 7 of the Charter.[21] In practice, the attitude of Canadian commentators toward the American experience has ranged from enthusiastic praise for judicial enforcement of constitutional rights in the United States[22] to warnings about misusing or misunderstanding American constitutional theory and experience.[23]

Judicial attitudes have been similarly mixed. In the Supreme Court's first Charter decision, *Law Society of Upper Canada v. Skapinker* (1984), Justice Willard Estey remarked that "it is of more than passing interest to those concerned with these new developments in Canada to study the experience of the United States courts."[24] Striking a more cautious note, Justice Antonio Lamer argued in the British Columbia *Motor Vehicle Reference* (1985) that the use of American jurisprudence must be tempered by judicial recognition of the "truly fundamental structural differences between the two Constitutions."[25] Similarly, in *Rahey v. The Queen* (1987) Justice Gérard La Forest suggested that "American jurisprudence . . . must be viewed as a tool, not as a master."[26] In 1988, Chief Justice Brian Dickson synthesized these attitudes when he wrote in *Simmons v. The Queen* that, while Canadian courts "must . . . be wary of adopting American interpretations where they do not accord with the interpretive framework of our Constitution, the American courts have the benefit of 200 years of experience in constitutional interpretation. This wealth of experience may offer guidance to the judiciary in this country."[27] Just as the American experience may guide the Canadian judiciary, so may it guide Canadian scholars in their quest to understand the relationship between judicial power and constitutional democracy. Consequently, this book places some emphasis on the manner in which Canadian and U.S. courts have dealt with similar constitutional questions.

The book is divided into three parts. Part I, containing the first two chapters, deals in general terms with judicial review and constitutional interpretation. Chapter One compares and contrasts the origins and development of judicial review in Canada and the United States, concluding with a discussion of the paradox created by judicial review in liberal constitutional democracies. Chapter Two examines the link between the scope of judicial power and various theories of constitutional interpretation. These theories are important because they provide the normative justification for various uses of judicial power. This chapter begins with a discussion of the debate between interpretivism and non-interpretivism in U.S. constitutional theory, and then moves to an examination of the tension between liberal individualist and communitarian interpretations of the Canadian Charter. An important feature of this chapter is its discussion of the influence that American jurisprudence has had on the development of the Canadian Supreme Court's approach to constitutional interpretation under the Charter.

The second part of the book forms its substantive core and encompasses Chapters Three through Five. These chapters canvass the Supreme Court's decisions concerning some of the most controversial and far-reaching sections of the

Charter: fundamental freedoms (Chapter Three), legal rights and fundamental justice (Chapter Four), and equality rights (Chapter Five). Each chapter discusses the Court's definition of the rights involved, the interpretive method employed in each case, the political impact of the decisions, and the contribution of these decisions to the evolving nature of judicial power in Canada. Readers will note that I have chosen not to include separate chapters on either democratic rights or language rights. This does not imply that I consider judicial enforcement of these rights to be unimportant. Indeed, judicial interpretation of democratic rights (section 3) raises fundamental questions about the nature of representative democracy; and judicial enforcement of language rights reveals much about the fundamental political tensions that characterize Canada. The actualization of both sets of rights also illuminates the relationship between judicial power and constitutional democracy. I have chosen, however, to explore the political impact of these guarantees in the context of a broader discussion of judicial policy-making and remedial powers under sections 1 and 24(1) of the Charter. Consequently, democratic and language rights decisions are considered primarily in Part III.

Part III consists of Chapters Six and Seven, which examine more closely the relationship between the structural characteristics of adjudication and the Charter's impact on public policy. Chapter Six considers the Supreme Court's application of sections 1 and 24(1) of the Charter, each of which involves the Court directly in policy considerations and raises significant questions of institutional capacity. Chapter Seven attempts to revive the legislative override provision of section 33 as a legitimate element of liberal constitutionalism. This chapter responds to criticisms of section 33 and offers suggestions about how this provision might be amended to enhance both its legitimacy and effectiveness. The book concludes with some reflections on the impact of the Charter on constitutional reform in Canada, and with some final thoughts on the modern tendency to resolve political disputes through legal means.

As this book amply demonstrates, it is always tempting to emphasize constitutional adjudication concerning individual rights and freedoms when discussing judicial power. One should not lose sight of the fact, however, that Charter cases constitute only about one-quarter of the Supreme Court's docket. Consequently, Supreme Court decisions concerning the fundamental freedoms, legal rights, and equality rights provisions of the Charter do not exhaust the ways in which judicial review generally, and Charter review in particular, influences Canadian politics. The exercise of judicial power also has a significant impact on the nature of Canadian politics through other public law decisions, as well as through cases involving private law matters. However, constitutional decisions set the parameters of political debate and are exceedingly difficult to alter. For these reasons, they raise a more crucial set of issues than other types of decisions. It is these issues that are the central concern of what follows.

PART 1

Judicial Review
and Constitutional Interpretation

CHAPTER 1

Judicial Review and the Paradox of Liberal Constitutionalism

On January 28, 1988, the Supreme Court of Canada delivered its decision in *Morgentaler, Smoling and Scott v. The Queen.*[1] At issue was the constitutionality of section 251 of the Criminal Code of Canada, which prohibited the procurement or performance of an abortion without prior approval from the therapeutic abortion committee of an accredited hospital. The complexity of the issue was evident in the four separate reasons for judgment rendered in the case, none of which commanded the support of more than two justices. What mattered most to opponents of the law, however, was that five of the seven justices who heard the case found a conflict between section 251 and the Canadian Charter of Rights and Freedoms. In what became the most influential opinion, Chief Justice Brian Dickson found that the procedure required under section 251 to obtain the necessary approval for a legal abortion imposed undue physical and psychological burdens on women, thereby limiting their right to "security of the person" as guaranteed by section 7 of the Charter. Dickson further found that this limitation was neither consistent with the "principles of fundamental justice" (as section 7 requires), nor reasonable and demonstrably justified in a "free and democratic society" (as required by section 1). With the exception of Justice Bertha Wilson, however, the justices who voted to strike down section 251 refrained from passing judgment on the substantive merits of abortion regulation. Although the decision nullified the means by which Parliament had regulated abortion since revisions to the Criminal Code in 1969, it did not immediately deny Parliament the authority to establish alternative methods for pursuing the same objective.

Despite the majority's attempt to strike down section 251 on as narrow constitutional grounds as possible, *Morgentaler, Smoling and Scott* attracted unprecedented public attention and provoked a minor legislative crisis. Indeed, it would not be an exaggeration to suggest that the decision paralysed the government of Prime Minister Brian Mulroney on this issue. After several months of indecision, the government finally asked Parliament, on July 28, 1988, to indicate its disposition toward several proposed abortion laws. To the chagrin of those who had welcomed the decision in *Morgentaler, Smoling and Scott,* the proposal that came closest to adoption was a pro-life resolution that would have restricted access to abortion even more than did section 251. This proposal was defeated by a vote of 118 to 105. No other proposal, including the one officially supported by the government itself, received more than seventy-six votes. Chastened by this outcome, the Mulroney government waited until after its re-election in November, 1988, to introduce new legislation. On May 29, 1990, the House of Commons passed Bill C-43, which attempted to redress the procedural deficiencies of section 251 identified in Chief Justice Dickson's reasons for judgment while keeping the regulation of abortion within the Criminal Code. The proposed law would have maintained the distinction between therapeutic and non-therapeutic abortions, but would have expanded the definition of health and liberalized the process of obtaining approval for legal abortions. However, as a result of a tie vote in February, 1991, the Senate failed to approve Bill C-43 on its third reading. The government subsequently announced that it would not attempt to enact new abortion legislation during the remainder of its mandate.

For students of the judicial process, three aspects of *Morgentaler, Smoling and Scott* merit special attention. First, the Charter's entrenchment in 1982 caused Chief Justice Dickson to alter his earlier views about the Court's proper role in the abortion controversy. In 1975, Dickson did not believe that the Court should participate in "the loud and continuous public debate on abortion."[2] By 1988, Dickson's reticence had been displaced by the Court's "added responsibilit[y]" of ensuring "that the legislative initiatives pursued by our Parliament and legislatures conform to the democratic values" expressed in the Charter.[3] A second aspect of *Morgentaler, Smoling and Scott* worth noting is that the Court's analysis of the conflict between section 251 and "security of the person" relied heavily on extrinsic evidence, a relatively unusual practice in Canadian constitutional jurisprudence. Finally, the Chief Justice's decision to restrict his reasons for judgment to the procedural aspects of section 251 suggests that he recognized the tension between the demands of Charter adjudication and the Court's traditional decision-making style.

Both the decision-making process and the outcome in *Morgentaler, Smoling and Scott* raise important questions about the constitutional legitimacy and institutional capacity of the Canadian Supreme Court's exercise of judicial review under the Charter. The constitutional questions include the basic legitimacy of judicial review in a political regime that places a premium on publicly accountable decision-making, as well as the permissible scope of judicial review once its basic legitimacy is established. The spectre of unelected officials, who hold their positions by virtue of extraordinary tenure,[4] second-guessing the decisions of elected legislators poses a special dilemma for liberal democratic theory. This dilemma takes on an added dimension when this review extends to the substance, or policy content, of legislation. These normative questions of legitimacy are closely linked to empirical questions concerning the institutional capacity of courts to gather, process, and evaluate the type of information necessary to perform adequately the role envisioned for the judiciary by Chief Justice Dickson in *Morgentaler, Smoling and Scott.* These normative and empirical questions are the central components of a paradox at the heart of liberal constitutionalism, a paradox the roots of which can be traced to the unique role of judicial institutions in constitutional democracies. The remainder of this chapter considers both the historical roots and the modern nature of this paradox by examining the evolution of constitutionally focused judicial review in Anglo-American jurisprudence.

The Development of American Judicial Review: From *Dr. Bonham's Case* To *Roe v. Wade*

The idea that judges might evaluate statutes according to the standards of a "higher law," and then refuse to enforce those they find wanting, was first set forth by Lord Coke in *Dr. Bonham's Case* (1610). For Coke, these higher standards were to be found in the common law:

> It appears in our books, that in many cases, the common law will control acts of parliament, and sometimes adjudge them to be utterly void: for when an act of parliament is against common right and reason, or repugnant, or impossible to be performed, the common law will control it and adjudge such act to be void.[5]

Although some British jurists endorsed the principle underlying Coke's *dictum,* they nevertheless refused to practise what Coke preached.[6] Consequently, Coke's argument had little impact on the evolving doctrine of parliamentary supremacy. Indeed, almost three hundred years after Coke's *dictum,* A.V. Dicey could state with confidence that "no person or body is recognised by the law of England as having a right to override or set aside the legislation of Parliament." Moreover, according to Dicey, the "expression 'unconstitutional' . . . as applied to an English Act of Parliament . . . cannot mean that the Act is either a breach of law or is void."[7]

While judicial review in the sense articulated by Coke made little headway in Britain, it did attract attention in the American colonies. Coke's *dictum* became a central part of American political discourse after a speech by James Otis in the *Writs of Assistance Case* (1761). Between 1755 and 1760 the Superior Court of Massachusetts issued several writs of assistance, which granted broad powers of search and seizure to customs officials. After the death of King George II, it became necessary for these officials to apply for new writs under the name of George III. However, the court's chief judge expressed doubts about the writs' legality and ordered legal arguments on the question in 1761. Although no one made an exact record of the proceedings, John Adams reported that, in the course of arguing against the writs' legality, Otis declared that "[a]n Act [of Parliament] against the Constitution is void: an Act against natural equity is void: and if an Act of Parliament should be made, in the very Words of this petition, it would be void. The Executive Courts must pass such acts into disuse."[8] Although Otis's argument ultimately failed in this instance, it found its way both explicitly and implicitly into several state court decisions prior to the Constitutional Convention of 1787. Courts in New Hampshire, North Carolina, Rhode Island, New Jersey, and New York all issued decisions inspired by Otis's admonition to judges to measure the validity of ordinary statutes against some higher law.[9]

Although not without ambiguities, these state precedents persuaded both popular and informed opinion that judges could check legislative power by refusing to enforce statutes they found constitutionally deficient. Indeed, delegates brought this conviction to the Philadelphia Convention, and evidence of it is scattered throughout both the general debates about legislative power and the specific discussions concerning the Council of Revision proposed in the constitutional plan submitted by Virginia's representatives.[10] Virginia's proposal would have created a joint executive-judicial body charged with the responsibility of reviewing congressional acts before they went into effect. While the idea failed, the discussion of it produced several comments recognizing some form of judicial review. Speaking against the proposal, Elbridge Gerry of Massachusetts conceded that it was quite legitimate for judges to "set aside laws as being ag[ainst] the Constitution," but he argued adamantly that it "was quite foreign from the nature of [th]e office to make them judges of the policy of public measures." Similarly, Luther Martin argued that including the judiciary in a Council of Revision would give it a "double negative," since it already possessed the power to nullify unconstitutional laws by virtue of its "proper official character." Other participants in the convention, including Rufus King, James Wilson, George Mason, and Gouverneur Morris, also alluded to judicial review.[11] However, that these allusions were not entirely clear, or unanimously accepted, is evident in the contemporary persistence of the argument that the framers of the U.S. Constitution never contemplated the creation of a power of judicial review.[12]

Whatever the Convention participants' actual view of judicial review, one thing is clear: they did not explicitly include it among the federal judiciary's enumerated powers in Article III of the U.S. Constitution. Nevertheless, Raoul Berger has argued that such a power may be inferred from two constitutional provisions. One is the provision in Article III granting the federal courts jurisdiction over "cases . . . arising under this Constitution"; the second is the supremacy clause of Article VI, which declares that "the Judges in every state shall be bound" by the supreme law of the Constitution, "any Thing in the Constitution or Laws of any State to the Contrary notwithstanding." While Article VI clearly implies that state courts may review state legislation for conformity with the federal Constitution, Berger argues that it also implies a similar power for federal courts with respect to both state and federal legislation. Berger's argument may be summarized in the following way: Article VI provides that laws made pursuant to the Constitution are supreme; the question whether a law is pursuant to the Constitution is one arising under that document; federal courts have jurisdiction over cases arising under the Constitution; therefore, federal courts are authorized to review the constitutionality of federal and state statutes. Although Berger is thus able to claim textual support in the Constitution for judicial review, it is support for a type of limited judicial review inherent in any federal constitution.[13]

However persuasive Berger's argument, the salient point is that the constitutional foundations of a now common judicial function are at best ambiguous. In the absence of clear constitutional provisions, the power of judicial review exercised by U.S. federal courts derives its principal legitimacy from two extra-constitutional sources. The first is Alexander Hamilton's reflections on judicial power. Hamilton was responding to Anti-Federalist complaints that the constitutional provisions for a national judiciary made the power of this branch of government "superior to that of the legislature." Indeed, the Anti-Federalists detected in the potential power of judicial review the "seeds of arbitrary government" rather than additional protection for individual rights.[14] In the Anti-Federalists' eyes, the proposed Constitution was seriously defective in granting broad jurisdiction and powers to a politically unaccountable institution.

One reason for the national judiciary's unaccountability, according to the Anti-Federalists, was life tenure, which was the subject that Hamilton ostensibly addressed in *The Federalist,* No. 78. Hamilton's defence of the national judiciary began by stressing, in direct opposition to the Anti-Federalists, that the judiciary was inherently weak. The judiciary, in Hamilton's famous phrase, would be the branch "least dangerous to the political rights of the Constitution," largely because it would have "no influence over either the sword or the purse." Hamilton argued, moreover, that this inherent weakness rendered the judiciary vulnerable to encroachments on its power and authority by the other branches of government, a situation he found intolerable in a government of constitutionally limited powers where judicial independence played a crucial role.[15] Hamilton thus defended special protections for the judiciary – such as life tenure – as being necessary to guarantee the judiciary's independence.[16]

What made the relationship between judicial independence and constitutionally limited government so important in Hamilton's eyes was his understanding that it would occasionally be the responsibility of courts to declare laws made contrary to the Constitution "null and void." Although he acknowledged the fear that this doctrine might imply "a superiority of the judiciary to the legislative power," Hamilton asserted that without it "all the reservations of particular rights or privileges would amount to nothing." For Hamilton, the Constitution embodied the permanent will of the people, which was necessarily superior to the transient popular will reflected in the legislative enactments of the people's representatives. Consequently, the service rendered by courts as "the bulwarks of a limited Constitution against legislative encroachments" justified the extraordinary tenure granted to federal judges by the Constitution.[17]

U.S. Supreme Court Chief Justice John Marshall provided a second extra-constitutional justification for judicial review when he gave practical effect to Hamilton's argument in *Marbury v. Madison* (1803).[18] *Marbury* was the product of a political dispute between outgoing President John Adams's Federalist Party and the incoming Jefferson administration. During the transition of power, the Federalist-controlled Congress commissioned forty-two new justices of the peace for the District of Columbia. Adams nominated members of the Federalist Party, including William Marbury, to fill each of these posts. However, during the final days of the Adams administration, then Secretary of State John Marshall failed to deliver Marbury's commission. Jefferson's Secretary of State – James Madison – subsequently refused to deliver the commission, leading Marbury to bring suit in the Supreme Court to compel its delivery. Although only four of six justices heard the case, and despite Marshall's own close involvement with the matter, Marbury's suit became the occasion for the Court to establish its power of judicial review.[19]

Marbury rested his case on section 13 of the Judiciary Act of 1789, which, he asserted, purported to give the Court original jurisdiction over cases involving "public ministers," as well as remedial power to issue writs of *mandamus* ordering officials to undertake certain actions. In Marshall's view, Marbury's claim raised three questions: whether Marbury had a right to the commission he was demanding; whether, assuming the right's existence, there was any remedy in law for its violation; and, finally, whether a writ of *mandamus* issued by the Supreme Court was the appropriate remedy. Although Marshall answered the first two questions in the affirmative, he refused to issue the writ because he found a conflict between section 13 of the Judiciary Act and Article III, section 2 of the Constitution. Accepting Marbury's assertion that the Court had indeed been given original jurisdiction in the matter by section 13, Marshall held that Congress had thereby altered the Court's original jurisdiction, a power not granted to it under Article III. This rendered section 13 of the Judiciary Act unconstitutional.

This finding led Marshall to consider whether the Court was under any obligation to enforce a law that it found to be in conflict with the Constitution. Noting that "whether an act repugnant to the Constitution can become the law of the land, is a question deeply interesting to the United States," Marshall considered two issues: whether unconstitutional laws are void, and whether, notwithstanding their invalidity, courts are obliged to uphold them. "If," Marshall argued, "courts are to regard the Constitution, and the Constitution is superior to any ordinary act of the legislature, the Constitution and not such ordinary act, must govern the case to which they both apply." Drawing heavily on Hamilton's discussion of the judicial role, Marshall concluded that laws contrary to the Constitution are void, and that the Court is under no obligation to enforce them; in fact, its duty and responsibility are precisely the opposite. So emerged the Court's practical power of judicial review.

Important as they are, the arguments of Hamilton and Marshall offer only qualified support for judicial review. For example, Hamilton excluded the executive from his discussion of judicial review. More importantly, he described a very narrow set of circumstances in which nullification of legislative enactments would be appropriate. Indeed, he cited only two examples of situations where judicial review would be necessary. If Congress passed bills of attainder or *ex post facto* laws, according to Hamilton, it would be the duty of the "courts of justice" to void such laws for violating "the manifest tenor of the Constitution." Hamilton warned federal judges that if they went beyond specific constitutional provisions of this type they would be usurping "the authority of the legislature" and would render themselves liable to impeachment. Hamilton's reflections on the necessity of a separate bill of rights, which is now the principal source of cases inviting judicial review under the U.S. Constitution, also reveal much about his understanding of judicial review. He believed that such a declaration of rights was unnecessary because the Constitution, in reflecting the people's reasoned choice of how they wished to be governed, was "itself, in every rational sense, and to every useful purpose, A BILL OF RIGHTS."[20] In Hamilton's view, the internal structure of the government created by the Constitution would be a better safeguard of rights than any judicially enforceable "parchment barrier."

Similarly, the conflict Marshall purported to find between section 13 of the Judiciary Act and Article III of the Constitution arguably resulted from a misconstruction of the statute in question. Contrary to Marshall's finding, two aspects of section 13 suggest that it probably *did not* extend the Court's original jurisdiction to cases like Marbury's.[21] First, the provision for the Court's original jurisdiction over "suits or proceedings against . . . public ministers" appears in a context suggesting that this phrase ("public ministers") referred to foreign diplomatic personnel, not to domestic government officials like Madison. Second, the reference to writs of *mandamus* in section 13 appears in provisions concerning the Court's appellate jurisdiction, over which Congress has plenary power under Article III. Marshall could therefore have dismissed Marbury's suit for want of jurisdiction, but this would have given the Jeffersonians an important political victory. By accepting jurisdiction, and then denying Marbury any remedy, Marshall simultaneously expanded judicial power, scored political points against his opponents, and avoided a potentially destructive confrontation between the executive and the judiciary. Finally, even if one accepts Marshall's construction of section 13, there is nothing in Article III to suggest that Congress may not *augment* the Court's original jurisdiction, only that it may not be diminished. Judicial review emerges in *Marbury,* as in *The Federalist Papers,* as a judicial defence against legislative and executive encroachments on the status and authority of courts, not as a broad power to review the other branches' actions with respect to their own responsibilities.

Despite the less than firm footing of federal judicial review in constitutional text and law, the U.S. Supreme Court experienced little difficulty in gradually applying it to supervise the development of state legislation.[22] In fact, judicial review has proved to be a very malleable power, and it has evolved significantly in terms of both subject matter and style. From 1789 until the Civil War, the Court concerned itself primarily with establishing and defending the powers of the national government against the centrifugal forces of state power; from the Civil War until 1937, it protected various rights of economic liberty and the doctrine of laissez faire; and from 1937 to the present, the Court has used judicial review primarily to defend and expand political and civil rights.[23] In terms of style, a distinctively modern approach to judicial review has emerged, the aim of which is the "specification of vague constitutional generalities." This modern approach is largely legislative in character, de-emphasizing rules of interpretation and focusing on questions of degree.[24] In its most extreme form, modern judicial review is "non-interpretivist," a concept that will be discussed in greater detail in Chapter Two.

The modern era has witnessed not only a significant change in the style of judicial review, but also in its political supporters. The use to which the Court put judicial review between 1803 and the 1950s made it unattractive to progressive intellectuals.[25] After *Marbury,* the Court refrained from nullifying any federal statute until *Dred Scott v. Sandford* (1857), in which it declared that "persons of the Negro race" could not be United States citizens.[26] As a result, the Court declared section 8 of the Missouri Act of 1820 unconstitutional and denied Congress any power to prohibit the expansion of slavery into federal territory. The Court was undaunted by the fact that in the Act's thirty-four years of existence no one had seriously questioned its validity, with the possible exception of those who actually believed that slavery was a positive good.[27]

The Court's impact on racial equality was similarly negative throughout the era of post-Civil War reconstruction in the nineteenth century. It exercised judicial review to undercut the Fourteenth Amendment's "privileges and immunities" clause, to deny Congress any power to enforce the Fourteenth Amendment through prohibitions against private discrimination, and to constitutionalize state-enforced segregation.[28] Having undermined efforts to advance civil rights, the Court turned to economic regulation in the twentieth century. Using the newly articulated doctrine of substantive due process, the Court denied to the state and federal governments the power to set maximum hours and minimum wages, as well as to regulate the working conditions of women and children.[29] Finally, the Court mounted an assault against Franklin Roosevelt's New Deal legislation.[30] Needless to say, these decisions created a distinct impression that judicial review was an impediment to social progress.

The Court finally shed its anti-progressive image in *Brown v. Board of Education* (1954).[31] The moral soundness of *Brown* granted new legitimacy to judicial review in American political life.[32] For two decades, *Brown* served as the source of a strong positive consensus concerning the legitimacy and proper scope of judicial review. As one Canadian commentator noted shortly after the entrenchment of the Charter of Rights and Freedoms, *Brown* was "such a moral supernova in civil liberties adjudication that it almost singlehandedly justifies the exercise."[33] This consensus began to deteriorate, however, in the wake of the U.S. Court's decision in *Roe v. Wade* (1973),[34] in which it extended the right to privacy articulated in *Griswold v. Connecticut* (1965)[35] to include abortion. In *Griswold,* the Court struck down a Connecticut statute prohibiting the use of contraceptives on the grounds that the law violated the implicit constitutional right to privacy that the Court purported to discover in the "penumbral emanations" of several provisions of the Bill of Rights. According to the Court, these amendments[36] each protected an aspect of personal privacy that, viewed in their entirety, pointed to a general right to privacy. In *Roe,* seven justices agreed that this general right "is broad enough to encompass a woman's decision whether or not to terminate her pregnancy." The Court held that this right is absolute during the first trimester of pregnancy, but that states may regulate abortion in the interests of maternal health during the second trimester and prohibit it entirely during the third in order to protect the "potential" life of fetuses.

The Court's inability to demonstrate convincingly that either the general right to privacy or the specific right to abortion could be found in the express words or "manifest tenor" of the Constitution and Bill of Rights was a critical blow to the constitutional legitimacy of modern judicial review. In the eyes of Justices William Rehnquist and Byron White, who dissented from the majority in both *Roe* and its companion case *Doe v. Bolton* (1973), the abortion decisions amounted to "judicial legislation" and "an exercise of raw judicial power."[37] Moreover, *Roe* resurrected to an even greater degree than did *Griswold* the discredited doctrine of substantive due process, on which the Court had relied in its decisions striking down progressive labour and economic legislation.[38] For these reasons and others, the decision distressed even constitutional scholars sympathetic to the liberalization of state abortion laws.[39] *Roe v. Wade* thus re-opened in rather dramatic fashion a normative debate about judicial power that *Brown v. Board of Education* appeared to have brought to an end, since the decision was such a bold exercise of judicial power that it did not easily fit within either Hamilton's or Marshall's justifications for judicial review.

Judicial Review in Canada:
Federalism, the Bill of Rights, and the Charter

At least one important observation can be made about the development of judicial review in Canada in light of its evolution in the United States: the basic legitimacy of judicial review has been less controversial in Canada for both historical and structural reasons.[40] The imperial context of the 1867 British North America Act, as well as the need to enforce the division of powers between the federal and provincial governments, provided a foundation on which justifications for judicial review could be built.[41] The reference procedure, which provides

Canadian courts with a much broader jurisdiction than their American counterparts, also adds to the legitimacy of judicial review.[42] Even with its inherent limitations and timid enforcement by Canadian courts, the 1960 Bill of Rights spurred at least one Supreme Court justice (Bora Laskin) to call for an extension of judicial power. Finally, the acknowledgement of constitutional supremacy in section 52(1) of the Constitution Act, 1982 and the explicit provision for judicial enforcement of guaranteed rights in section 24(1) of the Charter further entrench judicial review as a legitimate component of Canada's constitutional order.

Although Canada inherited the doctrine of parliamentary supremacy from Britain when it adopted "a constitution similar in Principle to that of the United Kingdom," Canadian parliamentary sovereignty has always been qualified by various limitations. As Peter Hogg reminds us, Confederation did not entail independence; the imperial Parliament at Westminster retained significant control over Canadian affairs. One of the principal mechanisms through which Westminster exercised this control was the Colonial Laws Validity Act, 1865, which remained in force until repealed by the Statute of Westminster, 1931. The Act stipulated that colonial laws "repugnant" to imperial statutes – which the Act defined narrowly to include acts of the imperial Parliament "extending to the colony . . . by the express words or necessary intendment" of the specific statute – were void. Although the Colonial Laws Validity Act actually enhanced the power of Canada's Parliament by affirming its capacity to alter received statutes and the common law, the Act underscored the qualified nature of Canadian parliamentary supremacy by confirming that, in some matters at least, Canadian statutes were subject to a higher authority.[43]

Of more lasting importance have been the qualifications imposed on parliamentary supremacy by the Constitution Act, 1867 (the BNA Act), of which the most important have been those related to federalism and the division of powers. These qualifications are important for at least two reasons. First, they represent *substantive* limitations on the sovereignty of each level of government in that, by dividing power between the federal and provincial governments, they categorically exclude some powers from each jurisdiction.[44] Each level of government, in other words, is denied outright the power to legislate in certain substantive policy areas. Second, these qualifications have provided the bulk of constitutional grist for the judicial mill. Although some evidence suggests that Prime Minister Sir John A. Macdonald thought the division of powers was sufficiently clear (and the powers of disallowance and reservation sufficiently potent) to render judicial review on federalism grounds unnecessary,[45] history has shown this judgment to have been overly optimistic. Indeed, until the modern advent of co-operative and executive federalism, decisions of the Judicial Committee of the Privy Council and the Supreme Court monopolized the forces shaping Canadian federalism.

The complex realities of the division of powers inevitably meant that the judiciary would be forced to become the "umpire" of federalism. In order to perform this function, both the Judicial Committee and the provincial courts adopted an argument similar to the one advanced by John Marshall in *Marbury* to assert their right to review the validity of enactments made by Canadian legs. lative bodies. As an imperial statute, these judicial bodies argued, the Constitution Act, 1867 took precedence over colonial legislation; consequently, legislation found contrary to the Act was invalid and unenforceable by the courts. This power to nullify legislation was subsequently adopted by the Supreme Court after its creation in 1875.[46]

The Judicial Committee of the Privy Council (JCPC) served as Canada's final court of appeal until 1949. In general, the JCPC exercised judicial review in a way that strengthened the constitutional status of the provinces and gradually transformed Canada from a quasi-federal state to one characterized by co-ordinate federalism.[47] The Judicial Committee assisted this transformation in two ways. First, it narrowly interpreted the scope of federal power over trade and commerce, as well as the federal residual power "to make Laws for the Peace, Order, and good Government of Canada" in matters not "assigned exclusively to the Legislatures of the Provinces." At the same time, the JCPC provided a very generous interpretation of provincial power over property and civil rights (which in this context referred primarily to proprietary, contractual, and tortious rights).[48] This combination of contracted federal powers and expanded provincial authority redefined the character of Canadian federalism in a manner consistent with the interests of provincial rights advocates.[49]

The direction in which the Judicial Committee directed Canadian federalism made it the subject of harsh criticism by Canadian scholars.[50] After surveying developments in Canadian federalism, F.R. Scott accused the Privy Council of being "too handicapped by its ignorance of Canada to be able to give good judgments in Canadian constitutional law." Scott concluded that only through constitutional amendment could the "evil" perpetrated by the Judicial Committee be undone.[51] In Scott's view, the negative consequences of the JCPC's jurisprudence became particularly evident during the Great Depression, when it "weaken[ed] the central government, and so . . . postpon[ed] indefinitely any further attempts at government regulation of the economy in the interests of stability and security."[52] Similarly, Bora Laskin argued that, particularly under the stewardship of Viscount Haldane, the Judicial Committee's decisions concerning federal power were "uninformed and unnourished by any facts of Canadian living," leading to a constitutional jurisprudence characterized by "rigid abstractions." In Laskin's judgment, this jurisprudence produced at best a Pyrrhic victory for the advocates of provincial autonomy. It limited the nation's ability "to meet economic and social problems of inter-provincial scope," while assuring that "the citizens of a province are citizens of the Dominion for certain limited purposes only."[53]

Although the precise nature of the Judicial Committee's impact on Canadian federalism remains a controversial subject,[54] it is evident that the perceived distortion of federal power by the Judicial Committee played an important role in the eventual elevation of the Supreme Court to Canada's final court of appeal. To be sure, nationalist sentiments had favoured the abolition of JCPC appeals since Confederation; but the belief that the Supreme Court would favour national power, as it had shown in early decisions,[55] provided additional impetus for the abolition movement. In 1947, the Judicial Committee itself affirmed that the federal Parliament's power to legislate with respect to "a general court of appeal for Canada" also included the power "to deny appellate jurisdiction to any other court," including the JCPC.[56] Thus, despite ambivalent public opinion and provincial fears of a centrally biased Supreme Court, Parliament passed legislation abolishing all JCPC appeals in 1949.[57]

The Supreme Court began to fulfil the expectations of its centralist supporters almost immediately after the abolition of JCPC appeals. The Judicial Committee had established several tests for determining the validity of legislation enacted under the federal government's "peace, order, and good government" powers. The earliest of these was a fairly liberal "national dimensions" test, but this was soon replaced by the restrictive view that this federal power could only be exercised in emergency situations. Finally, in one of its last Canadian decisions, the JCPC adopted a moderate "inherent national importance" test.[58] Although this last test did not carry the same authority as the emergency test, the Supreme Court adopted it in 1952 to grant broader scope to the federal government's powers.[59] After this breakthrough the Court continued to support broad federal regulatory powers and to limit provincial activity in similar fields throughout the 1960s and 1970s.[60]

These shifts in the Court's attitude toward the federal government's residual power surfaced in the *Anti-Inflation Reference* (1976).[61] At issue was the federal government's plan to control wages, prices, and profits in important areas of the private sector, as well as in the federal public sector and the public sectors of provinces that opted in to the plan. Since this legislation intruded on powers normally reserved to the provinces, the federal government defended its action under the "peace, order, and good government" clause. Although the Supreme Court rejected the national dimensions and inherent national importance tests in favour of the emergency doctrine, it did not hold the federal government to a very strict standard of "emergency." According to Justice Beetz, the federal government could rely on its residual power in two circumstances.[62] Under normal conditions, this power could be invoked to support federal legislation in narrowly defined areas of national concern where gaps exist in the distribution of powers. In addition, Beetz argued, the federal government may invoke this power to legislate in areas of provincial jurisdiction in extraordinary circumstances that constitute a national emergency. What made the Court's decision to uphold the impugned legislation in the *Anti-Inflation Reference* a liberal application of this doctrine is that a seven-to-two majority held that it was in no position to second-guess Parliament's judgment that inflation constituted an emergency. The implication of this result – that Parliament could legislate in areas of provincial jurisdiction simply by declaring an emergency – greatly concerned the provinces.

Some commentators during this period began to suggest that a distinctive Canadian institution – executive federalism – would eventually overtake judicial review as the principal means of resolving jurisdictional disputes.[63] For the most part, this judgment proved premature.[64] Indeed, perhaps the most outstanding examples of the vitality of judicial review in resolving federal-provincial disputes were the Supreme Court's three decisions concerning constitutional amendment.[65] In 1980, the Court sided with the provinces in declaring that the federal Parliament could not unilaterally amend the Constitution in a manner that altered the essential character of the Senate. One year later, the Court straddled the political fence by holding that the federal government could *legally* patriate the Constitution unilaterally and add to it a domestic amending formula and the Charter of Rights and Freedoms, while warning that constitutional *convention* counselled against proceeding without "substantial" provincial consent. Finally, in 1982 the Court held that substantial provincial consent did not necessarily have to include Quebec. These three decisions set the conditions under which the most important changes to Canada's constitution since 1867 could take place.

Contrary to Macdonald's expectations, therefore, judicial review became, for political as well as legal reasons, a principal mechanism for mediating federal-provincial disputes.[66] It would be wrong, however, to leave the impression that this has been the only use to which judicial review on federalism grounds has been put. Indeed, the division of powers has also served to provide judicial protection for individual liberties. For example, during the 1930s and 1940s Quebec passed several laws restricting the rights of religious and political minorities (specifically, Jehovah's Witnesses and Communists). The Supreme Court was able to rely on the division of powers to strike down these laws by declaring that they constituted provincial invasions on powers reserved to the federal government, such as the criminal law power.[67] Although these decisions restricted the provinces' power to limit civil liberties, they did not provide any absolute protection for religious or political freedom. In general, the impact of legislation on civil liberties was of only secondary importance in determining its constitutionality; enactment of restrictive legislation by the proper level of government was the threshold issue.[68] Consequently, despite these decisions, judicial review of the division of powers provided limited protection for liberties not expressly guaranteed by the Constitution Act, 1867.

In the absence of sufficient protection from express guarantees or the division of powers, some justices of the Supreme Court purported to discover in the origins and structure of the Constitution Act, 1867 an "implied" bill of rights.[69] First raised as a possibility by Chief Justice Lyman Duff in the *Alberta Press Case* (1938), the implied bill of rights theory received its most explicit articulation by Justice Douglas Abbott in *Switzman v. Elbling* (1957).[70] The justices offered two justifications for this theory. First, they argued that the reference to "a Constitution similar in Principle to that of the United Kingdom" in the preamble to the BNA Act incorporated into the Act an unspecified set of civil liberties enjoyed in the United Kingdom in 1867. Legislation contrary to these liberties, the theory averred, could be struck down on that ground alone. The justices found a second justification for the theory in the Act's establishment of representative parliamentary democracy. In particular, they argued that freedom of political speech was indispensable to the effective operation of democratic institutions. Consequently, the courts could refuse to enforce laws curtailing this particular civil liberty even if enacted by the proper level of government. Despite these claims, the implied bill of rights theory ultimately failed to provide a solid foundation for judicial review on civil liberties grounds. Finally, in 1978 Justice Jean Beetz declared for a majority of the Court that no civil liberty, including those inherited from the United Kingdom, "is so enshrined in the Constitution as to be beyond the reach of competent legislation."[71] Ironically, Beetz partially resurrected the implied bill of rights theory in 1987, arguing that neither level of government could "enact legislation the effect of which would be to substantially interfere with the operation of the basic constitutional structure" of parliamentary government.[72]

By the end of the 1970s it was also apparent that the Court had no intention of giving judicial teeth to a third potential source of judicial review on purely civil liberties grounds – the 1960 Bill of Rights. Enacted through the legislative leadership of Prime Minister John Diefenbaker, the Bill of Rights was part of the worldwide post-World War Two movement to declare the existence of fundamental rights and freedoms.[73] Section 1 recognized individual rights to life, liberty, security of the person, and enjoyment of property. Canadians possessed these rights, the Bill declared, regardless of race, national origin, colour, religion, or sex; moreover, individuals could not be deprived of these rights except by due process of law. Section 1 also recognized an individual right to equality before the law, as well as freedom of religion, speech, assembly, association, and the press. Section 2 provided that, absent an express declaration to the contrary, federal laws should "be so construed and applied as not to abrogate, abridge, or infringe" any of the rights set out in the Bill. This section also added to the rights enumerated in section 1 a set of procedural rights designed to protect persons arrested for, and accused of, criminal offences.

Despite the principles expressed in the 1960 Bill of Rights, its utility as a tool for judicial review was hampered from the outset by several factors. First, it applied exclusively to the federal government, leaving provincial actions unaffected. Second, its recognition of rights and freedoms that "have existed and shall continue to exist" discouraged judicial creativity in the definition and enforcement of civil liberties. Finally, and most importantly, the Bill of Rights lacked constitutional status, which weakened any claim that it could be used legitimately to nullify other federal legislation.

Although these structural features of the Bill of Rights placed hurdles in the path of judicial review, they became insurmountable obstacles only because the Court as a whole viewed them as such. The Supreme Court's conservative approach to the Bill first became apparent in *Robertson and Rosetanni v. The Queen* (1963).[74] At issue was whether Sunday-closing provisions of the federal Lord's Day Act conflicted with the Bill's declaration of religious freedom. In considering the matter, Justice Roland Ritchie declared that the Bill of Rights was "not concerned with 'human rights and fundamental freedoms' in any abstract sense, but rather with such 'rights and freedoms' as they existed in

Canada before the statute was enacted."[75] In Ritchie's view, Canadian history and jurisprudence suggested that religious freedom could co-exist with the Lord's Day Act. He therefore concluded that nothing in the Act infringed the actual religious freedom enjoyed by Canadians.

The Court's cautious construction of the Bill is perhaps best illustrated in its approach to the concept of equality in two cases from the 1970s: *Lavell v. A.-G. Canada* (1973) and *Bliss v. A.-G. Canada* (1975).[76] In *Lavell,* the Court upheld a status provision of the Indian Act stipulating that Indian women who married non-Indians lost their Indian status, while Indian men in a similar situation did not. A majority of the Court defined "equality before the law" narrowly as "equality of treatment in the enforcement and application of the laws."[77] Since the impugned provision was enforced and applied equally against all Indian women, it did not conflict with this definition of equality. At issue in *Bliss* was a provision of the Unemployment Insurance Act that denied regular benefits to women who interrupted their employment because of pregnancy. The Court denied Bliss's claim that the denial constituted discrimination on the basis of sex, with Justice Ritchie concluding that "any inequality between the sexes in this area is not created by legislation but by nature."[78] The Court's narrow reading of "equality before the law" in these two decisions would later play a significant role in the drafting of the Charter's equality rights section, and they are the subject of more detailed discussion in Chapter Five.

The Court's approach to the Bill of Rights signalled to potential litigants that it was not a particularly valuable instrument for challenging federal statutes. Consequently, between 1960 and 1982 the number of cases to reach the Supreme Court involving claims based on the Bill, as well as the success rate of those claims, was small.[79] Moreover, on only one occasion did the Court actually strike down provisions of a federal statute because of a conflict with the Bill of Rights.[80] At issue in *R. v. Drybones* (1969) was the consistency of the equality provisions of the Bill of Rights with provisions in the Indian Act restricting the right of Indians to consume alcohol in ways not applicable to non-Indians. In a significant departure from its decision in *Robertson and Rosetanni,* the Court admitted that the Bill could be used to expand rights beyond the meaning they had prior to 1960. Consequently, the Court declared the impugned provisions of the Indian Act inoperative. As *Lavell* and *Bliss* clearly demonstrate, however, the Court did not follow this path very far.

It would be wrong to leave the impression that the entire Court was uninterested in breathing life into the Bill of Rights. In particular, Justice (and eventually Chief Justice) Bora Laskin attempted to raise the Bill to "quasi-constitutional" status to provide a sounder basis for holding federal laws found to be incompatible with the Bill inoperative.[81] In a significant departure from traditional Canadian practice,[82] Laskin relied extensively on U.S. Bill of Rights jurisprudence in undertaking this project.

Citations of U.S. cases were prominent in Laskin's concurring and dissenting reasons for judgment in several criminal law cases.[83] Three of these decisions involved challenges to the Criminal Code under the 1960 Bill of Rights. In

Appleby v. The Queen (1972), Laskin cited two U.S. Supreme Court decisions, *Coffin v. United States* (1895) and *Leland v. Oregon* (1952),[84] while concurring with his colleagues that reverse onus clauses were compatible with section 2(f) of the Bill of Rights. However, in *R. v. Burnshine* (1974) Laskin cited a combination of U.S. federal and state court decisions in dissenting from the majority's conclusion that a provision in the federal Prisons and Reformatories Act, which subjected offenders below the age of twenty-two to indeterminate sentences, did not unlawfully discriminate on the basis of age.[85] In *Morgentaler v. The Queen* (1975), Laskin cited *Roe v. Wade* (1973) and a state court decision in dissenting from the Court's judgment upholding the Criminal Code's abortion provisions.[86] Finally, Laskin relied on a number of important Warren Court decisions concerning criminal procedure to support his contention in *Curr v. The Queen* (1972) that the Court could infer a guarantee of non-compellability of testimony from section 2(d) of the Bill of Rights.[87] More importantly, despite citing the decision in which the U.S. Court finally abandoned its doctrine of substantive due process in economic matters,[88] Laskin raised the possibility in *Curr* that Canadian courts could legitimately engage in substantive judicial review under a constitutionally entrenched charter of rights.[89]

Perhaps Laskin's most important use of U.S. citations, however, appeared in his majority reasons for judgment in *Thorson v. A.-G. Canada* (1975), the first of the Court's important trilogy of decisions on the rules governing standing to challenge legislation.[90] In *Thorson,* Laskin held for a majority of the Court that ordinary taxpayers could be granted standing without showing any direct personal harm from a statute's enforcement if they were seeking a declaration concerning the constitutional validity of that statute.[91] In reaching this conclusion, Laskin followed the example set by the U.S. Supreme Court in *Flast v. Cohen* (1968).[92] The majority in *Flast* held that taxpayers could challenge congressional spending if it emanated directly from the taxing and spending powers of Congress, and if they could show a link between their status as taxpayers and a specific constitutional limitation on the spending power.[93] By importing this significant development in American jurisprudence into Canada, Laskin prepared the ground for an even greater liberalization of the Canadian rules of standing with which, ironically, he disagreed (perhaps because of his personal disagreement with the use to which these new rules were being put by pro-life advocates). Thus, since 1981, individuals can be granted standing to challenge legislation either by showing that they are directly affected by the legislation, *or* by showing that they have "a genuine interest in the validity of the legislation and that there is no other reasonable and effective manner in which the issue may be brought before the Court."[94]

The liberalization of standing rules on the eve of the Charter's enactment is highly significant. Standing, along with similar doctrines like mootness, ripeness, and political questions, is one of the threshold requirements that courts may invoke to deny litigants access to the judicial process. Although the decision to grant standing in specific cases is always within a court's discretion, any liberalization of the general principles governing standing has important political implications. "Relaxation of standing requirements," argued U.S. Supreme Court Justice Lewis Powell, "is directly related to the expansion of judicial power. It seems to me inescapable that allowing unrestricted taxpayer or citizen standing would significantly alter the allocation of power . . . with a shift away from a democratic form of government."[95] The existence of liberal standing rules under the Charter makes litigation easier and multiplies whatever anti-democratic tendencies the document might contain.

In comparing the pre-Charter development of Canadian judicial review with similar U.S. developments, several important differences are apparent. The most obvious is that judicial review has had a different impact on the nature of federalism in the two countries. By explicitly enumerating the national government's powers, by establishing a powerful upper legislative chamber originally controlled directly by the states, and by assigning unenumerated, residual powers to the states, the U.S. Constitution sought to create a regime in which the national government would be powerful within a limited sphere. Largely under the influence of John Marshall, the U.S. Supreme Court gradually expanded the boundaries of national power. This stands in direct contrast to Canada, where the original federal structure was framed in the wake of the U.S. Civil War. To avoid disputes over the relative strength of the two levels of government, the BNA Act attempted to make the federal government's predominance clear. Informed by a different conception of the "federal principle," however, the Judicial Committee of the Privy Council sharply limited federal powers to the benefit of the provinces. Although the Canadian Supreme Court managed to push the pendulum back toward national power after 1949, there is little evidence of a radical shift toward centralization in judicial decisions.[96]

A second difference concerns the subject matter and style of judicial review. The existence of a constitutionally entrenched Bill of Rights in the U.S. has meant that constitutional questions concerning federalism have always shared time on the judicial stage with civil liberties questions. Indeed, during the past two generations federalism issues have faded into the background, leading a majority of the Supreme Court to declare that federal courts are not the proper forum in which states should defend their interests.[97] In Canada, federalism has been the principal source of constitutional litigation; and while some Canadian justices searched for a theory to justify judicial review on civil liberties grounds, it remained a problematic area for judicial intervention. It is therefore of more than passing interest that, in the absence of strong constitutional authority for the judicial protection of rights, Canada's civil rights record, even with its notable blemishes, is remarkably good.

To some degree, the failure to establish judicial review in the civil liberties field was a product of the Judicial Committee's and the Supreme Court's tendency to treat constitutional and quasi-constitutional documents in a highly legalistic fashion. The Privy Council approached its interpretation of the BNA Act as it did any ordinary statute; neither historical context nor underlying social conditions were considered relevant to the interpretive task. Later, the Supreme Court would adopt a similarly legalistic approach to the Bill of Rights. While it would be wrong to diminish unduly the political importance of this style of review, it would not be inaccurate to claim that legalistic judicial review on federalism grounds produces more limited and less permanent political consequences than creative judicial review on civil liberties grounds.[98] Indeed, contemporary concerns about judicial review in the United States have arisen in response to decisions enforcing judicially defined substantive rights of individuals against various forms of state and federal regulation.

This leads to a final difference. While Canadian jurists refused to build much of substance on rather firm foundations for judicial review, U.S. courts transformed a very ambiguous power into something extremely far-reaching. The historical reluctance of Canadian courts to follow the lead of their U.S. counterparts in this respect makes the fact that the Canadian Supreme Court has switched gears and adopted a very broad conception of its review powers under the Charter even more significant. This development is the result of at least two factors, each of which is discussed in subsequent chapters. First, most of the groups that testified before the Joint Committee of the Senate and House of Commons on the Constitution in 1980-81 lobbied for "a charter with terms which were as broad and potent as they could be."[99] These demands proved politically easy to satisfy, producing a generously worded document open to liberal judicial construction. The second factor has been the incorporation of several important facets of American judicial review. This has occurred as the Canadian Court has employed U.S. constitutional jurisprudence in grappling with the problems of interpretation and application unique to constitutionally entrenched declarations of rights.[100] The Canadian Court's citation of U.S. Supreme Court decisions has increased significantly since 1984. Moreover, the largest proportion of these citations has been drawn from the modern era of U.S. judicial review, when the most celebrated decisions have resulted from the noninterpretivist approach to constitutional jurisprudence. Not surprisingly, this is also the period during which the tension between constitutional democracy and judicial power has been most pronounced in the United States.

The Paradox of Liberal Constitutionalism

Section 52(1) of Canada's Constitution Act, 1982 and section 24(1) of the Charter of Rights and Freedoms explicitly establish a political regime of constitutional (as opposed to legislative) supremacy in which constitutional limits on political power are enforced through judicial review of statutes, regulations, and official conduct.[101] Such judicial enforcement of constitutionally entrenched individual rights has become a crucial component of liberal democracy for two reasons. The most obvious is that judicial review is by its very nature countermajoritarian. Liberated from the direct control of political majorities, courts are often the only institution capable of safeguarding minority rights, although as the pre-1954 history of American judicial review reminds us, this is not universally the case. A second relevant characteristic of judicial review is the attractiveness of adjudication as a technique for resolving complex political and moral disputes. The atmosphere of impartiality surrounding adjudication lends considerable moral legitimacy and authoritativeness to the decisions of courts on such issues. Unfortunately, these characteristics cut two ways. Counter-majoritarianism and judicial finality are the very reasons why judicial review continues to be controversial in liberal democracies.

Judicial review is, however, an indispensable and key element of liberal constitutionalism. The paradox of modern liberal constitutionalism lies in this: if judicial review evolves such that political power in its judicial guise is limited only by a constitution whose meaning courts alone define, then judicial power is no longer itself constrained by constitutional limits. Contrary to liberal constitutional theory, the modern development of American judicial review suggests that judicial supremacy can easily overtake constitutional supremacy.[102] The paradox is that judicial enforcement of rights in the name of liberal constitutionalism may destroy the most important right that citizens in liberal democracies possess, i.e., the right of self-government. This danger was perhaps never better expressed than in Abraham Lincoln's first inaugural address: "If the policy of the government, upon vital questions, affecting the whole people, is to be irrevocably fixed by decisions of the Supreme Court, the instant they are made, in ordinary litigation . . . the people will have ceased to be their own rulers."[103] Lincoln's purpose in uttering these words was to justify his refusal to be bound by the constitutional principle articulated in *Dred Scott,* but its message remains relevant precisely because it went unheeded by courts and their political allies. In fact, contemporary North American constitutional scholarship is dominated by the quest for theories of constitutional interpretation that might justify increasingly more expansive uses of the power of judicial review.

To be sure, readers sceptical about this argument would be correct to point out that, in the sentence following the passage quoted above, Lincoln went on to say that his criticism of the type of judicial power wielded by the U.S. Supreme Court in *Dred Scott* should not be taken as a general "assault upon the court or the judges."[104] The same qualification applies to my argument: the paradox of liberal constitutionalism is not found in the existence of the institution of judicial review *per se,* but in the particular form that this institution has taken during the past two generations. It is too late in Canadian constitutional development to question whether the Charter should have been entrenched. Indeed, it is precisely because that question was resolved in favour of the Charter that attention must be paid to the manner in which judges interpret and apply this document of open-ended rights subject to broad judicial construction. For what concerned Lincoln most, and what should concern contemporary Canadian commentators, is the effect of judicial errors made in the course of modern constitutional litigation, in which litigants frame their unmet policy expectations as violations of private individual or group rights and ask courts for remedial action.[105] Unfortunately, judges are no more infallible than legislators or other policy-makers in transforming competing demands into public policy. These errors, if effectively incapable of correction, permeate the entire political landscape and may produce policy consequences that undermine, rather than advance, the public interest. That judges should review government action and pass judgment on its constitutionality is a relatively uncontroversial proposition; that the proper functioning of liberal constitutionalism requires these judgments to be, for all practical purposes, final is debatable.

Sceptical readers might still object, however, on two additional grounds. First, between 1984 (when the Court decided its first Charter case) and 1989, the Supreme Court relied on the Charter to nullify federal and provincial statutes in whole or in part on only sixteen occasions.[106] Moreover, in cases of great significance, the Court has left intact mandatory retirement exemptions contained in provincial human rights legislation,[107] as well as the hate literature and anti-solicitation provisions of the Criminal Code.[108] At first glance, this appears to be the record of a cautious Court sensitive to the potentially far-reaching nature of its judicial review powers under the Charter. From a comparative perspective, however, the Court's activity has a different appearance. The U.S. Supreme Court, for example, overturned only one federal statute and eighteen state laws during the first *thirty-four years* that it claimed to exercise judicial review.[109] While the early Charter Court has not asserted its new powers as forcefully as the U.S. Court did during its most activist period (1953-86), it has adopted the interpretive tools necessary to match its American counterpart's record. Judicial deference to government policy in specific cases should not be confused with judicial restraint in exercising the political power of judicial review.

A second objection is that the Supreme Court has been careful to concede the inappropriateness of judicial policy-making and to assure observers that the checks on judicial power contained in sections 1 and 33 of the Charter provide adequate protection against judicial usurpation of legislative responsibilities. On their face, these sections would appear to do precisely that, but their actual effectiveness is uncertain. The major weakness of the intended internal check contained in the "reasonable limits" clause of section 1 is that its meaning and application are determined by the Court itself. Indeed, as will become evident in Chapters Two and Six, the Court has interpreted this section in a way that arguably expands judicial power. Although intended as a means by which courts might save otherwise unconstitutional legislation, as interpreted by the Supreme Court section 1 allows courts to re-evaluate the policy decisions of legislatures while simultaneously affirming the exclusive right of legislatures to formulate policy in controversial areas. Moreover, in its first 100 Charter decisions, the Court used section 1 to "save" only 15 per cent of the constitutional violations it detected.[110] The problem with the external check on judicial power contained in the legislative override provision of section 33 is that its political legitimacy has been seriously undermined, resulting in calls for its removal from the Charter. Indeed, what comes in the following chapters is ammunition for the next Charter-related constitutional battle, which will be fought over the survival of this provision. Whether by explicit amendment or through the emergence of a new constitutional convention, there is a real possibility that section 33 will become a non-operative part of the Charter.[111] As I argue in the final chapter, this would be a serious blow to the development of liberal constitutionalism in Canada.

There are two final arguments that might be made against the claim that judicial supremacy so threatens liberal constitutionalism that it exposes a paradox at the core of this doctrine. One argument, which Robert Dahl first advanced in the American context in 1958, is that the moral insights of judges cannot remain out of step with the moral insights of society as a whole for very long.[112] A second argument is that, notwithstanding the possible enfeeblement of section 33, the negative impact of constitutional decisions can be addressed either by crafting new legislation or by directly amending the constitution. As I shall argue more fully in Chapter Seven, each of these arguments has its weaknesses. For example, significant social harm can occur while waiting for the convergence of judicial and popular moral insight. Similarly, constitutional amendment and legislative redrafting are clumsy responses that are themselves subject to judicial interpretation and review. In the final analysis, the problem of judicial supremacy remains a serious one within the political theory of liberal constitutionalism.

CHAPTER 2

The Dimensions of Constitutional Interpretation

The interpretation and application of constitutional guarantees of individual rights and freedoms is a complex enterprise. While some constitutional provisions are precisely worded and narrowly applicable to specific situations, most are subject to an almost infinite variety of interpretations and applications. Broad, open-ended phrases like "freedom of expression," "freedom of conscience and religion," "equal protection and equal benefit of the law," and the right not to be deprived of "liberty and security of the person except according to the principles of fundamental justice" inevitably require that judges inject substantive content into vague constitutional guarantees.[1] At some point in the performance of this task, however, judges risk going beyond constitutional enforcement to constitutional creation. Recognizing this possibility, jurists and constitutional scholars in both Canada and the United States have devoted considerable attention to elaborating general theories of constitutional interpretation designed to provide guidelines for determining the specific meaning that should be attached to indeterminate constitutional language.

The principal cleavage among American scholars in this area is between "interpretivist" and "non-interpretivist" theories of judicial review.[2] Interpretivist theories hold that "judges deciding constitutional issues should confine themselves to enforcing norms that are stated or clearly implicit in the written Constitution." According to interpretivists, there is a clearly defined line between constitutional enforcement and constitutional creation, and courts exercise their powers illegitimately when they cross that line. Consequently, judicial nullification of legislation is permissible only if the legislation contradicts specific constitutional provisions or violates rights clearly inferable from the document's language. Non-interpretivist theories, by contrast, counsel judges to "enforce norms that cannot be discovered within the four corners of the [constitutional] document." This approach does not perceive any inherent conflict between constitutional enforcement and constitutional construction, viewing the task of constitutional interpretation as a creative one of identifying and applying novel rights to determine the validity of legislation.

In Canada, the interpretivist/non-interpretivist dimension of constitutional theory is complicated by a cleavage between liberal-individualist and communitarian theories of judicial review. Although recognizing that liberal individualism is a significant component of both Canadian political culture and the Charter, communitarians argue that Canada is more committed than the United States to "collectivist, organic values."[3] This commitment is embodied in the Charter itself, which protects the collective rights of linguistic groups, aboriginal peoples, and cultural communities.[4] In addition, section 1 (the reasonable limits clause) and section 33 (the legislative override clause) of the Charter protect the collective interests of society as a whole. Communitarian theories of judicial review warn that Canadian courts must take this feature of Canadian constitutionalism into account when exercising judicial review under the Charter; not to do so risks transforming post-Charter judicial review into "another branch-plant operation of an American head office."[5]

In this chapter, I examine where the Canadian Supreme Court's interpretation of the Charter falls along the interpretivist/non-interpretivist continuum, as well as the extent to which the Court's understanding and use of judicial review under the Charter have been influenced by American constitutional jurisprudence. The chapter's first two sections set out the broad contours of interpretivism, non-interpretivism, liberal individualism, and communitarianism as theories of judicial review. In the third section I make the claim that the Supreme Court's reading of American constitutional jurisprudence has contributed significantly to its adopting the basic principles of a very potent form of non-interpretivist judicial review. In particular, the Court has embraced substantive judicial review while largely divorcing its interpretation of the Charter from the meaning provided by the document's drafters. The question of where the Court's approach lies on the liberal-individualist/communitarian spectrum is taken up in later chapters.

Interpretivism and Non-Interpretivism

In a speech before the American Bar Association on July 9, 1985, U.S. Attorney-General Edwin Meese III called on the federal judiciary, and the justices of the U.S. Supreme Court in particular, to embrace a "jurisprudence of original intention."[6] According to Meese, the objective of constitutional interpretation should be "to judge policies in light of principles, rather than remold principles in light of policies." The only way to ensure this, he argued, is for the Supreme Court to ground its constitutional jurisprudence in the meaning that the Constitution's framers originally attached to the language used in the document. Meese asserted that this is the only theory of constitutional interpretation consistent with the "sanctity of the rule of law" and the system of "limited yet energetic powers" established by the U.S. Constitution. The Attorney-General promised that the Justice Department would "endeavor to resurrect the original meaning of constitutional provisions and statutes as the only reliable guide for judgment" in cases in which the department became involved.

Meese's speech elicited a harsh and unusually public response from two Supreme Court sitting justices, William J. Brennan, Jr., and John Paul Stevens.[7] Justice Brennan attacked Meese's concept as "arrogance cloaked as humility," and described as "facile historicism" the "chorus of lamentations calling for interpretation faithful to 'original intention'." In Brennan's eyes, the Constitution embodied a "vision of human dignity" whose dynamic character requires that the document not fall captive "to the anachronistic views of long-gone generations." Justice Stevens's more pedestrian criticism was specifically directed against Meese's implicit rejection of the incorporation doctrine, through which the Court has applied the Bill of Rights to the states. For Stevens, the Civil War and Reconstruction era amendments profoundly altered the federal-state relationship in a way that made incorporation not only constitutionally possible but politically desirable and necessary.

The reactions by Brennan and Stevens forced Meese to clarify what he meant by a "jurisprudence of original intention." "Where the language of the Constitution is specific," Meese argued, "it must be obeyed. Where there is demonstrable consensus among the framers and ratifiers as to a principle stated or implied by the Constitution, it should be followed. Where there is ambiguity as to the precise meaning or reach of a constitutional provision, it should be interpreted and applied in a manner so as to at least not contradict the text of the Constitution itself."[8] Meese's "intentionalism," as Robert Bork called it in joining Meese's side in the debate, meant that "the text, structure, and history of the Constitution provide . . . a premise [which] states a core value that the framers intended to protect." The judge's task is to supply "the minor premise in order to protect the constitutional freedom in circumstances the framers could not foresee." For Bork, the key point was that the Constitution is a law that constrains the actions of judges, as well as legislators, executives, and citizens.[9]

The exchanges among these adversaries during the summer and fall of 1985, as well as during the confrontation over Robert Bork's nomination to the Supreme Court two years later,[10] were important public manifestations of a long-standing academic debate about the source from which the U.S. Supreme Court draws the authority for its constitutional decisions. Unfortunately, the language in which the two sides expressed themselves focused attention on only a limited aspect of this debate: the degree to which the constitutional deliberations of 1787 to 1791 (and later 1865 to 1870) should serve as the source of contemporary constitutional law in the United States. "Original intent" became identified with the record of the Constitutional Convention at Philadelphia, causing sceptics to raise three very legitimate questions: Why should framers' rather than ratifiers' intent be binding? Is it possible to discover a common intent among either the framers or ratifiers? Should this intent, even if ascertainable, matter in the late twentieth century?[11] For many critics, the difficulty of answering these questions became a sufficient reason to reject the more general idea that constitutional law should be firmly anchored to the text of the Constitution itself. [12]

The principles at issue in this controversy are clearly evident in the debate surrounding John Hart Ely's attempt to formulate a theory of judicial review falling somewhere between interpretivism and non-interpretivism. The principal motivation for Ely's 1980 book on judicial review, *Democracy and Distrust,* was his dismay with the Supreme Court's 1973 abortion decision, *Roe v. Wade.* [13] Although Ely agreed in principle with liberalizing state abortion laws, he was profoundly disturbed by the Court's failure to connect its decision in *Roe* to "any value the Constitution marks as special," or even to provide any indication that it thought it had an obligation to make such a connection. [14] Moreover, Ely did not even find the decision persuasive as an exercise in judicial policy-making. In his view, the Court's judgment that fetuses are not legal persons was entirely irrelevant to the question of whether states could legislatively protect their existence; as he pointed out, states legitimately interfere with individual conduct to protect the lives and existence of many things (like animals) that no one would remotely consider legal persons. [15] Concerned that *Roe* would have a long-term negative impact on an institution and practice he respected, Ely undertook to articulate a theory of judicial review that would preserve the Supreme Court's important role in American politics while avoiding the destructive judicial policy-making characteristic of the discredited era of substantive due process.

Despite Ely's fear that judicial power might spin out of control in the wake of *Roe,* he rejected "clause-bound interpretivism" as the solution to the problem. According to Ely, this concept holds that "provisions of the Constitution be approached essentially as self-contained units and interpreted on the basis of their language, with whatever interpretive help the legislative history can provide, without significant injection of content from outside the provision." Ely viewed this approach as not only unwise, but impossible. In his view, several constitutional provisions invite interpreters "to look beyond their four corners" in order to inject meaning into them from outside sources. In particular, the Ninth Amendment's recognition of unenumerated rights and the "due process," "privileges or immunities," and "equal protection" clauses of the Fourteenth Amendment provide such an invitation. [16]

At this point in the argument there is little difference between Ely's rejection of clause-bound interpretivism and the results-oriented jurisprudence of non-interpretivism. The distinction emerges, however, in Ely's contention that the Constitution itself illuminates the external meaning that can legitimately be injected into the Ninth and Fourteenth Amendments. Ely argued that the U.S. Constitution is fundamentally a process-oriented document that is primarily concerned with formal decision-making procedures rather than with substantive outcomes. He thus asserted that the Ninth and Fourteenth Amendments should be interpreted in ways that reinforce the process of representation, clear the channels of political change, and facilitate the representation of minorities. This "representation-reinforcing" approach to judicial review, Ely contended, is legitimate because of its consistency with both the Constitution's principal purpose and with the special procedural expertise of judges.[17] The same cannot be said, according to Ely, about the "value-protecting" approach of non-interpretivist judicial review.

In contrast to "clause-bound interpretivism" or "intentionalism," Ely designed his theory not to prevent judicial activism, but merely to restrict activism to its proper sphere. What underlies his theory is the assumption that a consistent failure by the political process to respond adequately to the concerns of certain groups signals a breakdown in the representative institutions of pluralist democracy. When this occurs, the Supreme Court is justified in actively intervening in the political process to repair the structural defects in these institutions and enhance the political status of underrepresented interests.

The non-interpretivist advocates of broader judicial activism reacted to Ely's narrow emphasis on decision-making processes by arguing that the purpose of constitutional adjudication should be to go beyond structural concerns to discover the fundamental values that the Constitution is meant to achieve and advance those values by giving specific meaning to vague constitutional language.[18] Arthur Selwyn Miller, for example, argued that the systematic exclusion of certain groups and interests from the political process not only supports Ely's representation-reinforcing theory of judicial review, but also justifies the active intervention of judges "in the governing process, so as to substitute their judgment for that of federal and state political officers."[19] Michael Perry's reaction to Ely was even more direct. He asserted that most of the decisions in the area of human rights for which the Court has been praised have been the product of non-interpretivist judicial review. The "status of constitutional human rights" in the United States, Perry argued, "is almost wholly a function, not of constitutional interpretation, but of constitutional policymaking by the Supreme Court."[20] To follow Ely's theory would be to undermine progress in the area of human rights.

Perry thus undertook to defend the legitimacy of non-interpretivist judicial review even in the absence of either historical or textual justification for any form of non-interpretivism. In his view, the principal justification for non-interpretivist review in human rights cases is functional, and that function is to remedy "a serious defect in American government – the absence of any policymaking institution that regularly deals with fundamental political-moral problems other than by mechanical reference to established moral conventions." Non-interpretivist review, according to Perry, constitutes a "tolerable accommodation" between the democratic commitment to electorally accountable policymaking and the American conviction "that there may indeed be right answers – *discoverable* right answers – to fundamental political-moral problems." What emerges from non-interpretivist review, asserted Perry, is a dialogue between electorally accountable decision-makers, whose policy choices are the captives of conventional morality, and the justices of the Supreme Court, whose evaluation of those choices may be informed by a more sophisticated and progressive moral vision. According to Perry, this dialogue generates a more self-critical and mature political morality.[21]

As Perry's justification for non-interpretivism suggests, one of his principal criticisms of interpretivists like Robert Bork and Supreme Court Chief Justice William Rehnquist is that their approach to constitutional interpretation derives from a profound moral scepticism.[22] This scepticism, according to Perry, leads interpretivists to deny that there exists any principled ground on which judges can nullify or alter the moral vision reflected in the policies enacted by electorally accountable decision-makers other than that the vision directly contradicts specific constitutional language. Where no such contradiction exists, the moral principles adopted by the majority must prevail. In Perry's view, therefore, the essential deficiency of interpretivism is that it denies the possibility of moral growth. To put this point in Miller's language, the framers intended the Constitution to be a "delegation of power to later generations of Americans to write their own fundamental laws."[23] As Perry and Miller describe it, the debate between interpretivism and non-interpretivism is a debate between morally impoverished legal positivism and morally prophetic judicial statesmanship.

Formulating the debate in these terms, however, oversimplifies the relationship that exists in liberal constitutionalism between attachment to legal positivism and faith in the capacity of human reason to discover universal moral principles. Liberal constitutions do not deny the possibility of moral growth; indeed, they provide for this growth by granting legislatures sufficient power to create new rights, and by providing for an amendment process through which moral progress may be written into fundamental law. For example, despite the narrow interpretation given to the concept of equality by the Canadian Supreme Court under the 1960 Bill of Rights, every jurisdiction in Canada eventually enacted human rights legislation designed to protect various minority groups from both public and private discrimination.[24] Furthermore, the experience provided by this legislative creation and protection of rights had a significant impact on the fundamental law of equality entrenched by the Charter.

The history of suffrage in the United States provides another example of moral progress in the absence of judicial participation. Article I of the U.S. Constitution initially left the determination of the qualifications necessary to vote in elections for the U.S. House of Representatives entirely within the policy discretion of state legislatures, imposing as a sole requirement that anyone qualified to vote in elections for the most numerous branch of the state legislature must also be qualified to vote in elections for the House of Representatives. Nothing in Article I prohibited individual states from restricting the suffrage as much as they thought appropriate or from extending it as far as they desired. Consequently, several states extended the right to vote to women long before female suffrage became a constitutional requirement. Gradually, the national polity concluded that it was fundamentally unjust to deny the vote to blacks, women, and persons over the age of eighteen. As a result, several constitutional amendments and federal statutes were enacted to remove the states' policy discretion in this area. Moral progress thus became part of the positive constitutional law enforceable by the courts.

The essence of liberal constitutionalism is that judges, like legislators and executives, must be bound by the positive law of a constitution that embodies, however imperfectly, universal and eternal principles of moral justice. The claim is not that the rights protected by liberal constitutions at any particular time are exhaustive, but that liberal constitutionalism requires that judges enforce only those rights that a constitution authorizes them to enforce. The task of rendering liberal constitutions more perfect properly belongs to the citizens who must live under them. This process of moral change is obviously slow and often produces results limited in their scope; but such is the quest for absolute moral principles in pluralist liberal democracies. The real complaint of non-interpretivists like Perry and Miller is that moral progress does not proceed far enough, fast enough. However, to follow their advice and grant judges the sole, or even primary, responsibility for changing fundamental constitutional principles to reflect moral progress is to create the possibility that the moral dialogue that commentators like Perry wish to establish between the courts and the polity will simply become a judicial monologue. Recognizing this problem, Perry to his credit advocated the aggressive use of the devices available in Article III of the U.S. Constitution to control judicial power.[25] While sound in theory, however, these structural checks on judicial power have proved to be very weak in practice for reasons that will become evident in Chapter Seven.[26]

This is not to say that interpretivism, in either Meese's "intentionalist" or Ely's "representation-reinforcing" form, provides a better check on judicial power. Indeed, both versions of interpretivism are variations on the theme of judicial self-restraint; but self-restraint is precisely what the framers of the U.S. Constitution, and thus of liberal constitutionalism more generally, refused to rely on as the principal device for controlling political power. What they attempted to do was to supply "by opposite and rival interests, the defect of better motives." Federalism and an overlapping separation of powers in which each branch of government possesses the "constitutional means . . . to resist encroachments of the others" constituted the "republican remedy for the diseases most incident to republican government."[27] Consequently, to rely on a "jurisprudence of original intention" to control judicial power ironically contradicts the actual intentions of the framers of the U.S. Constitution.[28] The general point is that, by its very nature, liberal constitutionalism relies on structural arrangements to control political power.

Like all theories of judicial review, the competing sets of constitutional theories included within the general categories of interpretivism and non-interpretivism perform two complementary tasks. First, these theories "attempt to provide justifications for the exercise of the power of judicial review in a democracy."[29] Second, constitutional theory attempts to restrain this aspect of judicial power by providing a means of identifying when judges exceed its legitimate boundaries. To paraphrase Madison, achieving these two goals is part of a larger objective of enabling judges to control legislators and executives while obliging them to control themselves.[30] Constitutional theory alone, however, is inadequate to this task. Despite the efforts of Perry, non-interpretivist theories of judicial review cannot escape the problem of constitutional legitimacy. The function that Perry assigns to non-interpretivist review properly belongs elsewhere in liberal constitutional democracies. Interpretivist theories of review, on the other hand, are not particularly effective as checks on judicial power because their implementation depends on the very officials (judges) that these theories are designed to control. At most, interpretivism might prevent the boldest exercises of judicial power, such as *Roe v. Wade*. Non-interpretivism, of course, both justifies and encourages such decisions.

While obviously complex, most of the antagonists in the American debate about the legitimacy of rights-based judicial review at least share in common a commitment to the proposition that rights belong primarily, and perhaps exclusively, to individuals. Even affirmative action, which is a group-based remedy for discrimination, is usually represented as a means of protecting and expanding *individual* rights. Among Canadian theorists, however, there is almost universal scepticism about the idea that protecting individual rights should constitute the principal objective of political life. The American concern with individual rights is either denigrated as an impediment to real social and political progress or depreciated in importance by emphasizing the equal significance of *collective* rights and *communitarian* values in Canada.

Liberal Individualism and Communitarianism

Many Canadian scholars have been attracted by Ely's argument that a broad form of interpretivist review is necessary both to constrain judicial power and to protect the rights of those whose access to the political process is limited.[31] A leading example is Patrick Monahan's 1987 book, *Politics and the Constitution,* in which he criticized the Canadian Supreme Court's early Charter decisions for maintaining an artificial and untenable distinction between "legal" and "political" analysis. According to Monahan, the Court's emphasis on legal analysis permits it to understate its inevitable concern with the policy rationality of legislation. Although this tends to produce impoverished decision-making, it is an understandable consequence of the normative and empirical vacuum in which Charter adjudication takes place.[32] Monahan presents his own theory of judicial review as a remedy for at least the normative vacuum in which Charter review takes place.

Monahan approaches judicial review in much the same way as Ely. While he accepts the proposition that "courts under the Charter can never escape the task of evaluating the policies chosen by the legislature," he also argues that judges should restrict their evaluation to the consistency of those policies with values explicitly contained in the constitutional document. According to Monahan, one of the fundamental values underlying the Charter is its commitment to representative democracy. Thus, like Ely, he argues that judicial interpretation of the Charter should ensure "that there are no arbitrary and permanent boundaries around the scope of political debate." For Monahan, judicial review should be "a mechanism to protect existing opportunities for democratic debate and dialogue as well as to open new avenues for such debate." Again following Ely, Monahan criticizes "value-reinforcing" or "justice-based" theories of judicial review because, by "inviting judges to test the substantive fairness of political outcomes against some independent normative standard, justice-based theories limit the opportunities for popular participation and control."[33] Implicit in this criticism is the view that Charter review should only be exercised over government policies that impede participation in the political process, or over policies that are clearly the product of a process in which full participation was absent. In this sense, Monahan's theory of judicial review is consistent with Ely's process-oriented theory.

Where Monahan differs from Ely is in recognizing a second, more substantive value embodied in the Charter. Drawing on the work of Gad Horowitz and Seymour Martin Lipset, Monahan argues that, in contrast to the profound individualism and strict separation of private and public activity embodied in the U.S. Constitution, Canada's constitutional arrangements reflect a much stronger commitment to the collectivist values of communitarianism.[34] The essence of this doctrine is that the "good of the individual is not conceivable apart from some regard for the good of the whole"; consequently, "restraints on individuals are natural rather than contractual, flowing from the very duties and rights which are implicit in membership in a larger community."[35] One important feature of this communitarian spirit is the absence of any "necessary tension between the state and freedom."[36] Communitarianism, unlike liberal individualism, produces a more tolerant and participatory regime in which "collectivist or organic conceptions of society" can flourish. Citizens in such regimes recognize themselves as "part of some cosmic order" and a "culture which elaborates and maintains the vocabulary of [their] self-understanding."[37]

The conclusion that Monahan draws from these characteristics of Canadian political culture is that judicial review under the Charter should not simply be "representation-reinforcing" (i.e., democratic) but should also be *communitarian*. According to Monahan, judges "must regard attempts by the community to embody its fundamental beliefs in law as something more than the imposition of one person's 'external preferences' on another." Judicial review, in other words, should not protect individual rights at the expense of reducing the capacity of communities "to define their common identity [and] enrich the lives of individuals in those communities." This requires both "negative" judicial review, which ensures that the Charter does not adversely affect communities, and a positive strategy, which extends the collective rights of specific communities or groups already entrenched in the Charter. In Monahan's theory of judicial review, the collective rights-oriented language provisions (sections 16 to 23), interpretive clauses (sections 25 and 27), and the guaranteed rights of denominational schools (section 29) become crucial components of the Charter. Similarly, the reasonable limits (section 1) and legislative override (section 33) provisions protect the larger political community's right to advance its interests through the democratic process.[38]

The communitarian aspects of Monahan's theory of judicial review raise both historical and theoretical questions. The historical question is whether Monahan's theory accurately reflects the Canadian legal and political tradition. As Robert Vipond has demonstrated, individual liberty and collective self-governance in communities have both been important values in Canadian political arrangements.[39] Indeed, the framers of Canada's constitution envisioned mechanisms such as disallowance, reservation, and judicial review as means through which individual rights (especially property rights) could be protected against encroachments by provincial governments acting under powers inferred from section 92(13) of the Constitution Act, 1867 in pursuit of a collective good that was hostile to those rights. The theoretical question concerns the inevitable necessity of reconciling conflicts between different communities. In essence, the issue here is which community's collective rights ought to prevail when such conflicts occur. An example from Alberta illustrates the historical point, while one from Quebec illuminates the theoretical issue.

In 1935, Albertans reacted to the depression by electing a Social Credit government dedicated in part to bringing market forces under the control of political power.[40] Shortly after taking power, the new government passed several statutes designed to provide relief from the depression, to address the province's revenue shortfalls, and to bring the province's debt under control. The initial legislation included statutes designed to "bring about the equation of consumption to production, and to afford each person a fair share in the cultural heritage of the people of the Province" (Social Credit Measures Act); to reduce the rate of interest payable on the provincial debt (Provincial Loans Refunding Act); to control monetary policy (Alberta Credit House Act, Credit of Alberta Regulation Act); and to implement other measures thought necessary to achieve the broader objectives of social credit (Bank Employees Civil Rights Act, Judicature Act Amendment Act). On August 17, 1937, however, the federal government disallowed the Credit of Alberta Regulation Act, the Bank Employees Civil Rights Act, and the Judicature Act Amendment Act. As J.R. Mallory put it, one important reason for this unexpected revival of the disallowance power "was the alarmed insistence of the chartered banks that the legislation was intolerable."[41] That this should have been the case is not surprising: Sir John A. Macdonald had stipulated years before that the federal government would be justified in using its power of disallowance against provincial legislation that unduly infringed contractual and property rights.[42]

Alberta responded to the federal government's action by passing three new legislative measures. First, it enacted a new Credit of Alberta Regulation Act that was virtually identical to the first, with the exception that all references to "banking" and "banks" were replaced by "credit" or "business of dealing in credit." The purpose of this change was to avoid a direct conflict between the statute and the federal government's authority under section 91 of the British

North America Act to legislate with respect to banking. A second statute was the Accurate News and Information Bill, which gave the government broad power to force newspapers to publish official statements designed to correct public misperceptions about provincial policies. Finally, the Bank Taxation Act was a largely punitive, retaliatory measure directed against the banks, which had been instrumental in pushing for disallowance of the earlier legislation. Like the earlier legislation, however, none of these acts survived federal scrutiny. On October, 6, 1938, the Lieutenant-Governor of Alberta refused to grant royal assent to any of the bills; and in January, 1938, the Supreme Court of Canada ruled that the statutes were *ultra vires* the Province's legislative competence.[43] Thus, in the space of two years, disallowance, reservation, and judicial review were deployed in favour of relatively advantaged, national economic interests against the needs of "a class of debtors who lived in the midst of economic ruin."[44] The collective interest of these Albertans did not long survive once it clashed with the individual proprietary rights of interests situated outside the province.

The example from Quebec concerns judicial review of various laws enacted by the province to restrict the activities of Communists and Jehovah's Witnesses.[45] In 1937, Quebec passed An Act to Protect the Province Against Communist Propaganda, which became known as the Padlock Act. This statute prohibited the publication and distribution of Communist "propaganda" and permitted the Attorney-General to evict the occupants and padlock any house used to propagate communism. Similarly, between 1936 and 1959 Quebec sought to repress the Jehovah's Witnesses through various statutes and legal harassment. One Quebec City by-law, for example, prohibited the Witnesses from distributing their literature without the prior permission of the police chief. On another occasion, Premier Maurice Duplessis ordered that a Witness restaurateur have his liquor licence revoked in perpetuity because he posted bail for other Witnesses charged with violating restrictive legislation. Eventually, the Supreme Court of Canada declared many of these statutes and official conduct against Communists and Jehovah's Witnesses unconstitutional on division of powers grounds.[46]

Although the Supreme Court's decisions against Quebec in these cases can be understood in communitarian terms as vindicating the collective rights of marginal communities to express and act on their beliefs, they more likely reflect an individual rights perspective in which the Court properly acted to defend the freedom of expression and religion enjoyed by dissentient individuals. Indeed, one might even defend Quebec's action against these dissenters on communitarian grounds by arguing that its restrictive laws were necessary measures to enable an otherwise fragile community to assert its collective right to defend itself against ideas it perceived as hostile. In fact, this was implicit in the position taken by three justices in *Saumur v. Quebec* (1953) who held that freedom of religious practice was subject to provincial regulation.[47]

The Quebec example points to the theoretical question raised by communitarianism, the essence of which is the value of any theory of collective rights in societies characterized by a plurality of collectivities or communities. If, as Monahan suggests, liberalism exaggerates the tension between individuals and the community,[48] then communitarianism equally understates the potential conflict between competing communities in heterogeneous societies. To put this another way: a theory of collective rights must provide some mechanism for protecting groups and individuals who do not belong to the dominant community without at the same time hampering that dominant community from asserting its collective rights over the objections of dissenters. According to communitarians like Monahan, the Charter strikes this delicate balance between pure liberalism and authoritarianism by granting special protection to various collective rights of certain marginal communities. However, if the rights of the members of these communities are defined solely in terms of common group characteristics, they remain vulnerable in circumstances beyond those covered by the Charter's special protections. Consequently, some protection of individual rights is necessary.[49]

What concerned Monahan in 1987, and now profoundly disturbs likeminded commentators such as Allan Hutchinson and Andrew Petter,[50] is the potentially chilling effect that the Charter's liberal-individualist core might have on any proactive judicial role in creating *additional* collective rights. In the specific case of Hutchinson and Petter, their concern is the Court's failure to protect the collective rights of "labour" against the rights claims of individual workers and owners of capital and other property. The first Supreme Court decision to draw harsh criticism from communitarians was *RWDSU v. Dolphin Delivery* (1986).[51] In this decision, the Court upheld an injunction prohibiting secondary picketing in a labour dispute against a claim that the injunction violated freedom of expression. Among the reasons the Court gave for its decision was the Charter's inapplicability to private litigation and to the common-law regulation of private relationships. The Court also held that, even if the Charter did apply to the situation, the injunction would constitute a reasonable limit on expression under section 1. Thus, the Court affirmed the existence of a "wall of separation" between the private and public spheres, and refused to use the Charter to protect the rights of labour.

According to Hutchinson and Petter, the Court's acceptance in *Dolphin Delivery* of a distinction between public, state power (which is subject to the Charter) and private power (which is not controlled by the Charter) reflected the flawed assumption of liberal legal positivism that judges can objectively identify the dividing line between the public and private spheres. The flaw in this assumption, according to Hutchinson and Petter, is to believe that such a distinction even exists. In their view, the distinction is entirely illusory, since private, individual rights – especially the rights to property and freedom of contract – exist only because they are enforced by state power. Consequently, any distinction that judges draw in this respect will inevitably be arbitrary and non-neutral. To be more precise, it will always be defined on a case-by-case basis in a manner that serves the interests of entrenched private power. The perpetuation of this distinction, therefore, constitutes "a formal fraud that perpetuates a substantive injustice," particularly by destroying "the hopes and opportunities of working people for an improved life."[52]

In making this criticism, however, Hutchinson and Petter are guilty of the same oversimplification of liberal constitutionalism that plagues the arguments advanced by Perry and Miller. There is indeed a strong element of positivism in liberalism, but liberal constitutionalism also contains a complex relationship between natural rights and positive law. In fact, liberal constitutions originated in the attempt to express the "laws of nature and of nature's God" in a positive law form. Moreover, liberal constitutions embody a concept of equality according to which no individual possesses a *natural* right to rule over another. All right to rule, in other words, is conventional and depends on the consent of those over whom it is exercised. This natural equality is the source both of the positive right of self-government through majoritarian political processes, and of the negative individual rights that limit majoritarian political power.[53] Liberal constitutionalism strives to achieve the delicate task of balancing these two types of rights.

Which is not to say that *Dolphin Delivery* does not deserve to be criticized. Perhaps the most pernicious feature of the decision was that the Court held that the Charter does not apply to the judicial branch of government.[54] More than anything else, this shows the extent to which Canada has been exposed to the paradox of liberal constitutionalism. The problem is not that courts improperly enforce individual rights (as the communitarians might argue), but that in the name of performing this function they exempt themselves from constitutional limits on their own power in a way that undermines the positive right of self-government. Nowhere has this been more evident than in the Supreme Court's adoption of non-interpretivism and substantive review.

Non-Interpretivism and the Emergence of Substantive Review Under the Charter

Non-Interpretivism and the Influence of American Constitutional Jurisprudence

Although constitutional history and doctrine ensured the basic legitimacy of judicial review in Canada when the Charter came into existence in 1982, it was still necessary for the Supreme Court to define the precise scope of this power under the Charter. In a concerted effort to escape the criticism of narrow legalism that greeted its Bill of Rights jurisprudence, the Court has enthusiastically embraced non-interpretivism by relying on key elements of both U.S. and domestic jurisprudence. This trend began in the Supreme Court's first Charter decision, *Law Society of Upper Canada v. Skapinker* (1984), when Justice Willard Estey sought guidance from "the techniques of interpretation to be applied in construing a Constitution" that U.S. Chief Justice John Marshall had articulated in *McCulloch v. Maryland* (1819).[55] Estey repeated Marshall's assertion that, while the specific meaning of broadly worded constitutional phrases should be deduced from the "nature" of the Constitution's "important objects," judges "must never forget, that it is *a constitution* [they] are expounding."[56] This meant that courts "must allow the legislative branch to exercise that discretion authorized by the Constitution."[57] Chief Justice Dickson later relied on these "classical principles of American constitutional construction" to declare in *Hunter v. Southam* (1984) that the Charter calls for a "broad, purposive analysis, which interprets specific provisions of a constitutional document in the light of its larger objects."[58] Dickson defined this approach further in *R. v. Big M Drug Mart* (1985), where he argued that judges should generously interpret the Charter to guarantee and secure for Canadians its "full benefit" by focusing on the purposes of, and interests protected by, specific Charter provisions. Nevertheless, echoing Marshall's concerns, Dickson pointed out that courts should not "overshoot the actual purpose of the right or freedom in question."[59]

As in the United States, however, the Canadian Court soon began to abandon the more cautious elements of Marshall's interpretive principles. For example, while Dickson's admonition to engage in a purposive interpretation of Charter rights is routinely cited, his accompanying caution not to go too far is almost never cited. Moreover, in *Reference re Section 94(2) of the Motor Vehicle Act (B.C.)* (1985), Justice Antonio Lamer implicitly associated Justice Estey's use of Marshall in *Skapinker* with the "living tree" metaphor of Canadian constitutional interpretation first articulated by Lord Sankey in *Edwards v. A.-G. Canada* (1930).[60] In *Edwards,* Sankey relied on this metaphor to declare that the word "person" in section 26 of the BNA Act was broad enough to include women, permitting the appointment of women to the Senate. Citing Lord Sankey directly in the British Columbia *Motor Vehicle Reference,* Lamer offered the following warning: "If the newly planted 'living tree' which is the Charter is to have the possibility of growth and adjustment over time care must be taken to ensure that historical materials . . . do not stunt its growth."[61] Similarly, applying both *Edwards* and *McCulloch* in *Morgentaler, Smoling and Scott v. The Queen* (1988), Chief Justice Dickson concluded that the Supreme Court is "charged with the crucial obligation of ensuring that the legislative initiatives of our Parliament and legislatures conform to the democratic values expressed in the Canadian Charter of Rights and Freedoms."[62]

The lesson that the post-Charter Court has drawn from *McCulloch* and its domestic equivalent *Edwards* is that constitutional interpretation is an exercise in judicial creativity. This vision of judicial review, however, is not the only, or even the most accurate, interpretation of *McCulloch* or *Edwards*. F.L. Morton and Rainer Knopff have persuasively argued that, by taking the "living tree" metaphor out of its original context and applying it to Charter adjudication, the Court has effected a subtle transformation in its meaning. According to Morton and Knopff, the "living tree" metaphor originally functioned to provide Parliament with sufficient flexibility to meet new problems and pursue novel policy objectives. When applied to the law of rights, however, the same metaphor functions to encourage judicial creativity in constructing new rights and in actively nullifying legislative policy choices. This application of the metaphor, Morton and Knopff assert, seriously undermines the very concept of constitutionalism: "Broad wording is used to ensure the degree of flexibility necessary for a constitution to endure, but if there is to be anything to *endure,* the language cannot be so general as to constitute a 'blank cheque' to posterity, on which each generation of judges can scrawl what it likes."[63] The danger is that, when misused, the "living tree" can become a noxious weed that chokes off legislative and executive power that might be used to pursue valuable objectives.

Morton and Knopff's interpretation of *Edwards* and its misapplication is also applicable to *McCulloch.*[64] Two constitutional questions were at issue in this case: whether Congress had the power to establish a national bank; and whether the state of Maryland could tax that bank. The provisions of the U.S. Constitution under consideration, therefore, concerned the scope of federal legislative power and its relationship to state power. Although not expressly granted the constitutional authority to charter banks, Congress defended its decision to establish the Second Bank of the United States in 1816 as consistent with the "necessary and proper" clause of Article I, section 8 of the U.S. Constitution. Maryland, on the other hand, argued that this clause should be interpreted as a restriction on national legislative power that prevented Congress from exercising *implied* powers beyond those minimally necessary to carry out its *enumerated* powers. Marshall disagreed, arguing instead that a narrow construction of the "necessary and proper" clause would unduly restrict Congress's ability to accomplish the ends for which the Constitution had been adopted. Consequently, Marshall established the following principle: "Let the end be legitimate, let it be within the scope of the constitution, and all means which are appropriate, which are plainly adapted to that end, which are not prohibited, but consist with the letter and spirit of the constitution, are constitutional."[65]

Considered within its proper context, therefore, Marshall's decision to interpret the "necessary and proper" clause liberally, like Sankey's "living tree" metaphor, has a far different meaning than the one attributed to it by Estey and Dickson in *Skapinker* and *Southam.* Instead of justifying judicial creativity in constructing new rights and additional restrictions on legislative power, Marshall's argument suggests that the broad, open-ended language of constitutional documents may also be understood as a means of ensuring that constitutions do not unduly limit a legislature's flexibility to enact laws designed to meet circumstances unforeseen at the time of the document's writing.[66] This difference between *McCulloch*'s original meaning and the Canadian Court's understanding of Marshall's opinion is particularly evident in the criteria established by the Court to measure the validity of legislation under section 1 of the Charter. Unlike Marshall, who argued for a liberal approach in defining the legitimate means that could be employed to achieve constitutionally valid legislative objectives, the presence of "pressing and substantial" legislative objectives is not in itself sufficient to justify legislation under section 1. The legislature must also show that the statute in question is "rationally connected to the objective," restricts the rights protected by the Charter as little as possible, and will produce social benefits large enough to offset the costs of limiting individual rights.[67]

Driven by the interpretive principles set out by Marshall, as well as the common understanding among Marshall's contemporaries that there are well-defined limits to judicial power, the traditional approach to judicial review in the United States placed an emphasis on clear rules of interpretation, intelligible standards, and the wisdom of relying on judicial review infrequently. By contrast, the modern approach to judicial review is characterized by the frequent use of a judicial power that is no longer guided by set interpretive rules or standards. Consequently, one major difference between these two approaches is their respective understanding of where the responsibility lies for defining the grey areas created by the necessarily broad and general language of constitutions. The traditional understanding, exemplified in Marshall's *McCulloch* decision, is that this responsibility lies primarily with the legislature; the modern view is that it belongs to the judiciary. To be even more precise, the traditional American view of judicial review saw constitutional interpretation as a collaborative enterprise in which the executive and legislative branches had as strong a claim to participate as the judiciary. In the modern era, constitutional interpretation has become a judicial monopoly in which legislative or executive disagreement with judicial declarations of rights is viewed as approaching tyranny. Although the Canadian Court has relied on such venerable U.S. authorities as *McCulloch* (and to a lesser degree *Marbury v. Madison*) to support its vision of constitutional interpretation, the theory of judicial review developed by the Canadian Court from *Skapinker* to *Morgentaler, Smoling and Scott* shares most of the characteristics of the modern version of American judicial review, which has been especially prominent in U.S. constitutional litigation since 1937.[68]

Nowhere was the influence of this modern view of judicial review more evident than in the interpretive principles articulated by Justice Bertha Wilson. Like Dickson, Justice Wilson also took account of American jurisprudence in developing her understanding of judicial review under the Charter. In *Big M Drug Mart,* for example, she relied on the U.S. Supreme Court's decision in *Griggs v. Duke Power Co.* (1970) to argue that the Charter is "first and foremost an effects-oriented document."[69] Wilson meant by this that the Court has the power to review not only the intent or purpose of legislation for constitutional defects, but also the constitutionality of the legislation's effects. Quoting from Chief Justice Warren Burger's majority opinion in *Griggs,* Wilson contended that the "starting point for any analysis of a civil rights violation is 'the *consequences* of the [discriminatory] practices, not simply the motivation.'"[70] In advancing this principle, which was accepted by Chief Justice Dickson in *Big M Drug Mart* and applied by him in *Morgentaler, Smoling and Scott,* Wilson considerably broadened the scope of judicial review.

As in the case of her colleagues' interpretation and application of *McCulloch,* however, Wilson took *Griggs* out of its original context. *Griggs* was a non-constitutional case involving judicial construction of the Civil Rights Act of 1964.[71] Consequently, the U.S. Court in *Griggs* was not using an "effects-oriented" approach to determine the constitutionality of legislation but to evaluate the employment procedures and testing mechanisms of a company with a long history of racially discriminatory hiring and promotion practices. Had Congress disagreed with the Court's construction of the Civil Rights Act, it could simply have amended the statute to make the legislation's intent less ambiguous. Thus, in contrast to its use by Wilson in the constitutional context of the Charter, *Griggs* had virtually no impact on the balance of power between the legislative and judicial branches of the U.S. federal government. Indeed, the U.S. Court has consistently refused to apply an "effects-oriented" test to the constitutionality of government action under the equal protection clause of the Fourteenth Amendment precisely because such a test would subject a vast array of legislation to constitutional challenge on adverse impact grounds.[72] Proponents of non-interpretivist judicial review, however, have been critical of the U.S. Court's reluctance to extend the *Griggs* approach into the realm of constitutional law.[73] Wilson thus took Charter review even farther along the non-interpretivist path.

Justice Wilson's second major excursion into American jurisprudence for clues about the nature of judicial review appeared in her concurring reasons for judgment in *Operation Dismantle v. The Queen* (1985), which provided the basis for the entire Court's rejection of a "political questions" doctrine that would have placed executive decisions concerning foreign and defence policy beyond judicial review.[74] Although recognizing that this doctrine constituted a "well established principle of American constitutional law" derived from the separation of powers doctrine,[75] Wilson found a sufficient number of exceptions to this principle to question its actual impact on judicial review.[76] In Wilson's view, these examples of the U.S. Court's deciding politically contentious issues suggested that "courts should not be too eager to relinquish their judicial review function simply because they are called upon to exercise it in relation to weighty matters of State."[77] In reaching this conclusion, Wilson did not so much reject the American political questions doctrine as choose between the two different interpretations of its application offered by Justices Felix Frankfurter and William Brennan. By adopting Brennan's interpretation, Wilson chose the position most consistent with non-interpretivist review. Consequently, she rejected the value of judicial self-restraint implicit in Frankfurter's willingness to grant the legislative and executive branches wide discretion in certain policy areas outside the normal range of judicial expertise.

By embracing and even extending the principles of the modern era of American judicial review – the most celebrated decisions of which have been the products of non-interpretivism – the Canadian Court has carved out a theory of constitutional interpretation that envisions a strong and creative judicial role in defining the norms embedded in the Charter.[78] One of the key issues raised by this non-interpretivist approach concerns the source of the unenumerated democratic rights and values the Court intends to uphold through Charter adjudication. As Ely has argued, discovering the fundamental values implicitly protected by constitutions is a problematic enterprise. The central danger is that, in the hands of modern judges, each of the available alternatives – natural law, reason, tradition, consensus, and "neutral principles" – can easily collapse into some version of judicial policy preference.[79] What makes this problematic is that personal policy preferences are not sufficient to legitimate the decisions of such electorally unaccountable institutions as courts. Although the Court has attempted to address this issue by identifying the "basic tenets of our legal system" as the source of many of the values that it intends to uphold, the justices have not yet articulated any objective means of determining what those tenets are.[80] The problem of constitutional legitimacy thus remains. Moreover, of particular interest to Canadian commentators is whether the adoption of American-inspired non-interpretivist review will lead the Canadian Court to define these democratic values in a manner consistent with the philosophical assumptions of U.S. constitutional jurisprudence, or whether non-interpretivism will acquire a uniquely Canadian character.

The Emergence of Substantive Review

Non-interpretivist review is especially potent when it reaches to the substantive policy of legislation. The question of substantive review first reached the Canadian Supreme Court in the British Columbia *Motor Vehicle Reference* (1985).[81] At issue was the constitutionality of a provision in the British Columbia Motor Vehicle Act that defined the act of driving with a suspended licence as an absolute liability offence punishable by mandatory imprisonment and a fine. The effect of defining the prohibited act in this way was to remove from British Columbia the burden of establishing *mens rea* prior to conviction and punishment. Section 94(2) of the Act provided that guilt of the proscribed conduct could be established simply "by proof of driving, whether or not the defendant knew of the prohibition or suspension." Speaking for a majority of the Court, Justice Antonio Lamer held that this provision violated section 7 of the Charter because it deprived individuals of their liberty in a manner contrary to the principles of fundamental justice. Justice Lamer further found that this particular infringement of the Charter could not be reasonably justified under section 1.

The province's interference with individual liberty in section 94(2) was obvious in the section's provision for mandatory imprisonment as a sanction against the proscribed conduct. Its violation of fundamental justice was less clear, particularly since there was no challenge to the procedural scheme by which British Columbia proved the act of driving with a suspended licence. Nevertheless, Justice Lamer found that section 94(2) violated a *substantive* principle of fundamental justice that now prohibits provinces from establishing absolute liability offences.[82] Lamer contended, moreover, that section 7 grants the Court the power to strike down provincial legislation on such substantive grounds. Although the case evoked minor differences among some of the justices, all agreed with Justice Lamer's proposition that the principles of fundamental justice permit substantive judicial review.[83]

Justice Lamer began his reasons for judgment by stressing the importance of "an open-minded approach to determining the meaning of 'principles of fundamental justice'."[84] He argued that it was misleading to frame the issue in terms of a strict separation between procedural and substantive review, which he described as a peculiarly American dichotomy that had developed in a constitutional context that included neither the explicit authorization for judicial review found in section 52 of the Constitution Act, 1982 and section 24(1) of the Charter, nor the checks on judicial power contained in sections 1 and 33 of the Charter.[85] American courts, Lamer averred, had been forced to develop elaborate theories of constitutional interpretation to justify even very limited powers of judicial review.

In Lamer's view, the different constitutional context of judicial power in Canada meant that Canadian courts were not so constrained as their American counterparts by clumsy distinctions between different forms of judicial review. The task of Canadian courts, Lamer argued, is "not to choose between substantive or procedural content *per se* but to secure for persons 'the full benefit of the Charter's protection' under section 7, while avoiding adjudication of the merits of public policy."[86] Using Justice Dickson's "purposive analysis" to define the rights protected by section 7, Justice Lamer determined that the Court would deny Canadians the full benefit of the Charter's protection if it simply imposed procedural restraints on government interference with life, liberty, and security of the person. Judicial review of legislation according to substantive principles of fundamental justice was necessary to avoid the danger that "individuals may be deprived of these most basic rights."[87] According to Lamer, therefore, substantive review is legitimate whenever it is functionally necessary to secure the benefit of the Charter's guarantees in specific instances.

Given the legislative history of section 7, Justice Lamer's conclusion that the phrase "principles of fundamental justice" addressed the substance, as well as the administration, of provincial penal law was indeed remarkable. The initial draft of the general legal rights section of the Charter required that infringements of life, liberty, and security of the person be consistent with "due process of law." At meetings held during the summer of 1980, provincial officials attacked this language on the grounds that it could be used by Canadian courts, as it had been by their American counterparts, to develop a doctrine of *substantive* due process.[88] In the U.S. context, this doctrine came to mean that courts could legitimately review the reasonableness, or policy content, of legislation. Laws that the courts found "arbitrary, oppressive, and unjust" were unconstitutional, even when they were otherwise within the legitimate police powers of the states.[89] First used against a federal law in *Dred Scott v. Sandford* (1857), and against state legislation in *Allgeyer v. Louisiana* (1897),[90] substantive due process later became a powerful judicial weapon against economic regulation.

The federal government responded to this concern by striking the phrase "due process" from section 7 and replacing it with "principles of fundamental justice." Although not a term of art in Canadian jurisprudence, the meaning of "principles of fundamental justice" was not entirely indeterminate in 1980. It appeared in section 2(e) of the 1960 Bill of Rights, which prohibited the federal government from depriving "a person of the right to a fair hearing in accordance with the principles of fundamental justice for the determination of his rights and obligations." In *Duke v. The Queen* (1972), the Supreme Court defined this phrase to mean that "the tribunal which adjudicates upon his rights must act fairly, in good faith, without bias and in a judicial temper, and must give him the opportunity adequately to state his case."[91] To the officials in the Justice Department responsible for drafting the Charter, this procedural definition was sufficient to indicate that the phrase "principles of fundamental justice," even abstracted from the specific context in which it originally appeared, did not have any substantive connotation in Canadian law, whatever its ultimate procedural meaning.[92]

During testimony before the Special Joint Committee on the Constitution in 1981, the assistant deputy minister of justice for public law, Barry L. Strayer, summarized the Canadian history of this phrase and explained that, in the department's view,

> the words "fundamental justice" would cover the same thing as what is called procedural due process, that is the meaning of due process in relation to requiring fair procedure. However, it in our view does not cover the concept of what is called substantive due process, which would impose substantive requirements as to the policy of the law in question.[93]

During these same hearings, Minister of Justice Jean Chrétien also reported to the Committee that the phrase "principles of fundamental justice" did not confer the same power "to the courts over the substance of the legislation" as did the phrase "due process."[94] Strayer took this definition so seriously that he adhered to it after his appointment to the Federal Court bench.[95] Lower courts also consistently refused to attach a substantive meaning to "fundamental justice" in early Charter adjudication.[96]

Given the apparent intent of the Charter's drafters not to create a power of substantive judicial review, one aspect of the legislative history of section 7 is puzzling. As Justice Lamer noted in the *Motor Vehicle Reference,* the Charter's drafters could have replaced "due process" with "natural justice," a known term of art with a clear and relatively narrow procedural meaning.[97] By using "natural justice," the section's drafters might have avoided any confusion about whether section 7 permitted substantive judicial review; conversely, the decision not to employ it supported the opposite interpretation. What may explain this puzzle is the fact that although "natural justice" traditionally referred to procedural justice in judicial and quasi-judicial proceedings, its meaning was in flux as the Justice Department drafted the Charter. During the 1970s, courts began to expand natural justice to include a broader concept of "fairness," which applied to administrative proceedings as well as to judicial and quasi-judicial proceedings. Moreover, courts were beginning to use the concept of fairness to review both the procedural and substantive merits of administrative decision-making.[98] Indeed, Deputy Minister of Justice Roger Tassé indicated at the Joint Committee hearings that his department was concerned about the implications of entrenching these developments in the constitution through the use of "natural justice" in section 7.[99]

Although conceding that evidence about the legislative history of section 7 was relevant to the questions at issue, Justice Lamer rejected the argument that his decision should be significantly guided, if not entirely determined, by that history. He minimized the importance of section 2(e) of the Bill of Rights and the meaning attached to it in the Court's *Duke* decision on the grounds that, unlike section 7, the Bill of Rights placed the words "principles of fundamental justice" squarely in the context of a "right to a fair hearing."[100] Similarly, he argued that comments made during the Special Joint Committee hearings should be given minimal weight, since statements by civil servants were not sufficiently indicative of the intentions of the legislative bodies that adopted the Charter. Most importantly, Justice Lamer averred that "casting the interpretation of section 7 in terms of the comments made by those heard at the joint committee proceedings" might lead to the conclusion that the rights protected by the Charter are "frozen in time to the moment of adoption with little or no possibility of growth, development and adjustment to changing societal needs."[101] This understanding of rights and freedoms had proved to be a major obstacle to the emergence of a creative judicial role under the Bill of Rights, and the Court's reticence to undertake such a role had been the subject of severe criticism. In the *Motor Vehicle Reference,* the post-Charter justices appeared intent on avoiding the same criticism.

It would be wrong to leave the impression that Justice Lamer was totally unaware of the path down which substantive review might lead the Court. In fact, he attempted to articulate a relatively narrow standard for determining the scope and content of the principles of fundamental justice. These principles, Lamer argued, "are to be found in the basic tenets of our legal system. They do not lie in the realm of general public policy but in the inherent domain of the judiciary as guardian of the justice system."[102] The irony of Lamer's "basic tenets" formulation should not go unremarked, however. According to the Justice Department, one of the most "basic tenets of our legal system" in 1981 was that the "principles of fundamental justice" were purely procedural in nature. What Lamer's decision shows is the extent to which judges are potentially free to create whatever principles are necessary to reach their intended result. The Court's power to declare absolute liability offences contrary to substantive fundamental justice and violations of the Charter (when such offences are enforced by imprisonment or probation) had no source other than judicial will.

Interpreting Section One

Section 1 of the Charter, which provides that the rights and freedoms set out in the document are "subject only to such reasonable limits prescribed by law as can be demonstrably justified in a free and democratic society," recognizes that constitutionally guaranteed rights cannot be absolute in a functioning society; and since the definition and application of these rights has become largely a judicial function, section 1 can serve to limit the potential excesses of non-interpretivist, substantive judicial review. Section 1 has not had this effect, however, for two very important reasons. First, as a result of significant criticism between

1980 and 1982, the Charter's drafters altered section 1 to dilute its strength as a limitations clause. These changes included adding the phrase "prescribed by law"; substituting the phrase "as can be demonstrably justified" for "as are generally accepted"; and removing an explicit reference to "a parliamentary system of government." Proponents of a powerful Charter argued that these amendments were necessary to soften the restrictive impact of section 1 on guaranteed rights.[103]

The impact of section 1 on judicial power has also been limited because, like every provision of the Charter, its operational meaning is subject to judicial definition. The Supreme Court has limited the effectiveness of this provision in three distinct ways: by distinguishing between the *limitation* of rights (which can be justified under section 1) and their complete *abrogation* (which cannot be so justified); by narrowly defining the phrase "prescribed by law"; and by establishing a relatively rigid test for determining when limits are "reasonable" and "demonstrably justified."[104] For the most part, this last aspect of the Court's approach to the limitations clause gives judicial review of legislation and other legal rules under section 1 of the Charter its basic character.

The Court fully articulated its analytical approach for determining reasonable and demonstrably justified limits for the first time in *R. v. Oakes* (1986).[105] This so-called *Oakes* test of reasonableness and demonstrable justification contains two elements. First, the government seeking to defend the limit in question must show that its legislative objective relates "to concerns that are *pressing and substantial* in a free and democratic society" (emphasis added). Second, the limit itself must be proportionate to the legislative objective, which courts are to determine according to a three-pronged proportionality test. To pass the first prong of this test, the limit must be rationally connected to the legislative objective. Next, the government must show that, by impairing the relevant right or freedom as little as possible, the limit in question represents the least restrictive means of achieving this objective. Finally, it must be clear that the benefits gained from limiting the right or freedom outweigh the costs of the impairment.

Technical details aside, the general tenor of the *Oakes* test is perfectly consistent with the modern approach to judicial review in the United States, where "balancing" has become a principal mode of constitutional adjudication. This descriptive metaphor "refers to theories of constitutional interpretation that are based on the identification, valuation, and comparison of competing interests." While some exercises in balancing establish "a substantive constitutional principle of general application" (definitional balancing), others identify the balancing process as a constitutional principle itself (*ad hoc* balancing).[106] What makes balancing controversial is that its emphasis on interest balancing and cost-benefit analysis fits uncomfortably within any traditional conception of the judicial function. Moreover, the balancing process raises important questions about whether courts are institutionally equipped to engage in this traditionally legislative function. Both of these issues of constitutional legitimacy and institutional capacity are explored at greater length in Chapter Six.

Conclusion

The controversy surrounding constitutional interpretation under the Charter reflects a more general uncertainty about the political theory underlying the Charter. For communitarians, the Charter embodies an antiquated and morally bankrupt political theory of atomistic individualism that ignores the reality "that society comprises a thick web of interdependent relations."[107] From this perspective, judicial enforcement of this political theory only serves to exacerbate the harmful consequences of the Charter's liberalism. Non-interpretivists, on the other hand, either fail to find any coherent political theory in the Charter at all, or they argue that whatever theory it does contain provides inadequate answers to contemporary social problems.[108] In either case, non-interpretivism views constitutional interpretation as a process of injecting a political theory into the Charter in order to solve pressing social problems through constitutional adjudication. That this view is now firmly entrenched in Charter jurisprudence is evident in the Supreme Court's contention that legislation must conform to "democratic values" derived from "changing societal needs" rather than from principles articulated by the Charter's framers. The consequence of this approach to Charter review is the subject of the next three chapters.

PART 2

The Supreme Court and the Charter

CHAPTER 3

Fundamental Freedoms

Section 2 of the Charter of Rights and Freedoms sets out those guarantees of individual liberty deemed minimally necessary for the existence of a free society. These guarantees are spelled out in four subsections, which protect freedom of conscience and religion [2(a)]; freedom of expression and the press [2(b)]; freedom of peaceful assembly [2(c)]; and freedom of association [2(d)]. Supreme Court decisions concerning section 2 have had a significant impact on specific legislation, and have been instrumental in defining several important principles of Charter interpretation. In *R. v. Big M Drug Mart* (1985), for example, the Court affirmed and expanded its earlier ruling that corporate entities are entitled to some Charter protection; declared that the meaning attached to rights and freedoms under the 1960 Bill of Rights should not determine their meaning under the Charter; and identified a "broad, purposive" analysis as the best means of determining the meaning of Charter guarantees.[1] Similarly, in *Retail, Wholesale and Dept. Store Union v. Dolphin Delivery* (1986), the Court identified the type of public, or government, action subject to Charter regulation.[2]

Given the extensive American jurisprudence on such First Amendment issues as freedom of speech and religion, it is hardly surprising that section 2 decisions have also been distinguished by their citation of American constitutional law. Although the Canadian Supreme Court has found U.S. First Amendment jurisprudence useful in considering the questions raised in these cases, its general attitude has been that Canadian constitutional doctrine and the structure of the Charter itself mandate a somewhat different approach to these questions in specific cases. The terms in which certain fundamental freedoms like expression and conscience are enumerated, for example, are more open-ended than the language employed in the First Amendment. Moreover, section 2 expressly protects freedoms that are only implicitly protected in the United States (e.g.,

65

freedom of association). Finally, section 1 of the Charter explicitly instructs the Court to balance the constitutional protection afforded fundamental freedoms against important ("pressing and substantial," in the Court's terms) governmental objectives. In one sense, this structure simplifies the process of Canadian judicial review. While the U.S. Court has been forced to debate the very legitimacy of balancing values under the First Amendment and to engage in complex definitional manoeuvres to undertake such balancing, the Canadian Court has for the most part avoided complex debates about the definitional scope of section 2 freedoms and focused most of its attention on applying section 1 analysis to legislation that limits very broadly defined liberties of expression, religion, and the like. As a result, the Court has been able in most cases simply to accept the broadest possible meaning of the right in question and devote most of its energy to section 1 issues.

Freedom of Religion

The contribution of freedom of religion decisions to the development of the general principles according to which the Charter is interpreted and applied is particularly evident in *R. v. Big M Drug Mart* (1985) and *Edwards Books and Art v. The Queen* (1986), both of which concerned Sunday-closing laws.[3] At issue in *Big M Drug Mart* was the constitutionality of the federal Lord's Day Act,[4] which prohibited the performance of most forms of work and commercial activity on Sunday.[5] This was not the first occasion on which legislation of this nature had been challenged. Indeed, the passage of the Lord's Day Act in 1906 stemmed directly from decisions by the Judicial Committee of the Privy Council and the Supreme Court that existing Sunday observance legislation did not fall within provincial regulatory power over property and civil rights within the province, nor under provincial authority over other merely local or private matters. The Privy Council held in *A.-G. Ontario v. Hamilton Street Railway* (1903) that, since the primary purpose of such legislation was to promote public order, safety, and morals, it fell within the federal government's power over criminal law.[6] The Supreme Court followed this precedent in *Reference re Legislation Respecting Abstention from Labour on Sunday* (1905).[7] Consequently, it fell to the federal government to legislate restrictions on commercial activity on Sunday, which it did with the Lord's Day Act.

The Lord's Day Act itself became the subject of a more substantive challenge in *Robertson and Rosetanni v. The Queen* (1963).[8] The appellants in this case asserted that the guarantee of religious freedom enumerated in the 1960 Bill of Rights rendered the most important sections of the Act inoperative. In rejecting this argument, the Supreme Court held that the Bill of Rights did not guarantee religious liberty in the abstract, but only as it concretely existed in Canadian law in 1960. In addition, the Court argued that it was not the Act's purposes that mattered in determining its consistency with the Bill of Rights but the effects of the statute. Although the Court found the Act's purpose to be clearly religious in substance, it viewed its effects as "purely secular and financial."[9] Since the

Court did not observe any direct impact of the Act on the ability of Canadians to hold whatever religious beliefs they wished, or to affirm those beliefs publicly, it did not find the statute inconsistent with the religious freedom protected by the Bill of Rights.

In using *Big M Drug Mart* to strike down the Lord's Day Act as inconsistent with the religious freedom guaranteed by section 2(a) of the Charter in 1985, Justice Brian Dickson (as he then was) rejected the proposition that the meaning attached to religious liberty in *Robertson and Rosetanni* could determine "the meaning of 'freedom of conscience and religion' under the Charter."[10] Dickson rejected *Robertson and Rosetanni* as a binding precedent because to do otherwise would be to rely on the discredited "frozen concepts" theory of rights, according to which the meaning of fundamental freedoms is determined solely "by the degree to which that right was enjoyed by Canadians prior to the proclamation of the Charter." Instead, he argued that the meaning of Charter guarantees should be determined by a generous, rather than legalistic, interpretation of their broader purposes. According to Dickson, the purpose of section 2(a) was to protect "expressions and manifestations of religious non-belief and refusals to participate in religious practice," as well as to allow individuals "to hold and to manifest whatever beliefs and opinions [their] conscience dictates."[11] This generous interpretation of the purposes of section 2(a) led Dickson to conclude that, at a minimum, "government may not coerce individuals to affirm a specific religious belief or to manifest a specific religious practice for a sectarian purpose."[12] This was, in his view, the essential purpose of the Lord's Day Act, thus rendering it inconsistent with the Charter.

Dickson's understanding of the purposes underlying section 2(a), as well as any protection for fundamental freedoms generally, stemmed in large part from his finding that the "ability of each citizen to make free and informed decisions is the absolute prerequisite for the legitimacy, acceptability, and efficacy of our system of self-government." The "rights associated with freedom of individual conscience," Dickson asserted, are central "both to basic beliefs about human worth and dignity and to a free and democratic political system." In his view, this accounted for their being designated in the Charter as "fundamental" and for their primacy among the rights protected by the U.S. Bill of Rights. Indeed, Dickson pointed out, these rights are included among those protected by the *First* Amendment to the U.S. Constitution.[13]

At least one comment is necessary about this part of Dickson's judgment. In stressing the inclusion of religious freedom among the rights protected by the First Amendment, Dickson uncritically adopted a rhetorical device often used by U.S. civil libertarians. In fact, the First Amendment carries that designation as a result of historical accident rather than by conscious design. The free speech and religion clauses were originally contained in the third of twelve amendments submitted by Congress to the states for ratification in September, 1789. When the states failed to ratify the first two amendments on the original list, the amendment containing the religion clauses became the first amendment.[14] Thus, whatever the relative importance of religious freedom in the U.S. Bill of

Rights, no conclusions about its status can be drawn from its placement in the First Amendment.

In addition to relying on questionable history, Dickson's emphasis on the importance of religious freedom in American jurisprudence was highly ironic. As Dickson noted in *Big M Drug Mart,* the earlier decision in *Robertson and Rosetanni* had been consistent with several U.S. Supreme Court decisions sustaining the constitutionality of state Sunday observance legislation against challenges brought under the First Amendment.[15] In majority decisions authored by Chief Justice Earl Warren, the U.S. Court upheld such legislation despite finding that its *original* purpose violated the First Amendment's prohibition against laws "respecting an establishment of religion." What saved the legislation was Warren's generous construction of its *contemporary* purpose and effect. In Warren's view, the laws in question no longer aimed at religious purposes, but had become secular measures for the regulation of labour.[16] Moreover, according to Warren, none of the legislations' direct effects could be construed as invidiously discriminating among religions, or as interfering with the free exercise of religion. Consequently, state Sunday observance legislation violated neither of the First Amendment's religion clauses.

In considering the relevance of these U.S. cases to the constitutional questions surrounding the Lord's Day Act, the Crown's argument forced Dickson to compare the structure of the First Amendment to that of section 2(a) of the Charter. The Crown argued that section 2(a) provides less protection for religious freedom than the First Amendment because it does not contain an "establishment" clause. In the absence of such a clause, the Crown averred, there could be no conflict between the Charter and the legislative purpose underlying the Lord's Day Act. In rejecting this argument, Dickson argued that the American establishment and free exercise categories were "not particularly helpful in defining the meaning of freedom of conscience and religion under the Charter," largely because he found a tendency for these categories to overlap in the American jurisprudence.[17]

Dickson saved his most important observations about the First Amendment, however, for the U.S. Court's treatment of the legislative purposes underlying Sunday observance statutes. Dickson agreed with Warren's proposition that legislation promoting constitutionally prohibited purposes must be rejected by virtue of that fact alone. He refused, however, to apply Warren's "evolving purpose" doctrine to the Lord's Day Act. In Dickson's view, this doctrine clashed with at least two fundamental principles of Canadian constitutional law. First, the "theory of shifting purpose" did not accord with the Canadian conception of "Parliamentary intention," in which "purpose is a function of the intent of those who drafted and enacted the legislation at the time, and not of any shifting variable."[18] Second, since the determination of legislative purpose constitutes a crucial component of division of powers jurisprudence, a "shifting purpose" theory, Dickson argued, "could effectively end the doctrine of *stare decisis* in division of power cases."[19] Left unsaid by Dickson was that the Court could still strike down the Lord's Day Act even if it accepted Warren's evolving purpose doctrine by declaring that the Act now constituted a federal infringement on provincial power. However, this would have meant a lost opportunity to employ the newest and most powerful weapon in the Court's arsenal of judicial review.

Having rejected the U.S. Court's evolving purpose doctrine, Dickson characterized the Lord's Day Act as a law whose primary purpose "is the compulsion of sabbatical observance";[20] and since this legislative purpose was in direct conflict with the purpose of section 2(a) of the Charter, Dickson declared the Act unconstitutional. In addition, although it was unnecessary for him to comment on the matter, Dickson explicitly accepted Justice Wilson's proposition that legislation enacted in pursuit of otherwise constitutionally valid purposes might nevertheless be invalid because of its effects.[21] *Big M Drug Mart* thus established the principle that a statute may violate the Charter by virtue of either unconstitutional purposes or effects. However, Dickson allowed that where the constitutional violation is a function of the legislation's effects, the statute may be upheld by reference to section 1 of the Charter. The Court's duty at this stage of the analysis would be to balance the importance (not simply the constitutionality) of the legislation's purpose against its deleterious effects.

The opportunity to apply the second part of this principle to judicial review of legislation similar to the Lord's Day Act came less than two years later. At issue in *Edwards Books and Art* was the constitutionality of Ontario's Retail Business Holidays Act, which contained provisions prohibiting most retail stores from opening on Sundays and other holidays.[22] At first glance, the statute appeared to suffer from the same constitutional deficiency (provincial intrusion on federal power) as the legislation struck down by the Judicial Committee and the Supreme Court in *Hamilton Street Railway* and *Re Legislation Respecting Abstention from Labour on Sunday.* However, in *Edwards Books and Art,* the Court characterized the purpose of the Retail Business Holidays Act as secular in nature. The Court found that, by allowing "employees to enjoy a common day of rest and recreation," the Act constituted a valid regulation of labour under Ontario's power to legislate with respect to "civil rights" within the province.[23] Having affirmed the constitutional validity of the Act's purpose, the Court shifted its focus to the effects of the Ontario statute.

At this point in his reasons for judgment, Chief Justice Dickson turned to the U.S. Supreme Court's discussion of the First Amendment's "free exercise" clause in Sunday observance decisions. The relevant question here was whether, regardless of intent, the laws in question imposed a burden on the exercise of religions whose day of worship falls on days other than Sunday. Dickson's survey of the American decisions revealed unanimous agreement among the U.S. justices that Sunday observance laws did, in fact, impose an indirect economic burden on retailers whose religion requires a day of rest other than Sunday. The Chief Justice's analysis of the impact of Ontario's Retail Business Holidays Act produced roughly the same conclusion. Dickson identified four classes of individuals who might be affected by Sunday closing legislation: non-observers,

Sunday observers, Saturday observers, and observers of another day of the week. In his judgment, any impact on non-observers would be purely secular in nature; Sunday observers benefited from the legislation; and at least some Saturday observers suffered a competitive disadvantage. Dickson added that the legislation also imposed a burden on Saturday-observing consumers. [24]

Was this burden on certain Saturday-observing retailers and consumers sufficient to invalidate the Act? Dickson again turned to the relevant American jurisprudence, where he found the U.S. Supreme Court divided on the question of whether indirect economic burdens rendered Sunday-observance legislation unconstitutional. [25] U.S. Chief Justice Earl Warren and five other justices held that there was no means of achieving the constitutionally valid objective of the legislation without imposing an economic burden on non-Sunday observers. Justices William Brennan and Potter Stewart held that the legislation was unconstitutional in the absence of any accommodation for non-Sunday observers. Finally, Justice William Douglas articulated an absolutist interpretation of the First Amendment that prohibited the enactment of any law even remotely connected to religion.

In summary, a majority of the U.S. Supreme Court agreed that Sunday observance legislation is valid despite the economic costs it imposes on the exercise of religious beliefs, and despite the absence of any legislative effort to accommodate non-Sunday-observing retailers. [26] Among the factors the majority considered in reaching this conclusion were the interest of employees in enjoying a common day of rest, the interest of employers in avoiding the costs of Sunday observance legislation, and the possibility that any attempt to accommodate non-Sunday observers might require undesirable state-sponsored inquiries into the sincerity of individually held religious beliefs. [27]

Although Dickson conceded the relevance of these factors, he rejected the majority U.S. conclusion that these administrative burdens remove from legislatures any duty to exempt some groups and individuals from Sunday-closing legislation. Instead, Dickson adopted the Brennan-Stewart position requiring reasonable accommodation. Dickson accepted this position because it most closely resembled the balancing process called for by section 1 of the Charter. [28] Thus, for Dickson, the question in *Edwards Books and Art* became whether the Retail Business Holidays Act included exemptions sufficient to accommodate the right of Saturday-observing retailers to freedom of religion, thereby satisfying the criteria necessary to justify limits on Charter guarantees under section 1. Dickson accepted Ontario's claim that the provision of a common day of rest for retail workers was sufficiently important to justify limiting religious freedom, and that the statute in question was rationally connected to the achievement of that objective. Dickson also agreed that no alternative legislative scheme could accomplish this objective with less impairment of the freedom in question. Consequently, the Chief Justice declared that the Act embodied a "serious effort . . . to accommodate the freedom of religion of Saturday observers," rendering it constitutional by virtue of section 1. [29]

The principles articulated in *Big M Drug Mart* and *Edwards Books and Art* illustrate an important difference between judicial review under the Canadian Charter and judicial review under the U.S. Bill of Rights. In practice, no government can function without imposing constraints on the actions of its citizens. Courts must necessarily be sensitive to this feature of governance when interpreting and applying constitutionally entrenched declarations of rights. The absence of a "reasonable limits" clause in the U.S. Bill of Rights forces American courts to build these limits into the substantive definition of rights. By contrast, section 1 of the Charter allows Canadian courts to balance the rights and freedoms guaranteed by the Charter against other considerations without necessarily limiting the substantive scope of the Charter's provisions. The significance of this difference lies in the relationship between balancing and modern judicial review. Section 1 of the Charter constitutionalizes this relationship, and may arguably provide Canadian judges with greater freedom to recalculate the legislative determination of reasonable limits than their American colleagues currently enjoy.

This is not to say, of course, that the presence of section 1 in the Charter precludes judicial disagreement over the interpretation and application of Charter guarantees. A good example of this is *Jones v. The Queen* (1986).[30] Like *Big M Drug Mart* and *Edwards Books and Art, Jones* was a freedom of religion case in which American jurisprudence played a significant role. At issue in *Jones* were certain provisions of the Alberta School Act that impose punitive sanctions on parents who fail to send their children to public schools or to private schools approved by the Department of Education.[31] The actual dispute arose over an exception to this regulation whereby parents whose children follow a provincially certified program of efficient home instruction are exempt from sanctions. The appellant was the pastor of a fundamentalist church who opted to educate his children and others privately, but who refused to comply with the province's requirement of departmental certification. Charged with violating the School Act, Jones was initially acquitted in Alberta Provincial Court.[32] The Crown appealed to the Alberta Court of Appeal, which imposed conviction after allowing the province's appeal. Jones sought relief in the Supreme Court on several grounds, including the claim that the Act's compulsory attendance provisions and certification requirements violated the Charter's guarantee of freedom of conscience and religion.

The Court split four to three on this question, with Justices La Forest, Lamer, and Chief Justice Dickson finding that the provisions in question did indeed interfere with the freedom guaranteed by section 2(a). Justice La Forest acknowledged the purely secular objectives underlying the Act but accepted Jones's contention that the effect of the provisions in question was to limit his freedom of conscience and religion. According to Jones, the requirement of registration or certification forced him, contrary to his religious beliefs, to recognize the Alberta government rather than God as having ultimate authority over the education of his children.[33] Justice La Forest declared that, since the Supreme Court is "in no position to question the *validity* of a religious belief," it must assume the sincerity of any religious conviction.[34] Consequently, La

Forest agreed that "the effect of the School Act does constitute some interference with the appellant's freedom of religion." However, since the interference flowed from legislative effects, rather than purposes, the School Act could be saved by section 1.

La Forest's use of American jurisprudence thus occurred in the context of balancing Jones's religious interest in providing for his children's education free from state interference against the province's interest in maintaining uniform educational standards. Citing *Brown v. Board of Education* (1954), La Forest noted that education "is today a matter of prime concern to government everywhere"; consequently, he acknowledged that provinces could place reasonable limits on religious freedom to maintain high educational standards.[35] La Forest also found American decisions useful for determining the permissible scope of such limits, as well as the extent to which they must accommodate religious beliefs. Citing decisions of the Michigan Court of Appeal and the New Jersey Supreme Court, La Forest concluded that it was unnecessary for provinces to exempt individuals entirely from educational regulations in order to accommodate their religious convictions.[36] La Forest warned, however, that without proper administration, the limits imposed by these regulations might infringe religious freedom.[37]

In contrast to La Forest, Justices Wilson, Beetz, McIntyre, and Le Dain found that the provisions in question did not offend section 2(a). Like La Forest, Justice Wilson began by considering the legislative purpose of the statute in question. Wilson also followed La Forest in surveying the relevant American jurisprudence, choosing to focus on three criteria established by the U.S. Supreme Court for measuring the validity of legislation under the First Amendment's religious establishment clause. These criteria included whether the legislation's purpose is secular or religious; whether its primary effect is to advance or inhibit religion; and whether it creates excessive "government entanglement" with religion.[38] Wilson found that in applying these criteria, U.S. courts had reached the consensus that legislatures may constitutionally impose standards of efficient instruction on religious schools because those standards have "the secular purpose and effect of ensuring a knowledgeable and competent citizenry."[39] While recognizing the difficulties the U.S. Court has faced in applying this principle to specific state policies, Wilson did not have any difficulty applying it to the Alberta statute.[40] In measuring the School Act against this standard, Wilson found that its regulation of private schools and home instruction advanced the constitutionally valid secular purpose of ensuring that children receive an adequate education.

Given the constitutionality of the statute's purpose, Wilson concluded that Jones's real complaint was about the effect of the regulations on his religious beliefs.[41] Despite her own affinity for an effects-oriented approach to the Charter, as well as the use of an effects-based test of constitutionality by American courts in the area of religious freedom, Wilson refused to accept this part of Jones's argument. Wilson noted that the U.S. Supreme Court had restricted the applicability of its effects-based test to direct burdens on religious observance;

and although she found aspects of this component of the U.S. Court's effects-based test problematic, she agreed that the impact of legislation on religious observance must be substantial to infringe the Charter. According to Wilson, "[t]o state that any legislation which has an effect on religion, no matter how minimal, violates the religious guarantee 'would radically restrict the operating latitude of the legislature'."[42] Unlike Chief Justice Dickson, who implied in *Edwards Books and Art* that the Charter's fundamental freedoms are in themselves absolute and may only be limited by section 1, Wilson held that such limits could be included within the substantive definition of the guaranteed freedom.[43]

Justice Wilson's view in *Jones* was that the Charter does not apply to legislation whose purposes or effects conflict in a trivial manner with the objectives embodied in specific Charter guarantees. Similarly, Wilson (unanimously supported by her colleagues) held in another freedom of religion case that the Charter could not be applied to invalidate other provisions of the constitution. At issue in *Reference re An Act to Amend the Education Act (Ontario)* (1987) was whether Ontario could implement a policy of full public funding for Roman Catholic high schools in the province.[44] Opponents of the proposal argued, *inter alia,* that public funding of denominational schools would violate section 2(a) of the Charter.[45] As Justice Willard Estey pointed out in concurring reasons for judgment, the consensus among counsel on both sides of the issue was that, if the Charter applied in the circumstances, the proposed legislation would be in violation of section 2(a) because it would constitute government support for a specific religious denomination to the exclusion of all others.[46] Supporters of the legislation argued, however, that such support would be consistent with powers expressly granted elsewhere in the constitution, and it was therefore shielded from Charter review.

Section 93 of the Constitution Act, 1867 grants exclusive plenary power over education to the provinces, subject only to provisions expressly preserving the rights and privileges of denominational schools already existing by virtue of statutory enactments at the time of union.[47] In 1928, however, the Judicial Committee interpreted these rights so narrowly as to give the provinces a broad regulatory power to control public funding of denominational schools;[48] and on the basis of this decision, Ontario provided public funding to Roman Catholic schools only to the Grade 10 level. In 1984, the government of retiring Premier William Davis announced that it intended to provide public funding for the entire Roman Catholic secondary education program. Although this proposal was politically explosive, all three political parties supported it in the 1985 provincial election; and following the election, the victorious Liberal Party enacted Bill 30 in order to implement the policy. Faced with political opposition articulated in the form of constitutional objections, the government referred the legislation to the Ontario Court of Appeal, where a majority upheld the legislation. The Ontario court held that the province was acting under its section 93 authority to create additional rights for denominational schools, and that these rights were shielded from Charter review by section 29 of the Charter.[49]

In the Supreme Court, Justice Wilson accepted the Ontario government's submission that the extension of full public funding to Roman Catholic secondary schools in 1987 did not create any new rights, but was a legitimate remedial measure designed to restore "rights constitutionally guaranteed to separate schools by s.93(1) of the Constitution Act, 1867."[50] Although this "special treatment guaranteed by the constitution to denominational, separate or dissentient schools . . . sits uncomfortably with the concept of equality embodied in the Charter because not available to other schools," it was nevertheless unimpaired by the Charter. "It was never intended," according to Justice Wilson, "that the Charter could be used to invalidate other provisions of the Constitution, particularly a provision such as s.93 which represented a fundamental part of the Confederation compromise."[51] The rights protected from provincial plenary power over education are so central to the character of Canada's constitution, in other words, that legislation enacted pursuant to them is entirely insulated from Charter review.

The principal lesson to draw from the *Education Act Reference* is that, whatever purposes are embodied in the Charter, the repeal of other constitutional provisions, however discriminatory those provisions might be, is not among them. It is, however, significant that the decision implicitly held that public funding for Roman Catholic secondary schools would violate section 2(a) were it not for section 93 of the Constitution Act, 1867. Nevertheless, the Ontario *Education Act Reference* is more important for the general principle it articulated concerning the relationship between the Charter and other elements of the constitution than for what it says about freedom of religion.

The freedom of religion decisions illustrate the extent to which the Charter brings the central dilemmas of liberal constitutionalism to the foreground in Canadian politics. On the one hand, one of the central aims of liberalism is to avoid the destructive consequences that flow from the transformation of religious conflicts into political conflicts. Liberalism attempts to achieve this objective by relegating religion to the private realm, hence the development of constitutional provisions designed to keep religious matters from becoming the subject of public policy. On the other hand, as Alexis de Tocqueville pointed out, secular democracies need some commitment to religious principles in order to moderate the liberal understanding of self-interest, as well as to counteract the democratic taste for materialism and individualism.[52] Prior to 1982, Canada had developed an imperfect yet workable compromise between these two competing principles. While the Constitution Act, 1867 removed certain aspects of religion from political debate, it did not prevent the secular authorities from favouring religion over non-religion or from publicly supporting specific religious sects. Section 2(a) of the Charter brings that compromise into question by changing the political status of religion in Canada. Overall, this analysis of the freedom of religion cases offers mixed evidence about whether the blunt instrument of judicial review is up to the task of establishing a new and effective compromise.

Freedom of Expression and the Press

Retail, Wholesale & Department Store Union, Local 580 et al. v. Dolphin Delivery (1986) has proven to be one of the most controversial Charter decisions rendered by the Supreme Court.[53] At issue in *Dolphin Delivery* was the constitutionality of an injunction issued by the British Columbia Supreme Court, enjoining secondary picketing by members of a trade union in a labour dispute. The appellants challenged the injunction on the grounds that their activity was protected under section 2(b) of the Charter. However, in addition to this substantive issue, the Court also found itself forced to decide the extent to which the Charter applies to the common law and to private litigation. Although Justice McIntyre's majority reasons for judgment actually dealt with this question *after* considering the freedom of expression issue, the answer he provided to it became the central focus of debate about the decision.

The question of the Charter's applicability to the common law presented little difficulty for McIntyre. Section 52(1) of the Constitution Act, 1982, he observed, provides that "any law that is inconsistent with the provisions of the Constitution is, to the extent of the inconsistency, of no force or effect." According to McIntyre, this language was sufficiently broad to include the body of the common law among the rules subject to the Charter's guarantees. Since the common law "in great part governs the rights and obligations of the individuals in society," to find otherwise, he asserted, "would be wholly unrealistic and contrary to the clear language employed in s.52(1) of the [Constitution] Act."[54]

The Charter's applicability to private litigation presented the more complex question of "whether or not an individual may found a cause of action or defence against another individual on the basis of a breach of a Charter right." Reviewing the appropriate literature and case law, McIntyre concluded that the Charter does not apply to purely private litigation.[55] McIntyre also found that section 32(1) of the Charter clearly declares that the Charter applies only to the Parliament and government of Canada, and to the legislatures and governments of the provinces and territories. Determining that the Charter does not apply to private litigation was only the first step toward a complete answer to the question, however; it still remained to define the precise boundary between private and public, as well as the meaning of the term "government" in section 32.

In McIntyre's view, the actors specified by section 32 were the legislative, executive, and administrative branches of government, whose actions are subject to the Charter whether implicated in public or private litigation. This is the case, McIntyre asserted, whether those actions are taken pursuant to statutory authority or by virtue of the common law. Thus, the Charter applies to common-law rules governing the relationship between individuals and the state, whether invoked in private or public litigation. McIntyre declared, however, that the Charter does not apply to common-law rules governing the relationship between private individuals where those rules are not the basis of some governmental action.[56]

There remained one further issue to consider before finally answering the central question. As McIntyre conceded, the "element of a governmental intervention necessary to make the Charter applicable in an otherwise private action is difficult to define."[57] In particular, the Court had to decide whether an order issued by a court in private litigation under common-law rules constitutes "governmental intervention" sufficient to implicate the Charter. While acknowledging that from a "political science" perspective the judiciary forms an integral part of government, McIntyre refused to "equate for the purposes of Charter adjudication the order of a court with an element of government action."[58] Otherwise, McIntyre averred, the Charter would apply to virtually all private conduct, since any aspect of private relationships can be the subject of litigation. This would give courts – rather than legislatures – ultimate responsibility for setting the rules that govern private interactions.

McIntyre's discussion in *Dolphin Delivery* of the relationship between court orders and state action was precisely the opposite of the U.S. Supreme Court's decision in *Shelley v. Kraemer* (1948),[59] and the background and nature of that American decision may shed light on the issues raised in *Dolphin Delivery*. At issue in *Shelley* was the constitutionality of racially restrictive covenants, which barred owners of property from selling it to members of specified racial or religious groups (generally African-Americans and Jews). As private agreements, these covenants had escaped constitutional scrutiny because of the "state action" doctrine established in the *Civil Rights Cases* (1883).[60] According to this doctrine, which the U.S. Court had used to deny the U.S. Congress power to enact legislation prohibiting private discrimination, the Fourteenth Amendment applies only to racial discrimination resulting from state action. The Court finessed this doctrine in *Shelley* by unanimously holding that *judicial enforcement* of restrictive covenants is state action contrary to the Fourteenth Amendment. In contrast to Justice McIntyre, the U.S. Court declared that "the action of state courts and of judicial officers in their official capacities is to be regarded as action of the State."[61] To use the language of contemporary Charter jurisprudence, the U.S. Court declared that a sufficient nexus exists between judicial enforcement of private contracts and government action to invoke constitutional guarantees.

Although *Shelley* might be praised for advancing the interests of a vulnerable minority in the absence of legislative action, there are good reasons to commend Justice McIntyre for not following the same path. The racially discriminatory conduct that the U.S. Court sought to remedy in 1948 owed its existence in part to the Court of 1883. Unlike *Dolphin Delivery,* which invoked the government action doctrine to exclude implementation of Charter principles through judicial regulation of private relationships, the *Civil Rights Cases* used the state action doctrine to deny similar implementation of Fourteenth Amendment principles through *legislative* regulation of private agreements. Had the Court of 1883 left Congress's power to enforce the Fourteenth Amendment intact, it might not have been necessary to expand the definition of state action in *Shelley*. Indeed, the U.S. Supreme Court would hold in 1976 that the Civil Rights Act of 1866 had in fact prohibited racial discrimination in private contracts.[62] Had the U.S. Court exercised judicial restraint in 1883, judicial activism might not have been necessary in 1948.

Justice McIntyre did not declare in *Dolphin Delivery* that private conduct should not be consistent with the principles of the Charter, but only that the responsibility for achieving this consistency belongs to legislators rather than judges. In seeking to limit the reach of judicial review under the Charter, McIntyre adopted an attitude of judicial self-restraint in order to constrain judicial power within its constitutional boundaries. Nevertheless, his judgment in *Dolphin Delivery* illustrates both the limits of judicial restraint and the paradox of judicial power in liberal constitutional theory. By excluding the judicial branch from the organs of government to which the Charter applies, McIntyre acted consistently with the modern proposition that courts are somehow above the constitutional documents they enforce, since they ultimately define the meaning of those documents. Courts, according to McIntyre, are indifferent to the outcome of constitutional disputes, since they apply the law as "neutral arbiters, not as contending parties involved in a dispute."[63] Although perhaps less bold than some of his colleagues, McIntyre accepted the view that courts must monopolize the process of constitutional interpretation largely because of their lack of interest in the outcome of these cases.

This last point is clearly illustrated in the largely anticlimactic discussion of freedom of expression in *Dolphin Delivery,* as well as in *British Columbia Government Employees' Union (B.C.G.E.U.) v. A.-G. British Columbia* (1988).[64] In *Dolphin Delivery,* the Court had to decide whether the term "expression" was broad enough to encompass the right to picket during labour disputes. In answering this question for the Court, Justice McIntyre began by noting the importance of free speech and expression in creating the marketplace of ideas from which democratic government derives its strength.[65] McIntyre thus accepted the appellant's use of American cases to support the assertion that picketing is a form of expression entitled to constitutional protection.[66] The key case among those cited by the appellant was *Thornhill v. Alabama* (1940), in which the U.S. Supreme Court struck down a state law prohibiting all picketing by unions on the grounds that peaceful picketing to publicize labour disputes is constitutionally protected by the First Amendment's free speech clause.[67] Finding the American jurisprudence persuasive on this point, McIntyre concluded "that the picketing sought to be restrained would have involved the exercise of the right of freedom of expression."[68]

According to McIntyre, however, the social cost of industrial conflict is sufficiently high to justify regulating and limiting the right to picket implicitly guaranteed by section 2(b). In particular, he found it "reasonable to restrain picketing so that the conflict will not escalate beyond the actual parties." McIntyre held, therefore, that the injunction issued against secondary picketing in *Dolphin Delivery* constituted a reasonable limit on the right to picket under section 1 of the Charter.[69] McIntyre reached this result without restricting the substantive definition of expression; by contrast, the U.S. Supreme Court has been able to justify similar state picketing regulations only by establishing a distinction between speech and conduct.

A similar issue arose in *B.C.G.E.U.,* which involved another British Columbia Supreme Court injunction enjoining picketing during a legal strike. This time, however, the union chose the province's courts as its target, producing a harsh response from Chief Justice Brian Dickson. Dickson began his reasons for judgment by questioning the union's attempt to claim Charter protection for an activity whose intent was to limit access to the courts. According to the Chief Justice, it is impossible for courts to "independently maintain the rule of law and effectively discharge the duties imposed by the Charter if court access is hindered, impeded or denied." The effect of the union's action, therefore, was to render the Charter's protections illusory; indeed, it undermined the entire document.[70] The union's picket line fundamentally interfered with the administration of justice, thereby constituting conduct falling within the definition of criminal contempt. It was therefore proper, Dickson concluded, for the British Columbia Court of Appeal to have upheld the Supreme Court's injunction against the picketing.[71]

In defence of its action, the union invoked section 2(b) of the Charter. Following *Dolphin Delivery,* Chief Justice Dickson agreed that the injunction had to "comply with the fundamental standards established by the Charter," and that "picketing in the context of a labour dispute contains an element of expression which attracts the protection of s.2(b)."[72] It thus became necessary under section 1 to balance the public values served by the injunction against the right to picket. Dickson found this balance easy to strike, since "without the public right to have absolute, free and unrestricted access to the courts the individual and private right to freedom of expression would be lost."[73] Finding that the injunction rationally and proportionately served a "pressing and substantial" public objective, the Chief Justice declared it to be a reasonable limit on the union members' right to picket. Concurring with Dickson's conclusion, Justice McIntyre went even further: he asserted that no activity that interferes with access to the courts, and thus with the proper protection of Charter rights, is in any way protected by the document.[74] Like *Dolphin Delivery,* the central message of *B.C.G.E.U.* was the impossibility of preserving Charter rights without unhindered judicial activity.

Although the type of expression to which the Court extended Charter protection in both *Dolphin Delivery* and *B.C.G.E.U.* was largely "economic" in nature, neither case required the Court to determine the Charter's applicability to purely commercial expression. An opportunity to decide this question did arise in *Rio Hotel Ltd. v. New Brunswick (Liquor Licence Board)* (1987), in which the appellant attempted to persuade the Court that "nude entertainment" is protected expression under the Charter. Finding the record on this question in the court below "woefully inadequate," the Court refused to consider it.[75] The Court finally dealt with this question in the much more politically volatile case of *Ford v. Quebec (Attorney-General)* (1988).[76] At issue in *Ford* was the constitutionality of Quebec's requirement that public signs, posters, and commercial advertising be solely in French, except as otherwise provided by the province's *Charte de la langue française.* Although Quebec Premier Robert Bourassa had promised to eliminate this requirement in his successful 1985 election campaign, the issue proved too politically controversial. While this promise succeeded in attracting significant Anglophone support for Bourassa's Liberal Party, it also alienated many Francophones. Faced with a difficult policy choice, Bourassa decided to wait and see whether pending constitutional litigation would resolve the issue for him.

Ford raised a number of complex constitutional questions, including the extent to which section 2(b) protects commercial speech. Prior to *Ford,* the answer to this question was uncertain. Although commentators had argued that commercial expression should be protected by the Charter,[77] lower courts were divided on the subject.[78] The question had also been the subject of litigation in the U.S. Supreme Court, which held in *Virginia State Board of Pharmacy v. Virginia Citizens Consumer Council* (1976) that commercial expression deserves First Amendment protection.[79] In their unsigned opinion in *Ford,* Chief Justice Dickson and Justices Beetz, McIntyre, Lamer, and Wilson decided to follow their U.S. counterparts' general principle that commercial speech merits constitutional protection, if not to the same degree as political speech. Under U.S. constitutional doctrine, the Canadian Court noted, commercial speech can be regulated to achieve substantial state interests if such regulation is narrowly tailored to achieve the purpose in question.[80] Interestingly, the U.S. Court found that the constitutional value of commercial expression lies primarily in the benefits it confers on consumers rather than in the freedom it gives to commercial enterprises.

In *Ford,* the case for constitutionally protecting commercial expression was made by retailers who objected to Quebec's language regulations. The Court agreed with their argument, holding that section 2(b) includes a right to engage in commercial expression in the language of one's choice. The Court thus found that the impugned legislation violated the Charter, bringing into consideration section 1. Although the Court found that the objective of the legislation at issue in *Ford* – to preserve and promote the French language and culture in Quebec – was serious and legitimate, it held that Quebec had not demonstrated "that the requirement of the use of French only is either necessary for the achievement of the legislative objective or proportionate to it."[81] As in *Dolphin Delivery,* the structure of the Charter allowed the Court to discuss the constitutionality of legislative limitations on implicitly protected rights without engaging in complex definitional considerations.

The Court affirmed the Charter's applicability to commercial expression four months later in *A.-G. Quebec v. Irwin Toy Ltd.* (1989).[82] On this occasion, however, the Court upheld by a slim margin regulations limiting certain types of commercial expression. At issue in *Irwin Toy* was a Quebec law prohibiting commercial advertising directed at persons under thirteen years of age. While the Court unanimously held that the statute violated section 2(b), it divided three to two on whether the law could be justified under section 1. Writing for himself and Justices Lamer and Wilson, Chief Justice Dickson found the legislation both rationally and proportionately connected to its objective, which was to protect a particularly vulnerable group (children) from undue commercial manipulation. In dissent, Justices McIntyre and Beetz could not find any rational connection between a ban on commercial advertising and the promotion of children's welfare. Moreover, they argued that a "total prohibition of advertising aimed at children below an arbitrarily fixed age makes no attempt at the achievement of proportionality."[83]

The Court continued its discussion of commercial expression in *Royal College of Dental Surgeons of Ontario v. Rocket and Price* (1990).[84] At issue in *Rocket and Price* was the constitutionality of regulations governing professional advertising by dentists. In deciding this issue for a unanimous Court, Justice Beverly McLachlin made two important contributions to the Court's commercial expression jurisprudence. First, citing U.S. jurisprudence, McLachlin conceded that there might be a sufficient distinction between commercial advertisements for standardized retail products and "more subjective claims as to the quality of services involving the exercise of professional judgment" to justify enhanced regulation of the latter.[85] McLachlin admitted, in other words, that in addition to the basic distinction between highly protected political and less well-protected commercial expression, there might be differences among types of commercial expression that could affect the level of constitutional protection available under the Charter.

McLachlin's second contribution was to summarize the judgments in *Ford, Irwin Toy,* and *Dolphin Delivery* in order to articulate a three-pronged test for determining when regulations governing professional advertising conflict with the Charter.[86] According to McLachlin, the first prong of this test is to determine whether professional advertising constitutes "expressive" activity in the sense that it aims at conveying a meaning. Answering this question in the affirmative, McLachlin turned to the test's second prong, which is to determine whether the expressive activity takes a prohibited form like violence or threats of violence. Finding that the advertising in question took perfectly acceptable forms, McLachlin addressed the third prong of the test to determine whether the regulation's purpose is to restrict the substantive content of the expression. Concluding that the regulations at issue explicitly restricted the type of information that dentists could make available to the public, McLachlin declared that the impugned regulations violated section 2(b). Although McLachlin determined that this limit on freedom of expression pursued the important governmental objectives of "promoting professionalism and avoiding irresponsible and misleading advertising," she found that its effects were disproportionate to these goals and struck them out in accordance with section 52 of the Constitution Act, 1982.[87]

Commercial expression of a different sort was at issue in *Reference re ss. 193 and 195 of the Criminal Code* (1990).[88] Also known as the *Prostitution Reference,* this case involved provisions of the Criminal Code designed to control street solicitation by prohibiting communication in "a public place or in any place open to public view . . . for the purpose of engaging in prostitution or of obtaining the sexual services of a prostitute." Unlike the decisions in *Ford, Irwin Toy,* and *Rocket and Price,* the plurality opinion by Chief Justice Dickson (for himself and Justices La Forest and Sopinka) did not find much constitutional protection for the expressive activity prohibited by this provision. "It can hardly be said," Dickson argued, "that communications regarding an economic trans-action of sex for money lie at, or even near, the core of the guarantee of freedom of expression."[89] Moreover, according to Dickson, whatever slight impairment the law might impose on this freedom could be easily justified as a reasonable limit under section 1. By contrast, the dissenting reasons for judgment by Jus-tices Wilson and L'Heureux-Dubé asserted that the impugned provisions aimed at restricting the content of certain expressive activities in the hope of eliminat-ing their negative consequences; and in their view, this was clearly contrary to the purpose of section 2(b).[90] Wilson and L'Heureux-Dubé also failed to see how this infringement of expression was proportional to the legislative objec-tive of eliminating the social nuisance caused by street solicitation.[91]

Along with the Court's freedom of religion decisions, *Dolphin Delivery, B.C.G.E.U., Ford, Irwin Toy, Rocket and Price,* the *Prostitution Reference,* and other decisions under section 2(b)[92] clearly illustrate the importance and conse-quences of a clause like section 1. Even where individual justices find no viola-tion of a Charter guarantee, as Chief Justice Dickson in the *Prostitution Refer-ence,* they find themselves compelled to discuss the rationality and propor-tionality issues raised by section 1. More importantly, the presence of this sec-tion more frequently allows Canadian courts to define fundamental freedoms in nearly absolute terms. In practice, any governmental interference with rights that are conceptually absolute requires an extraordinary legislative rationale. Indeed, a majority of the Court has found it relatively easy to detect a violation of freedoms guaranteed by sections 2(a) and 2(b) of the Charter. Only in cases like *Jones* and a relatively minor freedom of the press case under section 2(b) has the Court refused to include some activity within the meaning of the freedom in question.[93] In virtually every other case, the question of constitutional validity is ultimately resolved through section 1 analysis. Such analysis, however, dupli-cates a task that legislatures presumably undertake, whether explicitly or not, prior to enacting any statute. While there are good reasons to ask courts to review the legislative calculus of reasonable limits, it is less obvious why the judicial calculus should be accepted as final.[94] Yet this is precisely what section 1 encourages by transforming the results of judicial balancing into constitution-al law.

The significance of this structural feature of the Charter is more evident as the interests at stake in this balancing process become more important. Such was the case in *R. v. Keegstra* (1990), where the Court considered the constitutionality of the Criminal Code's hate literature provisions.[95] James Keegstra served as a high school teacher and principal in Eckville, Alberta, for nearly ten years, dur-ing which time he used this position to disseminate anti-Semitic conspiracy theories to his students. In 1984, the Crown charged Keegstra under section 319(2) of the Criminal Code with unlawfully promoting hatred against an identifiable group.[96] Convicted by a jury in the Alberta Court of Queen's Bench, Keegstra successfully appealed his conviction in the Alberta Court of Appeal on the grounds that this provision of the Criminal Code violated the Charter. A seven-judge panel of the Supreme Court heard the Crown's appeal of this decision in December, 1989, and one year later upheld the constitutionality of section 319(2) by a single vote.

None of the seven justices had any difficulty finding that section 319(2) infringed freedom of expression. Speaking directly for himself and Justices Wilson, L'Heureux-Dubé, and Gonthier, Chief Justice Dickson determined that section 319(2) violated freedom of expression by prohibiting the communication of meaning considered repugnant by virtue of its content rather than form, a conclusion with which Justices McLachlin, Sopinka, and La Forest separately agreed.[97] The Court split four to three, however, on whether this infringement was a reasonable limit under section 1. To be more precise, the Court divided on the minimal impairment prong of the *Oakes* proportionality test.

Led by Dickson, the majority found "that s.319(2) possesses definitional limits which act as safeguards to ensure that it will capture only expressive activity which is openly hostile to Parliament's objective" of preventing the general and specific harm caused by hate propaganda, as well as of promoting the individual equality of Canadians guaranteed by section 15 of the Charter.[98] Moreover, the majority found sufficient protection for legitimate political expression in the four defences available under section 319(2).[99] Finally, the Dickson majority was not persuaded that the existence of parallel enforcement measures under human rights legislation rendered the Criminal Code provisions redundant or overly restrictive. The majority acknowledged that legislatures could employ a variety of means to pursue the same pressing and substantial objective.[100] The majority could have added that the likelihood of legislatures employing multiple means to achieve a single objective would arguably increase in proportion to the importance of the pressing and substantial objective.

The three justices in the minority were of a quite different mind. Although conceding the narrowing effect of the impugned provision's defences, McLachlin, Sopinka, and La Forest still found section 319(2) to be "overbroad in that its definition of offending speech may catch many expressions which should be protected."[101] In their view, the term "hatred" signified a concept so broad and subjective that triers of fact would be simply incapable of reaching a dispassionate verdict. Indeed, the McLachlin-led minority argued that judges and juries would be tempted to define as "hatred" any speech that was merely unpopular. In addition, the minority expressed concern that section 319(2) does not require the Crown to demonstrate that any concrete harm actually resulted from the communication of "hatred."[102] Finally, McLachlin and the others worried that regulation through the Criminal Code would have little impact on dedicated hatemongers but might deter ordinary individuals from expressing unpopular opinions. These factors combined to lead the dissenting justices to argue that the legislation's danger is that it might "have a chilling effect on legitimate activities important to our society by subjecting innocent persons to constraints born out of a fear of the criminal process."[103]

Closely decided freedom of expression cases like *Keegstra* and *Irwin Toy* illustrate an important feature of what the Supreme Court actually does when it applies its section 1 "reasonable limits" analysis: it draws inferences about the general operation of policies either without any empirical evidence whatsoever, or on the basis of the limited evidence contained in the facts of one or a few specific cases. In *Keegstra,* for example, the minority relied on hypothetical examples, as well as instances in which groups simply made requests (generally unheeded) for official action against certain novels or succeeded in temporarily delaying the distribution of books and films. While each of these incidents raises justifiable concerns about how the policy embodied in section 319(2) might be administered in specific cases, it tells us nothing about the general deterrent effect of the criminal law on the expression of idiosyncratic or unpopular ideas. Similarly, in *Irwin Toy* the dissenting Supreme Court justices found that the Quebec legislature had overregulated by prohibiting *all* commercial expression aimed at children below the "arbitrarily fixed age" specified in the statute; and in the Quebec Court of Appeal, the statute in fact fell because a majority disagreed with the legislature's judgment about the age at which children cease to be vulnerable to the effects of commercial expression. It is unclear, however, what *legal* principle would dictate either a more refined definition of prohibited expression or a different age that should be protected from it. Indeed, it is precisely because these are complex policy questions about which reasonable people can disagree that the Court is so closely divided on them. The general implications of this characteristic of section 1 analysis will be explored in more detail in Chapter Six.

Freedom of Association

In view of the conceptual absolutes and legislative balancing that have characterized decisions under sections 2(a) and 2(b) of the Charter, it is significant that the most important decisions concerning section 2(d) have imposed substantive limits on the concept of association. In particular, a majority of the Court has rejected the argument that the Charter's guarantee of freedom of association extends constitutional protection to collective bargaining and the right to strike. Consequently, these decisions have been extremely important in prompting the development of communitarian theories of judicial review. According to the communitarian critics of the majority's approach to association in these decisions, the adoption of a liberal-individualist perspective toward the Charter has led to the false conclusion that the labour movement exists primarily to advance the individual economic rights of union members to sell their labour. Instead, these critics aver, freedom of association is specifically guaranteed by the Charter in order to protect the collective ability of trade unions to counterbalance the inherent inequalities of the employment relationship.[104] Liberal-individualist judicial review, they conclude, undermines this capacity to the benefit of the economically powerful.

This liberal-individualist/communitarian debate reached the Supreme Court for the first time in a trilogy of labour cases decided simultaneously in 1987: *Reference re Public Service Employee Relations Act (Alberta Labour Reference)* (1987); *Public Service Alliance of Canada v. The Queen* (1987); and *Retail, Wholesale and Department Store Union (Saskatchewan Dairy Workers) v. Saskatchewan* (1987).[105] At issue in the key *Alberta Labour Reference* were three Alberta statutes that prohibited certain classes of employees from engaging in collective bargaining; that prohibited lockouts and strikes in certain areas of the public service; and that substituted compulsory arbitration for other forms of negotiation. The Court decided in a four-to-two decision that prohibiting lockouts and strikes does not violate section 2(d) of the Charter, but it did not find sufficient evidence in the record to determine whether restrictions on collective bargaining violate the Charter.

The central question in the *Alberta Labour Reference* was whether section 2(d) protects the simple right of individuals to form associations or whether it also protects those activities of associations that are deemed necessary for the pursuit of their collective objectives. This question produced three separate reasons for judgment, with Justice Le Dain writing for a plurality of the Court consisting of himself and Justices Beetz and La Forest. Le Dain began his rather brief reasons by warning his colleagues that, in view of the "wide range of associations or organizations" – each pursuing a variety of objectives through various means – to which freedom of association might apply, they should consider seriously the "implications of extending a constitutional guarantee . . . to the right to engage in a particular activity on the ground that the activity is essential to give an association meaningful existence." What might be valuable in the context of labour relations, he suggested, could have very negative unintended consequences in other contexts. In particular, Le Dain worried about the possibility of extending *prima facie* constitutional protection to the activities of openly racist associations.[106]

What ultimately persuaded Le Dain to reject the assertion that freedom of association protects the rights to bargain collectively and to strike, however, was his determination that these rights are not in any sense fundamental. Both of these rights, he argued, are "the creation of legislation, involving a balance of competing interests in a field which has been recognized by the courts as requiring a specialized expertise." Constitutionalizing these rights as part of freedom of association, he continued, would subject the relevant balances struck by legislatures to judicial review under section 1. According to Le Dain, this would entangle the Court "in a review of legislative policy for which it is really not fitted."[107] For Le Dain, institutional capacity became the principal reason for exercising judicial restraint in this instance. To a large degree, however, Le Dain's reasons for judgment were peripheral to the main debate between Chief Justice Dickson and Justice McIntyre concerning the substantive meaning of association.

The Chief Justice began by declaring that, at a minimum, freedom of association "is the freedom to combine together for the pursuit of common purposes or the advancement of common causes." For Dickson, the central question was whether this "constitutive" definition of freedom of association could be broadened to include the freedom to engage in those activities necessary to achieve the association's common purposes or causes.[108] Dickson's discussion of this question was entirely consistent with the two general principles of Charter adjudication he had articulated in earlier decisions concerning fundamental freedoms. First, he emphasized the limited relevance of pre-Charter domestic jurisprudence for determining the meaning of Charter guarantees. Second, because of both different wording and the presence of section 1, he cautioned against uncritically accepting American jurisprudence, which had imposed substantive limits on rights similar to those protected by the Charter.

Dickson's rejection of pre-Charter jurisprudence on the meaning of freedom of association was important, since that jurisprudence supported a constitutive definition of association. The leading Privy Council decision was *Collymore v. Attorney-General* (1970), which held that the freedom of association guaranteed by the constitution of Trinidad and Tobago did not protect the right to strike.[109] In *Collymore,* the Privy Council accepted the lower court's judgment that, although freedom of association includes the "freedom to enter into consensual arrangements," it does not confer either right or licence "for a course of conduct or for the commission of acts which in the view of Parliament are inimical to the peace, order and good government of the country."[110] Although courts in several provinces, as well as the Federal Court of Appeal, followed *Collymore* and adopted a constitutive definition of association after 1982,[111] Dickson did not find the judgment persuasive in determining the meaning of association under the Charter. Finding the constitution of Trinidad and Tobago to be similar to the Canadian Bill of Rights in recognizing existing rights rather than in providing "a source of new constitutional protections," Dickson repeated his argument that "the Charter ushers in a new era in the protection of fundamental freedoms. We need not ground protection for freedom of association in pre-existing freedoms."[112] The Chief Justice found support for a broader definition of association, moreover, in decisions by courts in both Ontario and Saskatchewan.[113]

Turning to American jurisprudence, Dickson noted two important differences between the Charter and the U.S. Bill of Rights, each of which limited the relevance of American case law. First, unlike the Charter, the U.S. Bill of Rights does not provide explicit protection for freedom of association. This right is entirely a product of judicial creation, designed to extend implicit constitutional protection to the collective exercise of activities explicitly protected by the First Amendment. The second difference noted by Dickson was the absence in the U.S. Bill of Rights of a provision similar to section 1. Consequently, freedom of association in the United States was weakened by its status as an implied right and by the necessity of imposing internal limits on its definition in order to balance it against other important public interests. Thus, although the U.S.

Supreme Court had granted unions the rights to organize, to select representatives for collective bargaining, and to secure legal representation for their members, it had refused to extend similar constitutional protection to strike activity in the public sector.[114] To Dickson, then, the peculiar character of the constitutional protection accorded freedom of association in American jurisprudence diminished its applicability to the questions at issue in the *Alberta Labour Reference.*

Having rejected the "frozen rights" theory implicit in *Collymore,* as well as the definition of association developed in American case law, Dickson sought to determine the meaning of section 2(d) through the "purposive" analysis approach he had articulated in *Big M Drug Mart.* The first step in this analysis was to reject the purely constitutive definition of association as inconsistent with the purposes of section 2(d). According to Dickson, to extend constitutional protection to the formation of associations, but not to the pursuit of the activities for which they are formed, would make the freedom "legalistic, ungenerous, indeed vapid."[115] In addition, such a definition would defeat the central purpose of section 2(d), which Dickson declared to be the recognition of "the profoundly social nature of human endeavours and [protection of] the individual from State-enforced isolation in the pursuit of his or her ends." Citing Alexis de Tocqueville and John Stuart Mill, and echoing the arguments of Monahan and Mandel, Dickson stressed the importance of communal action as a means by which individuals may counter the influence of "larger and more powerful entit[ies], like the government or an employer." "What freedom of association seeks to protect," Dickson declared, is "the freedom of individuals to interact with, support and be supported by, their fellow humans in the varied activities in which they seek to engage."[116]

For Dickson, this underlying purpose of freedom of association meant that section 2(d) protects more than simply the collective pursuit of inherently individual activities; it also protects activities that are collective in their very nature. In Dickson's view, this was precisely the nature of strikes: "The refusal to work by one individual," he asserted, "does not parallel a collective refusal to work." Similarly, collective bargaining is more than simply the aggregation of numerous individual bargains: it is "one of the integral and primary functions of associations of working people." Nor, Dickson averred, is the importance of these activities diminished by their economic character. The collective interests of labour, the Chief Justice explained, "go far beyond those of a merely pecuniary nature"; they also protect "an essential component of [individuals'] sense of identity, self-worth and emotional well-being." For all of these reasons, Dickson found the rights to strike and to bargain collectively constitutionally protected by the Charter.[117]

Although Dickson's references to both Tocqueville and Mill are worth noting in this context, his use of Tocqueville is especially revealing of the hazards that modern judges confront during their frequent forays into the unfamiliar terrain of social philosophy. Dickson cited the following passage from *Democracy in America,* which he employed to underscore the central importance of freedom of association in democratic societies:

The most natural privilege of man, next to the right of acting for himself, is that of combining his exertions with those of his fellow creatures and of acting in common with them. The right of association therefore appears . . . almost as inalienable in its nature as the right of personal liberty. No legislator can attack it without impairing the foundations of society.[118]

However, in the sentence immediately following this passage, Tocqueville warned that, "if the liberty of association is only a source of advantage and prosperity to some nations, it may be perverted or carried to excess by others, and from an element of life may be changed into a cause of destruction." In fact, Tocqueville explained, this was precisely what had occurred in Europe, where individuals abandon "the exercise of their own judgment and free will" in uniting together. The genius of political associations in the United States, Tocqueville asserted, is their ability "to promote a common undertaking" while recognizing the "independence of each individual" member. Contrary to Dickson's interpretation, Tocqueville did not idealize associations as organic bodies with greater importance than their individual members. Indeed, he praised the essentially individualistic nature of American associations.

Despite quoting the same passage from Tocqueville and following similar interpretive steps as Dickson, Justice McIntyre reached precisely the opposite conclusion. McIntyre began by accepting the proposition that "the Charter should receive a broad and generous construction consistent with its general purpose"; however, he also warned that it "should not be regarded as an empty vessel to be filled with whatever meaning we might wish from time to time."[119] According to McIntyre, the purpose underlying section 2(d) was to constitutionalize the proposition that "the attainment of individual goals, through the exercise of individual rights, is generally impossible without the aid and co-operation of others." In addition, McIntyre argued, by allowing individuals to form groups to pursue various objectives, freedom of association "strengthens the general social order." Finally, by making "possible the effective expression of political views," freedom of association "supports the healthy functioning of democratic government."[120]

Despite the important functions served by freedom of association, McIntyre stressed that it is a freedom "belonging to the individual and not to the group formed through its exercise." "People, by merely combining together," McIntyre argued, "cannot create an entity which has greater constitutional rights and freedoms than they, as individuals, possess." According to this view, a group may "exercise only the constitutional rights of its individual members on behalf of those members. If the right asserted is not found in the Charter for the individual, it cannot be implied for the group merely by the fact of association."[121] In making this assertion, McIntyre proposed an entirely different view of the Charter than the one implicit in Chief Justice Dickson's reasons for judgment. While both McIntyre and Dickson recognized that certain Charter guarantees obviously belong to groups rather than to individuals, McIntyre was unwilling to follow the Chief Justice and read a collective component into guarantees of primarily individual rights. For McIntyre, the Charter contained mutually exclusive sets of individual and collective rights that must be interpreted accordingly.

This did not mean, however, that the meaning of association had to be restricted to the one articulated in *Collymore*. According to McIntyre, this was only one of at least six possible definitions of freedom of association, which include:

1. A right to associate with others in common pursuits or for certain purposes [the *Collymore* definition].
2. The freedom to engage collectively in those activities which are constitutionally protected for each individual [the definition adopted in U.S. jurisprudence].
3. The right of individuals to do in concert with others that which they may lawfully do alone, implying that individuals and organizations have no right to do in concert what is unlawful when done individually.
4. A right to engage in collective action considered fundamental to our culture and traditions and which by common assent are deserving of protection.
5. A right to engage in all activities which are essential to the lawful goals of an association.
6. Constitutional protection for all acts done in association, subject only to limitation under s. 1 of the Charter.[122]

According to McIntyre, the fourth, fifth, and sixth definitions of freedom of association clearly surpassed the intended scope of section 2(d);[123] on the other hand, the first and second were acceptable definitions.[124] In McIntyre's view, the third definition should also be accepted, since it provided the same constitutional protection to groups and individuals without elevating group activity to a higher constitutional status than individual activity.[125]

In view of these considerations, McIntyre concluded that freedom of association means that "Charter protection will attach to the exercise in association of such rights as have Charter protection when exercised by the individual," as well as to those activities "which are lawful when performed alone."[126] Having thus defined freedom of association, McIntyre turned to whether this definition includes the right to strike. "Since the right to strike is not independently protected under the Charter," McIntyre began, "it can receive protection under freedom of association only if it is an activity which is permitted by law to an individual." However, McIntyre rejected the argument that individual employees may lawfully cease work during the course of an employment contract; nor did he find any analogy between "the cessation of work by a single employee and a strike conducted in accordance with modern labour legislation." Ironically, McIntyre found support for this finding in Chief Justice Dickson's emphasis on the absence of any individual equivalent to a strike. Strikes, according to McIntyre, are inherently collective actions used by trade unions primarily, although not exclusively, to advance their economic interests.[127] In McIntyre's view, therefore, the right to strike claimed by the appellants conflicted with two important facets of the Charter: its emphasis on individual rights and its lack of concern with economic or property rights.

It is hardly surprising that McIntyre's reasoning, which also determined the outcome in the *Public Service Alliance of Canada* and *Saskatchewan Dairy Worker* cases, would disturb labour rights activists.[128] Their dissatisfaction with McIntyre increased substantially, moreover, after he suggested in *Law Society of Alberta v. Black* (1989) that section 2(d) provides constitutional protection for certain types of associations formed to pursue essentially economic objectives.[129] In particular, without discussing (or even citing) the *Alberta Labour Reference,* McIntyre argued that freedom of association precludes provincial law societies from prohibiting resident members from forming partnerships with non-resident members. McIntyre presumably reasoned that, since the practice of law is a lawful activity when performed by individuals, its performance by any association of individuals may not be unduly restricted. However, the practice of law is not a lawful activity for *every* individual; all provinces impose requirements of education, training, and ethical conduct on lawyers. One might infer, therefore, that not every association formed for the practice of law is protected by section 2(d). It is a singular weakness of McIntyre's reasons for judgment in *Black* that he neglected to provide a more thorough explanation for his rather offhand extension of freedom of association to interprovincial law firms.

In the final analysis, the various reasons for judgment in the labour trilogy reflect two competing visions of judicial review under the Charter. The vision articulated by Dickson is that, although any single Charter guarantee may protect predominantly collective or individual rights, every guarantee embodies characteristics of both types of rights. In McIntyre's view, the Charter indeed contains both collective and individual rights, but these guarantees do not overlap in such a way that individual rights confer constitutional status on the inherently collective activities of groups formed by individuals. Indeed, in McIntyre's vision, the Charter's individual rights should always prevail over the collective rights of specific groups. What concerns communitarians is that, in the context of labour relations, this vision necessarily creates a tension between the collective rights of trade unions and the individual rights of union members in ways that will irrevocably harm the labour movement. Indeed, this vision was evident in the judicial creation of a "freedom of non-association" in the courts of at least one province.[130] Thus, while McIntyre's vision certainly appears to be the narrower (or more interpretivist) one, it has broader (or non-interpretivist) implications.

Nevertheless, there are two important qualitative differences between the predominantly individual rights guaranteed by the Charter and those rights usually designated as "collective," each of which tends to support McIntyre's general approach to the relationship between collective and individual rights in the Charter. First, many of the collective rights provisions are written in the declaratory language of the "frozen rights" formulation of the 1960 Bill of Rights. This is true of certain rights pertaining to official languages (sections 21 and 22), aboriginal rights and freedoms (section 25), and the rights of denominational schools (section 29). All of these sections arguably declare that the Charter protects either existing rights or rights that may be acquired by political means, rather than inviting judicial creation of additional collective rights.

The second difference is that these collective rights tend to be defined in very specific terms, implying that they apply to a very narrow range of circumstances. Sections 16 to 20, which define certain rights of French and English linguistic groups, fall into this category. An even clearer example is the minority-language educational rights guaranteed by section 23, some of which only come into play "where numbers warrant." Indeed, one purpose of this phrase is arguably to prevent *minority* tyranny by ensuring that public funds need not be expended to supply minority-language instruction or facilities for a very small number of children. The only collective right that does not fit comfortably into either of these categories is section 27, which requires that the Charter be interpreted "in a manner consistent with the preservation and enhancement of the multicultural heritage of Canadians." This might allow courts to confer unenumerated collective rights on certain cultural communities. With this exception, however, the Charter's collective rights are not written in the same open-ended language as, for example, the fundamental freedoms. One plausible conclusion, therefore, is that the Charter's drafters signalled the special importance of individual rights over collective rights by leaving more room for judicial expansion of individual rights.

There is a second reason to be sceptical about the communitarian critique of the Court's general reluctance to expand collective rights: the Charter contains a second category of collective rights that protect the collective interests of society as a whole and are defined in section 1. As the Court's willingness to engage in the balancing process of section 1 suggests, the justices have been sensitive to this aspect of the Charter's more communitarian aspects. Or have they? With the exception of its adoption of McIntyre's position in the freedom of association cases, the Court's decisions under section 2 reveal some important elements of the relationship between judicial power and the concept of limited constitutional government under the Charter. The pattern in these decisions is for the Court to articulate a broad interpretation of the Charter's substantive provisions, which inevitably leads it to find some inconsistency between the Charter and either the purpose or effect of an impugned statute. It then becomes necessary for the government concerned to justify the statute as a reasonable limit under section 1. What this demonstrates is the central importance of section 1 as a tool for judicial review rather than as a concession to legislative flexibility. Section 1 has been transformed from a provision designed to give constitutional recognition to the principle that rights must be limited for effective government into a constitutional grant of power to courts not only to interpret and apply Charter provisions, but also to determine the importance, rationality, and proportionality of certain legislative measures. Under the pattern of judicial decision-making evident in the Court's section 2 decisions, legislatures must justify the technical details of important policy decisions not only to the electorate, to which they are directly accountable, but also to a panel of judges who possess no special expertise in the areas to which these policies are addressed. Indeed, the case can be made that section 1 has had the effect of emboldening, rather than constraining, judicial power.

Perhaps even more important for understanding the emerging relationship between judicial power and constitutionalism under the Charter is Justice McIntyre's surprising – indeed, almost shocking – declaration in *Dolphin Delivery* that the judiciary does not form part of government. This statement carries the Court a long way toward embracing the modern notion that the role played by courts in enforcing constitutional limits on political power requires that they generally be exempt from these same limits. That this declaration should have come from the justice best known for judicial restraint serves as further evidence of how entrenched the modern view of judicial power has become in Charter adjudication.

CHAPTER 4

Legal Rights, Fundamental Justice, and Criminal Procedure

Like the U.S. Bill of Rights, a significant portion of the Charter of Rights and Freedoms is devoted to protecting the general legal rights of Canadians and the specific procedural rights of accused persons. These rights are enumerated in sections 7 to 14 of the Charter and are expressed in terms similar to the Fourth, Fifth, Sixth, and Eighth Amendments to the U.S. Constitution. Section 7, which resembles the due process clauses of the Fifth and Fourteenth Amendments, provides that "[e]veryone has the right to life, liberty and security of the person and the right not to be deprived thereof except in accordance with the principles of fundamental justice." Sections 8 and 9 prohibit unreasonable searches and seizures, as well as arbitrary detention or imprisonment. Section 10 identifies several rights available on arrest or detention, including the right to be informed promptly of the reasons for the arrest or detention; the right to retain and instruct counsel without delay and to be informed of that right; and the right to *habeas corpus*. Section 11 enumerates several rights available to persons charged with an offence, including the right to be tried within a reasonable time; the right to be presumed innocent until proven guilty; and protection against double jeopardy. Section 12 prohibits cruel and unusual treatment or punishment, while sections 13 and 14 grant rights against self-incrimination and to an interpreter in judicial proceedings.

Since the development of procedural rules is considered to be "a traditional policy area of judicial responsibility . . . where judicial expertise is at its highest,"[1] the definition and application of these rights should in principle be one of the easier tasks of Charter adjudication. For the same reason, this task should also be less plagued by the same normative tensions that characterize the enforcement of other rights guaranteed by the Charter. Indeed, this perceived expertise and legitimacy encourage both judges and litigants to frame a variety of constitutional issues in procedural terms whenever possible.[2] In practice, however, this task is not so straightforward as it appears, since the interpretation and application of procedural rights involves substantive questions about the purpose and scope of these rights, as well as empirical questions about the likely impact of judicial definitions of these rights on the behaviour of non-judicial participants in the criminal justice system.

The U.S. Supreme Court has faced these questions both in defining the specific content of the procedural guarantees of the Bill of Rights and in determining the extent to which these guarantees apply to the states by virtue of the Fourteenth Amendment's due process clause. Although the incorporation problem does not arise in Charter adjudication, sections 8 to 12 raise the same definitional and policy questions as their U.S. equivalents. Moreover, since there are no counterparts in the text of the U.S. Bill of Rights to sections 11(d) (right "to be presumed innocent until proven guilty . . . by an independent and impartial tribunal") or 14 (right to an interpreter), the Canadian Court must deal with certain indigenous questions. Section 7 also poses a number of unique interpretive questions, including the scope of individual conduct and entitlements protected by "liberty" and "security of the person" and the precise meaning of the phrase "principles of fundamental justice."[3] Indeed, after the Court decided that "fundamental justice" permits substantive, as well as procedural, judicial review in the British Columbia *Motor Vehicle Reference* (1985), commentators turned their attention to whether "liberty" means more than simply the absence of physical coercion and whether "security of the person" protects rights to welfare benefits and to some forms of property.[4] The answers that the Canadian Supreme Court gives to these questions are important for understanding the relationship between constitutionalism and judicial power in the post-Charter era, since a combination of substantive review and broadly construed, open-ended, legal/procedural rights significantly enhances judicial power. This potent combination became particularly apparent in what has been perhaps the most politically contentious case decided thus far under the Charter's legal rights sections (or, indeed, any section) – the Court's abortion decision in *Morgentaler, Smoling and Scott v. The Queen* (1988).[5]

Legal Rights and Fundamental Justice

As we saw in Chapter Two, Justice Lamer attempted to formulate a relatively narrow conception of substantive review in his reasons for judgment in the *Motor Vehicle Reference.* Nevertheless, his *dicta* suggested the possibility that this power could be used in more extensive ways. As Lamer indicated, substantive violations of fundamental justice infringe the Charter only if they also restrict the rights protected by section 7. While imprisonment and probation constitute obvious infringements of liberty, Justice Lamer speculated that absolute liability offences enforced by other types of sanctions might also infringe section 7, depending on the content given to security of the person in future decisions.[6] This openness to future expansion of the circumstances under which substantive review might be appropriate suggested that the Court might expand the list of government actions that are inconsistent with substantive principles of fundamental justice in the course of broadening the meaning of liberty and security of the person. Moreover, it meant that, as liberty and security of the person become more broadly defined, substantive review might occur more frequently in areas outside the traditional boundaries of the judicial process. Both of these phenomena have been evident in subsequent section 7 decisions.

Principles of Fundamental Justice

The Supreme Court of Canada has decided numerous cases under section 7 of the Charter. In many of these cases, the Court has considered applications for relief from government interference with narrowly conceived rights to physical liberty and security of the person as a result of alleged violations of both procedural and substantive fundamental justice.[7] As a whole, these applications were only moderately successful during the Charter's first decade. The Court granted relief in five procedural cases, but in two of these cases the Crown itself conceded that the statute in question violated procedural principles of fundamental justice.[8] The Court has also granted relief in three substantive cases, with two of these cases having a significant impact on the traditional powers of Parliament and the provincial legislatures.[9] Neither of the cases encompassing both types of claims succeeded.

The Court's general reluctance to grant relief in the relatively small number of procedural cases it has heard under section 7 is largely a function of the specific procedural rights available to criminal defendants in sections 8 to 14 of the Charter. The enumeration of these specific rights, which are closely linked to traditional legal values and sufficiently open-ended to provide the Court with broad supervisory powers over the administration of justice, makes them a logical source of procedural challenges to government conduct. In fact, cases brought under sections 8 (prohibiting unreasonable search or seizure) and 10 (enumerating rights available on arrest or detention) have produced the most successful Charter litigation to date.[10] This pattern suggests that procedural applications for relief brought under the general provisions of section 7 probably have little support in even very generous interpretations of the specific rights enumerated in sections 8 to 14. The likely weakness of these claims, particularly when made in the context of criminal proceedings whose administration is explicitly governed by sections 8 to 14, suggests that it would be unusual if the Court frequently granted relief in such cases. In the context of criminal procedure, the principles of fundamental justice appear to be primarily a source of residual rights.

A brief glance at some of the cases in which the Court has denied procedural relief under section 7 illustrates this characteristic.[11] At issue in *Spencer v. The Queen* (1985) was whether it offends fundamental justice for the Crown to compel testimony from a witness in a trial when such testimony would be contrary to provisions of foreign law. In *Spencer,* the manager of a Canadian bank in the Bahamas who had acquired information about a defendant's financial affairs in that capacity argued that testifying in the defendant's tax evasion trial would violate the Bahamas Bank and Trust Companies Regulation Act, which prohibits bank officers from disclosing information about financial transactions without a client's consent. The Court held, however, that the Crown's actions in the case did not violate the Charter, since no infringement of section 7 rights would result from the operation of Canadian law. The Court further held that upholding the fundamental justice claim in this case would permit foreign law to frustrate the administration of justice in Canada, as well as infringe on Canadian sovereignty.[12]

While the alleged violation of procedural justice in *Spencer* was somewhat exotic, the Court has also denied procedural claims in more conventional cases. In *Albright v. The Queen* (1987), the Court considered the procedures by which provinces impose enhanced penalties for impaired driving. The British Columbia statute in question provided for such penalties in cases where the defendant had been previously convicted of the same offence, and it permitted the Crown to prove the existence of prior convictions by entering into evidence a certified extract of provincial driving records. The alleged deficiency in this procedure was the absence of any requirement that the Crown give prior notice of its intent to rely on the certificate. The Court rejected this argument and held that failure to provide advance notice of the Crown's intentions did not violate fundamental justice, since it did not affect the accused's ability to challenge the certificate's accuracy at trial.[13] Finally, at issue in *R. v. Vermette* (1988) was whether section 7 imposes any procedural requirements on jury selection. While section 11(f) of the Charter grants the right to trial by jury where serious offences are involved, it is silent about the criteria governing jury selection. Although this is the type of issue to which a residual procedural rights section might perhaps be most relevant, the Court simply declined to decide the question.

While the Court has appeared reluctant to use section 7 to impose procedural restraints on criminal proceedings beyond those enumerated in sections 8 to 14, it has indicated more sympathy for section 7 procedural claims where the administration of non-criminal proceedings is at issue. In *Re Singh and Minister of Employment and Immigration* (1985) the Court considered the constitutionality of procedures established by the Immigration Act, 1976 for determining "Convention refugee" status.[14] The Act provided for the determination of refugee status by the Minister of Immigration, following an initial recommendation by the Refugee Status Advisory Committee. In the event of a negative decision, the Act granted refugee claimants the opportunity to apply in writing to the Immigration Appeal Board for a redetermination of their status. The Act granted the Appeal Board virtually unlimited discretion to allow or deny the application for redetermination.[15] Although all six justices who participated in the judgment found these procedures inadequate, they divided evenly on whether the procedures violated section 7 of the Charter or section 2(e) of the Bill of Rights. Writing on behalf of herself, Chief Justice Dickson, and Justice Lamer, Justice Bertha Wilson held that the procedural mechanisms of the Act offended fundamental justice by denying refugee claimants an adequate opportunity to present their case for refugee status. The precise deficiency, she argued, was the Act's failure to provide for oral hearings prior to the Appeal Board's decision. Although she conceded that exclusive reliance on written submissions might be adequate under other circumstances, Justice Wilson said that in this instance they did not offer sufficient opportunity for refugee claimants to articulate their own case and to challenge the case brought against them.

In Justice Wilson's view, the impugned provisions of the Act were inadequate primarily because the determination of refugee status depended to a large degree on the credibility of the evidence offered by both sides in the dispute. It was difficult, she asserted, "to conceive of a situation in which compliance with fundamental justice could be achieved by a tribunal making significant findings of credibility solely on the basis of written submissions."[16] Moreover, the Act's procedural mechanism forced refugee claimants to prepare their written submissions without any knowledge of the government's case against their claim. Justice Wilson held that, "as a matter of fundamental justice," refugee claimants are entitled to discovery of the Crown's case prior to the redetermination hearing.[17] Both of these conclusions about the requirements of fundamental justice in these circumstances flowed from Justice Wilson's characterization of redetermination proceedings as adversarial in nature.[18]

The decision by three justices to rely on the constitutionally entrenched concept of fundamental justice, rather than the equally applicable statutory concept as elaborated in *Duke v. The Queen* (1972), indicated their desire to transcend the limitations of the 1960 Bill of Rights and enhance the public law role of the Court.[19] In articulating the principle that fundamental procedural justice requires, at a minimum, oral hearings and full discovery in adversary proceedings where significant issues of credibility are at issue, Justice Wilson rejected a narrower approach to procedural review in which faithful adherence to decision-making procedures established by statute satisfies the principles of fundamental justice in non-criminal cases. Instead, she adopted an approach that requires the Court to measure legislatively defined procedures against independent standards of fundamental justice established by the Court itself. Finally, she declared that Parliament could not ignore these requirements for the sake of administrative convenience or cost.[20]

Justice Wilson's approach to the procedural elements of section 7 in *Singh* advanced the proposition that fair procedure should be determined on a case-by-case basis according to the specific nature of the proceedings under review and the rights at stake in those proceedings. This approach significantly augments judicial power to write codes of procedure for various types of proceedings, and it suggests that the procedural character of non-criminal adversary proceedings may evolve independently of the procedural rights enumerated in sections 8 to 14. While this will probably mean that less rigorous standards will apply to such proceedings, changing definitions and shifting judicial evaluation of the importance of the rights protected by liberty and security of the person could lead in some instances to greater rigour.

The Court's adaptation of this interpretive approach to the procedural elements of section 7 in *Lyons v. The Queen* (1987) provides one indication of its flexibility.[21] At issue in *Lyons* were the "dangerous offender" provisions of the Criminal Code. These provisions allow for indeterminate detention where an accused is declared to be dangerous following a conviction for a serious personal injury offence that is shown to be part of "a pattern of repetitive behaviour, . . . a pattern of persistent aggressive behaviour, . . . or of such a brutal nature as to compel the conclusion that his behaviour in the future is unlikely to be inhibited by normal standards of behavioural restraint."[22] In addition to several substantive arguments, the appellant advanced three section 7 procedural challenges to the dangerous offender provisions.[23] These included the claim that dangerousness must be determined by a jury, that it must be proved beyond a reasonable doubt, and that the Crown must give notice of its intention to invoke the dangerous offender provisions prior to the entering of a plea. The Court rejected each of these arguments, holding that although section 7 entitles defendants to a fair hearing, "it does not entitle [them] to the most favourable procedures that could possibly be imagined."[24] Instead, the procedural requirements of fundamental justice "vary according to the context in which they are invoked. Thus, certain procedural protections might be constitutionally mandated in one context but not in another."[25] What this conclusion suggests is that, under the interpretive standard articulated in *Singh,* some aspects of criminal proceedings may indeed be subject to less rigorous procedural requirements than non-criminal proceedings.

The appellant in *Lyons* was also unsuccessful in his application for *substantive* relief from the dangerous offender provisions, in which he argued that indeterminate preventive detention constitutes punishment without a finding of *actus reus.* To be more precise, Lyons challenged the dangerous offender provisions on the grounds that they permit courts to impose criminal sanctions for crimes defendants have not committed. Led by Justice La Forest, a majority of the Court found two reasons to reject this argument. First, Justice La Forest denied the assertion that the dangerous offender provisions permit punishment without proof of *actus reus.* The provisions only become relevant, he noted, following the accused's conviction of a specific crime.[26] More importantly, the majority accepted the Crown's argument that "it cannot be considered a violation of fundamental justice for Parliament to identify those offenders who, in the interests of protecting the public, ought to be sentenced according to considerations which are not entirely reactive or based on a 'just deserts' rationale."[27] In other words, Justice La Forest found that the principles of fundamental justice do not impose any general constraint on Parliament's power to use various combinations of incapacitation, deterrence, retribution, and rehabilitation in the development of its criminal sentencing policies.[28]

Lyons and *R. v. Milne* (1987)[29] are two of several decisions in which the Court has refused to declare certain actions of Parliament contrary to substantive principles of fundamental justice. Other decisions in this category have involved extradition proceedings,[30] the relationship between fundamental justice and equality rights,[31] fingerprinting requirements under the Identification of

Criminals Act,[32] and two cases in which the Court left the development of substantive fundamental justice open by finding other grounds on which to deny relief from alleged government infringement of section 7 rights.

In one of the cases falling within this last group, *Krug v. The Queen* (1985), the Court considered whether provisions of the Criminal Code violate substantive fundamental justice by allowing simultaneous conviction of the same accused for armed robbery and the more specific offence of using a *firearm* while attempting to commit an indictable offence.[33] On behalf of a unanimous Court, Justice La Forest argued that it was within Parliament's power "to create an aggravated form of robbery, [and] to punish more severely an accused who uses a firearm in perpetrating that offense by imposing an additional penalty including a mandatory period of imprisonment."[34] Justice La Forest did not decide, however, whether there might be circumstances in which fundamental justice would prohibit Parliament from declaring that a single event constitutes a series of offences. He also declined to decide whether mandatory sentences *per se* offend fundamental justice.[35] Justice La Forest's desire to maintain flexibility by leaving both of these questions open for further deliberation is understandable, since the Court had not yet established the legitimacy of substantive review when it decided *Krug.*[36]

Although the Court's power of substantive review was firmly established by the time it heard *Stevens v. The Queen* (1988), it simply remained silent about the requirements of substantive fundamental justice by choosing to deny a substantive application for relief without considering its actual merits.[37] At issue in *Stevens* was the constitutionality of the Criminal Code's definition of statutory rape as an absolute liability offence. Because the acts for which the appellant had been convicted occurred prior to the Charter's coming into force, a majority of the Court dismissed the appeal on the grounds that the Charter did not have retroactive application. Justice Wilson, with the support of Justices Lamer and L'Heureux-Dubé, argued in dissent that retroactive application of the Charter is permissible and that the Court should decide the issue on its merits.[38] She argued, moreover, that, as a matter of substantive fundamental justice, section 7 "prohibits the existence of offences that are punishable by imprisonment and that do not allow the accused as a minimum a due diligence defence."[39] In her view, the impugned section of the Criminal Code violated section 7 in a manner that could not be justified under section 1 of the Charter.

As Justice Wilson's *Stevens* dissent and the *Motor Vehicle Reference* illustrate, substantive fundamental justice claims appear to be most persuasive when they challenge the legislative definition of criminal offences. This was clearly evident in *R. v. Vaillancourt* (1987), in which the Court considered the level of *mens rea* necessary to impose liability for murder.[40] *Vaillancourt* involved the Criminal Code's constructive murder provisions, which allowed for murder convictions where an accused caused the death of a person during the commission of another offence (in this case robbery) whether the accused intended to cause death or not. In resolving this issue, Justice Lamer relied on the *Motor Vehicle Reference* to declare that, although Parliament retained its traditional "power to define the elements of a crime" after the Charter's entrenchment in 1982, section 7 conferred on courts the duty "to review that definition to ensure that it is in accordance with the principles of fundamental justice."[41] In this case the question was not whether the definition of crimes in general must contain some mental component, but the exact level of *mens rea* constitutionally required to define an act as murder. Although Lamer believed that "a conviction for murder cannot rest on anything less than proof beyond a reasonable doubt of subjective foresight," he was content to decide the case more narrowly and hold that conviction for murder requires proof beyond a reasonable doubt of at least *objective* foreseeability.[42] As Justice Wilson noted in her *Stevens* dissent, *Vaillancourt* affirmed the principle that section 7 had "elevated the requirement of *mens rea* from a presumption of statutory interpretation to a constitutionally mandated element of a criminal offence."[43] This became very clear in *R. v. Martineau* (1990), when Lamer finally persuaded a majority of his colleagues to accept the more restrictive *mens rea* requirement that he had not been able to impose in *Vaillancourt.*[44] Through its decisions in *Vaillancourt* and *Martineau,* the Court succeeded in removing the concept of constructive murder from the Criminal Code.

There are at least two explanations for the Court's propensity to use substantive review to alter key definitional elements of criminal offences. First, these issues constitute a significant component of criminal justice policy, whose development by courts is less hampered by concerns about judges overextending their decision-making competence or undermining the legitimacy of courts. The second explanation is that the substantive questions the Court has decided in these cases have to a considerable degree resembled procedural issues. The level of *mens rea* necessary to produce a murder conviction, for example, is closely related to procedural questions concerning the Crown's burden of proof. If the general contours of criminal justice policy are considered a traditional area of judicial expertise, then this is especially true of criminal procedure. In these fundamental justice cases, therefore, the Court's most activist decisions have involved issues where the line between procedure and substance has been very unclear.

The Court wove together various strands of its principles of fundamental justice jurisprudence in its May, 1991, decision in *Swain v. The Queen.*[45] At issue in *Swain* was the constitutionality under section 7 of a common-law rule allowing the Crown to raise evidence of insanity over an accused's objections, as well as the constitutionality of provisions of the Criminal Code mandating automatic, indeterminate detention of persons found not guilty by reason of insanity. In a six-to-one decision (L'Heureux-Dubé dissenting), the Court held that both the common-law rule and the Criminal Code provisions violate section 7. According to the principal reasons for judgment by Chief Justice Lamer (as he had become), the common-law rule interfered with the accused's right to control his or her own defence. Lamer conceded, however, that this right is not absolute; and he allowed that the Crown could advance such evidence where the accused's conduct raised questions about mental capacity.

On the statutory issue, Lamer held that the impugned provisions were deficient primarily because of their mandatory nature. Fundamental justice, he asserted, requires that no one be denied liberty without a hearing, in this case a hearing concerning the accused's mental state sometime after the commission of an offence. Lamer also criticized the substance of the provisions as defective, since they imposed arbitrary detention contrary to section 9 of the Charter. Significantly, Lamer did not rely on section 9 directly; he read its substantive limit on government action into section 7. However, taking account of the potential consequences of striking down these provisions, Lamer permitted them to remain valid for a temporary period of six months as long as no period of detention exceeded sixty days. *Swain* reflects several characteristics of section 7 jurisprudence: the constitutional domestication of the common law; the creation of new procedural rules; caution in applying these rules in the criminal context; and the use of a specific procedural Charter provision to inject substantive content into section 7. This last characteristic suggests that Canada may develop its own version of the American incorporation doctrine, in which specific procedural guarantees are said to be incorporated into the principles of fundamental justice.

Despite the Court's apparent restraint, its decisions under the fundamental justice clause of section 7 have had a significant impact on both public policy and judicial behaviour. These decisions have prohibited the use of absolute liability offences in provincial penal law and federal criminal law; prohibited reliance on writs of assistance to authorize searches under the Narcotic Control Act; required that oral hearings and full discovery rights be granted to individuals in adversarial administrative proceedings; placed constitutional limits on certain common-law rules; and significantly altered the manner in which the criminal justice system must deal with defendants acquitted on the grounds of insanity. Moreover, the Court has disassociated the development of this component of section 7 from both its Bill of Rights jurisprudence and the intentions of the Charter's drafters. Finally, the principles of fundamental justice now appear also to incorporate more specific constitutional guarantees.

Liberty and Security of the Person

The Court's interpretation of the requirements of procedural and substantive fundamental justice has generally occurred in cases involving a narrow range of matters. With the exception of *Singh,* which involved a dispute over the possible denial of security of the person in non-criminal immigration proceedings, these applications for relief have arisen in the context of state interference with physical liberty through the application of the criminal law. In addition to these matters, however, the Court has also decided several appeals under section 7 in which broader conceptions of liberty and security of the person formed the basis of the alleged Charter violation.[46] Although the Court has denied relief in all but one of these appeals, it has established the general principle that liberty and security of the person have more than merely a physical meaning. Moreover, even in denying relief the Court has acknowledged that these rights may be infringed by government decisions and actions outside the traditional boundaries of the administration of justice.

For example, in *Operation Dismantle v. The Queen* (1985) the Court rejected an attempt by a coalition of disarmament groups to prevent the federal government from allowing the United States to test cruise missiles over Canadian territory. The coalition alleged that the federal cabinet's decision to permit such testing increased the risk of nuclear conflict and therefore violated the rights to life and security of the person guaranteed by the Charter. Consequently, these groups filed a statement of claim in the trial division of the Federal Court in which they sought a declaratory judgment that the cabinet's decision was unconstitutional, injunctive relief to prohibit the testing, and damages. The federal trial court denied a Crown motion to strike the statement of claim prior to a hearing on the merits, but the Federal Court of Appeal reversed this decision and struck out the statement of claim. The Operation Dismantle coalition then appealed to the Supreme Court to reinstate its claim in order to proceed with a trial on the merits.

Although it ultimately dismissed Operation Dismantle's appeal, the Supreme Court established two important principles in its discussion of the questions involved. First, as discussed in Chapter Two, the Court refused to formulate a "political questions" doctrine that would have excluded certain disputes from litigation, either because they encompass issues that are inherently political or because they entail excessive judicial invasion of exclusively executive or legislative powers.[47] Writing on behalf of four other justices, Chief Justice Dickson "agree[d] in substance with Madame Justice Wilson's discussion of justiciability," and held that "disputes of a political or foreign policy nature may be properly cognizable by the courts."[48] The second important principle established in *Operation Dismantle* was that the meaning of security of the person extends beyond physical security. Chief Justice Dickson found that the key component of Operation Dismantle's claim was not that cruise missile testing in Canada would lead directly to a nuclear attack and cause "actual deprivation of life and security of the person," but that such testing might increase the "general insecurity experienced by all people in Canada as a result of living under the increased *threat* of nuclear war."[49] In the Chief Justice's view, government interference with security of the person in this indirect psychological sense is as inconsistent with the rights guaranteed by section 7 as are more direct physical intrusions.

By establishing that executive decisions are subject to judicial review under the Charter and that security of the person refers to psychological as well as physical security, Chief Justice Dickson conceded at least a *prima facie* legal basis for Operation Dismantle's claim. He avoided the claim's substantive merits, however, by focusing on its *empirical* basis. Dickson argued that, in order to prove that the Cabinet's decision violated even this psychological component of security of the person, Operation Dismantle would have to demonstrate that the decision to allow cruise missile testing actually increased the risk of nuclear war. Meeting this burden at trial, he continued, required that the group prove numerous "assumptions and hypotheses about how independent and sovereign nations, operating in an international arena of radical uncertainty, and continually changing circumstances, will react to the . . . decision to permit the testing of the cruise missile."[50] Dickson argued that such proof was beyond the fact-finding capacity of courts, and he thus concluded that the "causal link" between the cabinet's decision and the alleged violation of section 7 rights "is simply too uncertain, speculative and hypothetical to sustain a cause of action."[51]

While the majority of the Court dismissed Operation Dismantle's appeal on the grounds that the causal link between the cabinet's decision and the alleged infringement of section 7 rights could not be proved at trial, Justice Wilson argued that it was improper for the Court to pre-judge the issue.[52] In her view, the proper reason for dismissing the appeal was constitutional: even if the facts alleged in the statement of claim were true, the decision to test cruise missiles did not constitute a breach of section 7. Justice Wilson asserted that "there must be a strong presumption that governmental action which concerns the relations of the State with other states, and which is therefore not directed at any member of the immediate political community, was never intended to be caught by section 7 even although such action may have the incidental effect of increasing the risk of death or injury that individuals generally have to face."[53] Thus, while agreeing with her colleagues that section 7 protects individuals from more than arbitrary arrest or detention and that cabinet decisions are reviewable under the Charter, she argued that section 7 could not protect Canadians from the indirect and hypothetical consequences of this particular executive decision.[54]

In *Operation Dismantle* the Court demonstrated its willingness to interpret section 7 rights broadly, but then exhibited restraint in refusing to apply the expanded interpretation to the facts of a specific case. A similar ambivalence is evident in other cases where the Court has considered applications for relief based on broad definitions of liberty. In *Re Eve* (1986),[55] the Court grappled with the question of whether the mother of a mentally disabled woman should be authorized to consent to the non-therapeutic sterilization of her daughter. This case raised a complex set of issues concerning the criteria according to which decisions may be made on behalf of mentally incompetent individuals, as well as the constitutional question of whether the right to liberty protected by section 7 includes a fundamental right to procreative choice.[56] Speaking for a unanimous Court, Justice La Forest found it unnecessary to decide whether section 7 protects this right, choosing instead to deny the mother's request by narrowly construing the *parens patriae* jurisdiction of provincial courts.[57]

Broad conceptions of liberty were also invoked by the litigants in two of the freedom of religion cases discussed in Chapter Three. In *Jones v. The Queen* (1986), the appellant challenged provisions of the Alberta School Act that impose punitive sanctions on parents who fail to send their children to public schools or approved private schools. After his conviction for truancy,[58] Jones sought relief partly on the grounds that the School Act infringed both his narrow right to liberty (by imposing imprisonment as a sanction for the offence) and his broader liberty right to raise his children as he saw fit. He contended that these infringements of liberty were inconsistent with procedural fundamental justice because the Act allowed for only one means of proving effective home instruction (a certificate from a provincial education inspector).[59] Six of seven justices again found it unnecessary to decide whether the liberty clause of section 7 extends this far. The sole exception was Justice Wilson, who found that liberty as used in section 7 protects the right of parents to raise their children in accordance with conscientiously held beliefs, if not entirely as they see fit.[60] In *Edwards Books and Art v. The Queen* (1986), the appellants argued that the right to liberty in section 7 protects a right to choose when to transact business.[61] The Court unanimously rejected this argument, with Chief Justice Dickson holding that liberty "is not synonymous with unconstrained freedom" and thus does not confer "an unconstrained right to transact business whenever one wishes."[62]

Another case that led the Court to consider a claim based on a broad right to liberty was *B.C.G.E.U. v. British Columbia* (1988).[63] At issue here was the constitutionality of an *ex parte* injunction issued by the Chief Judge of the British Columbia Supreme Court to prevent striking provincial employees from disrupting the business of provincial courts through picketing. In addition to arguments based on sections 2 and 11 of the Charter, the employees' union argued that the injunction's enjoinment of picketing infringed a specific right included within the general right to liberty guaranteed by section 7. Chief Justice Dickson's treatment of this claim on behalf of a majority of the Court was brief: he held that even "assuming . . . that the effect of the injunction was to deny the Union members' right to liberty protected by section 7, the denial of that right was fully in accordance with the principles of fundamental justice."[64] The judge's use of an *ex parte* injunction, according to Dickson, was, under the circumstances, "a minimal interference with the procedural rights" of striking provincial employees whose picketing would interfere "with the legal and constitutional rights of all citizens of British Columbia."[65]

The Court has thus been given the opportunity in cases brought under the liberty clause of section 7 to declare that liberty includes the freedom to raise one's children without government interference, freedom of absolute procreative choice, the freedom to decide when to conduct business, and the right to picket. With one exception, the Court's reaction to these claims has been silence, neither denying nor vindicating the broad rights to liberty claimed by the appellants in these cases. Few generalizations are possible on the basis of these decisions, with the exception that the justices appear to recognize that liberty, like security of the person, has more than simply a physical meaning. The Court appears reluctant, however, to expand the meaning of liberty unnecessarily.

In general, cases decided under section 7 have established two very important principles to guide future constitutional development. The first is that the reference to fundamental justice in section 7 makes the Court responsible for measuring the substantive, as well as procedural, consistency of legislation with the "democratic values" entrenched in the Charter. The second principle is that "liberty" and "security of the person" are sufficiently open-ended to give the Court considerable power to define precisely what these democratic values are. This power is especially important since the Court has rejected the Charter's drafters as an authoritative source of those values without at the same time articulating any alternative source other than its own understanding of the "basic tenets" of Canada's system of justice. Moreover, the Court has not yet provided a comprehensive justification of why its interpretation of these basic tenets is superior to, and should prevail over, the interpretation of these values offered by Parliament and the provincial legislatures. Despite the apparent judicial restraint in some of the Court's section 7 decisions, the emergence of substantive review under section 7 and the Court's willingness to use liberty and security of the person to identify additional values against which legislation must be measured belie the assurances given by the justices of the Canadian Supreme Court that they will refrain from interfering with policy decisions.

Criminal Procedure

In contrast to the United States, where both the federal and state governments exercise jurisdiction over criminal law and procedure, in Canada these matters are largely within the exclusive jurisdiction of the federal government. The sole exception is provincial authority over the administration of justice within the province, which can be exercised to regulate some aspects of criminal investigations and procedure.[66] Prior to the enactment of the Charter, common-law rules that could be modified by statute determined the substance of criminal procedure. In the area of search and seizure, for example, Canadian legislatures used this statutory authority to create additional search and seizure powers for government officials, as well as to suspend common-law rules prohibiting warrantless searches in certain circumstances.[67] To a large degree, this approach to criminal procedure reflected the values of what Herbert S. Packer called the *crime control* model of criminal procedure. According to Packer, this model views "the repression of criminal conduct [as] the most important function to be performed by the criminal process." To achieve this purpose, it focuses attention on "the efficiency with which the criminal process operates to screen suspects, determine guilt, and secure appropriate dispositions of persons convicted of crime." Consequently, the crime control model tends to de-emphasize the formal adversary components of the criminal process in favour of the pre-adjudicative, investigative phase of the process.[68] Police, prosecutors, defence lawyers, and judges work together to ensure the efficient administration of criminal justice and the rapid processing of criminal cases.

The principal effect of the Charter is to impose constitutional limits on the traditionally unfettered legislative power to alter criminal procedure. The Charter accomplishes this in two ways: first, by virtue of sections 8 to 11, the Charter grants courts extended supervisory powers over criminal procedure; second, section 24(2) explicitly authorizes courts to enforce these constitutional guarantees by excluding evidence obtained illegally from trial. In so doing, the Charter embraces elements of the *due process* model of criminal procedure that Packer contrasted with the crime control model. This approach to criminal procedure is deeply concerned with the factual integrity and accuracy of the criminal process, and it aims at eliminating the possibility of erroneous fact-finding. This leads the due process model to reject "informal fact-finding processes as definitive of factual guilt and to an insistence on formal, adjudicative, adversary fact-finding processes in which the factual case against the accused is publicly heard by an impartial tribunal."[69] The due process model is sceptical of the motivations and fact-determining skills of law enforcement agencies and prosecutors: rigorous procedures are considered to be the best instruments for guaranteeing correct outcomes.

The best place to begin evaluating the extent to which the Supreme Court has operationalized the Charter's conceptual shift to the due process model is with American judicial experience in this area. As in the case of the Charter's fundamental freedoms provisions, U.S. criminal procedure decisions have been frequently cited in Canada since 1982.[70] The basic assumptions underlying the due process model were at the core of the U.S. Court's incorporation of the Bill of Rights into state criminal proceedings under the leadership of Chief Justice Earl Warren during the 1960s.[71] Indeed, the Warren Court's concern with maintaining the factual integrity of the criminal process led it to extend the protections of the Bill of Rights to the earliest stages of criminal investigation. To ensure that the fact-finding process would not be tainted by evidence gathered illegally, for example, the Court applied the federal exclusionary rule to state criminal proceedings as a way of deterring law enforcement officers from violating the Fourth Amendment's prohibition against unreasonable searches and seizures. Although this rule first emerged in *Weeks v. United States* (1914), the Court explicitly refused to impose it on the states in *Wolf v. Colorado* (1949).[72] The Court's rationale in *Wolf* was that the exclusionary rule was simply a practical remedy, without constitutional status, developed as part of the Court's general supervisory power over the federal judiciary.[73] The Warren Court abandoned this position in *Mapp v. Ohio* (1961), holding that the exclusionary rule was necessary to ensure that no defendant would be convicted by evidence obtained through constitutionally prohibited means.[74]

In reaching this conclusion, the Court in its *Mapp* decision made several assumptions about the likely behaviour of criminal investigators and prosecuting attorneys. Although the exclusionary rule is designed to deter illegal police behaviour, it most directly affects prosecutors whose cases are undermined by the exclusion of evidence at trial. Consequently, for the rule to operate properly there must be a high level of communication between prosecutors and law enforcement officials. The evidence suggests, however, that the Court mistakenly assumed that such communication exists uniformly across jurisdictions. Since this is not the case, the expected benefits of the rule have not always exceeded the costs associated with its implementation. Moreover, the rule has on occasion had the ironic consequence in some jurisdictions of *increasing* illegal police behaviour by encouraging harassment and police perjury.[75] The exclusionary rule has only been partially successful in promoting the objectives of the due process model because it affected non-judicial behaviour in unanticipated ways.

The Canadian exclusionary rule found in section 24(2) of the Charter is textually more limited, and has been aimed at different purposes, than the *Mapp* rule. These two differences are both products of the instruction to judges in section 24(2) that evidence should be excluded only if its admission "would bring the administration of justice into disrepute." Consequently, the implementation of section 24(2) has not been concerned primarily with deterring illegal police behaviour but with maintaining the integrity of the criminal justice system.[76] The result is that the Court attempts to determine whether a "reasonable person" would view admission of the evidence as impeding the fairness of a trial, with one element of fairness being whether the illegally obtained evidence is "real" – that is, existed independently of the infringement of rights – or whether it owes its existence entirely to the rights violation. Nevertheless, despite these textual and judicial qualifications, the Charter's exclusionary rule has revolutionized the law of evidence in Canada. Indeed, in several cases the Court has excluded evidence that would have been admitted prior to the Charter.[77]

By broadening the supervisory powers of the Canadian Supreme Court in the area of criminal procedure, and especially by explicitly entrenching the exclusionary rule (albeit in a qualified form), the Charter has clearly created the potential that Canadian criminal procedure will converge with the American procedural jurisprudence inspired by the due process model.[78] That the Supreme Court of Canada is gradually realizing this potential is evident in the fact that the Charter's impact on criminal justice has been greatest with respect to the preadjudication, investigatory phase of the criminal process.[79] By the end of 1989, for example, the Court had upheld eight of seventeen challenges to government conduct brought under the section 8 prohibition against unreasonable searches and seizures. Moreover, on no occasion where the Court found a violation of section 8 did it find the search or seizure justified under section 1.[80] More dramatically, challenges brought under section 10(b) (guaranteeing the right on arrest or detention to retain and instruct counsel without delay and to be informed of that right) were successful in thirteen of sixteen cases. Finally, the Court found that evidence should have been excluded in eleven of the thirty-six cases in which section 24(2) was invoked.

Although the Court has rejected specific components of the American version of the due process model,[81] it has relied fairly extensively on Fourteenth Amendment due process jurisprudence to find legal rights violations in cases like the British Columbia *Motor Vehicle Reference, Vaillancourt v. The Queen,* and *Gamble v. The Queen.*[82] An even more obvious adoption of the due process approach to legal rights surfaced in Justice Wilson's reasons for judgment in *Singh,* which imposed various aspects of adversary hearings on proceedings to determine convention refugee status under the Immigration Act, 1976.[83] Noting the broad meaning of liberty developed under the Fourteenth Amendment and dismissing Crown submissions that adversary hearings would create excessive administrative burdens, Wilson significantly restructured these proceedings.[84] Consistent with the due process model, her objective was to eliminate the possibility of error regardless of administrative costs.[85]

In addition to procedural cases like *Singh,* the Canadian Court has also been willing to explore the outer boundaries of due process. One reason why the Warren Court preferred a blanket exclusionary rule to the common-law practice of undertaking a case-by-case determination of the reliability and relevance of evidence, or even to a more qualified exclusionary rule, was its adoption of an additional aspect of the due process model that is largely unrelated to the model's instrumental value in guaranteeing the factual integrity of the criminal process. During the Warren Court era, commentators began to argue that the strict procedural requirements of the due process model also have an intrinsic value because they equalize the relationship between individuals and the state and provide individuals with an opportunity to express "their dignity as persons."[86] According to this "dignity enhancement" aspect of the due process model, the interpretation of procedural rights should maximize the capacity of individuals to make decisions free from state coercion.[87] This approach was particularly influential in the development of Fifth Amendment jurisprudence concerning the privilege against self-incrimination, in which the U.S. Court sought to eliminate tactics that "strip individuals of their self-respect" on the grounds that "forcing an individual to be the instrument of his own undoing degrades the dignity of man."[88]

The Warren Court's concern with dignity enhancement reached its apex in *Miranda v. Arizona* (1966).[89] Referring to several police interrogation manuals, Warren argued that modern interrogation practices are "psychologically rather than physically oriented." Custodial interrogation (i.e., "incommunicado interrogation of individuals in a police-dominated atmosphere"), Warren continued, "exacts a heavy toll on individual liberty and trades on the weakness of individuals." This results in "inherently compelling pressures which work to undermine the individual's will to resist and to compel him to speak where he would not otherwise do so freely." All of this Warren found inconsistent with the privilege against self-incrimination, whose "constitutional foundation . . . is the respect a government must accord to the dignity and integrity of its citizens."[90] As the Court would elaborate one year later in *In re Gault* (1967): "The roots of the privilege tap the basic stream of religious and political principle because [it] reflects the limits of the individual's attornment to the state . . . and insists upon the equality of the individual and the state."[91] To ensure that individual dignity would be protected in the coercive atmosphere of custodial interrogation, the Court in *Miranda* developed a constitutional rule that law enforcement officers must fully inform arrested suspects of their Fifth and Sixth Amendment rights.

Canada's Supreme Court has been willing to adopt this "dignity enhancement" component of the due process model, with *Hunter v. Southam* (1984) providing an early indication that such concerns might influence the Court's approach to the legal rights protected by the Charter. At issue in *Southam* was the meaning of the term "unreasonable" in the section 8 guarantee of freedom from unreasonable search or seizure. Applying the purposive mode of analysis developed earlier in the decision, Justice Dickson (as he then was) declared that the purpose of section 8 is to "protect individuals from unjustified State intrusions upon their privacy."[92] In so construing section 8, Dickson relied extensively on the U.S. Supreme Court's decision in *Katz v. United States* (1967), in which Justice Potter Stewart interpreted the Fourth Amendment's guarantee against unreasonable searches and seizures as protecting "people, not places."[93] In other words, the Fourth Amendment and section 8 of the Charter protect the personal privacy of individuals rather than the integrity of the physical space they occupy. Dickson also followed Stewart in holding that the purpose of section 8 could "only be accomplished by a system of *prior authorization,* not one of subsequent validation."[94] According to Dickson, this conclusion was consistent "with the apparent intention of the Charter to prefer, where feasible, the right of the individual to be free from State interference to the interests of the State in advancing its purposes through such interference."[95]

Although dignity enhancement did not explicitly appear as *Katz*'s underlying rationale, the timing of the decision, along with its emphasis on privacy rights and prior authorization, was consistent with the Warren Court's general concern with advancing human dignity through due process. Consequently, although Dickson warned that "American decisions can be transplanted to the Canadian context only with the greatest caution," his use of *Katz* implicitly incorporated similar concerns into Canadian legal rights jurisprudence. The impact of this incorporation became evident eight months later in the reasons for judgment of Justice Gerald Le Dain in *R. v. Therens* (1985).[96] At issue in *Therens* was the meaning of the right guaranteed by section 10(b) of the Charter to retain and instruct counsel upon arrest or detention. In finding that a request to accompany a police officer to a police station and submit to a breathalyzer test constitutes detention under section 10, and therefore requires notification of the right to retain and instruct counsel, Le Dain echoed the concern with psychological coercion that motivated the U.S. Court's *Miranda* decision. "The element of psychological compulsion, in the form of a reasonable perception of suspension of freedom of choice," Le Dain argued, "is enough to make the restraint of liberty involuntary."[97] In *Therens,* the Court went even further than its U.S. counterpart, however, since the fact situation in *Therens* was not one that would have required *Miranda* warnings. To be precise, there was an absence in *Therens* of the "custodial interrogation" necessary to trigger the *Miranda* requirement.[98]

The dignity enhancement element of procedural rights implicit in *Southam* and *Therens* became explicit in *R. v. Oakes* (1986), in which the Court considered the constitutionality of the reverse onus provision of the Narcotic Control Act.[99] In reasons for judgment by Chief Justice Dickson, the Court unanimously held that the impugned provision of the Act violated the presumption of innocence guaranteed by section 11(d) of the Charter. Again employing his purposive approach to Charter interpretation, Dickson described this presumption as a "hallowed principle lying at the very heart of criminal law" that protects "the fundamental liberty and human dignity of every person accused . . . of criminal conduct."[100] The crucial procedural guarantee of this presumption, Dickson argued, is the requirement that the state prove its accusations beyond a reasonable doubt. By shifting the legal burden of proof from the Crown to the accused, the reverse onus provision of the Narcotic Control Act violated the presumption of innocence.[101]

Dickson's view of the relationship between the presumption of innocence and the state's burden of proving guilt beyond a reasonable doubt relied in part on the U.S. Supreme Court's decision in *In re Winship* (1970).[102] Written by Justice William Brennan (an articulate proponent of the dignity enhancement approach to due process),[103] the decision in *Winship* imposed the requirement of proof beyond a reasonable doubt on juvenile delinquency proceedings. In deciding *Oakes,* Dickson cited with approval Brennan's rationale for the constitutional protection accorded this requirement,[104] which Brennan attributed to the important interests criminal defendants have in maintaining their freedom and avoiding unwarranted stigmatization.[105] The importance of the reasonable doubt standard in protecting these interests, Brennan argued, had long been recognized in the United States. Citing two well-known common-law treatises on evidence, Brennan traced the origins of this standard to at least 1798.[106] This suggested to Brennan that the reasonable doubt standard should be elevated to a constitutional requirement, despite its absence from the U.S. Bill of Rights.

If Dickson had exercised the cautious approach to American decisions that he had recommended in *Southam,* however, he might have noticed that Brennan's analysis of the reasonable doubt standard in *Winship* was somewhat problematic.[107] First, contrary to Brennan's assertion, this standard had not been developed to provide greater protection for criminal defendants but to ease the burden of persuasion placed on prosecutors by an older "any doubt" test. The reasonable doubt standard, in other words, was originally intended to make convictions easier to obtain by limiting the grounds on which juries could acquit. Second, although the standard first appeared in the United States even earlier than Brennan's authorities indicated (1770), it did not become the dominant standard of proof in criminal cases until well into the nineteenth century. Consequently, the reasonable doubt standard was not a settled component of American jurisprudence when the due process clauses of the Fifth and Fourteenth Amendments were written. Whatever its merits, the constitutional importance of the reasonable doubt standard is not easily derived from its historical origins.

Despite the difficulty of establishing either empirical or historical links between due process and individual dignity, the dignity enhancement approach to interpreting and applying procedural rights remains influential in Canadian courts.[108] To a large degree, the Supreme Court has followed its *Southam* decision in linking individual human dignity to some level of personal privacy protected by section 8 of the Charter.[109] In *Simmons v. The Queen* (1988), for example, Justice Wilson emphasized that the freedom against unreasonable searches and seizures "is tied to a broader concern reflected in many of the legal rights in the Charter to prevent the citizen from being overborne by the much greater power of the state."[110] This approach echoed her earlier decision in *Clarkson v. The Queen* (1986), where Wilson stressed that "the adjudicative process must arrive at the truth in a way which does not reflect an abuse by the police or the Crown of its dominant position vis-à-vis the individual."[111] At issue in *Clarkson* was the admissibility of an accused's confession while under the influence of alcohol. Two justices held that the trial judge had properly excluded the statement on the basis of common-law principles, making it unnecessary to consider whether the accused's Charter rights had also been violated. Writing on behalf of a majority, however, Justice Wilson chose to decide the case on Charter grounds. Focusing on the accused's alleged waiver of the right to counsel, Wilson cited a series of U.S. decisions in holding that a valid waiver of rights must be premised on a true appreciation of the consequences of the waiver.[112] More importantly, by emphasizing Charter rights over common-law principles, Wilson's decision echoed the underlying rationale of *Miranda* and other U.S. decisions that constitutionally derived procedural rules protect individual dignity more effectively than common-law rules of evidence. Ironically, Wilson repeated her earlier error with respect to *Griggs v. Duke Power Co.* (1970) by misapplying the U.S. jurisprudence: her reasons for judgment applied Sixth Amendment jurisprudence to a situation actually covered by the Fifth Amendment.[113]

The importance of the dignity enhancement approach to legal/procedural rights is that it gives even the most procedurally oriented Charter provisions a substantive dimension that inevitably involves judges more visibly in "overtly political matters."[114] This transformation in the underlying rationale for procedural safeguards also reflects a profound theoretical shift from a utilitarian view of rights to one dominated by contemporary versions of the Kantian proposition that individuals must be treated as ends in themselves rather than merely as means to some other end. According to John Rawls, for example, the most important primary good that any society can promote is self-respect, which leads him to reject the utilitarian assertion that individual claims to liberty can be subordinated to the need to maximize average social utility.[115] In a utilitarian theory of procedural justice, procedural rules exist because they contribute to accurate decision-making; but efficiency and cost considerations can be weighed against any additional gains in accuracy that might be produced by more stringent procedures. From a Rawlsian perspective, the state owes its citizens the most extensive procedural safeguards available consistent with their right to equal self-respect; consequently, no procedure that trades off reliability for efficiency is tolerable. It is this Rawlsian principle that is implicit in the rationale underlying Justice Wilson's articulation of more rigorous procedures for determining refugee status in *Singh*.[116] This presents a problem not because the enhancement of human dignity is not a goal worth striving for, but because it provides few concrete and judicially manageable standards against which government action can be measured.

During the 1980s, the principal bias introduced into the administration of criminal justice by Charter litigation was toward stricter procedural standards. By 1990, litigants also sought to combine speedier case processing with the more stringent process required by the due process model. These two somewhat contradictory demands collided in *Askov v. The Queen* (1990), where the Court found that, under certain circumstances, delays of six to eight months between laying charges and bringing a case to trial violate the right to be tried within a reasonable time guaranteed by section 11(b) of the Charter.[117] According to Justice Peter Cory's purposive analysis of this provision, unreasonable delays are prohibited for two reasons. First, these delays have an adverse psychological impact on accused persons, witnesses, and victims. Consistent with the dignity enhancement approach to due process, such psychological effects must be eliminated or significantly reduced. Second, unreasonable delays have the practical effect of reducing the reliability and factual integrity of the criminal process because of their impact on the memories of witnesses and the quality of physical evidence. This leads to more acquittals and engenders community "frustration with the judicial system and eventually . . . contempt for court procedures."[118] Whether the product of inefficiency or inadequate resources, unreasonable delays frustrate the quest for error-free proceedings in which the dignity of every participant is maintained.

One of the ironies of the *Askov* decision is that the strict adherence to every element of the formal adversarial process required by the due process model is bound to produce the very delays that Justice Cory's decision attempted to eliminate. Indeed, one of the reasons why participants in the lower levels of the criminal justice process adopt the crime control model is to process cases expeditiously within the constraints of limited resources. As a result of *Askov* and other decisions, this solution is no longer permissible: provinces must simply allocate greater resources to the administration of justice. As in *Singh,* administrative costs cannot justify inadequate implementation of the due process model.

Legal Rights and Federal Economic Regulation: The Case of Competition Policy

A principal reason for the low regard in which many American scholars held judicial review prior to *Brown v. Board of Education* (1954) was the U.S. Supreme Court's use of the constitutionally questionable doctrine of substantive due process to frustrate state and federal regulation of the economy. During the early twentieth century, to cite only a few examples, the U.S. Court struck down state minimum wage/maximum hours legislation in *Lochner v. New York* (1905), nullified federal child labour legislation in *Hammer v. Dagenhart* (1918) and *Bailey v. Drexel Furniture Company* (1919), and voided federal minimum wage legislation for women workers in *Adkins v. Children's Hospital* (1923).[119] Three generations later, the drafters of the Charter took pains to ensure that this history could not be repeated in Canada. First, as discussed earlier in Chapter Two, they attempted (unsuccessfully in the end) to prevent a substantive interpretation of the principles of fundamental justice. Second, under pressure from provincial governments and the federal NDP, they refused to provide explicit protection for property rights in the Charter.[120]

Given these relatively clear intentions, the degree of uncertainty among Canadian courts about the extent to which the Charter protects economic rights and controls economic regulation has been surprisingly high. Although lower courts have generally refused to extend Charter protection to economic and property rights, this has not universally been the case.[121] Similarly, although the Supreme Court has refused to find substantive protection for economic rights against provincial economic regulation under either sections 2 or 7,[122] it has been willing to entertain procedural limits on regulatory schemes enacted under the federal government's criminal law power such as the Combines Investigation Act in cases such as *Hunter v. Southam* (1984) and *Thomson Newspapers v. Canada* (1990).[123] In *Southam,* of course, the Court held that corporations are entitled to protection under section 8 and that certain investigation procedures authorized by the Combines Investigation Act constitute unreasonable search and seizure. In *Thomson Newspapers,* the Court upheld the constitutionality of other investigation procedures in the Act, but in a closely divided decision that has probably created more confusion than clarity.

At issue in *Thomson Newspapers* was the constitutionality of sections 17 and 20(2) of the Combines Investigation Act under sections 7 and 8 of the Charter. Section 17 of the Act allows officials of the Restrictive Trade Practices Commission to order individuals to give testimony under oath and/or to produce various documents deemed relevant to an investigation of alleged violations of the Act. Section 20(2) buttresses this provision by prohibiting witnesses from refusing to testify or to produce documents on the grounds that such testimony or evidence might tend to incriminate them. The section provides partial protection for witnesses, however, by guaranteeing that *directly* incriminating oral evidence may not be used against them in future criminal proceedings. Nevertheless, this provision does put witnesses at some risk by not providing *derivative use immunity,* which means that evidence obtained as an indirect result of oral testimony may be used in subsequent criminal proceedings. Determining the constitutionality of these provisions proved to be just as complicated as it appears, with the five justices who heard the case producing five separate reasons for judgment totalling 194 pages in the *Dominion Law Reports.* Consequently, sorting through the appellant's arguments and the justices' responses to them is not an easy task.

Thomson Newspapers challenged the compulsory requirement in section 17 to produce documents on the grounds that it constituted an unreasonable seizure within the meaning of section 8 of the Charter. The five justices responded to this argument in three different ways. Justice John Sopinka disagreed with the basic claim that the impugned provision authorized *any* type of seizure, reasonable or otherwise. In his view, the fact that individuals and companies could challenge subpoenas issued under section 17 before surrendering documents meant that no seizure took place; consequently, Thomson Newspapers could not invoke section 8 of the Charter.[124] Although the remaining four justices did not have any real difficulty determining that the requirements in section 17 constituted a seizure, they divided evenly on whether the seizure was unreasonable. According to Justice Wilson, with whom Justice Lamer concurred, the fact that documents obtained under section 17 could be used in a criminal prosecution made the compulsory production of such evidence by subpoena rather than by a judicially authorized warrant unreasonable. Since Wilson found it difficult to understand how an "unreasonable" seizure could simultaneously be a "reasonable limit" on section 8 rights, she refused to uphold section 17 of the Act on section 1 grounds.[125] Justices La Forest and L'Heureux-Dubé, on the other hand, found the seizure completely reasonable in the regulatory context of anti-combines legislation.[126] La Forest and L'Heureux-Dubé thus joined with Sopinka to produce a slim three-to-two majority to reject Thomson Newspapers' section 8 argument.

Thomson Newspapers also argued that the power in the Combines Investigation Act to compel testimony in *non-criminal* proceedings without providing adequate protection against prosecution in future *criminal* proceedings violates liberty and security of the person in a manner inconsistent with the principles of fundamental justice. Thomson relied on this section 7 argument because neither of the Charter's self-incrimination provisions (sections 11(c) and 13) were directly relevant. On the one hand, the limited protection offered to witnesses under the Act was consistent with section 13; on the other hand, section 11(c) refers specifically to the right of defendants to refuse to testify in their own criminal trials. Thomson Newspapers thus had to argue that section 7 encompasses a residual right against self-incrimination, and that the principles of fundamental justice require derivative-use immunity as well as direct-use immunity.

Once again the five justices produced three different responses to this argument, with Justices Lamer and Sopinka reversing their positions. On this question, Sopinka concurred with Wilson that the Act unreasonably limited a residual section 7 right against self-incrimination. As in many of her criminal procedure decisions, Wilson reached this conclusion by invoking the important goal of protecting "the privacy and personal autonomy and dignity of the individual."[127] In her view, this was sufficient reason to use section 7 to extend the applicability of sections 11(c) and 13 of the Charter. Like Wilson and Sopinka, Justices La Forest and L'Heureux-Dubé agreed that section 7 implicitly extends the protections afforded by sections 11(c) and 13; they found, however, that the principles of fundamental justice are satisfied by direct-use immunity.[128] Justice Lamer provided the most curious judgment, agreeing completely with Justice Wilson's analysis but rejecting Thomson Newspapers' claim on the grounds that the company had selected the wrong section of the Act for Charter scrutiny.[129] Consequently, the Court again rejected Thomson Newspapers' argument by a three-to-two margin.

Government regulation of the economy has been the source of a significant proportion of the Supreme Court's constitutional decision-making throughout Canadian history. For the most part, the Court has allocated political responsibility for this activity to the provincial governments, although the federal role has been enhanced in recent decisions.[130] Nevertheless, the federal government possesses a relatively limited arsenal of policy instruments with which to regulate the economy, and criminal legislation such as the Combines Investigation Act is one of the few instruments through which federal regulatory power can be unambiguously exercised. Although *Thomson Newspapers* did not involve a substantive challenge to the Act, the fact that some members of the Court were willing to nullify elements of this important legislation because of inconsistency with the procedural standards of the due process model of criminal justice is an important indicator of the qualitative change in judicial power that has taken place under the Charter. Given the general difficulty of enforcing anti-combines legislation, the impact of imposing even more rigorous enforcement procedures could have been devastating to the legislation's policy objectives. Moreover, judicial interference with these objectives could not be justified on the usual grounds that the parties affected by the legislation (in this case, large corporations) constitute a vulnerable group with little or no influence in the political process. Finally, the justices who declared the Act deficient were able to do so without adopting the controversial "substantive fundamental justice" doctrine. As the Court demonstrated in its 1988 abortion decision, the line between procedure and substance is indeed narrow.

Legal Rights, Fundamental Justice, and the Abortion Question

Like its U.S. counterpart, the Supreme Court of Canada has found that the abortion question raises a particularly vexing set of issues for judicial review. Since 1988 the Court has decided three cases concerning abortion, among which *Morgentaler, Smoling and Scott v. The Queen* stands out as the most important.[131] At issue in this case was the constitutionality under section 7 of the Charter of section 251 of the Criminal Code, which regulated the conditions under which women could legally obtain abortions. Section 251 had been added to the Criminal Code in 1969 as a means of liberalizing access to legal abortions in Canada. Prior to 1969 the Criminal Code treated abortion as a form of homicide to which the only possible defence was the traditional common-law defence of necessity, which applied in only limited circumstances. In contrast to this approach, section 251 created two categories of abortion: therapeutic abortions, which could be performed legally; and non-therapeutic abortions, which remained subject to criminal penalties.

At the core of this provision was a set of procedures designed to identify and to approve legitimate requests for therapeutic abortions. To achieve this objective, section 251 permitted only those abortions approved by a therapeutic abortion committee of an accredited hospital. It further stipulated that this committee must include three physicians other than the physician wishing to perform the abortion and that abortions could be approved only where necessary to protect the health of the woman seeking the abortion. Failure to meet the conditions set forth in section 251 constituted an indictable offence with maximum punishments of two years' imprisonment for women procuring (or self-performing) abortions and life imprisonment for other individuals performing abortions. In 1975, these regulations survived a challenge from pro-choice advocates based on the 1960 Bill of Rights.[132]

The three appellants in the 1988 challenge were physicians who had been charged with conspiring to perform illegal abortions in Ontario. The physicians' counsel challenged the constitutionality of section 251 on the grounds that, as used in section 7 of the Charter, "liberty" encompasses "a wide-ranging right to control one's own life and to promote one's individual autonomy." In the view of counsel, this included a "right to privacy and a right to make unfettered decisions about one's own life," which encompasses a woman's decision to terminate her pregnancy.[133] Although this argument offered a clear opportunity to explore the outer boundaries of both liberty and judicial policy-making, all but one justice refused to take this opportunity. Justice William McIntyre offered the most adamant refusal in his dissenting reasons for judgment. In his view, it was entirely inappropriate for the Court to inquire into the liberty interests of pregnant women in a case in which none of the defendants was either pregnant or a woman.[134]

Only Justice Wilson adopted the physicians' concept of liberty in her concurring reasons for judgment. Indeed, her judgment in *Morgentaler, Smoling and Scott* represents an important application of the dignity enhancement interpretation of legal rights that she had found so compelling in criminal procedure cases. Relying on American decisions concerning privacy and abortion, Wilson agreed with the appellants' counsel that "the right to liberty contained in section 7 guarantees to every individual a degree of personal autonomy over important decisions intimately affecting their private lives."[135] She asserted, moreover, that this "right to make fundamental personal decisions without interference from the state" is an important component of the individual human dignity protected by section 7.[136] She concluded, therefore, that the central issue in *Morgentaler, Smoling and Scott* was reproductive freedom, which constituted "an integral part of modern woman's struggle to assert her dignity and worth as a human being."[137] By depriving women of significant choice in the matter of abortion, section 251 infringed this crucial aspect of the right to liberty.[138] Although quite broad, Wilson's reasons for judgment in *Morgentaler, Smoling and Scott* did concede that Parliament could regulate abortion to protect fetal life, but only in a manner sensitive to the level of fetal development at differing stages of pregnancy. In this sense, Wilson generally proposed incorporating into Canadian constitutional law the principle of *Roe v. Wade* (1973) that all government regulation of abortion during the early stages of pregnancy should be prohibited.

In contrast to Justice Wilson, Chief Justice Dickson considered it "neither necessary nor wise" to "explore the broadest implications of section 7" in analysing the constitutionality of section 251.[139] Instead, he found it sufficient to focus on the scope of protection offered to individuals by "security of the person" and the consistency of section 251 with certain principles of fundamental justice.[140] The Chief Justice began his reasons for judgment by weighing the appellants' argument that security of the person provides "an explicit right to control one's body and to make fundamental decisions about one's life" against the Crown's submission that "it at most relates to the concept of physical control, simply protecting the individual's interest in his or her bodily integrity."[141]

The distinction between these two positions was that the Crown's argument suggested that section 7 simply limits what governments can do to individuals, while the appellants' position viewed section 7 as also prohibiting state interference with what individuals choose to do to themselves. Although Chief Justice Dickson ultimately chose a meaning closer to the Crown's and restricted its application to criminal justice matters, he extended the definition of security of the person to include protection against "state-imposed psychological stress."[142]

The Chief Justice had little difficulty determining that section 251 violated security of the person by interfering "with a woman's bodily integrity in both a physical and emotional sense."[143] The key piece of evidence for this determination was the 1977 Report of the Committee on the Operation of the Abortion Law (the Badgley Report), which concluded that the requirement that therapeutic abortion committees approve all abortions produced significant delays in obtaining the permission necessary for an abortion, as well as uncertainty among women about whether permission would even be granted. The Badgley Report further indicated that these delays resulted in higher complication and mortality rates for women who qualified for permission. Chief Justice Dickson thus held that these delays created a clear threat to physical security of the person, and that the uncertainty accompanied by these delays also infringed security of the person by damaging the "psychological integrity of women seeking abortions."[144] He concluded, therefore, that "s.251 is a law which forces women to carry a foetus to term contrary to their own priorities and aspirations and which imposes serious delay causing increased physical and psychological trauma to those women who meet its criteria."[145]

Chief Justice Dickson based his analysis of section 251 on security of the person because he was unwilling to accept the broad concept of liberty offered by the appellants' counsel. Among the many questions this analysis raises is whether it was even necessary for Dickson to go this far. There was at least one other alternative to the appellants' broad liberty claim: Dickson could have simply found that the terms of imprisonment provided for in section 251 infringed the narrow concept of liberty protected by section 7. This analysis, however, would have pre-empted an inquiry into the indirect impact of Parliament's regulation of abortion on women as a group. Although intent on avoiding the implications of the broad argument offered by the appellants, Dickson's reasons for judgment suggest that he was at least somewhat dissatisfied with Parliament's decision to interfere with a woman's decision to terminate her pregnancy. He clearly wanted to establish that section 251 clashed with something more than a mere right not to be unfairly imprisoned.

After establishing that section 251 violated one of the rights protected by section 7, Chief Justice Dickson shifted his inquiry to whether the impugned provisions of the Criminal Code comported with the principles of fundamental justice. Unlike Justice Wilson, who was willing to review section 251 on substantive grounds, Dickson decided to restrict his analysis to "various aspects of the administrative structure and procedure set down . . . for access to therapeutic abortions."[146] In his view, section 251 had the dual effect of criminalizing abortion and establishing a defence – in the form of a certificate of permission from a therapeutic abortion committee – against charges brought under the section's punitive provisions. Rather than consider whether the Criminal Code's criminalization of abortion was inconsistent with substantive principles of fundamental justice, Chief Justice Dickson focused on the impact of section 251's procedural mechanisms and administrative structure on the availability of the defence that Parliament had established against criminal charges brought under the section.

The Chief Justice's procedural analysis of section 251 convinced him that there were at least three characteristics of its administrative structure that restricted access to the defence it purported to establish.[147] First, the Badgley Report's finding that only 271 hospitals had therapeutic abortion committees in 1976, as well as Statistics Canada data indicating that the number of hospitals with committees had dropped to 261 in 1982, suggested to Dickson that one administrative deficiency of section 251 was its failure to ensure that hospitals would establish therapeutic abortion committees. Second, the section's requirement that therapeutic abortions only be performed in approved or accredited hospitals was another administrative flaw that restricted the availability of its exculpatory provisions, since provinces could refuse to accredit *any* hospital for performing abortions. Finally, Chief Justice Dickson criticized section 251 for its failure to provide a legislative definition of health that would identify the circumstances under which permission for therapeutic abortions should be granted. The combined effect of these administrative deficiencies, according to Dickson, was to make the exculpatory provisions of section 251 "practically unavailable to women who would *prima facie* qualify for . . . a defence that is held out to be generally available."[148] He found these barriers inconsistent with the "basic tenets of our system of criminal justice" and thus contrary to fundamental justice.[149] Dickson failed, however, to cite any authorities to support his contentions about the content of the "basic tenets" of Canadian criminal justice in this context.

Chief Justice Dickson's approach to *Morgentaler, Smoling and Scott* reveals how permeable the distinction between procedural and substantive review is, as well as the Court's desire to free itself from its restrictive Bill of Rights jurisprudence. Dickson did not overtly challenge Parliament's abortion policy, which was to allow abortions under limited circumstances by establishing a mechanism for distinguishing between permissible and impermissible abortions. What disturbed the Chief Justice was the effectiveness of this mechanism, which in his view unjustly denied some women the certificate of permission that constituted their defence to charges brought under section 251. In this respect, Chief Justice Dickson's view of fundamental justice in *Morgentaler, Smoling and Scott* resembled the originally narrow procedural meaning attached to the phrase in *Duke v. The Queen.* The operation of section 251, in other words, could have been interpreted as denying some women the opportunity to state their case adequately in criminal proceedings brought against them, contrary to the principle articulated in *Duke*. Instead of relying on this pre-Charter precedent, however, the Chief Justice resolved the case according to the interpretation of fundamental justice articulated in the decision in which the Court established its power of substantive judicial review (the *Motor Vehicle Reference*).

Morgentaler, Smoling and Scott illustrates two important characteristics of judicial forays into substantive policy-making. First, there is an incentive to conceal this activity by converting indeterminate substantive issues into procedural questions – a phenomenon with which American commentators are familiar. In this instance, Dickson transformed *Morgentaler, Smoling and Scott* from a case about substantive abortion rights into one about the procedural rights of criminal defendants. The advantage of this strategy for judges is that it simplifies decision-making and avoids certain questions of judicial legitimacy by enabling them to engage in policy-making behind the veneer of exercising traditional judicial functions. As Rachel Moran notes, "[b]y restating issues in narrow, legal terms courts can not only minimize the significance and visibility of broad, indeterminate social issues but also restructure their decisionmaking responsibility."[150] The danger of this restructuring, however, is that it increases the probability that courts will reach decisions on the basis of inadequate information or unwarranted assumptions.[151]

Morgentaler, Smoling and Scott also illustrates some of the information-processing limitations of adjudication. The core of Chief Justice Dickson's argument was that section 251 told women that they could obtain legal abortions, but then established an administrative scheme that denied many women who were otherwise entitled to these abortions the opportunity of undergoing the procedure. Presumably, the connection between this security-of-the-person argument and the criminal procedure issue on which the Chief Justice decided the fundamental justice question is that these women either failed to obtain the abortions to which they were entitled or opted for illegal abortions and risked unjust criminal prosecution. An appropriate question to ask in this context, therefore, is how many women were actually deterred from seeking an abortion or unjustly convicted under section 251 because of the general unavailability of the defence created by Parliament. Neither the facts of the specific case nor the aggregate data cited by Chief Justice Dickson spoke directly to this question. Moreover, Dickson did not consider the alternative hypothesis that Parliament's decision to allow local conditions to control abortion policy (by failing to define health in the Code, for example) permitted some women to obtain abortions contrary to the legislative intentions underlying section 251. It was possible, in other words, for local officials to violate the spirit of section 251 by granting *too many* abortions, as well as by unduly restricting access to the procedure. Finally, as Justice McIntyre noted in dissent, many of the problems attributed to the administrative structure of section 251 are equally prevalent in the more liberal abortion regime of the United States.[152] This suggests that the abortion controversy involves more than simply the "basic tenets" of Canadian criminal justice.

Legal formalities aside, defenders of broad judicial review might praise Dickson's decision as a legitimate action necessary to prod an intransigent and myopic legislative body into finally acting on an eleven-year-old report that had revealed serious flaws in the administration of the nation's abortion policy – unless, of course, the findings of the Badgley Commission did not reflect flaws at all, but were roughly consistent with the outcome Parliament intended. Although Parliament clearly intended to liberalize access to legal abortions in 1969, it just as clearly did not intend to remove all legal barriers to the procedure. Any system of government regulation of individual conduct is bound to produce delays and perhaps even prohibit that conduct; indeed, that is precisely why conduct is regulated. Similarly, by failing to define health, by failing to require the establishment of therapeutic abortion committees in all hospitals, and by leaving enforcement of section 251 within the general provincial power over the administration of justice, Parliament virtually guaranteed unequal access to abortions both among and within provinces. Given the social divisiveness of this issue, however, Parliament's action makes sense as part of a strategy to allow local conditions to control abortion policy to some degree. The general point is that the decision to regulate cannot be completely divorced from the method of regulation. Despite his claim to the contrary, Dickson's quarrel was as much with Parliament's substantive decision to regulate abortion as it was with the procedural components of section 251.[153] In this sense, Justice Wilson's reasons for judgment were at least candid enough to confront the substantive issue directly.

Perhaps the most important lesson of *Morgentaler, Smoling and Scott,* then, is that it is unnecessary for the Court to engage in explicit substantive review, or to attach particularly extravagant meanings to liberty and security of the person, to have a significant impact on public policy when deciding cases under section 7. The broad and open-ended nature of section 7 means that the Court can examine complex questions of substantive policy even in the course of deciding seemingly narrow issues of criminal procedure. This makes the Court's willingness to adopt the language of "non-interpretivism" in decisions like *Singh,* the *Motor Vehicle Reference,* and *Operation Dismantle* all the more unsettling. Although the Court has proceeded cautiously in individual cases, it has shown little reluctance in its section 7 decisions to carve out a new role in Canadian politics. As Chief Justice Dickson declared in *Morgentaler, Smoling and Scott,* the Court is "now charged with the crucial obligation of ensuring that the legislative initiatives of our Parliament and legislatures conform to the democratic values expressed in the *Canadian Charter of Rights and Freedoms.*"[154] The paradox of liberal constitutionalism emanates precisely from the fact that courts both define and enforce these "democratic values."

CHAPTER 5

Equality Rights

In *Democracy in America,* Alexis de Tocqueville observed that democratic communities have an "ardent, insatiable, incessant, invincible" passion for equality. To Tocqueville's keen eye, trained on the United States in the early nineteenth century, equality appeared to be the driving principle behind all democratic ideas. Tocqueville knew, however, that the passion for equality, like all passions, is a mixed blessing. Although it encourages personal independence and a desire for free political institutions, this dedication to the principle of equality also supports tendencies toward both anarchy and political servitude.[1] To some degree, the constitutional guarantee of equality found in section 15 of the Charter also represents a mixed blessing. As Alan Cairns has argued, by granting special constitutional status to certain identifiable groups, section 15 (along with other relevant Charter sections) has contributed to the erosion of the traditional constitutional dialogue between federal and provincial elites in favour of a multitude of constitutional discourses through which "social conflicts are played out."[2] While this development injects a new degree of openness and citizen participation into constitutional politics, it also carries with it the danger of constitutional and social disintegration. Competing claims of constitutional rights are more difficult to reconcile than competing claims of legislative interests precisely because constitutional claims are indivisible. One of the Supreme Court's most important tasks under section 15, therefore, is to manage these conflicts.

That the Charter's drafters were aware of the complex relationship between equality and liberal democracy is reflected in their decision to delay the implementation of the Charter's equality rights for three years to allow governments to adapt to these new requirements. By granting legal equality to all individuals in Canada, and by providing constitutional support for affirmative action programs designed to ameliorate the "conditions of disadvantaged individuals or groups," section 15 encompasses two sweeping objectives. The first of these is embodied in section 15(1), which guarantees four types of legal equality (equality before the law, equality under the law, equal protection of the law, and equal benefit of the law) without discrimination, in particular, without discrimination based on the specific characteristics of race, national or ethnic origin, colour, religion, sex, age, or mental or physical disability. The second objective is embodied in section 15(2), which can be understood as a justificatory provision for certain forms of legal inequality. That is, section 15(2) justifies denying legal equality to some individuals in order to promote substantive (or social) equality for disadvantaged individuals or groups.

Although the constitutionalization of affirmative action in section 15(2) directly addresses one of the most controversial equality issues currently facing liberal democracies, the Charter's guarantee of equality rights raises a number of other issues. These include the definition and scope of each type of equality guaranteed by section 15, as well as the meaning of the phrase "without discrimination"; the applicability of section 15 to systemic discrimination and to unspecified grounds of discrimination; and the potential utility of various "levels of scrutiny" in equality rights jurisprudence. While the Supreme Court has dealt with some of these issues in the context of human rights legislation, section 15 makes them issues of constitutional law rather than problems of statutory construction. As in other areas, the Charter's drafters expected this transformation to embolden the Court, whose equality rights jurisprudence under the 1960 Bill of Rights could be charitably described as cautious. Indeed, under this earlier document, the Court went out of its way to ensure that its interpretation of equality would not interfere unduly with important federal policies.

This chapter explores the extent to which this new basis for equality rights jurisprudence has invigorated the Canadian judiciary in general and the Supreme Court in particular. The first section of the chapter surveys various ways in which the liberal conception of equality has been defined, as well as the evolution of Canadian anti-discrimination and human rights legislation. The second section examines the pre-Charter attitude of Canadian courts to the concept of equality by surveying key judicial decisions concerning the common law, the 1960 Bill of Rights, and modern human rights legislation. Finally, the chapter discusses the legislative history and judicial interpretation of the Charter's equality rights provisions, including both lower court decisions and the Supreme Court's major section 15 decisions.

Equality and Public Policy

The importance of the concept of equality in political and legal thought is evident in the extraordinary effort that theorists have made to define equality and the conditions under which it can be achieved and maintained. Aristotle, for example, placed equality at the centre of his theory of justice. First in the *Nicomachean Ethics,* and then in the *Politics,* Aristotle defined justice as "a sort of equality" in which individuals of equal merit are entitled to equal shares of the "good." Equality in this sense is not absolute but refers to a relationship of relative proportionality. The attainment of justice in Aristotle's philosophy is perfectly consistent with an unequal distribution of the "good" so long as there exists equal treatment of equals or like treatment of like cases.[3] Aristotle recognized, of course, that it is no simple matter to determine the circumstances under which individuals are equal or when like cases are alike. Not every difference among individuals, in other words, is relevant in determining the distribution of various goods. Political justice, for example, may require the equal distribution of political power according to excellence (aristocracy), wealth or noble birth (oligarchy), or free birth (democracy).[4] Indeed, according to Aristotle, the essence of political speculation is precisely to sort through the various principles underlying equal treatment.

Although the modern liberal conception of equality contains important elements of Aristotelian thought, it is far more clearly anchored in the political philosophy of John Locke. Locke's principal concern was the problem of liberty – both with overcoming the disadvantages associated with the perfect freedom enjoyed by humans in the state of nature, and with preserving individual liberty in the civil society that must emerge to mitigate these disadvantages. Perfect freedom, however, also means perfect equality; and in the natural state of perfect equality no "creature of the same species and rank" can claim "superiority or jurisdiction . . . over another."[5] Locke did not mean by this that individuals are equal in every respect, but that they possess an equal right to exercise their "natural freedom, without being subjected to the will or authority of any other [person]."[6] In the state of nature, liberty and equality are complementary; all being born "with a Title to perfect freedom," every individual has equal access to the "Rights and Privileges of the Law of Nature." In civil society, however, natural equality must give way to conventional inequality as individuals transfer their legislative and executive power over the law of nature to a common sovereign. Nevertheless, by describing this inequality in the right to rule that must exist in civil society as merely "conventional," Locke's theory stresses the importance of consent. Moreover, natural liberty and equality limit the power of conventional rulers.

The American Revolution marked the first attempt to found a new political regime on Lockean principles. The American Declaration of Independence articulates in a fundamental way the founding principles of liberal constitutionalism, including its principle of equality. After announcing the necessity of justifying the American colonies' decision to separate from British rule, the Declaration asserts the "self-evident truth" that "all men are created equal." To be sure, this did not mean equality in social status or physical and intellectual attributes, but equality in the sense of being equally endowed by a common creator with certain "inalienable rights," such as "life, liberty, and the pursuit of happiness." "Governments," the Declaration continued, "are instituted among men to secure these rights"; but to ensure that governments do not, in fact, extinguish these rights in the name of securing them, the Declaration made it clear that governments derive their "just powers" only from the "consent of the governed."

Thomas Jefferson, the author of the Declaration, would explain to a friend in 1826 that its principle of equality embodied "the palpable truth that the mass of mankind has not been born with saddles on their backs, nor a favored few booted and spurred, ready to ride them legitimately, by the grace of God."[7] As in Locke, equality meant the absence of any natural right of one person to rule another. All right to rule is conventional and may be withdrawn by the ruled at any time.

The principle of legal equality that liberal theorists derived from these philosophical roots was crucial to the development of free political institutions. In Anglo-Canadian legal history this limited understanding of equality received its fullest articulation in A.V. Dicey's description of the concept of the "rule of law." According to Dicey, what distinguished English institutions from their continental counterparts was subordination to the "rule, supremacy, or predominance of law." In Dicey's view, this characteristic of the English constitution embodied three distinct elements. First, it referred to the absence of arbitrary executive power: individuals could be punished only for distinct violations of the law according to recognized procedures before the ordinary courts. Second, the rule of law meant legal equality in the sense that all social classes must be universally subject to the law. Most importantly, legal equality meant that government officials are under "the same responsibility for every act done without legal justification as any other citizen." Finally, Dicey meant by the rule of law that the protection of individual rights in England did not flow from formal constitutional provisions, but that the constitution itself derived from the judicial protection of these rights in the course of ordinary litigation.[8]

The practical implications of this principle in Canadian law are best illustrated by the Supreme Court of Canada's decision in *Roncarelli v. Duplessis* (1959).[9] At issue in *Roncarelli* was an attempt by Quebec Premier Maurice Duplessis to retaliate against a Jehovah's Witness restaurant owner who continuously posted bail for co-religionists arrested under various anti-Jehovah's Witness laws in the province. Acting in his capacity as attorney-general, Duplessis ordered the provincial liquor commission to suspend Roncarelli's liquor licence permanently. In upholding Roncarelli's suit for damages against Duplessis, the Supreme Court relied on all three elements of Dicey's rule of law. First, the Court declared that Roncarelli could not be punished for engaging in a practice (posting bail) that was not otherwise prohibited by law. Second, the Court invoked the rule of law to hold that government officials could not act arbitrarily against citizens but required specific legal authority for their actions. Finally, the principles established in this private action for damages acquired near constitutional status, and *Roncarelli* is usually included among the landmark cases in Canadian civil liberties jurisprudence.[10]

Although *Roncarelli* illustrates the potential power of the rule of law and its doctrine of legal equality to constrain government action, it also reveals the limitations of this doctrine. Had legislation existed in Quebec that allowed the attorney-general to direct the liquor commission to suspend the licences of individuals who, for example, "unduly obstructed the administration of justice," the legal equality embraced by the rule of law would have been of little help to

Roncarelli. Moreover, critics have argued that the rule of law's doctrine that all social classes are equally subject to the same laws and have the same rights before the law (which is derived from the liberal concept of natural equality) is not sufficiently sensitive to the effect of social class and other group differences on the capacity to exercise these rights. Consequently, the discussion of equality by theorists like Locke, Jefferson, and Dicey is no longer considered by some to be adequate for modern politics.

Unfortunately, contemporary legal discourse lacks the elegance of Jefferson's Declaration of Independence or Dicey's *Law of the Constitution,* preferring instead to speak in terms of *formal equality* and its principal competitor, *substantive equality.* The concept of formal equality is closely linked to Dicey's rule of law and the Aristotelian proposition that like cases must be treated alike. Formal equality accepts Dicey's assertion that everyone should be equally subject to the law, but it also recognizes the practical necessity of tailoring laws to meet the various needs of different individuals and groups. Consequently, formal equality accepts the existence of legislative classifications as long as these classifications are consistent with the principle of similar treatment for similarly situated persons. According to formal equality theory, law should at most aim at ensuring equal opportunity and fair competition among individuals by eliminating barriers to participation.[11] Once these private and public barriers are overcome, the law is then indifferent to the competition's outcome.

Critics of formal equality have raised two related objections to its scope and purpose.[12] First, they argue that the elimination of formal barriers to participation does nothing to compensate for the accumulated disadvantages of past exclusion. This leads to a second objection, which is that the superficial legal equality embodied in the rule of law masks deeper inequalities that are exacerbated by the neutral application of the law required by the doctrine of formal equality. The achievement of "real" equality, therefore, demands that the law be concerned more with substantive differences in the social and political condition of various groups than with the neutral application of formal rules to similarly situated individuals.[13] While formal equality provides an individual right to equal treatment before the law, substantive equality embraces a collective right to share equally in a society's available goods. More importantly, any maldistribution of these goods among social groups constitutes *prima facie* evidence that their right to equality (so defined) is being denied. From the standpoint of legislative policy, this substantive model of equality leads not only to the elimination of formal barriers, but also to positive policies designed to ameliorate conditions of disadvantage. As a theory of judicial review, the substantive equality doctrine instructs courts to examine closely the actual impact of apparently neutral laws, as well as to be flexible in accepting differential treatment of individuals where that treatment is part of a remedy for past disadvantage.

Canadian public policy, particularly since World War Two, has witnessed the gradual acceptance of this broader concept of substantive equality. In the immediate post-war period, Canadian policy-makers recognized that eliminating the vestiges of legal inequality in Canada required a dual strategy of first abolishing government-supported inequality found in discriminatory laws and administrative practices, and then of providing positive legislative support in the form of legal prohibitions against private discrimination in areas like employment, accommodation, and property exchange. These early legislative efforts included the Ontario Racial Discrimination Act (1944), which prohibited the publication or display of signs, symbols, or other representations expressing racial or religious discrimination, and the Saskatchewan Bill of Rights Act (1947), which prohibited discrimination with respect to accommodation, employment, land transactions, businesses, and enterprises.[14]

Early efforts to secure equality through legislation like that passed in Ontario and Saskatchewan suffered from the disadvantages associated with attempting to enforce these prohibitions through penal sanctions. The quasi-criminal nature of these laws led to several weaknesses, including the reluctance of victims to initiate proceedings, the difficulty of proving violations (including discriminatory intent) beyond a reasonable doubt, and the inadequacy of penal sanctions to remedy the discrimination suffered by the victim. These defects led the provinces to shift increasingly toward an administrative approach to anti-discrimination policy. This approach first emerged in the enactment of fair employment and accommodation statutes,[15] and it replaced quasi-criminal enforcement mechanisms with administrative proceedings of investigation, conciliation, and settlement. Nevertheless, the responsibility for initiating proceedings and seeking a remedy for discriminatory action remained with the victim.

The final stage in this development consisted of the enactment of comprehensive human rights codes, enforced and promoted by permanent human rights commissions. Ontario initiated this step in 1962 and the federal Parliament completed it in 1977 when it passed the Canadian Human Rights Act. Although human rights legislation prohibits most forms of private discrimination in employment, shelter, and access to other publicly available goods, it does include several exemptions. Religious associations and other non-profit social organizations, for example, are normally allowed to discriminate. Similarly, the employment of domestic labour and the rental of accommodation requiring close personal contact between tenants and landlords have also been excluded.[16] Nevertheless, the relative comprehensiveness and permanent enforcement machinery of modern human rights legislation facilitate the resolution of complaints and permit more proactive educational efforts. As the Supreme Court emphasized in 1985, these statutes are concerned more with providing relief for victims of discrimination than with punishing discriminatory acts.[17]

In addition to these structural and enforcement changes, modern human rights legislation is characterized by three other traits that distinguish it from earlier anti-discrimination legislation. First, there has been a vast increase in the number of prohibited grounds of discrimination. Rainer Knopff has calculated that contemporary anti-discrimination policies include thirty separate prohibited grounds of discrimination, ranging from such traditional grounds as race, colour, religion, and sex to more recent categories, including marital status, pregnancy, political beliefs, and sexual orientation. According to Knopff, this expansion reflects not only a quantitative increase but a qualitative shift from legislative concern with purely *stigmatic* traits (e.g., race and colour) to concern with *life-cycle* (e.g., marital status and pregnancy) and *lifestyle* (e.g., political beliefs and sexual orientation) traits.[18]

The extension of human rights legislation to cover discrimination based on lifestyle traits is a particularly important development. Traits such as sexual orientation and political belief differ from others because they can, in principle, be concealed. This means that the socially negative consequences of certain lifestyle choices can be avoided simply by not revealing those choices. However, fear of discrimination may unduly inhibit lifestyle choices and constrain political activity aimed at changing government regulations and policies that directly disadvantage participants in certain lifestyles. The inclusion of lifestyle traits in human rights legislation reflects an expanded theory of equality in which the state must maintain an attitude of moral neutrality toward specified lifestyle choices, as well as encourage a similar neutrality among private citizens. In more theoretical terms, this expansion reflects the philosophical assertions of writers such as John Rawls and Ronald Dworkin that the achievement of equality requires that everyone be accorded equal dignity and respect by both government and their fellow citizens.[19] From this perspective, the principle of equality is violated if individuals can avoid the public stigma that may be attached to certain lifestyle choices only through a process of concealment that denigrates those choices and diminishes the individual's sense of self-worth. The protection of these choices through human rights legislation thus has two purposes: it serves to mitigate the immediate, negative consequences of unpopular lifestyle choices; and it promotes long-term moral acceptance (or at least non-judgmental tolerance) of those choices. This theory, which obviously goes far beyond formal equality, also underlies the "dignity enhancement" approach to legal procedures discussed in the previous chapter.

The second distinctive characteristic of modern human rights legislation is its concern with systemic discrimination as well as direct discrimination. Systemic discrimination is said to result whenever apparently neutral laws, regulations, practices, or selection criteria have a disproportionately adverse impact on groups against whom direct discrimination is prohibited. Human rights commissions concern themselves with systemic discrimination both to prevent sophisticated forms of direct discrimination and to overcome the effects of past direct discrimination that may prevent most members of some groups from meeting neutral requirements. Consistent with the doctrine of substantive equality, human rights commissions attack this second form of systemic discrimination because it produces unequal access to public goods for certain groups.[20] Finally, modern legislation is distinctive in its reliance on affirmative action as a remedy for discrimination, particularly systemic discrimination. Affirmative strategies to promote greater social equality for specified target groups may include dismantling systemic barriers, implementing remedial programs, and using ameliorative preferences to achieve participation targets for specified groups.[21] Once again, substantive equality is the driving force behind affirmative action.

The anti-discrimination policies of the early post-war period recognized inequality or discrimination as an intractable feature of human relationships. These policies also embraced a more limited vision of what the law could achieve, focusing as they did on legal equality and the dismantling of formal barriers. Consequently, these anti-discrimination policies rested on the premise that inequality is a political and social problem that must be continuously managed and regulated but cannot be fully eliminated. Modern human rights legislation, on the other hand, takes this premise a step further by viewing inequality as a temporary phenomenon that can be eradicated through proper techniques of social policy.[22] These techniques, which are designed and implemented by human rights experts functioning within quasi-judicial human rights commissions, fall under the general rubric of affirmative action. Section 15 of the Charter takes the final step in this policy development by empowering judges to entrench these policies as constitutional law and to use their constitutional powers to further the cause of substantive equality. Before examining this feature of section 15 in detail, it is useful to look more closely at the contribution of Canadian courts generally, and the Supreme Court in particular, to the evolution of equality rights policy in the pre-Charter era.

Equality and Canadian Courts: The Pre-Charter Experience

Any survey of the role that Canadian courts, and especially the Supreme Court, played in the development of equality rights prior to the Charter's enactment must judge the performance as mixed. To be more precise, Canadian courts have traditionally exhibited a highly ambivalent attitude toward the role that they should play in expanding equality rights. On the one hand, the pre-Charter experience is marked by a general reluctance among Canadian jurists to invoke constitutional and quasi-constitutional guarantees to promote equality. Even the Supreme Court's use of the division of powers to overturn Quebec's restrictions on free speech and religious freedom during the 1950s had only a limited impact on equality rights, since these decisions did not affect the federal government's power to enact discriminatory legislation in these areas if it wished. Moreover, the Court did not entirely eliminate Quebec's ability to pursue these legislative objectives by other means.[23] On the other hand, Canadian courts have been more willing to enforce human rights legislation vigorously. The Supreme Court, in particular, appeared to be much more comfortable with enforcing explicit legislative equality guarantees against private entities than with enforcing more vaguely worded limitations against government action. Indeed, the Court has actively contributed to the expansion of human rights legislation.

These points may be illustrated in two ways. The first is by examining in more detail three key Bill of Rights equality decisions: *R. v. Drybones, A.-G. Canada v. Lavell,* and *Bliss v. A.-G. Canada.*[24] In only one of these cases (*Drybones*) did the Court vindicate an equality rights claim against the government, and then it did so only on the basis of a very restricted concept of equality. The second means of illustrating these points is to examine the Court's contribution to the acceptance of affirmative action and the goal of eliminating systemic discrimination as legitimate elements of human rights policy. Indeed, Court decisions established both the basic compatibility of affirmative action policies with human rights legislation and the power of human rights commissions to impose affirmative action remedies for past discrimination.

Equality and the 1960 Bill of Rights

As Justice McIntyre would note in the Supreme Court's first section 15 decision, the language chosen to express the Charter's commitment to equality reflects a profound dissatisfaction with the fate of that concept under the 1960 Bill of Rights. Granting his predecessors the benefit of the doubt, McIntyre attributed this fate to structural flaws in the document itself, rather than to any error in judicial interpretation or application.[25] According to this view, the development of equality rights jurisprudence under the Bill of Rights suffered from two principal weaknesses. The first was the ambiguous language of section 1 of the Bill concerning the nature of the enumerated rights and freedoms. In particular, the statute's recognition and declaration of rights and freedoms that "have existed and shall continue to exist" promoted a "frozen rights theory" of interpretation that discouraged judicial creativity in the definition and enforcement of equality. A second weakness was section 2 of the Bill, which merely directed Canadian courts to construe and apply laws so as "not to abrogate, abridge or infringe" any of the rights recognized and declared in the statute. This lack of a clear remedial mandate made it difficult for courts to nullify federal legislation found to be inconsistent with the Bill of Rights.

As the Court would reveal in *R. v. Drybones* (1969), however, these flaws were not necessarily fatal.[26] Although unique in Bill of Rights jurisprudence, *Drybones* demonstrated that it was possible for the Court to invalidate a portion of a federal statute for inconsistency with the Bill of Rights. At issue was whether section 94 of the Indian Act, which prohibited Indians from being intoxicated off reserves, violated the Bill's guarantee of equality before the law. Drybones's counsel argued that the impugned provision of the Act involved two types of unequal treatment. First, because section 94 prohibited intoxication in both private and public, while the relevant statute of general application (the Northwest Territories' Liquor Ordinance) only prohibited public intoxication, the Indian Act made it illegal for natives to do what other Canadians in the Northwest Territories could do lawfully. Second, unlike the Liquor Ordinance, section 94 imposed a minimum penalty; consequently, it exposed natives to more severe punishment than non-natives faced for committing a similar offence. In a stunning departure from a decade of precedent, the Court accepted these arguments by a six-to-three margin and held that section 1(b) of the Bill of Rights rendered section 94(b) of the Indian Act inoperative.

Despite the fact that the outcome in *Drybones* vindicated an equality rights claim, the decision attests to the Court's uncertainty about its role in promoting equality. This uncertainty is apparent in the fact that Chief Justice Cartwright and Justice Ritchie reversed the positions that they had taken earlier in *Robertson and Rosetanni v. The Queen* (1963).[27] In *Robertson and Rosetanni,* Cartwright had dissented from the Court's narrow interpretation of the Bill of Rights, arguing instead that the Bill authorized courts to refuse to apply any federal statute they found to be inconsistent with the document.[28] However, "[a]fter a most anxious reconsideration of the whole question," Cartwright declared in *Drybones* that his earlier conclusion was mistaken. According to Cartwright, had Parliament intended to "confer the power and impose the responsibility upon the Courts of declaring inoperative" provisions of federal statutes, it would have done so in clearer language than that found in section 2 of the Bill of Rights.[29] Cartwright thus abandoned his earlier broad interpretation of the Court's remedial powers under the Bill of Rights.

Justice Ritchie, on the other hand, underwent a conversion in the opposite direction. In contrast to his cautious reasons for judgment in *Robertson and Rosetanni,* Ritchie declared that Cartwright's dissenting judgment in *Robertson and Rosetanni* was sound and should be adopted as a general rule by the Court.[30] Writing for a majority of the Court, Ritchie found that courts could use the Bill of Rights to hold federal legislation inoperative to the extent that it conflicted with the Bill, unless Parliament expressly declared its intention to override the Bill. According to Ritchie, this finding did not directly contradict anything in *Robertson and Rosetanni,* since the Court had simply not found any inconsistency between the Lord's Day Act and the Bill of Rights. Moreover, an important factor that contributed to Ritchie's bold statement of the Court's remedial powers under the Bill was the relatively narrow violation of equality under consideration in *Drybones.* What Ritchie found objectionable about section 94(b) of the Indian Act was that it permitted unequal treatment of natives with respect to a matter that was unconnected to their special status under the Act. In this sense, section 94(b) violated the second element of Dicey's rule of law, and thus *Drybones* was not so radical a departure from the norms of Canadian jurisprudence as it might have appeared.

The Court's confusion over its power to promote equality under the Bill of Rights, aptly reflected in the reversal of Cartwright's and Ritchie's views in *Robertson and Rosetanni* and *Drybones,* became even more apparent in *Lavell* and *Bliss,* the Court's most infamous Bill of Rights equality decisions. What makes the Court's failure to vindicate equality claims in these two decisions even more noteworthy is that they were authored by the same Justice Ritchie who had raised commentators' expectations in *Drybones.*

As in *Drybones, Lavell* involved a challenge to provisions of the Indian Act – in this case section 12(1)(b), which provided that native women, but not native men, who married non-natives lost their status as Indians and the rights and privileges that this status entailed. Lavell argued that this provision constituted discrimination on the basis of sex. In making this claim, Lavell received legal support from non-native women's organizations and the Native Council of Canada, which represented non-status Indians. On the other side, the federal government's defence of section 12(1)(b) received the unanimous support of national, provincial, and territorial organizations representing status Indians, including the National Indian Brotherhood. The decision by these groups to support the government was made against the political background of the Trudeau government's 1969 proposal to dismantle the Indian Act and abandon the concept of special status for natives in favour of an individualized concept of equal Canadian citizenship. This fundamental change in policy would have transformed aboriginal peoples from a legally distinct group in Canadian society to simply another ethnic group within Canada's multicultural mosaic. Native groups had expended tremendous political energy to defeat this proposal, and they were unwilling to lose in the courts what they had worked so hard to retain in the political arena. While Lavell's claim did not represent the same challenge to the Indian Act that the Trudeau government's 1969 proposal did, it could have led potentially to the same outcome.

Justice Ritchie's majority reasons for judgment in *Lavell* began by asserting that Parliament's authority under section 91(24) of the British North America Act to legislate with respect to "Indians and Lands reserved for Indians" could not be exercised effectively without the establishment of legislative criteria for distinguishing "Status Indians" from the general population. Ritchie thus defined the issue presented in *Lavell* as whether the Bill of Rights could be construed as rendering inoperative one of the conditions imposed by Parliament for the use and occupation of Crown lands reserved for Indians. According to Ritchie, this would be an inappropriate construction of the Bill of Rights, since in his view Parliament could not have intended that such an important policy change be implemented through the broad and general language of the Bill of Rights.

This observation led Ritchie to a discussion of the general status of the Bill of Rights, as well as the specific meaning of its guarantee of equality before the law. Ritchie acknowledged that the Bill's primary concern was to ensure that the rights and freedoms recognized and declared in it should continue to exist for all Canadians, but that it could not be invoked unless one of the enumerated rights or freedoms had been expressly denied to an individual Canadian or group of Canadians. Echoing Dicey, Ritchie argued that the Bill of Rights did not enumerate a general right to be free from discrimination, only a right to equality in the administration or application of the law by law enforcement authorities and the ordinary courts. "Discriminatory" laws, in other words, could remain operative so long as they were applied equally to everyone against whom they discriminated. Applying this principle to the case before him, Ritchie concluded that section 12(1)(b) contributed to the valid federal objective of defining Indian status without discriminating against anyone to whom it applied: the law treated all native women who married non-natives equally. Ritchie distinguished this conclusion from *Drybones* on the grounds that section 12(1)(b) dealt with the internal administration of native affairs and with natives *qua* natives, while the public intoxication provision dealt with natives *qua* Canadian citizens.

Ritchie's judgment commanded the slimmest of majorities (four justices dissented), and women's groups in particular have cited it as evidence that the restrictive theory of formal equality must be replaced by the more results-oriented theory of substantive equality.[31] However, it is uncertain whether *Lavell* unequivocally supports the claim that the doctrine of substantive equality – which recognizes the legitimacy of special treatment for disadvantaged groups – necessarily resolves the liberal dilemma of equality more effectively than the theory of formal equality. The collective right to special treatment for certain groups inherent in the doctrine of substantive equality may achieve better results for those groups than adherence to formal equality makes possible, but it does so by creating conflicts of its own with both the individual rights of specific persons and the collective rights of other groups. In the political atmosphere of the early 1970s, native leaders considered the Indian Act, including the status provisions impugned in *Lavell,* a vital instrument for preserving their identity and ameliorating their disadvantaged condition. Under these circumstances, they thought it necessary to sacrifice the individual equality rights of some native women in order to advance the broader collective right of natives as a group to special status. The point here is not that this was the correct position for native leaders to take – indeed, amendments to the Indian Act enacted in 1985 demonstrate that section 12(1)(b) was not so integral to the Act as it had once seemed – but that the outcome in *Lavell* cannot simply be attributed to an undue emphasis on individual rights and formal equality: it is equally consistent with theories of collective rights and substantive equality. *Lavell* highlights the complex coexistence of individual and collective rights in liberal democracies, as well as the difficult choices that must be made in cases where they conflict.

Despite criticism of its approach to equality in *Lavell,* the Supreme Court maintained its narrow construction of this concept five years later in *Bliss.* At issue in this case were provisions in the Unemployment Insurance Act concerning newly established maternity benefits. The Act established three types of benefits, each with its own eligibility requirements covering loss of employment through ordinary circumstances, disability, and pregnancy. Stella Bliss left her job because of pregnancy, making her ineligible for the ordinary benefits for which she was otherwise qualified; nor did she qualify for regular disability benefits, since these did not include pregnancy within the definition of disability. Moreover, since Bliss had not worked the specified number of weeks prior to leaving her job that the Act required before collecting maternity benefits, the government rejected her application for unemployment compensation under this provision. Bliss sought relief in the courts on the grounds that, by mandating more stringent eligibility requirements for maternity benefits than for other types of benefits, the Act's eligibility structure discriminated on the basis of sex.

Justice Ritchie again wrote the Court's judgment, this time with the unanimous agreement of his colleagues. In rejecting Bliss's claim, Ritchie narrowly defined both "equality before the law" and "discrimination." With respect to the former term, Ritchie held that it did not in principle prevent Parliament from creating separate classifications of unemployment insurance benefits to which different eligibility criteria might apply. Echoing *Lavell,* Ritchie argued that "equality before the law" meant only that the eligibility criteria in each category be applied equally to every applicant for the relevant benefits, a standard that the government's action toward Bliss met. Similarly, Ritchie responded to the indisputable fact that only women would bear the burden of the more stringent eligibility requirements for maternity benefits by denying that this constituted discrimination on the basis of sex. His explanation of this conclusion, however, produced two of the most criticized statements ever made by a Supreme Court justice. "If," Ritchie averred, the Act "treats unemployed pregnant women differently from other unemployed persons, be they male or female, it is . . . because they are pregnant and not because they are women"; moreover, Ritchie continued, any inequality suffered by Bliss was "not created by legislation but by nature."[32] By holding that discrimination on the basis of pregnancy did not necessarily constitute sex discrimination, Justice Ritchie advocated a narrow view of discrimination in which only express intent is relevant.

Drybones, Lavell, and *Bliss* are paradigmatic of the Supreme Court's cautious approach to equality rights under the Bill of Rights. While this caution was partly a function of the grip that formal concepts of equality held on Canadian legal thinking during this period, it was also the result of judicial uncertainty about the Court's power to give the Bill of Rights paramountcy over other federal legislation. The Court thus sought to avoid creating a crisis of legitimacy by adopting the "frozen rights" theory, which discouraged judicial expansion of substantive rights, and the "valid federal objective" test, which provided a broad justification for federal legislation that violated even narrowly defined equality rights.[33] *Drybones* proved anomalous because its political impact was so negligible. When the political consequences became more serious, as in *Lavell* and *Bliss,* the Court retreated. Indeed, one could argue that *Drybones,* by raising the possibility of judicial nullification under the Bill of Rights, contributed to judicial caution. Once the Supreme Court and legal commentators recognized a broader remedial power to declare legislation inconsistent with the Bill of Rights inoperative, the justices became more reluctant to define the document's guarantees broadly.

Equality and Human Rights Legislation

Commentators aimed two principal criticisms at the Supreme Court's Bill of Rights decision-making: that it rested on an unduly narrow construction of the Bill's substantive provisions, and that it was overly deferential to federal legislation and regulatory decisions. Applied to human rights legislation, however, these alleged judicial vices became judicial virtues in many cases; and the same decision-making characteristics that weakened the impact of the Bill of Rights have helped to enhance the importance of human rights legislation. At the same time, the Court has exhibited a greater willingness to interpret the terms of human rights legislation broadly. Consequently, the Court's record in this area reflects a curious blending of judicial deference, strict construction, and judicial creativity.

One important illustration of the positive effects of strict construction is found in Justice Ritchie's reasons for judgment in *Re Athabasca Tribal Council and Amoco Canada Petroleum* (1981).[34] At issue in this case was whether it was within the jurisdiction of Alberta's Energy Resources Conservation Board to require the establishment of an affirmative action program as a precondition for the Board's approval of a major petroleum development project. Although the Court unanimously held that the Board did not have jurisdiction to impose this requirement, the case remains important because of what Justice Ritchie said about the general compatibility of affirmative action programs with Alberta's Individual Rights Protection Act.

Ritchie actually decided the appeal's main question in a fairly straight-forward manner, relying exclusively on the fact that the Board's enabling legislation (the Oil and Gas Conservation Act) only granted it jurisdiction over matters directly concerning the province's natural resources. Unless the province enacted express statutory language to the contrary, Ritchie concluded, the Board could not extend this jurisdiction to policies concerning "the social welfare of [Alberta's] inhabitants." While this conclusion was sufficient for five justices, Ritchie (on behalf of Chief Justice Laskin and Justices Dickson and McIntyre) also felt compelled to discuss the Alberta Court of Appeal's conclusion that the Board's attempt to implement an affirmative action policy itself constituted employment discrimination under the Individual Rights Protection Act.[35] In reaching a conclusion different from that of the Alberta court, Ritchie focused on a key provision in the Act that prohibited employers from "discriminating against" any person. Accepting the Alberta court's interpretation of this prohibition, Ritchie argued, would make any policy favouring an individual or group of individuals unlawful. In Ritchie's view, affirmative programs, designed to allow members of disadvantaged groups to compete equally for employment, could "not be construed as 'discriminating against' other inhabitants."

By narrowly interpreting the phrase "discrimination against" to mean direct exclusion of individuals from employment, Ritchie was able to reconcile racially based affirmative action programs with Alberta's human rights legislation. Consequently, although Alberta had amended its Individual Rights Protection Act in 1980 to clarify the status of affirmative action, Ritchie's *dictum* on this point served to legitimize affirmative action as being consistent with the overall policy objectives of human rights legislation. Moreover, Ritchie dismissed two key U.S. Supreme Court decisions concerning affirmative action as irrelevant to his discussion,[36] and suggested that Canadian courts might be well advised to avoid the complicated U.S. debate about whether such policies constitute "reverse discrimination." Without conferring undue importance on Ritchie's *dictum,* it simplified the affirmative action issue in Canada.

Both judicial creativity and deference to regulatory authority characterized two cases decided in 1985 affirming the applicability of human rights legislation to "adverse effect discrimination": *Re Ontario Human Rights Commission and Simpsons-Sears Ltd.* (1985) and *Re Bhinder et al. and Canadian National Railways* (1985).[37] Both of these cases involved complaints against otherwise neutral employment requirements on the grounds that they adversely affected the employment opportunities of members of religious minorities. In the *Simpsons-Sears* case, the complaint originated with Theresa O'Malley, whose conversion to Seventh-Day Adventism prohibited her from continuing to comply with her employer's requirement that full-time sales staff work on Saturday. Mrs. O'Malley thus exchanged her full-time position for a part-time position that offered less income and fewer benefits. The complainant in *Bhinder* was a member of the Sikh religion whose employer discharged him after he refused on religious grounds to comply with the company's requirement that safety helmets be worn on the job.

Both O'Malley's and Bhinder's complaints encompassed two questions: whether the adverse impact of these employment requirements constituted *prima facie* discrimination, and whether (in the event of discrimination) their employers had taken sufficient steps to alleviate the adverse impact. In O'Malley's case, a Board of Inquiry established by the Ontario Human Rights Commission held that intent was not a necessary element in proving discrimination under the province's Human Rights Code, which allowed O'Malley to show *prima facie* discrimination on the part of her employer. However, the Board of Inquiry ultimately dismissed O'Malley's complaint on the grounds that Simpsons-Sears had acted reasonably in the steps it took to accommodate her religious practices. O'Malley's complaint fared even worse on appeal to Ontario's Divisional Court and Court of Appeal: contrary to the Board of Inquiry, both courts held that it was necessary to establish intent in order to make a finding of discrimination under the Code.

The most important part of Justice McIntyre's reasons for judgment on behalf of a unanimous Supreme Court, therefore, concerned discrimination and the question of intent. McIntyre began by acknowledging that the special status of human rights legislation – "not quite constitutional but certainly more than the ordinary" – justified giving it "an interpretation that will advance its broad purposes." This had been done by some Ontario judges and inquiry boards, he continued, to the effect of recognizing "the principle that an intention to discriminate is not a necessary element of the discrimination generally forbidden in Canadian human rights legislation." McIntyre endorsed this interpretation, arguing that a narrower view in which discriminatory intent becomes the focus of inquiry would "place a virtually insuperable barrier in the way of a complainant seeking a remedy." Echoing the Aristotelian concern with proportionate treatment, McIntyre concluded that, given the difficulty of proving motive, the narrow interpretation might permit "injustice and discrimination by the equal treatment of those who are unequal."[38] McIntyre thus held that individuals could seek relief under human rights legislation from the adverse impact of apparently neutral employment requirements, a principle he also applied to

Bhinder's complaint against Canadian National Railways under the Canadian Human Rights Act.[39]

Justice McIntyre's decisions in these two cases, which reflected the views of the Court as a whole in most important respects, gave equal weight to the importance of interpretive flexibility and the expert judgment of provincial human rights officials in declaring that human rights legislation provides a remedy for adverse impact discrimination despite the absence of express statutory language to that effect. Precisely what types of remedies, and for what scope of adverse impact, remained an open question until the Court's decision in *Action Travail des Femmes v. Canadian National Railways* (1987).[40] At issue in this case was whether tribunals appointed under the Canadian Human Rights Act could order a company to undertake an employment equity/affirmative action program to remedy "systemic discrimination" of which the principal evidence was the disproportionately low representation of a certain group (women) among part of the company's work force. This question went beyond the issue that the Court had dealt with in the *Athabasca Tribal Council* case by not merely considering whether human rights legislation could accommodate affirmative action, but whether this legislation might require such action. Similarly, *Action Travail des Femmes* also went beyond the two adverse impact cases in that those cases involved specific employment requirements rather than more general employment conditions.

The evidence of employment discrimination against women by Canadian National Railways (CN) had three components. The first was a report prepared in 1974, which identified three problems with the company's attitude toward women's employment: lack of guidance from senior management; the persistence of traditional beliefs and stereotypes among middle management; and generally ineffective personnel policies and procedures. The second component consisted of testimony before the Human Rights Tribunal from thirteen women about the difficulties that they faced in pursuing "non-traditional" occupations at the company. Finally, the Court considered statistical evidence that, although women constituted 13 per cent of all blue-collar workers in Canada in 1982, they represented less than 1 per cent of the blue-collar workers at CN and only 5 per cent of the applicant pool for such positions. In Chief Justice Dickson's judgment, this low rate of female participation in blue-collar positions was not the result of mere chance. The other evidence convinced him, as it had the Tribunal, that CN's general recruitment, hiring, and promotional policies were the reason for this situation.[41]

In response to this finding of systemic discrimination against women at CN, the Human Rights Tribunal ordered the company to undertake a three-part employment equity program. The first part of this program required the elimination of all employment procedures and policies, including certain mechanical aptitude and physical strength tests, that affected women adversely and were not directly related to the positions for which they were applying. Second, the Tribunal ordered CN to undertake two "special temporary" affirmative action measures to increase the proportion of women in its blue-collar work force to the national level of 13 per cent. One measure was an informational campaign to publicize the availability of these positions to women and to invite their applications; the second measure was a requirement that 25 per cent of all blue-collar positions be filled by women until CN reached the 13 per cent level. Finally, the Tribunal required CN to file periodic reports covering various aspects of its non-traditional employment of women. Canadian National appealed both the Tribunal's findings of fact and its remedial order to the Federal Court of Appeal, which agreed with CN that the Tribunal had exceeded its jurisdiction by imposing a hiring quota on the company. With all parties deciding to concede the presence of discrimination, the legality of the "special temporary measures" ordered by the Tribunal became the principal question dealt with in Chief Justice Dickson's reasons for judgment in the Supreme Court.

After confirming that the "special nature" of human rights legislation invites a broad interpretive approach,[42] Dickson went on to discuss the relationship between the special temporary measures and the elimination of systemic discrimination. The point of contention here was whether the Tribunal's order constituted a *preventive* measure – which the Canadian Human Rights Act clearly authorized – or a *remedial* measure, the legality of which was more ambiguous. The Federal Court of Appeal had held that the order was remedial, and hence impermissible, because the "special temporary measures" were not directly aimed at eliminating the practices that caused the systemic discrimination. Dickson disagreed, arguing that the order fell within a broad interpretation of "preventive" because the affirmative action program required by the "special temporary measures" would prevent future systemic exclusion of women from blue-collar positions. This was the case, Dickson averred, because the program would negate future intentional discrimination against women, would break down discriminatory stereotyping by placing women in a position to demonstrate their competence at non-traditional jobs, and would create a "critical mass" of women in these positions that might eventually convert them from non-traditional to ordinary occupations for women.[43] In Dickson's view, the "special temporary measures" represented a "rationally designed" strategy to prevent future systemic discrimination against women with respect to blue-collar positions at Canadian National.[44]

Although *Athabasca Tribal Council, O'Malley, Bhinder,* and *Action Travail des Femmes* represent only a small fraction of the Supreme Court's decisions concerning human rights legislation, they fairly reflect the Court's generally liberal approach to these statutes. The justices took as their guidance for this approach both the overall purposes of the legislation and a specific provision in the Interpretation Act (section 12), which requires that legislative enactments "be deemed remedial, and shall be given such fair, large and liberal construction and interpretation as best ensures the attainment of [their] objects."[45] By progressively applying this rule of interpretation to human rights legislation, the Court significantly enhanced the discretionary power of human rights commissions to develop means for achieving the substantive equality of traditionally disadvantaged groups like religious minorities and women. However, while these decisions increased the power of human rights regulators and the scope of human rights legislation, they had no impact on the basic distribution of political power between the judiciary and other components of government. Had they so desired, the provincial and federal governments could have nullified these decisions simply by enacting appropriate amendments restricting the jurisdiction of human rights tribunals and commissions. In fact, governments usually took the opposite route by specifically amending these statutes to affirm the new powers to which the Court had given its blessing.

The Court itself perhaps best summarized its approach to human rights legislation in 1988, when it took the rare step in *Brooks v. Canada Safeway* (1988) of expressly overruling one of its own judgments.[46] At issue in *Brooks* was the legality under Manitoba's Human Rights Act of a disability plan that excluded pregnant women from benefits during a seventeen-week period. When complaints were first filed against this provision of the disability plan, the Manitoba statute did not expressly prohibit discrimination on the basis of pregnancy; and the complainants relied on the Act's general prohibition of discrimination on the basis of sex. This, of course, posed the same question that the Court had faced in *Bliss*: Does discrimination on the basis of pregnancy also constitute discrimination on the basis of sex? Again writing for a unanimous Court, Chief Justice Dickson held that a decade of hindsight and human rights jurisprudence indicated that "*Bliss* was wrongly decided" and that the inequality suffered by Stella Bliss had indeed been created by legislation.[47] In Dickson's view, any analysis of "pregnancy-based discrimination" must recognize the biological fact that the "capacity to become pregnant is unique to the female gender."[48] Thus, despite employing problematic language linking the "socially vital function of women" to procreation,[49] Dickson erased from Canadian jurisprudence one of the principal lightning rods for criticisms of the formal equality doctrine.

In the final analysis, since most jurisdictions (including Manitoba) had superseded *Bliss* with legislation, the Court's decision had mostly symbolic value. Nevertheless, it signalled that the Court had completely abandoned the narrow view of equality it had expressed in its Bill of Rights decisions. Moreover, the threads of substantive equality and the rejection of Bill of Rights equality decisions characteristic of human rights jurisprudence formed an important part of the context in which the authors of the Charter drafted the equality rights provisions of section 15. Consequently, many commentators claimed that the interpretive principles and substantive doctrines established in the Court's decisions concerning human rights legislation would provide the best guide for judicial decision-making under section 15 of the Charter.

Equality Rights and Section 15 of the Charter

Legislative History and Lower Court Litigation

Although the Special Joint Committee on the Constitution received more sub-missions concerning the constitutional entrenchment of official language rights, minority-language education rights, the rights of denominational schools, and native rights than the entrenchment of equality rights, the general pattern of the submissions concerning equality rights supports Peter Hogg's early observation that section 15 potentially constituted "the most intrusive provision of the Char-ter."[50] Indeed, almost 50 per cent of the general submissions concerning the Charter provisions discussed in this book involved the equality rights provi-sions; and of these twenty-five submissions, only two disagreed in principle with entrenching equality rights.[51] Moreover, section 15 was the subject of 28 per cent of the 411 submissions concerning the specific content of the Charter's fundamental freedoms, legal rights, and equality rights provisions.[52] Section 15 attracted this much attention because its potential impact directly affected dis-tinct groups of people. By contrast, the potential impact of the Charter's pro-posed legal rights and some fundamental freedoms was more diffuse.

Women's groups, in particular, were determined to ensure that the Charter constitutionalized the expansive equality principles of human rights legislation and its accompanying jurisprudence rather than the more restrictive principles and jurisprudence of the Bill of Rights.[53] Consequently, they succeeded in adding "equality under the law" and "equal benefit of the law" to the rights pro-tected by section 15(1). Moreover, although they failed to exclude section 15 from the "notwithstanding" clause (section 33) or to impose a structure on it that would provide special status for sex equality, women's groups eventually suc-ceeded in adding a separate section guaranteeing equal application of the Char-ter to men and women to which section 33 does not apply.[54]

The Joint Committee also considered amendments to add mental and physi-cal disability, marital status, sexual orientation, and political belief to the list of specifically prohibited grounds of discrimination; to replace the term "without discrimination" with "without unreasonable distinction"; to remove the term "disadvantaged" from the affirmative action clause of section 15(2); and to restrict affirmative action protection to groups rather than individuals. In addi-tion, two members of the committee proposed adding a third subsection to sec-tion 15 that would protect aboriginal peoples from any unforeseen negative con-sequences of equality rights protection.[55] With the exception of adding mental and physical disability to the list of specifically protected groups, all of these proposals to expand section 15 failed.

In the discussion concerning these amendments, members of the committee and officials testifying on behalf of the government exhibited somewhat contra-dictory views about the impact of section 15 on judicial power. For example, in discussing the possible addition of "political belief" to section 15, one member of the committee expressed concern that in some matters this would transform fundamentally political judgments into questions for judicial determination.[56] Similarly, Justice Minister Jean Chrétien generally opposed expanding the list of protected groups on the grounds that it was preferable to allow for legislative flexibility in attempting to solve social problems rather than to attempt to do so through the clumsy process of constitutional amendment. At the same time, however, he also defended his opposition to this expansion by citing the probability that additional prohibited grounds of discrimination would be defined by the courts.[57] In a sense, these remarks reflect the basic dilemma of liberal constitutionalism, which is the desire to provide legislative flexibility to cope with unexpected social and political problems when they arise, while ensuring that this flexibility does not unduly restrict protected rights.

Recognizing the potentially vast impact of section 15 on existing legislation, the authors of the Charter delayed its judicial enforceability by three years. During this period, the federal and provincial governments undertook, with varying levels of commitment, statutory audits to bring legislation into compliance with the equality guarantees. This proved to be a daunting task, because of both the sheer number of statutes and the absence of judicial interpretation of section 15 to guide those undertaking the audits. Nevertheless, assumptions about what equality under the Charter should mean had a profound impact on both the process and outcome of the audits. At the federal level, for example, the Justice Department determined that legislation in the post-Charter era should reflect a conception of equality that recognized the equal dignity and worth of all individuals, that did not equate equality with sameness, and that was substantive rather than merely procedural.[58] Thus, even before the courts rendered a single judicial decision, section 15 affected the type of legislative distinctions considered legitimate by federal policy-makers. While some distinctions violating these principles were easy to identify and remedy, others posed more complex social policy questions. The result was a relatively extensive process of public consultation.[59]

Once section 15 became judicially enforceable, it produced a flood of litigation. Indeed, according to data collected by the Women's Legal Education and Action Fund (LEAF) and the Canadian Advisory Council on the Status of Women (CACSW), Canadian courts decided 591 section 15 cases of some significance between April, 1985, and June, 1988.[60] For the most part these decisions did not require courts to consider issues too remote from their areas of greatest expertise. Nearly 41 per cent of the decisions concerned alleged inequalities in the administration of criminal and civil procedure, and 17 per cent involved questions about the substantive criminal law. However, about 40 per cent of the decisions did involve broader questions of economic and social policy, including economic regulation, collective bargaining, education, and social assistance/income security policies. Perhaps the most interesting finding of the LEAF/CACSW study, however, was that almost 80 per cent of the sex discrimination decisions under section 15 during this period involved claims brought by men. While men were less successful than women in making sex equality claims (37.5 per cent versus 50 per cent) and tended to make their claims as reactive defensive manoeuvres rather than as part of proactive litigation strategies, their use of section 15 illustrates the difficulty of controlling the social impact of rights-based constitutional litigation. Despite a concerted effort through provisions like section 15(2) to ensure that litigation under the equality rights provisions would act as a uni-directional ratchet on Canadian social policy, relatively non-disadvantaged groups have been able to invoke it to their benefit.

Among the lower court decisions on section 15, two stand out as particularly significant: *Re Blainey and Ontario Hockey Association* (1986) and *Schacter v. The Queen* (1988).[61] At issue in *Blainey* was whether section 15 prohibits private athletic organizations from excluding participants on the basis of sex, in this case a twelve-year-old girl prevented from playing on a boys' hockey team. Justine Blainey had initially failed to secure a remedy under Ontario's Human Rights Code because the Code contained an exemption to its general prohibition against sex discrimination that expressly permitted private athletic organizations to exclude participants on the basis of sex. Although the Ontario Court of Appeal held that the Charter did not directly apply to the actions of the hockey association, it found that the Code's statutory exemption permitted direct discrimination contrary to section 15. Moreover, the court rejected the argument that this exemption constituted such an integral part of the statute – indeed, one without which the legislature would not have enacted the Code – that its constitutionality could not be abstracted from the constitutionality of the Code as a whole. Consequently, the court declared that the Code must operate without any exemption for single-sex athletic organizations.[62]

Blainey's significance extends beyond its particular circumstances for several reasons. First, it articulated a set of principles concerning the Charter's applicability to private activity that the Supreme Court would later adopt in *Dolphin Delivery*. Indeed, the Court in *Dolphin Delivery* cited *Blainey* as evidence of "the manner in which Charter rights of private individuals may be enforced and protected by the courts" despite the general principle that the Charter applies only to government action.[63] Second, *Blainey* signalled that the delicate legislative compromises and complex social policy choices underlying human rights legislation were now subject to judicial review under the Charter. This provided the opportunity to challenge other types of exemptions, such as those permitting mandatory retirement policies. Finally, although *Blainey* itself represented a victory for women's sex equality claims, it had the unintended consequence of placing women on the intellectual and juridical defensive to justify their own single-sex associations.[64] *Blainey* thus illustrates the problematic consequences of constitutionally based judicial review of legislation concerning complex social policy issues.

A similar point might be made about the Federal Court of Canada's decisions in *Schacter*. At issue in this case were provisions of the Unemployment Insurance Act that provided natural parents with less extensive parental leave benefits than those available to adoptive parents. The Act provided fifteen weeks of maternity benefits to the natural mothers of children that could, in the event of the mother's disability or death, be transferred to the natural father. Adoptive parents of *either* sex, however, could claim fifteen weeks of parental leave benefits on the sole condition that the claimant demonstrate the reasonableness of remaining at home. Schacter argued that these provisions denied him the equal benefit of the law guaranteed by the Charter for two reasons. First, he claimed that the Act created a discriminatory distinction between adoptive parents of both sexes and natural fathers by making it easier for adoptive parents to claim parental leave benefits. Second, Schacter argued that the Act established an impermissible distinction between natural fathers and natural mothers through its presumption that women should be unconditionally entitled to maternity benefits.

The trial division of the Federal Court agreed with Schacter (who received support from LEAF) that this benefit scheme constituted discrimination on the basis of sex largely because its presumption in favour of natural mothers perpetuated sexual stereotyping by envisioning women as the primary caregivers for infants. According to the court, this violated the spirit of section 15, which reflected Canadian society's commitment "to equalizing the role of parents in the care of children as much as possible, for the benefit of the family in general and in particular for the achievement of greater equality in the work place for women."[65] The impugned provisions of the Unemployment Insurance Act thus discriminated as much against women as men because they impeded women's progress toward substantive equality by making it more difficult for natural fathers to share equally in caring for their infant children.

Having found unequal treatment contrary to section 15, the Federal Court faced a delicate remedial task. Following the advice of counsel for both Schacter and LEAF, the trial judge rejected the suggestion that he base his remedy on section 52 of the Constitution Act, 1982 and declare the relevant benefit provisions of the Unemployment Insurance Act invalid. The obvious consequence of choosing this route would have been to nullify all parental leave benefits, leaving everyone worse off than they were before the litigation. Instead, the court based its remedy on the authority granted under section 24(1) of the Charter to frame "such remedy as the court considers appropriate and just in the circumstances." In this case, the court concluded that the impugned provisions of the Act were "under-inclusive" and that the "appropriate and just remedy" consisted of extending to natural parents the same benefits available to adoptive parents until such time as Parliament otherwise amended the Act to bring it into conformity with the Charter.[66] As a result, the plaintiffs in *Schacter* were able to achieve a substantial alteration in the parental leave benefits policy of the Unemployment Insurance Act. The remedial aspects of *Schacter* are the subject of more detailed discussion in Chapter Six.

Blainey and *Schacter* are reflective of a more general characteristic of early equality rights litigation: for the most part, these cases involved subtle policy questions about the delivery of public goods rather than pernicious discrimination against a vulnerable group. In *Blainey*, these questions concerned legislation designed to deliver maximum equality within the constraints imposed by a widely recognized and generally accepted social consensus that exclusion is acceptable under certain well-defined conditions. Whether judicial interference with that consensus actually advanced the cause of equality is one of the central questions posed by *Blainey.* Indeed, while Justine Blainey and similarly talented individual female hockey players clearly benefited from the decision, some evidence suggests that women hockey players *as a group* might have been disadvantaged as a result.[67] In *Schacter* the policy questions involved a complex scheme of government financial support for individuals, primarily women, who wished to become parents while continuing their employment. Even this limited policy goal proved difficult to implement, requiring continuous legislative refinement of the Unemployment Insurance Act.[68] Determining how to achieve the separate and unique policy goal of equalizing the burdens of child care between men and women is a separate question that judicial refinement of parental leave benefits does not necessarily address.

If anything became clear during the first few years that section 15 operated in cases like *Blainey* and *Schacter,* it was that courts faced a daunting series of interpretive questions in undertaking their responsibility for determining precisely what "equality rights protect Canadians against"[69] or, alternatively, entitle them to receive. The importance of these questions was significantly enhanced by the clear indication from this early litigation experience that section 15 imposes another difficult judicial task: determining which claims to positive entitlements deserve recognition as equality rights. *Blainey* and *Schacter* provided answers to some of the more important of these questions, including some concerning the application of section 15 and the judicial power to devise extraordinary remedies for breaches of equality rights. Others remained, of course, including the relation of "equality" to "discrimination," the relative status of each of the enumerated grounds of discrimination, the status of unenumerated grounds of legislative classification, the types of legislative distinctions precluded by section 15, and the role of "reasonable limits" in equality rights litigation. After several years of uncertainty, the Supreme Court began to provide authoritative answers to these questions in 1989.

Section 15 in the Supreme Court

Although litigants presented the Supreme Court with arguments based on section 15 in several cases shortly after it came into force, the Court either ignored these arguments and based its judgment on other Charter sections, or it refused to consider them because to do so would require retroactive application of the Charter.[70] On February 2, 1989, however, the Court finally delivered its first equality rights decision. At issue in *Law Society of British Columbia v. Andrews and Kinersly* was the constitutionality of section 42 of the British Columbia Barristers and Solicitors Act, which prohibited permanent-resident non-citizens from admission to the British Columbia bar.[71] As the first case in which the Supreme Court would interpret section 15, *Andrews* attracted interventions from several groups with little or no interest in its specific issue, including LEAF, the Coalition of Provincial Organizations of the Handicapped, the Canadian

Association of University Teachers, and the Ontario Confederation of University Faculty Associations. Each of these groups had a strategic interest in promoting an interpretation of section 15 that would facilitate its own future equality rights claims. For the groups representing university faculty this interest was particularly urgent, since they were involved in very important equality rights litigation in the lower courts concerning mandatory retirement.

Although *Andrews* clearly involved legislation that imposed a direct disadvantage on a group of individuals, it did not involve any of the prohibited grounds of discrimination listed in section 15. As Andrews's own case illustrated, the citizenship requirement did not constitute a permanent barrier to the practice of law in British Columbia. Nevertheless, the Court united unanimously behind Justice McIntyre's discussion of the substantive meaning of section 15(1) to find a *prima facie* violation of equality rights. However, a majority of the Court disagreed with McIntyre's conclusion that the citizenship requirement constituted a reasonable limit on the right to equality. Led by Justices Wilson and La Forest, the majority found the impugned provision neither rationally nor proportionately connected to its purported objectives.

Justice McIntyre's reasons for judgment represented a relatively comprehensive survey of the major issues raised by section 15. His first task was to determine the meaning of the concept of equality guaranteed by section 15(1), and he began by emphasizing that the Charter could not guarantee abstract social equality or the equal treatment of individuals and groups in their private interactions. Section 15(1), he declared, is concerned only with equality in the application of the law.[72] According to McIntyre, however, this concern did not mean that courts must restrict themselves to enforcing a conception of formal equality in which the sole burden on government is to ensure that similarly situated individuals receive similar treatment. McIntyre rejected this narrow approach to equality because experience suggested that it too easily permitted two types of unjust results. Citing as examples laws passed in Nazi Germany and the "separate but equal" doctrine adopted by the U.S. Supreme Court in *Plessy v. Ferguson* (1896), McIntyre argued that the similarly situated test of formal equality could easily be applied to justify laws that discriminate equally against entire classes of individuals. At the same time, he argued that this test could also exclude socially desirable legislation by failing to recognize the injustice of "equal treatment of unequals." For McIntyre, the meaning of equality could not be defined by any rigid formula; instead, it required the sensitive accommodation of differences. From this perspective, courts faced two key tasks: first, to determine which legislative distinctions constitute permissible accommodation of differences and which are denials of equality; and, second, to determine whether the failure to make legislative distinctions under certain circumstances violates equality rights.[73]

As McIntyre noted, commentators and lower courts had articulated three separate theories to guide judges in their performance of these tasks. According to a theory first proposed by Peter Hogg, the best approach to section 15(1) would consider *all* legislative distinctions as *prima facie* violations of the right to equality, thus requiring legislatures to provide a separate justification for each distinction under section 1. A second theory, adopted by the British Columbia Court of Appeal in its consideration of *Andrews,* held that unequal treatment in itself did not constitute a *prima facie* violation of section 15(1) because that section's reference to "discrimination" meant that the Charter only prohibited "unreasonable" or "unfair" legislative distinctions. The principal difference between this theory and the one proposed by Hogg was that, by including the question of reasonableness within the substantive definition of equality, it would force equality seekers to prove "unreasonableness" in order to succeed in their claim.[74] Finally, a third theory, drawn from the judicial interpretation of human rights legislation, suggested that courts should focus primarily on legislative distinctions that disadvantage members of the enumerated groups and groups analogous to them, striking down those distinctions unless governments could justify them under section 1. Legislative distinctions *benefiting* these groups, or those disadvantaging groups that are neither enumerated nor analogous, would not usually violate section 15(1).[75]

Following the interpretive approach outlined by Chief Justice Dickson in *Big M Drug Mart,* McIntyre proceeded to choose among these theories by identifying which among them permitted the fullest achievement of the purposes underlying section 15.[76] According to McIntyre, section 15 encompassed two related objectives. First, it aimed at overcoming the narrow protection of equality provided by the 1960 Bill of Rights, the shortcomings of which had been revealed in *Lavell* and *Bliss.* McIntyre quite correctly took as evidence of this purpose the fact that section 15(1) added additional equality rights to the traditional protection of equality before the law found in the Bill of Rights, bringing the constitutional protection of equality into line with the broad definition of discrimination found in the language and judicial interpretation of federal and provincial human rights legislation. Moreover, in a particularly important passage, McIntyre inferred from this similarity between human rights legislation and section 15 that intent did not constitute an essential element of discrimination under the Charter.[77] The second purpose of this provision, McIntyre argued, was remedial in nature and justified legislative departures from formal equality in order to redress deeper inequalities. According to McIntyre, this objective explained the specific reference to discrimination in section 15(1) and the constitutional protection afforded affirmative action in section 15(2). Consequently, section 15 could not be interpreted in a way that might destroy legislation designed to address certain inequalities through differential treatment.

These considerations led McIntyre to reject Hogg's theory, as well as the approach adopted by the British Columbia Court of Appeal. The problem with Hogg's theory was that it treated all legislative distinctions identically and placed unnecessary (and unwise) constitutional obstacles in the way of ameliorative legislation. The British Columbia theory failed because it radically departed from the usual analytical approach to the Charter, which separates definitional issues from questions of justification.[78] This left the "enumerated and analogous grounds" theory, which McIntyre found to be the approach that "most closely accords with the purposes of s.15 and the definition of discrimination." Adopting this third theory, in other words, promoted a judicial interpretation of section 15 that best advanced its principal mandate of preventing future damage to disadvantaged groups and remedying past damage. However, consistent with his reputation for judicial restraint, McIntyre attempted to soften the potential policy impact of this theory by stressing that the presence of a distinction based on an enumerated or analogous classification would not in itself bring a statute into conflict with section 15. It was also necessary to examine the "effect of the impugned distinction or classification on the complainant" and demonstrate that this effect is indeed harmful.[79] Read in conjunction with McIntyre's conclusion that section 15 prohibits systemic discrimination, this qualification suggests that the most important element in equality rights jurisprudence is not legislative classification *per se* but the impact of such classification.

Applying this approach to the legislative provision at issue in *Andrews,* McIntyre began by determining whether the impugned ground of distinction (citizenship) could be considered analogous to any of the enumerated classifications. He concluded after a single paragraph of discussion that legislative classifications based on citizenship are among those prohibited by section 15, offering as his rationale for this decision the observation that non-citizens are "a good example of a 'discrete and insular minority' who come within the protection of s.15."[80] McIntyre adopted this phrase from a footnote in the U.S. Supreme Court's decision in *United States v. Carolene Products* (1938), where the term emerged to describe legislation that would be subject to "more searching judicial inquiry" than economic regulation.[81] Discrete and insular minorities differ from other social groups in that their members share a common characteristic that sets them clearly apart from the majority *and* imposes obstacles that render them incapable of defending or advancing their commonly shared interests through ordinary political action. In U.S. equality rights jurisprudence, African-Americans are the paradigmatic example of a discrete and insular minority, and legislation that classifies on the basis of race must meet the strict requirement that it rationally and proportionately advances a compelling state interest. Gender-based classifications, on the other hand, are subject to the less rigorous requirement that they be substantially related to important governmental objectives. Other legislative distinctions are subject to an even less restrictive "rational basis" standard.[82] Since non-citizens lack extensive political power, including the right to vote, it is understandable that McIntyre would describe them as discrete and insular.

According to McIntyre's analysis, the most important (and perhaps only) factor determining whether an unenumerated distinction is analogous to the enumerated classifications is whether it encompasses a discrete and insular minority. This conclusion about his judgment is supported by the fact that McIntyre did not declare "citizenship" to be directly analogous to any of the enumerated classifications, such as national or ethnic origin. Additional aspects of this analysis are evident in Justice Wilson's more elaborate conceptual discussion, in which she stressed that the appropriate context for determining whether a group constitutes a discrete and insular minority is its place "in the entire social, political and legal fabric of our society" rather than the specific context of the law at issue. According to Wilson, this had the practical implication of ensuring that "the range of discrete and insular minorities . . . will continue to change with changing political and social circumstances." In her view, this gave courts the flexibility necessary to "ensure the 'unremitting protection' of equality rights" in the future by allowing judges to recognize novel grounds of discrimination.[83]

On first reading, the Court's decision in *Andrews* appears to be a balanced effort to provide broad constitutional protection for equality rights while avoiding an interpretation that would expose every legislative distinction to constitutional challenge and require governments to justify these distinctions according to the exacting standards of section 1. Indeed, Justice McIntyre went so far as to suggest that these standards should be relaxed when applied to legislative distinctions concerning administrative and regulatory matters.[84] The role of "adverse impact" in defining discrimination is further evidence of this attempt at careful judicial statesmanship. Although this extended the application of section 15(1) to systemic discrimination, it also provided a standard by which courts could uphold legislative distinctions based on even the enumerated classifications. Finally, by restricting the list of unenumerated grounds of discrimination to those analogous to the enumerated grounds, the Court attempted to place an additional limit on the expansion of section 15(1).

Despite this apparent restraint, however, various features of the *Andrews* decision have far-reaching implications. First, by including systemic discrimination within the ambit of section 15 the Court significantly increased the number of statutes open to potential challenge as violating equality. Even universally applicable laws are bound to impact some groups differently than others; and if these laws adversely affect a group enumerated in section 15, this will probably constitute a *prima facie* denial of equality whether those laws pursue regressive or progressive policy objectives. There also is no guarantee that courts will evaluate these policy objectives correctly when they determine whether such laws are reasonable limitations on equality.[85] Second, a majority of the Court rejected McIntyre's suggestion that the usual section 1 analysis be relaxed with respect to certain legislative distinctions. In practice, this means that Canadian equality rights jurisprudence is based on a single level of scrutiny that bears close resemblance to the U.S. Court's strict scrutiny standard. How this will affect the fate of various distinctions before the Canadian Court is an important question, since the strict scrutiny standard has often been described as " 'strict' in theory and fatal in practice."[86]

A final problem concerns the focus on discrete and insular minorities as the factor determining whether unenumerated classifications should be added to section 15. The difficulty lies not so much with discreteness as with insularity: given universal suffrage and constitutional protection for political activity, there are few groups who are absolutely incapable of defending or advancing their interests in the political process. Moreover, even those groups with the least political resources (e.g., refugees) have advocates who *can* advance their interests. In the final analysis, discrimination on unenumerated grounds may eventually come to mean any failure by an identifiable group to achieve its policy objectives through the political process. In that case, equality rights litigation may no longer be a means of vindicating a right to "equal concern and respect," but simply an alternative method for advocating interests that, for one reason or another, have failed to prevail in the political process.

The Court has had two major opportunities to elaborate the meaning of its judgment in *Andrews*. The first came three months after *Andrews* in *R. v. Turpin* (1989), which concerned the constitutionality of several provisions of the Criminal Code that made jury trials mandatory in murder cases.[87] The equality rights question involved section 430 of the Criminal Code, which, until its amendment in 1985, contained a special exemption from the general jury trial requirement that allowed persons accused of murder in Alberta to elect trial by judge alone. Turpin was charged with murder in Ontario, and she challenged the proceedings against her on the grounds that this section of the Criminal Code violated her equality rights by denying her a procedural option available to those tried for murder in Alberta. Writing for a unanimous Court, Justice Wilson had little difficulty determining that this procedural distinction between Alberta and the other provinces violated the Charter's guarantee of equality before the law.[88] The key question, therefore, was whether this particular denial of equality resulted in discrimination against those whom it affected.

In answering this question, Wilson relied on Justice McIntyre's judgment in *Andrews* that discrimination exists when differential treatment imposes disadvantages on individuals because of personal characteristics that place them within a discrete and insular minority. In Wilson's view, this could best be determined by such "indicia of discrimination" as "stereotyping, historical disadvantage or vulnerability to political and social prejudice." Following McIntyre, Wilson declared that this approach best advanced the principal purpose of section 15 "in remedying or preventing discrimination against groups suffering social, political and legal disadvantage in our society."[89] Applying these standards to the case at hand, Wilson denied the claim that "accused of murder outside Alberta" constitutes a personal characteristic that defines a discrete and insular minority. Moreover, she also rejected the proposition that section 15 embodies the "fundamental principle" that the criminal law apply equally throughout Canada. Indeed, she rejected the very idea that section 15 states any absolute, fundamental principles. Instead, she argued that the vindication of equality requires a pragmatic case-by-case analysis to determine whether impugned legislation violates any of the four equality rights in a way that is either purposefully discriminatory or creates a discriminatory effect.

The Court finally faced its first claims of discrimination on one of the enumerated grounds in several cases involving mandatory retirement, of which *McKinney v. University of Guelph* (1990) is the most comprehensive and important.[90] These age discrimination cases raised several constitutional questions, including the Charter's applicability to universities and similar institutions, the constitutionality of the mandatory retirement provisions contained in the employment contracts of these institutions, and the constitutionality of provisions in some human rights legislation that limit the protection available against age discrimination. The complexity of these questions was clearly evident in *McKinney,* which produced five separate reasons for judgment by the seven justices who heard the appeal. Although the Court ruled by a five-to-two margin that the Charter does not apply to universities, six justices agreed that the mandatory retirement policies would have violated section 15(1) had the Charter in fact applied (Justice L'Heureux-Dubé decided it was unnecessary to resolve this question). All but Justice Wilson, however, considered this violation justifiable under section 1 of the Charter. Similarly, while the Court unanimously held that the limitations imposed on the prohibition against age discrimination in Ontario's Human Rights Code infringed the equality guarantees of section 15(1), only Justices Wilson and L'Heureux-Dubé found this to be unjustified under section 1. The end result was that the Court upheld the constitutionality of provincial policies that permit the inclusion of mandatory retirement provisions in private employment contracts.

Sorting through the various judgments in *McKinney* is a daunting task, but it is one that can be simplified somewhat by concentrating on the plurality judgment written by Justice La Forest and Justice Wilson's dissenting judgment. Significantly, neither of these judgments disagreed in principle about the correct answers to the substantive questions concerning the interpretation of section 15(1). Both La Forest and Wilson held that the discriminatory laws prohibited by section 15 include contractual obligations entered into by governments; both understood *Andrews* as rejecting the "similarly-situated test" as the benchmark for determining discrimination; and both agreed that, even if "'administrative, institutional and socio-economic' considerations" are the principal reason for mandatory retirement provisions, such provisions would still constitute adverse impact discrimination.[91] Similarly, neither La Forest nor Wilson encountered any difficulty in finding that section 9(a) of Ontario's Human Rights Code contravened section 15(1) because its protection against age discrimination in employment extended only to persons between the ages of eighteen and sixty-five.[92] Consistent with the Ontario Court of Appeal's decision in *Blainey,* the Supreme Court unanimously held that such qualifications to the protections afforded by human rights legislation constitute a *prima facie* denial of section 15(1) guarantees. Where La Forest and Wilson disagreed was in their analysis of the Charter's applicability to universities and of the section 1 issues raised by mandatory retirement provisions.

The debate between La Forest and Wilson about the Charter's applicability to universities and similar institutions represents one of the most interesting exchanges in the early history of Charter jurisprudence, since it involved questions about the nature of government, the state, and constitutionalism in Canada. As in *Dolphin Delivery,* these questions revolved around the proper interpretation of section 32 of the Charter, which specifies that it applies, at the very least,

to the legislative and executive organs of the federal and provincial governments. With the Charter's entrenchment, two dominant interpretive approaches
to this section emerged. One approach, which Justice McIntyre adopted in *Dolphin Delivery,* asserted that section 32 establishes a clearly identifiable dividing
line between governmental (public) and non-governmental (private) action.
According to this approach, this line creates two distinct categories, with the
Charter applying only to conventionally defined government activity. In contrast to this, the second approach treats government activity as a more fluid concept, flexible enough to encompass activities that might be considered private
according to more traditional analyses. From this perspective, determining
whether the Charter applies to the decisions or actions of any particular institution requires a close examination of its relationship to government.

In considering the Charter's applicability to the decisions and conduct of
universities, Justice La Forest opted for an interpretation of section 32 that
recognized a relatively impermeable dividing line between governmental and
non-governmental action. In his view, the decision not to include express protection against private discrimination in the Charter was a conscious choice by its
drafters, reflecting their conclusion that government posed the *least constrained*
threat to individual rights in 1982. La Forest conceded that private institutions
and activities, especially private concentrations of economic power, also
threaten individual freedom, but he argued that these threats are susceptible to
regulation. In relative terms, therefore, government itself posed the principal
threat to individual rights and liberties, which could only be countered by a
constitutionally entrenched declaration of rights.[93]

Critics of *Dolphin Delivery* had argued that this theory of government represented an inaccurate depiction of Canadian social and political reality, as well as
an unnecessarily limited vision of judicial review under the Charter. La Forest
responded to these critics with both normative and institutional arguments for
his proposition that Charter review should be restricted to public action. His normative response stressed the importance of maintaining an "area of freedom
within which individuals can act." In La Forest's judgment, subjecting private
conduct to the stringent requirements of the Charter could destroy the very realm
of individual freedom the Charter exists to protect. La Forest supplemented this
argument with the observation that Charter review of private conduct would also
impose an insurmountable institutional burden on the judicial process. In his
view, specialized agencies like human rights commissions are better suited to
regulating private infringements of basic rights and liberties than are courts.[94]

While La Forest's analysis of these issues illuminated his view of the proper
interpretive approach to section 32, it did not automatically determine whether
universities and similar institutions belong in the governmental or non-governmental category. Universities, in particular, occupy an ambiguous position. On
the one hand, they exist by virtue of statutory authority, receive most of their
funds from general government revenues, and provide an important public
good. On the other hand, as Justice La Forest emphasized, their autonomy is
highly valued, and several safeguards exist to ensure that public universities do

not become direct instruments of specific government policies.[95] La Forest found these latter characteristics sufficiently compelling to conclude that universities do not form any part of the traditional administrative apparatus of the state. This meant that universities were not among the institutions contemplated in section 32 of the Charter, despite the incontrovertible fact that they are statutory bodies that perform a public service and contribute to an important public purpose.

Justice Wilson rejected La Forest's analysis on the grounds that it reflected an outmoded concept of "constitutionalism" according to which governments are a necessary evil whose interference with private social and economic ordering represents the greatest threat to individual freedom. According to Wilson, while this "minimal state" theory of government was the driving force behind the development of constitutionalism in the United States, its already weak historical roots in Canada had been entirely eroded by political developments.[96] Surveying Canadian political history, Wilson concluded that government regulation and intervention have been a common feature of the Canadian political landscape, despite its changing nature and the obvious importance of private economic and social arrangements.[97] Indeed, this historical survey led Wilson to assert that, in contrast to the U.S. Bill of Rights, the Charter came into existence primarily to assist the Canadian state in eradicating the threat to human rights represented by "the accumulation of social, political and legal power in private entities." In Wilson's judgment, the "constitutionalism" represented by the Charter did not erect barriers to government action. Instead, it provided a blueprint of a "Canadian conception of a just society," the implementation of which is an important judicial task. In her view, Justice La Forest's version of "constitutionalism" was insufficient precisely because it interfered with this task by narrowing the scope of Charter review.[98]

Wilson reconciled this understanding of the Charter's "constitutionalism" with the clear language of section 32 by opting for a broad interpretation of "government," which she considered to be consistent with the prevailing purposive approach to Charter interpretation in general. The overarching purpose of the Charter's constraints on government action, Wilson argued, is the protection of individual dignity and autonomy. Rather than protect these values by carving out a private sphere of activity into which governments may not reach, she continued, the Charter established a set of constitutional norms that must be respected "when structuring important aspects of citizens' lives." To achieve its basic purpose, the Charter's norms must reach as far as possible: narrowing the definition of government action would limit the Charter's impact and diminish the level of protection it provides.[99] To avoid this result, Wilson proposed three flexible criteria for determining whether an institution's activities constitute government action. These included the level of direct or indirect government control over the institution, the type of functions performed by the institution, and the relationship between the institution's functions and the pursuit of government policy objectives. Wilson enhanced the flexibility of these criteria even further by stressing that "government is a constantly evolving organism" that may pursue its objectives through a variety of institutions.[100] Consequently, the Court could not categorically exclude any institution's activities from possible Charter review.

Although the positions articulated in this debate by La Forest and Wilson represent different visions of government and the role of the Court, both reject one important aspect of traditional liberal constitutionalism. In the traditional liberal view of society, one function of written constitutions is to define a sphere of private activity into which governments may not intrude without compelling reasons. Within this concept of constitutionalism, courts perform the important task of policing the boundary between the public and private spheres. In their own way, both La Forest and Wilson recognized that the modern Canadian state no longer fits this traditional view, since the permissible scope of government regulation of private activity has expanded to the point where the line between the public and private spheres is almost non-existent. La Forest and Wilson disagreed, however, in the conclusions they drew from this observation about the scope of judicial power. In La Forest's view, judicial oversight of private activity is less necessary because governments now possess legitimate power to regulate most private activity for socially desirable purposes. Indeed, La Forest took direct issue with Wilson's characterization of his position on the grounds that a narrow view of constitutionalism would require a broad understanding of government in order to ensure proper judicial enforcement of the public/private boundary.[101] According to Wilson, however, the effective expansion of the public sphere means that governments now influence the structuring of individuals' lives in numerous ways that traditional liberal constitutionalism did not contemplate, making judicial enforcement of the constitutional norms of individual dignity and autonomy an even more crucial task.

Consistent with her rejection of the political questions doctrine in *Operation Dismantle,* Wilson's position in *McKinney* contemplates far fewer constraints on the Court's power to promote substantive equality in a wide variety of social and political arrangements than does La Forest's position. In practical terms, however, the difference between their positions is not too significant. As the Court's unanimous analysis of section 9(a) of the Ontario Human Rights Code illustrates, the Charter has come to impose a duty on governments to pursue substantive equality aggressively; and failure to regulate private conduct in a manner sufficient to achieve this goal is suspect under section 15(1).

The principal lesson of the Supreme Court's decisions in *Andrews, Turpin,* and *McKinney* is that judicial review under section 15 should follow a three-step process. The first step is to determine whether impugned legislation, regulations, or official conduct involves classifications, differential treatment, or adverse impact on an identifiable group. The second step is to determine whether the classification, treatment, or adverse impact is "discriminatory." Making this determination forces courts to ask whether the impugned action imposes a disadvantage (intentional or not) on individuals who belong either to one of the protected groups listed in section 15 or to another group that constitutes a discrete and insular minority. In all likelihood, this means that action challenged on the basis of adverse impact will almost by definition be discriminatory, since the fact that a group suffers such an impact indicates that it is discrete and insular. Finally, if the first two steps indicate a violation of section 15, courts must then subject the violation to a section 1 analysis to determine whether it is reasonable and demonstrably justifiable in a free and democratic society. The most obvious implication of this process is that government action that explicitly targets any of the enumerated groups for discriminatory treatment will simply not survive constitutional scrutiny, which is as it should be. In the current political environment, however, such action will be rare to the point of being non-existent. Indeed, current legislative trends go in precisely the opposite direction; and if a political consensus ever emerged to reverse the modern concern for equality on which public support for judicial enforcement of constitutional guarantees of equality rests, it will be evidence of a deep political crisis. This suggests that the Supreme Court will most often be placed in the position of evaluating the unintended policy impact of government decisions on the relative status of a wide variety of groups claiming to be discrete and insular minorities, or the policy rationale for government action that permits – or fails to prohibit – discrimination by private institutions. As a result, equality rights jurisprudence will stretch considerably the Court's institutional capacity.

Conclusion

Both the textual structure and judicial interpretation of section 15 reflect the ascendancy of substantive equality as a fundamental principle of Canadian public policy.[102] As Tocqueville might have predicted, the quintessential liberal democratic balance between liberty and equality appears to have shifted permanently toward equality. At the level of constitutional jurisprudence, this is reflected in the assertion that such traditional liberties as freedom of association and expression have been superseded by the Charter's overarching commitment to equality. According to this view, only those associations and forms of expression with objectives that are consistent with the promotion of equality are entitled to Charter protection. These arguments have surfaced in cases involving the constitutionality of female-exclusive teachers' unions (*Re Tomen and Federation of Women Teachers' Associations of Ontario*) and the Criminal Code's hate literature provisions (*R. v. Keegstra*).[103] The Supreme Court has sent mixed signals about its receptivity to these claims. In *Keegstra,* both Chief Justice Dickson and Justice McLachlin rejected the paramountcy of section 15 in defining the substantive meaning of freedom of expression, yet both considered equality rights considerations relevant to their respective section 1 analyses of the hate literature provisions of the Criminal Code.[104]

Section 15 claims like those found in *Keegstra* and *Tomen* also reflect a gap between the rhetoric supporting the Charter's guarantee of equality and the political reality of section 15. The equality rights sections of the Charter are generally defended as a necessary mechanism for protecting vulnerable minorities from the malicious legislative acts of unconstrained majorities. The political purposes of section 15, however, are quite different. As both the affirmative action clause in section 15(2) and the desire to extend section 15(1) to cover systemic discrimination suggest, what the equality rights provisions actually do is grant constitutional status to the policy claims of various special interest groups. The advantages of this accomplishment to these groups are obvious. Strategically, it allows them to assert that governments are violating the constitution whenever they fail to accede to the groups' claims. Tactically, section 15 allows these groups to convert their policy claims into judicially enforceable constitutional rights through litigation. It is thus possible for these groups to avoid forming political coalitions that might force them to adjust their claims. The danger in this is that the necessity of coalition-building exerts a moderating influence on political conflict that is lost when competing policy claims clash in the zero-sum arena of constitutional litigation.

Perhaps most importantly, the Court's early approach to equality rights falls squarely within the realm of results-oriented jurisprudence. This is evident in the Court's assertion that section 15 is a remedial provision the implementation of which must be guided by a concept of substantive equality according to which social policy is judged by its contribution to individual autonomy and dignity. This approach encourages a theory of judicial review under section 15 in which the correction of government policies that hinder the achievement of substantive equality becomes the primary judicial task. If judges are to engage in social engineering of this type, it is absolutely crucial that they possess the information and technical tools necessary to weigh the complex variables in the substantive equality equation. That courts possess this capacity is highly questionable, however. The next chapter explores some of the structural impediments to effective judicial policy-making.

PART 3

Public Policy and the Charter

CHAPTER 6

Judicial Policy-making and the Constitutional Jurisprudence of Reasonable Limits and Appropriate Remedies

One of the important themes of this book is that the Supreme Court's policy-making role has been significantly enhanced since the advent of the Charter. Here I elaborate on this subject. It would be wrong to suggest, however, that judicial policy-making is an entirely new subject of discussion in Canadian constitutional jurisprudence or scholarship. In particular, federalism disputes concerning the distribution of legislative power to regulate the economy have also focused attention on the Court's evaluation of competing policy considerations, as well as on the policy impact of its decisions. For the most part, analysis of the Court's allocation of regulatory power between the federal and provincial governments has suggested that policy criteria have been largely absent from the decision-making process. To be more precise, critics have argued that the Court's jurisprudence in this area has suffered from two related weaknesses. First, it has been unduly driven by abstract conceptual distinctions rather than by functional considerations concerning the relative capacity of each level of government to perform the regulatory activity; second, it has failed to consider adequately the relative policy costs and benefits of national and provincial regulation.[1] Critics have thus argued for greater judicial sensitivity to policy analysis in federalism cases.

It is significant, therefore, that the Court has been more willing to infuse its decision-making process with policy considerations under the influence of the Charter. One reason for this change is the structure of the Charter itself. In the majority of Charter cases, the Court performs its most important task not in defining the substantive meaning of rights and freedoms, nor in measuring government action against those definitions, but in applying the section 1 test of reasonable limits. In particular, the most contentious issue within the Court in most Charter cases is whether the government in question has selected the least restrictive means of achieving its policy objectives. The Court can only resolve this question by taking into account important policy considerations.

A second reason for enhanced judicial policy-making under the Charter is that it contains a remedial alternative whose potential policy consequences are even greater than the provisions for judicial nullification of legislation found in section 52(1) of the Constitution Act, 1982 and exclusion of evidence from criminal proceedings found in section 24(2) of the Charter. Section 24(1) of the Charter, which authorizes "courts of competent jurisdiction" to redress Charter infringements by crafting remedies they consider "appropriate and just in the circumstances," is important from a policy perspective because it provides courts with the opportunity to shape and administer social policy directly through positive and prospective remedies. In particular, the broad remedial authority granted to lower courts under section 24(1) inevitably enhances their responsibility not only for reviewing the constitutionality of public policies, but also for designing and administering more "appropriate and just" policies.

Sections 1 and 24(1) force Canadian courts to adopt more explicitly what American commentators have labeled the public law litigation model. Unlike litigation concerning private disputes about private rights – in which lawsuits are bi-polar and self-contained, rights and remedies are interdependent, and the process is party-initiated and party-controlled – public law litigation resolves disputes about the operation of public policies through a process characterized by an amorphous party structure, by its dependence on legislative rather than adjudicative facts, and by its formulation of remedies the aim of which is to shape future behaviour rather than to compensate for past wrongs.[2] I use the phrase "adopt more explicitly" because the constitutional disputes concerning the division of powers with which students of Canadian courts are familiar come very close to this model as they usually involve a more amorphous party structure, and rely more heavily on legislative facts, than does private litigation. The difference between Charter litigation and federalism cases in this respect is largely one of degree. The principal substantive difference is that litigants in federalism cases seldom seek prospective remedial decrees but simply declarations concerning the constitutionality of statutes.

The question raised by the public law litigation model is whether the traditional information-gathering and -processing techniques of adjudication are compatible with the empirical demands of such cases. Some commentators argue that these traditional "attributes of adjudication" constitute a permanent barrier to effective judicial policy-making; others argue that the judicial process can be restructured to facilitate normative and political acceptability, technical competence, effective information-processing, and better representation of the interests affected by public law litigation.[3] The purpose of this chapter and the next is to examine these competing perspectives.

The Constitutional Jurisprudence of Reasonable Limits

Section 1 and Judicial Balancing

Although Chapter Two briefly discussed the general contours and interpretation of the declaration in section 1 that the Charter "guarantees the rights and freedoms set out in it subject only to such reasonable limits prescribed by law as can be demonstrably justified in a free and democratic society," it is necessary for the purposes of this chapter to expand on that discussion. Section 1 contains four distinct elements with separate meanings that affect the interpretation of the section as a whole: (1) "reasonable limits"; (2) "prescribed by law"; (3) "demonstrably justified"; and (4) "free and democratic society."[4] Two of these elements – "prescribed by law" and "demonstrably justified" – have raised relatively fewer interpretive questions than the others. The Supreme Court has interpreted "prescribed by law" to mean that any limitation of Charter rights must be expressly contained in legislation, regulations, or (under certain circumstances) court orders. Consequently, actions by government officials (e.g., law enforcement officers) that infringe Charter rights are not salvageable under section 1 unless those actions are expressly authorized by a law or regulation. The Court has defined "demonstrably justified" to mean that governments bear the burden of proving that the Charter infringements they seek to uphold are justifiable. The standard of proof that governments must meet in this instance is the civil one of "preponderance of probability."

The contrast between the Court's relatively narrow definition of "law" in section 1 and its more expansive definition of the same word in section 52 of the Constitution Act, 1982 deserves special mention. In interpreting section 52 – which provides that "the Constitution of Canada is the supreme law of Canada, and any law that is inconsistent with the provisions of the Constitution is, to the extent of the inconsistency, of no force or effect" – the Court has read "law" as synonymous with "state power" broadly understood.[5] As a result, the Court has given the Charter its broadest possible application to matters in the public realm. By contrast, in adopting a narrower meaning of "law" in the context of section 1, the Court has restricted the range of state power whose exercise may be justified under this provision. This difference suggests that section 1 does not actually control judicial review but simply changes the focus and method of the inquiry.

The meaning of a third element of section 1 – "free and democratic society" – has been somewhat more difficult to define. At one level, this term has been interpreted to mean that legislation limiting Charter rights should be compared to similar measures operating in other free and democratic societies. At a more general level, Chief Justice Dickson suggested in 1986 that this term means that Charter limitations should be measured against the "values and principles essential to a free and democratic society," which include "respect for the inherent dignity of the human person, commitment to social justice and equality, accommodation of a wide variety of beliefs, respect for cultural and group identity, and faith in social and political institutions which enhance the participation of individuals and groups in society."[6] Overall, however, neither concrete comparisons between Canada and similar regimes nor the application of abstract democratic principles have been singularly determinative factors in resolving section 1 issues. At most, they have provided a framework for the Court's analysis.

The Court has focused most of its attention on the term "reasonable limits," which it began to define in *A.-G. Quebec v. Association of Quebec Protestant School Boards* (1984).[7] At issue was the constitutionality of the "Quebec Clause" in the province's *Charte de la langue française* (Bill 101), which limited access to English-language education in Quebec to the children of Anglophone parents who had received their own education in English in the province. By channeling new immigrants into the French-language education system and by discouraging English-speaking Canadians from moving into the province, these provisions formed an integral part of the Parti Québécois strategy to control the expansion of the province's English-speaking minority.[8] However, the "Quebec Clause" conflicted directly with section 23(1)(b) of the Charter, which guarantees that all French- and English-speaking Canadians have the right to educate their children in their mother tongue in any province, regardless of that language's status in the province. The conflict between this so-called "Canada Clause" and the "Quebec Clause" was not accidental: section 23(1)(b) had been included in the Charter precisely to override these provisions of Bill 101.

The Quebec government could thus do nothing but concede that its legislation infringed the rights guaranteed by section 23(1)(b) and then attempt to defend that infringement under section 1. The Supreme Court refused to entertain Quebec's section 1 arguments, however. It found instead that the "Quebec Clause" constituted a total abrogation, rather than a mere limitation, of the Charter rights in question. To clarify this distinction between the absolute denial and mere limitation of rights, the Court offered the example of a statute that purported to "impose the beliefs of a state religion" on all Canadians. Legislation of this character, according to the Court, would constitute a complete abrogation of the fundamental right to freedom of religion and would be declared invalid without considering section 1.[9]

The *Protestant School Boards* case represents the only occasion, however, on which the Court has invoked the abrogation/limitation distinction to resolve a Charter dispute. This should not really be surprising, since legislation that completely abrogates fundamental rights like religion will be virtually non-existent in properly functioning liberal democracies. As Rainer Knopff has argued, broad political acceptability of legislation that actually does abrogate rights would signal the existence of a profound crisis in the fundamental principles of any liberal democratic regime.[10] In most instances, moreover, the question of abrogation versus limitation is largely one of perception. Take, for example, legislation that restricts the right to vote guaranteed by section 3 of the Charter to individuals over the age of eighteen. From one perspective, this requirement is merely a limitation on the general right to vote; from the perspective of those below the age of eighteen, however, it represents an outright denial of their right

as citizens to vote. The precise point at which a limitation becomes an abrogation, in other words, is not entirely clear. As is the case with many modern rules
of interpretation, the abrogation/limitation distinction functions primarily as a
device through which courts may exercise significant discretion.

The Court provided its first definitive interpretation of reasonableness under
section 1 in *R. v. Oakes* (1986).[11] As Chapter Four discussed, the issue in *Oakes*
was whether a reverse onus provision in the Narcotic Control Act violated the
right to be presumed innocent. After finding that the provision in question constituted a *prima facie* violation of section 11(d) of the Charter, Chief Justice
Dickson considered whether the reverse onus provision could be justified under
section 1. Prior to *Oakes*, the Court had approached this question relatively
unsystematically, but now Dickson determined that a more precise test was necessary. According to Dickson, reasonableness should be determined through a
two-step process, with the first step focusing on the policy objectives of the
Charter limitation and the second on the means by which that objective is pursued. Under the *Oakes* test, limiting a Charter right may be justified only if the
limit is proportionately related to legislative objectives that the Court accepts as
"pressing and substantial" in a free and democratic society. Proportionality is
measured by whether the limitation is rationally connected to the objective,
whether it is the least restrictive means of achieving the objective, and whether
the benefits of limiting the Charter right outweigh the burdens of the limitation.[12]

While it represents a novel development in Canadian constitutional jurisprudence, the *Oakes* test has important antecedents. Indeed, in 1980, Bernard
Siegan, a libertarian proponent of broad constitutional protection for economic
rights in the United States, outlined an almost identical test that could serve as
the core of a modern version of economic substantive due process.[13] More generally, although some commentators would disagree, the *Oakes* test belongs to a
category of judicial review known as "balancing."[14] As a method of interpretation, balancing seeks to resolve constitutional disputes through a process that
identifies, evaluates, and compares competing interests or rights. In some cases,
this process produces a single principle that can be applied categorically to allow
one interest or right to override another in all circumstances. Perhaps the best
example of this type of balancing is the U.S. Court's decision in *Roe v. Wade*
(1973), in which it weighed the competing claims of three distinct interests (the
liberty interest of women, the state's interest in their health, and the state's interest in the potential life of fetuses) at various stages of pregnancy to resolve the
constitutional dispute over abortion.[15] More often, however, the balancing process gives constitutional recognition to several interests, forcing judges to
weigh the competing claims of these interests on a case-by-case basis in the context of specific legislation or government action. For example, the U.S. Court
weighs competing interests to determine whether various forms of speech are
protected by the First Amendment.

The *Oakes* test, which requires that courts weigh the collective right of the
majority to pursue its conception of the general welfare against claims for the

protection of individual rights, contains elements of both types of balancing.[16] Consistent with the categorical approach, the Court has held that considerations of administrative efficiency and cost carry no constitutional weight in the balancing of collective and individual interests.[17] In addition, the Court has held that greater constitutional weight should be given to the interests of particularly vulnerable groups like non-unionized workers and children.[18] For the most part, however, the Court has granted equal weight to individual and collective claims. It has acknowledged the importance of individual rights by defining most of the Charter's substantive provisions broadly; and it has recognized the importance of collective concerns by routinely accepting government claims that the reasons for limiting individual rights are pressing and substantial. The Court has instead focused its analysis on the "least-restrictive-means" component of the proportionality test, weighing the impact on individual rights of the actual means used to achieve important policy objectives against the probable impact of alternative measures on those same rights.

The least-restrictive-means analysis in which the Court generally engages is well illustrated by its decisions in *Ford v. A.-G. Quebec* (1988) and *A.-G. Quebec v. Irwin Toy* (1989).[19] In *Ford,* there was very little dispute about whether Quebec's language provisions conflicted with freedom of expression or whether those provisions aimed at a pressing and substantial government objective. The principal question was whether this objective could be achieved through less restrictive means than a complete prohibition on the use of languages other than French on commercial signs. The Court decided that this was possible and even offered Quebec a formula with which to implement the justices' conclusion: the province could order that French be predominant on commercial signs as long as the legislation permitted the presence of other languages in the same proportion as those languages existed in the population. In *Irwin Toy,* there was slightly more controversy about whether the impugned regulation of commercial advertising toward children violated freedom of expression, but the main issue again came down to the least-restrictive-means question. On this occasion, however, the Court accepted (in contrast to the Quebec Court of Appeal) Quebec's claim that the central element of the legislation – the age below which commercial advertising could not be aimed – was the least-restrictive means of achieving the province's policy objectives. Neither of these analyses, however, could be connected to any pre-existing legal principle.

The principal normative justification for *Oakes*-style balancing is not that legislatures absolutely fail to seek the least restrictive means of pursuing their policy objectives but that flaws in the democratic process affect the accuracy of the legislative calculus of reasonable limits. According to David Beatty, for whom the *Oakes* test provides the foundation for a separate theory of judicial review, strict judicial adherence to this "principle of alternative means" avoids the deepest problems of normative legitimacy by leaving substantive policy choices in the hands of democratically accountable decision-makers. At the same time, it enhances the "progressive quality of the substantive policies" that governments choose to enact by re-evaluating their calculus of reasonable limits.[20] In Beatty's view, judicial review of legislation under the least-restrictive-means element of the *Oakes* test should be virtually automatic. Indeed, Beatty comes very close to suggesting that such review should become part of the legislative process itself. In this respect, his proposal elevates the Supreme Court to a position resembling the Council of Revision contained in the Virginia delegation's submission to the U.S. Constitutional Convention of 1787. Under that plan, members of the executive and judiciary would jointly exercise broad powers of veto and revision over legislation.

The major objection to the Council of Revision plan was that judicial competence does not extend to judging "the policy of public measures," and Beatty's theory is subject to the same criticism.[21] Indeed, his confident assertion that the means by which policies are implemented can be separated easily from their objectives is extremely problematic. Take, for example, the abortion regulations struck down on procedural grounds in *Morgentaler, Smoling and Scott* (1988).[22] Section 251 of the Criminal Code embodied a complex legislative objective: to liberalize access to abortion in a controlled fashion, with responsibility for exercising that control conferred on local authorities in order to make the policy sensitive to the diversity of moral views toward abortion found in communities across Canada. In this instance, the procedural means of implementing the policy were closely connected to one of its important substantive objectives. By nullifying the procedural scheme of section 251, the Court in essence held that local diversity in the application of a national abortion policy is an illegitimate policy objective.[23] The important point is that, contrary to Beatty's argument, it is as difficult to sever means from ends as it is to separate procedure from substance.

An equally dramatic illustration of this point is the Court's judgment in *Seaboyer v. The Queen* (1991), in which it considered the constitutionality of Criminal Code provisions limiting a defendant's ability to introduce evidence concerning a complainant's previous sexual conduct in sexual assault trials.[24] Under common-law rules of evidence, questions about such conduct were admissible to show the complainant's propensity to consent, as well as to attack the complainant's credibility. Parliament's first attempt to alter these rules by legislation in 1976 proved unsatisfactory, and in 1982 it replaced these earlier provisions with those under scrutiny in *Seaboyer*. Writing for a seven-justice majority, Justice Beverly McLachlin declared that these provisions constituted a *prima facie* infringement of the right to a fair trial guaranteed by sections 7 and 11(d) of the Charter. She conceded, however, that Parliament had enacted the limitations to achieve a pressing and substantial objective and that the provisions were rationally connected to this objective. Nevertheless, she struck down the provisions on the grounds that they did not represent the least restrictive means of achieving Parliament's objective.

In McLachlin's view, *categorical* prohibitions against the use of certain types of evidence by the defence could not be justified. Instead, the least-restrictive-means test required that the decision to admit such evidence be left to judicial discretion on a case-by-case basis. However, as Justice L'Heureux-Dubé pointed out in her dissenting judgment, society's dissatisfaction with the exercise of judicial discretion in these cases had motivated Parliament to enact the impugned provisions. The perceived need to eliminate, or at least severely curtail, judicial discretion was precisely the reason that Parliament had adopted the rules governing the admissibility of sexual conduct evidence found in sections 276 and 277 of the Criminal Code. Justice McLachlin implicitly asserted in *Seaboyer* that Parliament could not, as a matter of policy, relieve courts of their traditional power to determine the relevance and reliability of evidence. Nowhere, perhaps, is the paradox of liberal constitutionalism more apparent than in this conclusion by the *Seaboyer* majority. According to McLachlin, once the concept of a "fair trial" becomes constitutionally entrenched, only judges are capable of determining, both generally and in specific cases, what constitutes fairness. In essence, the Court has effectively used the Charter to amend the Constitution Act, 1867 in a manner that removes Parliament's legislative power over criminal procedure that section 91(27) of the Act originally contained.

In any legislative scheme, both the substantive policy objective and the means selected to implement that objective are part of a single political compromise among competing interests. Whenever courts apply the *Oakes* test to legislation they cannot avoid passing judgment on the nature of that compromise as a whole. As we saw in Chapter Two, constitutional theory plays a crucial role in providing the normative justification for this judicial power to nullify or alter the political compromises made by electorally accountable decision-makers. In general, interpretivist theories consider it legitimate for courts to override political compromises only when the compromise is clearly inconsistent with either the constitution's express language or an interpretation of that language that is faithful to the intentions of its framers. By contrast, non-interpretivist theories consider this exercise of judicial power legitimate when the political compromise under consideration inhibits moral progress. Situated between these two sets of theories are the process-oriented approaches of John Hart Ely and Patrick Monahan, which consider it legitimate for judges to nullify political compromises when the process that produced them is substantially flawed.[25]

For reasons I discussed in Chapter Two, none of these theories can provide a completely satisfactory answer to the normative questions raised by the *Oakes* test. Even if these normative questions could be addressed adequately, however, there would still remain significant questions about the institutional capacity of courts to perform their self-imposed task under section 1. Judicial policy-making of the sort represented by the *Oakes* test forces courts to perform a role to which traditional adjudication is not well suited.[26] Policy-making is a bargaining process that relies on flexible and dynamic exchange to accommodate conflicting interests. Adjudication, by contrast, purports to resolve conflicts dispassionately through the authoritative application of rules derived from largely pre-existing principles.[27] Disputing parties have confidence in the outcome of the adjudicative process precisely because its decision-making techniques are designed to enhance its neutrality and reliability. These same techniques, however, limit the capacity of courts to analyse and resolve complex policy disputes.

The Oakes Test and the Attributes of Adjudication

Alexander Bickel was one of the first to note the conflict between the normative characteristics of adjudication and the empirical requirements of policy-making. In a book on American constitutional interpretation entitled *The Supreme Court and the Idea of Progress,* Bickel argued that the judicial process was not a good arena for deciding questions of policy because it

> is too principle-prone and principle bound – it has to be, there is no other justi-
> fication or explanation for the role it plays. It is also too remote from condi-
> tions, and deals, case by case, with too narrow a slice of reality. It is not acces-
> sible to all the varied interests that are in play in any decision of great conse-
> quence. It is, very properly, independent. It is passive. It has difficulty con-
> trolling the stages by which it approaches a problem. It rushes forward too
> fast, or it lags; its pace hardly ever seems just right. For all these reasons, it is,
> in a vast, complex, changeable society, a most unsuitable instrument for the
> formation of policy.[28]

According to Donald Horowitz, these characteristics of adjudication give the judicial process "its own devices for choosing problems, its own habits of analy-sis, its own criteria of the relevance of phenomena to issues, its own repertoire of solutions."[29] Adjudication, to be more precise, has certain distinctive attributes that affect the policy-making capacity of courts negatively.[30]

The most basic attribute of adjudication is that courts speak the language of rights.[31] Unlike legislatures, which are concerned with weighing the costs and benefits of different courses of action, the emphasis on rights and duties in adju-dication limits the alternatives available to courts and precludes an explicit con-cern with cost-benefit analysis: courts are supposed to provide remedies to vin-dicate violated rights, regardless of cost. As Lorraine Weinrib has argued, "constitutional rights . . . must receive a higher priority in the distribution of available government funds than policies or programmes that do not enjoy that status. A different preference for allocation of resources cannot justify encroachment on a right."[32]

Perhaps the best example of the consequences of judicial reluctance to make explicit cost-benefit calculations under section 1 is the Supreme Court's deci-sion with respect to refugee determination procedures in the *Singh* case. In this instance, the Court rejected a utilitarian approach to the legal rights protected by section 7 of the Charter and held that increased administrative efficiency and reduced cost do not satisfy the "pressing and substantial objectives" criterion of the *Oakes* test. The Court's decision to ignore these factors necessarily meant excluding certain relevant considerations from the analysis of these procedures. From a utilitarian perspective, the principal benefit of enhanced decision-mak-ing procedures where important rights are at stake, and where the consequences of mistakes are grave, is that these procedures enhance decision-making accu-racy. The adversarial process found in accusatorial systems of criminal justice, for example, is more reliable than the ancient practice of trial by ordeal in protecting the important right to liberty. However, when the Court defines legal rights in non-utilitarian terms, the justices avoid the need to consider complicated evidence about the accuracy of existing procedures and the marginal cost of increasing that accuracy. Nevertheless, this information is important, since the marginal reliability of an already highly accurate decision-making process can be increased only at a significant cost. New procedures, in other words, may provide very small gains in reliability while requiring tremendous implementation costs.

The social consequences of the Court's decision not to approach its analysis of refugee determination procedures from this policy-oriented approach are easily apparent to anyone reading the 1990 Auditor General's report, which includes a comprehensive review of the consequences of complying with the requirements set out in *Singh*.[33] According to this report, the number of refugee claims made from within Canada quadrupled from approximately 8,500 in 1985 to 35,000 in 1988, producing a backlog of 85,000 unprocessed claims by the end of 1988. In the Auditor General's view, the new "procedures did not provide effective means of dealing effectively and conclusively with claims that had no merit"; moreover, the "system was extremely prone to large-scale abuses." Finally, the audit found that the average direct cost of each claim under these procedures amounted to $2,600, for a total cost of $83 million in 1989-90 alone. Canadian taxpayers bore this cost without any evidence of greater accuracy in determining refugee status.

The Court's avoidance of important policy considerations in *Singh,* despite the presence of section 1, highlights the importance of a second attribute of adjudication. The judicial process is designed to ascertain *historical* or *adjudicative* facts rather than *social* or *legislative* facts. Adjudicative facts refer to the discrete events that occur between parties to a lawsuit, while legislative facts include information about the causal relationships and "recurrent patterns of behavior" on which policy decisions are based.[34] While the U.S. Supreme Court began to consider legislative facts in the early part of this century, the Canadian Court remained hostile to their use until the 1970s. Even after becoming more accepting of such evidence, however, the Court was still able simply to dismiss legislative facts as irrelevant in resolving the legal questions at issue in important cases. Indeed, although he pioneered the use of legislative facts in Canadian constitutional adjudication, Chief Justice Bora Laskin did precisely that in the *Anti-Inflation Reference* (1976) when he dismissed as irrelevant a technical submission by several economists that the law in question would have little impact on inflation. In his view,

the wisdom or expediency or likely success of a particular policy expressed in legislation is not subject to judicial review. Hence, it is not for the Court to say in this case that because the means adopted to realize a desirable end, i.e., the containment and reduction of inflation in Canada, may not be effectual, those means are beyond the legislative power of Parliament.[35]

Extensive reliance on legislative facts is absolutely required, however, by section 1 and the criteria established for its application in *Oakes*. Indeed, it is precisely the "expediency or likely success of a particular policy" that is reviewed under the proportionality element of the *Oakes* test. Consequently, the difficulties involved in communicating such facts through adjudication become more important. As Eleanor Wolf has argued, in trial courts these difficulties stem from the burden of communicating information in a forum that detracts from the information's comprehensiveness, quality, and integrity, that promotes unrealistic simplification, and that hinders the "logical order needed for a systematic consideration of findings on a specific topic."[36] The most important weakness of appellate court litigation is that it exaggerates the authoritativeness of information and encourages courts to treat hypothetical assertions as proven axioms.[37] Moreover, even when adequate information about social facts is available, judges find it difficult to evaluate and analyse that information.[38] Judicial reliance on legislative facts thus raises two related questions: do courts have good access to relevant information, and are they able to understand that information?

The Supreme Court recognized the difficulties faced by trial courts in this respect in *Operation Dismantle v. The Queen* (1985), where Chief Justice Dickson suggested that the answers to some questions are simply beyond the factfinding capacity of courts.[39] The Chief Justice argued that the claim of Operation Dismantle rested on a series of assumptions about events and their causes that could not be adequately tested by the information to which courts are accustomed. "In brief," Dickson wrote in his reasons for judgment, "it is simply not possible for a court, even with the best available evidence, to do more than speculate upon the likelihood of the Federal Cabinet's decision to test the cruise missile resulting in an increased threat of nuclear war."[40] Indeed, the appellants in *Operation Dismantle* did not submit a single exhibit or piece of evidence to support their statement of claim.

Despite recognizing how difficult it is for trial courts to acquire and analyse complicated legislative fact information, the Court has not shied away from the complex empirical demands that an analysis of such facts requires in its own Charter decisions. In *Morgentaler, Smoling and Scott,* for example, the Court relied extensively on the *Report of the Committee on the Operation of the Abortion Law* in determining whether the structure and decision-making criteria of section 251 of the Criminal Code violated the security of the person of women in a manner contrary to the principles of fundamental justice. The federal government commissioned this report, the Badgley Report, shortly after the Supreme Court's first *Morgentaler* decision in 1975. The government instructed the Committee "to conduct a study to determine whether the procedure provided in the Criminal Code for obtaining therapeutic abortions is operating equitably across Canada" and to "make findings on the operation of this law rather than recommendations on the underlying policy."[41] The Committee started its inquiry in November, 1975, and submitted its 474-page report in January, 1977. Among the Committee's several findings, the Court found two especially relevant to its evaluation of section 251 under section 7 of the Charter.

The first of these findings was that under the existing therapeutic abortion regulations there was an average interval of eight weeks between a woman's first medical consultation and the performance of an induced abortion. Since women waited on average about three weeks after the first indications of pregnancy before consulting a physician, therapeutic abortions were most often performed between the ninth and twelfth weeks of gestation.[42] What caught the Supreme Court's attention was the relationship between these delays and the complication rates of therapeutic abortions. According to data compiled in the Badgley Report, abortions performed between nine and twelve weeks of pregnancy were almost one and a half times more dangerous for women than those performed at less than nine weeks of gestation. This risk factor increased dramatically after the thirteenth week of pregnancy, with abortions performed between thirteen and sixteen weeks almost six times more dangerous than those performed at less than nine weeks.[43] In the view of the majority of the Court, therefore, the decision-making delays attributable to section 251 posed a real risk to the physical health of women seeking therapeutic abortions. This led the Court to find an infringement of security of the person.

The second important finding of the Badgley Report on which the Court relied concerned the Committee's investigation of the impact of provincial requirements and hospital practices on the distribution and availability of therapeutic abortions. The Committee found that 271 hospitals in Canada had established therapeutic abortion committees by 1976. This represented only one-fifth of all hospitals, and less than half of all the hospitals that met the basic provincial standards necessary for establishing a committee. As a result, according to the Report, 45 per cent of the Canadian population was not served by hospitals with therapeutic abortion committees. Moreover, access to "committee hospitals" varied among provinces and regions. In Newfoundland, for example, 77 per cent of the population was not served by committee hospitals; by contrast, only 35 per cent of the Ontario population did not have easy access to such hospitals. Similarly, the ratio of women between fifteen and forty-four years of age to committee hospitals in Quebec was four times higher than the national ratio.[44] Little wonder, then, that Chapter Six of the Badgley Report provided Chief Justice Dickson with his principal conclusion that "the procedure provided in the Criminal Code for obtaining therapeutic abortion is in practice illusory for many Canadian women."[45]

On the surface, the Badgley Report's findings, and the government's subsequent failure to respond directly to them, appear to provide unambiguous evidence of the desirability (and even necessity) of judicial action in the abortion field. On closer analysis, however, the picture is less clear. First, the Badgley Report did not include information about some relevant, though difficult to measure, facts, such as the number of women otherwise qualified for therapeutic abortions who failed to obtain them, or the number of women who obtained abortions contrary to the intentions of Parliament when it enacted the law. More relevantly, the Report made it clear from the outset that it was not the law itself that produced operational inequities and disparities in obtaining therapeutic abortions, but rather "the Canadian people, their health institutions and the medical profession."[46] Furthermore, the Report found significant improvement over the pre-1969 abortion regime in terms of both access and safety.[47] For example, the Report found that, with only two exceptions, the rate of legal, therapeutic abortions increased every year between 1970 and 1974 in every province and territory.[48] At the same time, the number of criminal charges and convictions for induced abortions decreased dramatically.[49] Despite its imperfections, section 251 created a safer and more liberal abortion regime than had previously existed in Canada.

The ambiguous nature of the Badgley Report's findings can be further illustrated by focusing on the situation in Quebec. By most measures, women in Quebec should have been worse off than women in other provinces. As indicated above, the ratio of women in their principal childbearing years to committee hospitals was much higher in Quebec than in other provinces. In addition, while Quebec women accounted for approximately 30 per cent of the Canadian female population between the ages of fifteen and forty-four years, the province had only 12 per cent of the nation's committee hospitals in 1976.[50] Nevertheless, women in Quebec enjoyed the shortest intervals between their initial medical consultation and the performance of an abortion. Almost 20 per cent of Quebec women had their operation within three weeks, and 65 per cent of women in the province had their abortions less than seven weeks into their pregnancies.[51] Quebec women, moreover, benefited from these shorter delays even before the government of Quebec decided not to enforce section 251 in the province. What the Quebec experience indicates is that the relationship between the distribution and availability of therapeutic abortion facilities and health-threatening delays was more complicated than the Supreme Court assumed on the basis of the Badgley Report. Indeed, what the Badgley Report as a whole indicates is that section 251 provided an historically superior, if not flawless, abortion regime whose imperfections were the result of factors that could not be easily overcome by simply nullifying the law as unconstitutional. Where section 251 obviously failed was in not providing as liberal an abortion regime as pro-choice activists demanded.

Morgentaler, Smoling and Scott illustrates one difficulty with the analysis of legislative facts in the judicial setting: the adjudicative arena inhibits the comprehensiveness necessary to reach adequate conclusions based on this evidence. A second difficulty is evident in the Supreme Court's 1990 *Askov* decision, which concerned unreasonable trial delays.[52] In a series of earlier decisions on this issue, a majority of the Court had consistently recognized that trial delays caused by limited institutional resources could be excused under certain circumstances.[53] In *Askov,* the appellants sought to show that the institutional delays in their case went far beyond anything the Court had allowed implicitly in earlier decisions. In order to support this assertion, they submitted an affidavit by Carl Baar, director of the Judicial Administration Programme at Brock University, which compared trial delays in several jurisdictions. The government of Ontario responded with an affidavit from its deputy attorney-general (Richard Chaloner), which contained information concerning the province's efforts to reduce court delays.

Professor Baar's affidavit consisted of three separate studies of court delays: two conducted in the context of preparing pre-Charter speedy trial legislation that proposed six-month time limits, and a third study conducted in 1987 of case dispositions in New Brunswick, six Ontario District Court jurisdictions, and two jurisdictions in British Columbia. In general, Baar's studies (which were also the subject of extensive discussion during oral argument) indicated that the Brampton District Court – from which *Askov* originated – had significantly longer institutional delays than comparable jurisdictions.[54] For example, the Brampton court took almost six times longer to process cases than courts in New Brunswick and four times longer than the court in London, Ontario. Moreover, even relative to the poor overall performance of the Brampton court, the delays in *Askov* were long. Indeed, according to counsel for the appellants, their trials were processed more slowly than 95 per cent of all cases in the district. These data thus offered significant support for the assertion that the trial delays attributable to institutional factors were intolerable in this district and case.

The data were much less revealing, however, about where the line should generally be drawn between justifiable and intolerable institutional delays, or about how these delays could be reduced. Indeed, counsel for Askov admitted in oral argument that it was impossible to "measure the point at which delay becomes intolerable by resorting to fixed standards." Counsel for Askov also conceded the Crown's point that expeditious case processing was not simply a function of available resources but of a combination of resources and good management.[55] From the perspective of Askov's counsel, the social science evidence contained in the Baar affidavit did not constitute a set of legislative facts that illuminated and explained the general problem of trial delay. Instead, the affidavit presented an important set of adjudicative facts that demonstrated the unreasonableness of the delay in their clients' cases. To the Supreme Court majority led by Justice Cory, however, the Baar affidavit supported the general conclusion that inadequate resources contributed significantly to institutional delays and that these delays offended the Charter when they exceeded a particular fixed standard of six to eight months.[56] The Court thus reached broad policy conclusions on the basis of social science evidence prepared and submitted by the appellants to support their own narrow adjudicative argument.

Since judicial policy-making is hampered by missing or inadequately analysed information, one might expect courts to benefit from the fact that judicial policy-making is "characterized by predominantly moral reasoning and an incremental, reactive style of problem-solving."[57] To be more precise, in ordinary litigation, courts contribute to the continual evolution of legal-moral principles by applying those principles to resolve disputes on a case-by-case basis. This attribute of adjudication enhances the decision-making capacity of courts in ordinary litigation, since, by allowing decision-makers to implement small changes, measure their impact, and respond quickly to new information, incrementalism works best precisely where information is scarce. Consequently, incrementalism can reduce the costs of large-scale policy errors.

There are two features of *constitutional* litigation, however, that cast doubt on the appropriateness of judicial incrementalism in the constitutional realm. First, constitutional litigation often requires the development of completely new moral principles in order to render "all or nothing" decisions that cannot easily be changed. Incrementalism is much less effective in this context than other, more comprehensive decision-making strategies.[58] Second, as the cases examined throughout this book suggest, Charter decision-making requires as much balancing of interests as other types of decision-making. Prudential reasoning, in other words, is as important in constitutional litigation as moral reasoning might be in ordinary litigation. Judicial policy-making in constitutional cases is thus characterized by the application of moral and prudential reasoning to solve problems on a comprehensive basis. Courts are hampered in pursuing what really amounts to "commission" or "ministry" policy-making (to use Ronald Manzer's terms[59]) by their slow reaction to new information, by their tendency to adapt to new information by qualifying prior decisions rather than engaging in a fresh consideration of the issue, and by their treatment of policy issues in isolation.[60]

Judicial incrementalism faces these hurdles to a large degree because the ability of courts to respond to new information and change policy direction is further affected by a fourth characteristic of adjudication. Courts are generally passive institutions in that they have little control over the cases litigated before them, depending on others to frame issues and gather necessary information.[61] This attribute is particularly relevant when litigation is used as a tool of social reform by interest groups.[62] The passivity of courts means that the constraints and incentives these groups face in designing litigation strategies are important factors in determining the effectiveness of judicial policy-making. Interest groups must ensure centralized control over litigation and devise strategies that take advantage of favourable venues and do not require unusual departures from established legal doctrine to reach the desired result.[63] The suitability of these strategies for the accurate communication of *policy*-relevant information is questionable, however. Since one of the most important consequences of the Charter has been an increase in litigation activity by interest groups like the Women's Legal Education and Action Fund, the National Citizens' Coalition, and the Canadian Civil Liberties Association, the factors determining the development of litigation strategies by these groups should become more important in Canadian constitutional scholarship.[64]

It is important, however, not to exaggerate the passivity of adjudication by failing to recognize that judicial control over court dockets allows judges to select cases on the basis of how important the issues implicated in them appear to be.[65] Indeed, some Canadian commentators have argued that courts are uniquely situated to review the substance of legislation because the cases tried before them reveal the direct effect of policies on individuals.[66] What this argument misses is that individual cases often do not represent general conditions. The Supreme Court faced this difficulty in its Sunday-closing decisions, where the facts of the specific appeals did not provide adequate information about the general impact of mandatory holiday regulations on various religious and ethnic groups.[67] Nor did the actual appeals provide any information about the impact of a different regime on strict Sunday observers, who would also constitute a minority despite their association with the majority religious group. Similarly, the facts in *Singh* were unrevealing about the overall performance of existing refugee determination procedures. Finally, although the Court in *Askov* received data concerning systemic trial delays in both the jurisdiction under immediate scrutiny and other jurisdictions, the Court made a number of questionable assumptions about the general policy consequences of its specific judgment in *Askov.* Just as conventional legal wisdom holds that hard cases often produce bad law, recent experience suggests that easy cases may result in bad policy.

The final attribute of adjudication that limits the policy-making capacity of courts is that it contains inadequate provisions for policy review. Courts tend to neglect *consequentialist* facts; that is, information relevant "to the impact of a decision on behavior."[68] This attribute is a function of adjudication's affinity for historical over social facts: the relative incapacity of courts to ascertain causal relationships and patterns of behavior limits their ability to predict the consequences of their decisions. Thus, courts are often forced to rely on questionable assumptions about how individuals and institutions will react to those decisions. The focus of adjudication on remedying past wrongs rather than on shaping future relationships provides little incentive for courts to test such assumptions systematically. The problem is not that judicial decisions have unintended consequences – so, too, do the decisions of legislatures and administrative agencies – but that the need to rely on litigants to initiate adjudication can make the process of discovering and responding to unintended consequences unusually cumbersome.[69]

The inability of courts to initiate policy review is especially important in view of the implementation difficulties that judicial policy-making faces. Both compliance (the degree to which a court's order is carried out) and impact (the degree to which the court's order alters behaviour) have been identified as weak elements of judicial policy-making.[70] Ironically, this weakness may stem from the very characteristics of adjudication that make it attractive to interest groups. Adjudication reduces the number of participants in decision-making, allowing courts to reach decisions on controversial issues more quickly and easily than legislatures. However, there is evidence that interest groups excluded at the adjudication phase of decision-making reappear later to block implementation.[71] Ultimately, poor compliance with and the weak impact of judicially formulated policies can be traced back to the judicial process's difficulty in gathering and processing the type of information necessary for policy-making. These difficulties hinder the communication of expected consequences to individuals and institutions affected by the decisions, leading to frustration and inhibiting compliance.[72]

The *Askov* decision again provides an excellent illustration of this point. The general principal articulated by Justice Cory for a majority of the Court in *Askov* was that trial courts must balance a complex set of factors when determining whether an accused's right to be tried within a reasonable time has been violated. These factors include the length of the delay, the specific reasons for the delay, whether the accused waived this right, and the degree of prejudice to the accused caused by the delay. Justice Cory further distinguished among three separate explanations for lengthy delays: (1) actions by the Crown; (2) delays caused by systemic or institutional factors; and (3) actions of the accused.[73] Comparing systemic delays in judicial districts in several provinces, Cory concluded that "a period of delay in a range of some six to eight months between committal and trial might be deemed to be the outside limit of what is reasonable."[74] Although Cory intended lower courts to apply this general balancing approach on a case-by-case basis rather than to follow the six-to-eight-month standard strictly, lower courts missed this message and began automatically to stay proceedings that exceeded the eight-month limit. In unprecedented public comments on the unanticipated consequences of *Askov,* Justice Cory expressed the Court's "shock" at the "rigidity of the interpretation" given to *Askov* by some lower courts. According to Cory, the justices were unaware of how extensive the impact of the decision would be.[75] Indeed, the Court found itself compelled to clarify in a subsequent decision that it only intended to articulate general guidelines in *Askov.*[76]

What might account for the initial miscommunication between the Supreme Court and lower trial courts? To some degree it reflects different perspectives toward the criminal justice process. The Supreme Court, which processes approximately 100 to 120 cases per year and is under no constitutional obligation to complete its deliberations expeditiously, enjoys the luxury of sufficient time in which to balance complex factors on a case-by-case basis. Criminal trial courts, to which *Askov* applies, face far different pressures. For example, between 1982 and 1989 Ontario criminal trial courts processed, on average, about 410 jury and non-jury trials *per week.*[77] Under these conditions, it is simply not feasible for them to engage in the case-by-case balancing of relevant factors called for by Justice Cory. Given their workloads and resource constraints, the rational decision for judges on these courts is to err on the side of caution and follow that aspect of Cory's judgment – the eight-month rule – with which it is easiest to comply. As a result, Justice Cory's concluding assertion that stays of proceedings "will be infrequently granted" as remedies for "unreasonable" delays proved to be a hollow one.[78]

The tension between traditional adjudication and Charter adjudication results from the fact that most of the questions put to the Supreme Court in Charter cases cannot be resolved through the authoritative application of pre-existing norms. As the *Oakes* test makes very clear, the Court must inevitably exercise political judgment in resolving its most important cases. The principal barrier to its performance of this task is that the attempt to solve complex and multi-faceted policy problems through decision-making techniques designed to resolve concrete private disputes strains the information-gathering, -processing, and -evaluating capacity of adjudication. To ease this strain, both litigants and courts tend to choose "easy" cases, to emphasize the familiar and highly visible procedural elements of those cases, and to avoid complex underlying issues. This increases the possibility of inadequate implementation and compliance, as well as the number of unintended consequences. Although legislatures and administrative agencies also face these problems, the limited capacity of courts for reviewing policy makes the judicial process more vulnerable to them.

Judicial Policy-making and Remedial Decree Litigation

Almost all of the cases discussed thus far in which the Supreme Court has applied the *Oakes* test have involved *proscriptive* judicial policy-making, in that the Court has indicated to Parliament and provincial legislatures what the Charter *prohibits* them from doing. Section 24(1), by contrast, creates the opportunity for *prescriptive* judicial policy-making by granting courts a broad power to dictate specific policy arrangements to governments. To be sure, the negative pronouncements of the Supreme Court in cases like *Singh* and *Morgentaler, Smoling and Scott* send important signals to legislators about the types of policies that will pass constitutional muster; nevertheless, section 24(1) supports much more positive judicial action. To be more technical, section 24(1) allows courts to shape public policy through remedial decrees issued in the form of mandatory injunctions. This means that courts can require governments to perform certain positive actions to remedy violations of Charter rights.

Remedial decree litigation has been a crucial element of constitutional adjudication in the United States for at least the past twenty-five years. Litigants have been successful in persuading U.S. federal courts to participate actively in shaping and administering policy in areas such as housing, social welfare, transportation, education, and the operation of complex institutions, including prisons and mental health facilities.[79] To cite two examples, consider the decisions by separate U.S. federal district courts in *Ruiz v. Estelle* (1980) and *Jenkins v. Missouri* (1987). In *Ruiz,* a U.S. district court in Texas ordered the Texas Department of Corrections (TDC) to remedy violations of inmates' constitutional rights by taking detailed actions designed "to reduce the inmate population at each prison, to increase the security and support staff, to furnish adequate medical and mental health care, and to bring all living and working environments into compliance with state health and safety standards." Among the court's specific orders were directives that the TDC divide its prisons into smaller "organizational entities" and refrain from locating new prisons far from large population centres.[80] In *Jenkins,* a federal court ordered the Kansas City school district to redress the effects of alleged past segregation by creating a magnet school to attract suburban children into the city and by making extensive capital improvements to existing schools. The combined cost of this remedial order was $460 million, and the court ensured that the resources would be available by ordering the district to raise its tax rates.[81] These two cases illustrate the extent to which courts can employ their remedial powers to exercise the powers of both the sword and the purse, contrary to the expectations of Alexander Hamilton in *The Federalist Papers.*

The Remedial Decree Litigation Model

Phillip J. Cooper has suggested that remedial decree litigation should be viewed as a process characterized by four key elements, which he describes as the trigger, liability, remedy, and post-decree phases of litigation.[82] Although these phases correspond to the chronological progression of ordinary lawsuits, Cooper argues that they are also analytically distinct categories whose attributes exert a unique influence on the ability of judges to resolve remedial decree cases successfully. Although the American and Canadian judicial processes differ in some important respects, they are similar enough to suggest that Cooper's model may prove useful in examining the issues raised by the broad remedial power granted to Canadian courts by section 24(1) of the Charter.

The trigger phase in Cooper's model includes both the general historical practices and specific triggering events that lead to the initiation of a constitutional rights case. These practices and events are the product of individual or group demands, local political forces, and conditions in the broader political system. According to Cooper, the importance of these factors to the trigger phase suggests that remedial decree litigation is as much reactive as it is the product of carefully planned reform strategies. During this phase of the process, one of the principal tasks facing litigants is to meet the threshold requirements necessary for continuing the lawsuit. At a minimum, this means gaining access to the courts. For parties directly involved in the dispute, the major hurdle is standing; for groups indirectly affected by the litigation, the major hurdle is to obtain intervener status. Although Canadian standing rules are among the most liberal in Western legal systems, it has been difficult until very recently for non-governmental parties to acquire intervener status.[83] This is an important factor in determining the outcome and effect of remedial decree cases, since the broad impact of these cases requires that as many interests as possible be represented in the proceedings.

As Cooper's model suggests, the fact that litigants must meet threshold requirements before proceeding from the trigger phase to the liability and remedy phases means that a significant degree of judicial choice is involved at the earliest stages of remedial decree litigation. Indeed, at the highest level of the judicial process courts have virtually complete control over their own dockets, which provides them with enough discretion to select the most appropriate cases for resolving complex policy issues. However, the pool of cases from which courts may choose often consists entirely of "outliers," in which the facts do not necessarily reflect general conditions. As suggested earlier in this chapter, the principal danger in this is that these cases may produce reforms "that prevent the worst case, but make things worse in most situations."[84]

The liability and remedy phases form the core components of remedial decree litigation. They may occur simultaneously or be the subject of separate proceedings. In addition, they may encompass certain elements of the trigger phase, such as determining whether litigants have met threshold requirements such as standing. The key aim of litigants at the liability phase is to persuade the court that there has been a violation of constitutional rights that merits a remedy. According to Cooper, several aspects of the liability phase affect the ultimate success of litigation.[85] Litigants must develop an adequate record to support the court's liability findings and subsequent remedial order, since successful litigation ultimately depends on a strong judgment with respect to liability issues. If a court equivocates in its liability findings, the subsequent remedy will be weak and may not survive scrutiny on appeal. These requirements impose considerable burdens on litigants in designing their litigation strategies. Indeed, poor litigation strategies may not only prevent interest groups from achieving their immediate policy goals but may also inflict serious damage on their long-term survivability. The peace groups belonging to the coalition responsible for *Operation Dismantle,* for example, were significantly hurt by their abortive court challenge to Canadian defence and foreign policy.

Once litigants have been successful in the liability phase, it becomes necessary to formulate a remedy. The remedial process often consists solely of negotiations between the parties to produce a remedy that is simply approved by the court. On other occasions, it is necessary for the court to impose a remedy following an adversary remedy hearing. Although lower federal court judges in the United States have significant discretion in crafting remedies, they are constrained to some degree by doctrinal limits imposed by the U.S. Supreme Court. For example, the U.S. Supreme Court has prohibited lower federal courts from ordering busing between suburban and inner-city school districts as a remedy for inner-city school segregation unless the suburban school districts have also engaged in legally mandated racial segregation of students.[86] Given the open-ended wording of section 24(1) of the Charter and the absence of Supreme Court decisions interpreting that provision, the extent to which Canadian lower court judges face similar constraints is unclear. An important question, therefore, is how creative Canadian litigants and judges are willing to be in suggesting and formulating "appropriate and just" remedies during the early years of Charter adjudication. If Canadian lower courts adopt the broadest American remedial alternatives prior to the Supreme Court's developing doctrinal limits on remedies, then the impact of section 24(1) will be even greater.

The remedy phase of remedial decree litigation also includes the appeals process. The principal element of this process is review of both the liability and remedy decisions rendered by lower courts. In some cases, appellate review of liability findings may occur while the lower court is still crafting its remedial decree. Under other circumstances, the implementation of remedies may be delayed while appellate review takes place. In still other cases, remedy implementation may proceed simultaneously with appellate review. Each of these scenarios introduces additional complexities into remedial decree litigation.

The post-decree phase of remedial decree litigation is concerned with the implementation, evaluation, and refinement of the initial remedy. This phase of the process is characterized by interaction between litigants and judges, with the degree of interaction determined by the nature of the initial remedy. Although courts may have access to several remedial alternatives, these remedies can only be imposed by coercive orders whose implementation depends on officials and institutions over which courts may exercise little direct control. According to Cooper, process-oriented remedies, in which the parties establish ongoing procedures for resolving their disputes, generally require less judicial supervision than do remedies specifying particular actions. However, when courts do order process remedies, and then limit their involvement in implementation and evaluation, additional litigation is often necessary to enforce the remedy. The final step in the post-decree phase, and in remedial decree litigation generally, is disengagement by courts from the dispute they were initially asked to resolve.

Remedial Decree Litigation Under the Charter

Remedial issues have been crucial in several Charter decisions. For example, in *Re Phillips and Lynch* (1986) the Nova Scotia Supreme Court found that a provision in the province's Family Benefits Act, which granted benefits to single mothers but not to single fathers, violated section 15(1) of the Charter in a way that could not be justified under either section 15(2) or section 1.[87] The court refused, however, "to assume the role of legislator" and use its powers under section 24(1) to amend the legislation by extending benefits to single fathers. Instead, the court relied on section 52(1) to nullify the impugned section, resulting in the temporary suspension of all relevant benefits under the Act.[88] The outcome in *Phillips* was one reason why Judge Strayer of the Federal Court chose to impose a more expansive remedy for a similar constitutional violation in the *Schacter* case discussed in the previous chapter. In Strayer's view, the "appropriate and just" remedy for the unconstitutional denial of benefits to certain groups of individuals is not to deprive those benefits to persons already receiving them but to entitle others to receive them as well.[89] The Federal Court of Appeal subsequently agreed with Strayer's decision that section 24(1) empowers "a court to extend benefits to groups aggrieved by an exclusion of benefits."[90]

The development of appropriate remedies has also been important in several language rights cases under section 23 of the Charter. While Canadian courts often refused to accept the broadest remedial claims of plaintiffs in early section 23 cases, many commentators argue that the remedial opportunities presented by language rights claims nevertheless constitute a revolutionary development in Canadian constitutional jurisprudence. This is because the language provisions require courts to enforce these rights through positive declarations concerning government obligations.[91] This became apparent in *Marchand v. Simcoe Board of Education* (1986), in which the Ontario High Court of Justice found that the plaintiffs had been denied their section 23 right to a full and complete publicly funded education in French. To remedy this rights violation, the court issued a mandatory injunction against the Board of Education ordering it to provide the facilities and funding necessary to make the level of education in its French secondary school equal to that in the English schools. In addition to this general order, the court also issued specific instructions concerning the industrial arts and shop programs at the French school.[92] Similarly, in *Lavoie v. Nova Scotia* (1988), the Nova Scotia Supreme Court made several positive orders in the context of section 23, including that the province design a program of French-language instruction, that the school board "designate a suitable education facility reasonably accessible to the students eligible for minority-language instruction," and that the board conduct a registration to determine the number of students who would enrol in the facility.[93]

The Supreme Court contributed significantly to these developments with its decision in *Mahé v. Alberta* (1990).[94] At issue in *Mahé* was whether the educational system in Edmonton, and the legislation under which it operated, satisfied the requirements of section 23. In particular, the Court had to determine the degree of "management and control" over instructional matters and educational facilities to which minority-language parents are entitled under section 23. In considering this issue, Chief Justice Dickson concluded for a unanimous Court that section 23 "confers upon a group a right which places positive obligations on government to alter or develop major institutional structures." Although Dickson conceded that these language rights thus require careful interpretation, he stressed that courts have an obligation to "breathe life" into section 23 and to implement "the possibly novel remedies needed to achieve that purpose."[95]

The extensive judicial involvement necessary for the remedial design of new institutional structures became apparent in Dickson's interpretation of the specific terms of section 23. According to the Chief Justice, the rights "where numbers warrant" to "minority language instruction" and to "minority language educational facilities" do not constitute two distinct rights differentiated by a specific numerical threshold. Instead, section 23 articulates a single right to unspecified minority-language educational services along a "sliding scale" from mere instruction in the minority language to management and control of distinct facilities through separate boards of education with their own taxation powers.[96] In so defining the rights contained in section 23, Chief Justice Dickson refused to formulate a single rule of general application to govern the implementation of section 23 rights. In his view, section 23 "simply mandates that governments do whatever is practical in the situation to preserve and promote minority language education."[97] Under his interpretation of section 23, however, no government can know with certainty what section 23 demands of it until a court "breathes life" into this provision. Taken to its logical conclusion, the analysis in *Mahé* implies a significant degree of judicial management of educational policy through remedial decrees.

The Court provided another glimpse into the potential remedial impact of the Charter in its June, 1991, decision on the constitutionality of Saskatchewan's electoral boundaries under section 3 of the Charter.[98] At issue was whether large discrepancies in the population size of rural and urban electoral ridings infringes the right to vote by diluting the value of urban votes relative to rural votes. Although the Court rejected the "one-person/one-vote" standard advanced in this challenge and thus upheld the province's electoral boundaries plan, it defined the right to vote broadly as meaning the right to "effective representation." By transforming the relatively straightforward word "vote" into the indeterminate phrase "effective representation," the Court laid the groundwork for a powerful and continuing judicial role in supervising the electoral system. The open-ended nature of this newly declared collective right to "effective representation" involves the Court in the difficult task of establishing judicially manageable standards for implementing qualitatively defined effective representation. This task also imposes significant remedial burdens, since it is not inconceivable that the Court might have to order that a certain number of seats in a legislature be reserved for groups whose historical exclusion from the political process have made them "discrete and insular minorities."

The precise nature of remedial decree litigation is best illustrated, however, by closely examining one of the most interesting cases of this type to make it through the judicial process: *Re Lavigne and Ontario Public Service Employees Union,* which broke new ground in the willingness of Canadian courts to explore their remedial powers under section 24(1).[99] The legal issues in *Lavigne,* which required four separate proceedings at three levels of the judicial process to resolve, concerned the formulation of a novel remedy to vindicate a broad interpretation of freedom of association. The story behind this case begins in 1974, when Mervyn Lavigne began teaching at the Haileybury School of Mines in Ontario. As a result of his appointment, Lavigne came within the jurisdiction of a bargaining unit represented by Local 653 of the Ontario Public Service Employees Union (OPSEU). Although Ontario's Colleges Collective Bargaining Act prohibited OPSEU from compelling individual members of the bargaining unit to join the union, the Act did require that non-members pay regular union dues. This arrangement was part of the so-called Rand Formula developed in 1945 by Canadian Supreme Court Justice Ivan Rand to resolve a labour dispute in the automotive industry. Under this formula, workers may refuse formal union membership but must still contribute financially to the union's collective bargaining efforts. Consistent with this arrangement, Lavigne paid compulsory dues to OPSEU without becoming a member of the union.

The principal dispute between Lavigne and OPSEU began on October 19, 1984, when the union initiated strike action against the community college system. Unhappy with this decision, Lavigne and similarly minded instructors defied the strike order and returned to teach their regular classes on November 5,

1984. The conflict between Lavigne and OPSEU attracted the attention of the National Citizens' Coalition (NCC), a politically conservative interest group. The NCC's political agenda opposed universal health care, official bilingualism, unemployment insurance, indexed pensions, and the National Energy Program. Although the organization claimed 30,000 members and sought public support for its agenda through newspaper advertising campaigns, it remained on the fringes of Canadian political life.

In 1984, however, the NCC achieved its most important political success in the courts, using Charter litigation to attack an amendment to the Canada Elections Act that prohibited anyone other than registered political parties or candidates from incurring election-related advertising expenses during national election campaigns. Seeking to launch a national advertising campaign against the New Democratic Party (NDP), the NCC challenged the amended provisions of the Act in the Alberta Court of Queen's Bench on the grounds that they infringed freedom of expression as guaranteed by section 2(b) of the Charter. The Alberta court rejected the government's contention that the impugned provisions actually encouraged the exchange of opinions and ideas, agreeing instead with the NCC's claim that the provisions imposed a *prima facie* limitation on freedom of expression that could not be justified under section 1.[100]

The NCC's victory convinced the organization that litigation could be a more productive strategy than traditional lobbying activities, and Mervyn Lavigne's dispute with OPSEU provided the NCC with an opportunity to aim this weapon at two favourite targets: organized labour and the NDP. As players in the same political game, organized labour and the NDP pursued policies diametrically opposed to those advocated by the NCC. Their capacity to participate in this game, however, depended on access to a portion of the compulsory dues collected by unions across the country. By successfully challenging the right of unions to spend compulsory dues on political causes, the NCC could potentially weaken a competing interest group and the political party that benefited most from that group's political activities. In section 2(d) of the Charter, which guarantees freedom of association, the NCC found a constitutional provision through which to pursue a litigation strategy designed to diminish the political strength of organized labour. Recognizing the broad implications of this case, the Canadian Labour Congress, the Ontario Federation of Labour, and the National Union of Provincial Government Employees intervened in the litigation on behalf of OPSEU.

Lavigne's conflict with OPSEU offered the NCC two tactical advantages during the trigger phase of the proceedings. First, since Lavigne had never belonged to OPSEU he could legitimately claim that his contributions to the union's political activities were truly involuntary. The union could not argue that Lavigne had tacitly consented either to the general use of compulsory dues for political purposes or to the specific causes to which the union had made contributions. More importantly, Lavigne's association with OPSEU also made it more likely that the NCC could meet the most crucial threshold requirement it faced during the litigation's trigger phase. Both parties agreed that the only way for the NCC to trigger liability and remedy proceedings was to persuade the court that Lavigne was attacking government action in his challenge to OPSEU's spending practices. Nevertheless, the only relevant precedent suggested that Lavigne's claim did not involve government action. In *Re Baldwin and B.C. Government Employees' Union* (1986), which involved similar constitutional issues and facts as *Lavigne,* the British Columbia Supreme Court had held that even public-sector unions make expenditure decisions in their capacity as private entities.[101] OPSEU similarly argued that its spending decisions constitute purely private action.

The NCC responded to this argument by shifting the focus of its constitutional challenge from OPSEU's spending decisions to the decision by the Ontario Council of Regents for Colleges of Applied Arts and Technology to enter into a collective agreement with OPSEU that failed to prohibit the union from using compulsory dues for political purposes. This argument rested on three assertions: (1) that the Council of Regents is a governmental actor; (2) that the provincial government and its agencies have a *positive duty* to act in a manner that protects Charter guarantees; and (3) that failure to do so constitutes government action in contravention of the Charter. Combining the general principles of Charter interpretation established by the Canadian Supreme Court in *Operation Dismantle* (1985) and *Big M Drug Mart* (1985), Judge John White of the Ontario Supreme Court concluded that "it is the purpose of the Charter to permit review of situations where a governmental actor acts in such a way that the effect of its action, whether such action be of a legislative or administrative nature, potentially infringes a value protected by the Charter."[102] Applying this conclusion to the question at issue, Judge White held that, by agreeing to include a compulsory dues provision in the collective agreement that effectively forced Lavigne to support OPSEU financially, the Council of Regents had engaged in government action that potentially infringed his Charter rights.[103] This conclusion brought the trigger phase of the litigation to its conclusion and granted the NCC access to the liability phase.

The threshold requirements that the NCC had to meet during the trigger phase significantly shaped the liability and remedy phases. In order to show government action, the NCC argued that the alleged infringement of the Charter did not occur when OPSEU expended its revenues but when the Council of Regents agreed to a collective agreement requiring compulsory payment of dues by non-members. However, since this provision in the Council's agreement with OPSEU originated in the Rand Formula, the NCC could not define the Council's liability in such unqualified terms without simultaneously challenging an inviolable element of Canadian labour relations. Instead, the NCC argued that the Council's liability occurred when it agreed to compulsory payment of dues *without also ensuring the adequate protection of non-members' freedom of association or expression.* By defining the Council's liability in this fashion the NCC found itself in the position of defending the novel proposition that the positive rights of freedom of association and expression should be interpreted to include negative rights of non-association and silence, and that these negative rights impose a positive, protective duty on government. Specifically, the NCC asserted that, if governments compel non-union members to pay union dues, then sections 2(d) and 2(b) of the Charter impose a corresponding duty to ensure that those dues are not used to support political causes with which non-members disagree.

At issue at this stage of *Lavigne* were OPSEU's financial contributions to the NDP, to disarmament campaigns, to a campaign opposing the expenditure of municipal funds for the Toronto SkyDome, to striking coal miners in the United Kingdom, to various groups in Nicaragua, and to pro-choice groups in the abortion debate.[104] The NCC submitted that the use of any portion of Lavigne's compulsory dues for these purposes created a "forced association" between him and the political causes supported by OPSEU. In addition, the NCC argued that these expenditures limited Lavigne's freedom of expression by implicitly forcing him to speak where he would prefer to remain silent. The NCC found support for its argument in the U.S. Supreme Court's decision in *Abood v. Detroit Board of Education* (1977), which declared that the use of compulsory union dues for political purposes violates an individual's First Amendment rights.[105]

OPSEU responded to the NCC's argument in three ways. First, the union asserted that, whatever the government's connection to the expenditures in question, the Charter does not impose a positive duty on governments or legislatures to act in a manner protective of fundamental freedoms under section 2. Second, OPSEU denied that the use of a small portion of Lavigne's compulsory dues forced him to associate with the union, embrace the causes OPSEU promoted, or refrain from expressing contrary views. Finally, OPSEU submitted that, even if the court found a breach of the Charter, the minimal limitation of Lavigne's section 2 freedoms could be justified under section 1 of the Charter as necessary for promoting the broader political and economic interests of workers.[106]

Judge White began his consideration of these liability issues by declaring that the Charter protects the fundamental freedoms listed in section 2 in order to maintain a free and democratic political system, as well as to promote individual self-worth and dignity. According to White, freedom of association serves the first of these purposes by allowing individuals to join together to pursue common political goals. In addition, by protecting voluntary private organizations, freedom of association serves the second purpose of section 2 by establishing a counterbalance to centralized state power.[107] Neither of these purposes would be meaningful, however, if governments could compel association where individuals opposed it. Consequently, Judge White concluded that "a right to freedom of association which did not include a right not to associate would not really ensure 'freedom'."[108]

The next step in the liability phase was to determine whether the compulsory dues provision forced Lavigne to associate with OPSEU. Judge White accepted the union's argument that the purpose of this provision was to prevent non-member employees from taking free advantage of the union's collective bargaining efforts. He found, however, that the provision effectively forced non-members to combine their financial resources with union members contrary to the negative right of non-association. White thus declared that, although unions may prevent free-riding on their collective bargaining efforts, they may not make non-members captive supporters of political causes. Consequently, he found a *prima facie* violation of Lavigne's freedom of association. [109]

The final step in the liability phase was for White to apply the *Oakes* test to determine whether the *prima facie* limitation of Lavigne's freedom of association was reasonable and demonstrably justified in a free and democratic society. White accepted OPSEU's claim that the compulsory dues provision aimed at promoting industrial peace through collective bargaining and the prevention of free-riding by non-members. He also agreed that these objectives constitute "a significant governmental objective that may warrant overriding individual rights to some extent." [110] This led White to the proportionality component of the *Oakes* test. [111] The compulsory dues provision easily passed the "rational connection" element of proportionality, but foundered on the requirement that it be the least restrictive means of achieving the objective in question. Reviewing legislation adopted in various industrialized nations, Judge White held that it would be possible to establish a dues payment scheme to finance collective bargaining and prevent free-riding without forcing those individuals to contribute to the political activities of unions. In essence, White held that the impugned compulsory dues provision was not sufficiently tailored to its purpose, since non-members were forced to pay more than was absolutely necessary to support OPSEU's collective bargaining efforts on their behalf. [112]

At the conclusion of his judgment in the liability phase of *Lavigne,* Judge White invited the NCC and OPSEU to make further submissions to assist him in crafting an appropriate remedy, which he then communicated to the litigants on July 7, 1987. Two general issues dominated White's preliminary discussion during this phase of the proceedings: the scope of his remedial powers under section 24(1) of the Charter and the relationship between those powers and section 1. In White's view, section 24(1) encouraged "a liberal view of a superior court's inherent power for the development of 'remedial methods'" and required, at the very least, "innovative adaptation" of the traditional repertoire of remedies available to superior courts. On the second issue, White argued that remedies are governed by the same section 1 principles that govern limitations on Charter guarantees. In particular, where a court has recognized an important governmental objective underlying the limitation of a Charter guarantee, its remedy should aim not at eliminating the limitation but at making it "reasonable" and "demonstrably justified in a free and democratic society." Consequently, in fashioning a remedy to protect Lavigne's future rights, Judge White sought guidance from the proportionality principles articulated in *Oakes.* [113]

White next turned to the two remedial alternatives offered by the NCC and OPSEU. The NCC argued that the union should bear the burden of obtaining explicit consent from non-members before using any portion of their compulsory dues for political purposes. This meant the inclusion of an "opt-in" provision in the collective bargaining agreement that would give union members and non-members alike the option of making additional contributions to support the non-collective bargaining activities of the union. OPSEU, on the other hand, argued that non-members should have the onus of explicitly objecting to certain uses of their compulsory dues. This meant the inclusion of an "opt-out" provision according to which individuals could compel the union to refund a portion of their dues. According to White, the form of his remedy had to maintain the integrity of the Rand Formula because that arrangement constituted an accepted principle of Canadian labour law and because its objective was sufficiently important to warrant limiting freedom of association. He also considered himself constrained by the "settled economic expectations of unions with respect to the dues received from non-members who are apathetic, neutral or indifferent."[114] Finally, since Lavigne had not brought his case as a class action, White was uncertain whether all non-members shared Lavigne's concerns. This was important, according to White, because the opt-in remedy would apply to all non-members, as well as some members, not simply to dissentient non-members like Lavigne.[115]

Taking these factors into account, White concluded that the opt-out alternative would best protect Lavigne's freedom of association, preserve the Rand Formula, and interfere as little as possible with the interests of OPSEU members.[116] White thus ordered OPSEU to establish mechanisms whereby objecting non-members could recoup a portion of their compulsory dues. In choosing this opt-out remedy, he obviously sought to soften the impact of his liability ruling on unions. Nevertheless, the outcome of both the liability and remedy phases of Lavigne struck a potentially significant blow at the NCC's political adversaries. For organized labour, the accounting and arbitration mechanisms required by the remedy could involve significant costs that might hamper non-collective bargaining activities even without a large reduction in revenues available for that purpose. For the NDP, Judge White's declaration that expenditures for non-collective bargaining include contributions to political parties posed a possible threat to its revenue. OPSEU and its political allies thus had an important incentive to appeal Judge White's rulings.

The next step in the remedy phase of *Lavigne* was the Ontario Court of Appeal's consideration of OPSEU's appeal of White's rulings and the NCC's cross-appeal of his failure to grant the entirety of its liability and remedy claims. The Ontario portion of this part of the litigation ended on January 30, 1989, when a three-judge panel of the Ontario Court of Appeal unanimously upheld OPSEU's appeal and reversed Judge White's liability and remedy findings. In terms of the remedial decree litigation model, the principal reason for this result was the appellate court's conclusion that the facts in *Lavigne* had not been sufficient to trigger the liability phase of the litigation. According to the appellate court, Judge White erred in accepting the NCC's threshold argument that OPSEU's use of compulsory dues for non-collective bargaining purposes involved government action. The court found that Lavigne's complaint was directed solely against the union's expenditure of funds, which the court found to be "private activity by a private organization and hence beyond the reach of the Charter." Moreover, the Court of Appeal disagreed with White that the

Council of Regents' failure to regulate the use of compulsory dues constituted government action.[117] By reinterpreting the nature of Lavigne's claim, the Court of Appeal was able to avoid adjudicating the substantive issues contained in it.

The Supreme Court wrote the final chapter in *Lavigne* on June 27, 1991, when it dismissed Lavigne's appeal of the Ontario Court of Appeal's decision. This means that *Lavigne* will never enter the post-decree phase, which in academic terms is unfortunate because this phase, with its emphasis on implementation and remedy refinement, involves some of the most interesting institutional capacity issues raised by remedial decree litigation. The fact that Mervyn Lavigne and the NCC ultimately failed to restructure the financial arrangements between unions and non-members through litigation does not, however, decrease the importance of understanding the process by which this case made its way through the courts. Indeed, in several important respects the Supreme Court agreed with Judge White's ruling rather than with the Ontario Court of Appeal's judgment. The seven justices who decided *Lavigne* unanimously agreed with White that the Charter applied to the membership arrangements at issue in the case. Moreover, three justices agreed that these arrangements infringed Lavigne's right to freedom of association. Where most of the disagreement between the Supreme Court and Judge White occurred was in their respective application of the *Oakes* test to this infringement. Consequently, *Lavigne*'s litigation history lends itself to some preliminary observations about remedial decree litigation under the Charter.[118]

On the positive side, the ability of groups like the Canadian Labour Congress, the Ontario Federation of Labour, and the National Union of Provincial Government Employees to intervene in *Lavigne* ensured reasonably adequate representation of the labour interests implicated in the case. Without such representation, Judge White might not have been so sensitive to the necessity of balancing Lavigne's Charter rights against the important purposes served by the Rand Formula. Indeed, the ability of diverse labour groups to bring important social fact information about the objectives of the Rand Formula to White's attention led him to narrow both his liability finding and remedial declaration. On the negative side, Judge White also narrowed his remedy ruling because he was unsure whether, as an individual plaintiff, Lavigne actually represented the interests of all non-members. White found himself able to assume only that Lavigne represented dissentient non-members. Had the case been brought as a class action, White might have selected the opt-in remedy preferred by the NCC. Inadequate representation of some of the interests affected by the decision thus had an important impact on the case's outcome. The important lesson here is that remedial decree litigation requires that courts strike a delicate balance between the need to accommodate an amorphous party structure and the necessity of ensuring judicial manageability of proceedings. In striking that balance, however, there is always the danger that important interests will be excluded, leading to flawed decisions.

In more general terms, *Lavigne* clearly illustrates the interdependence among each phase of remedial decree litigation. The conventional legal understanding of the Charter's applicability profoundly shaped the NCC's overall litigation strategy and tactics during the trigger phase of *Lavigne*. These tactical choices imposed constraints at the liability phase in terms of both defining the form and scope of the alleged Charter violation. While this facilitated the NCC's success during this phase, it also contributed to the formulation of a remedy less extensive than what the NCC desired. Finally, the legal issues around which the trigger phase revolved re-emerged to dominate the parallel appeals process. Indeed, Judge White's failure to articulate clearly the principles on which he based his finding that *Lavigne* concerned governmental action allowed the Ontario Court of Appeal to avoid entirely the substantive issues implicated by the NCC's claim.

Perhaps the most interesting question raised by *Lavigne* is a political one: Who benefits from remedial decree litigation under the Charter? Given the respective experiences of the NCC and organized labour in Charter litigation, one possible answer to this question is that politically marginalized groups have more to gain through litigation than more established interests. While organized labour is not as powerful as other interest groups, it does benefit from a formal association with a major political party and legislatively supported coercive authority over a significant number of individuals. By contrast, prior to its litigation activities, public support for the NCC's political agenda was small, and no political party actively articulated its interests. Isolated from the ordinary policy-making process, litigation was a natural path for the NCC to take. In the final analysis, the NCC's initial success in *Lavigne* illustrates the ambiguous political nature of remedial decree litigation. In particular, it calls into question one of the most important assumptions underlying support for remedial decree litigation: that remedial decree plaintiffs act in the name of a "public interest" that is either misunderstood or ignored by political actors in the legislative and executive organs of government. However, it is equally possible that what is often described as "public interest" remedial decree litigation is, in fact, litigation on behalf of private interests who have simply lost in the political process.

Conclusion

The survey of judicial implementation of sections 1 and 24(1) of the Charter presented in this chapter should raise questions about the popular view of judicial decision-making under the Charter. At the core of this perception is the understanding that Charter decision-making represents the discovery and confirmation of the fundamental principles of our political order in which principle triumphs over policy. In fact, Charter cases are more likely to involve more practical questions, such as whether a legislature acted properly when it decided to set thirteen as the age dividing vulnerable children from mature individuals for the purposes of controlling certain types of advertising, as was the case in *Irwin Toy*.[119] Once courts accept the basic assertion that legislatures may regulate such activities, there is no single legal or constitutional principle against which to evaluate the specific form of the regulation.[120] To be sure, there is always a danger that legislatures may act completely arbitrarily; but such arbitrariness would be so transparent that politically accountable decision-making bodies would rarely engage in it. Moreover, if such arbitrary decisions were to become frequent and beyond political control, then the political order would face a crisis that could not be resolved in any way by judicial enforcement of a written constitution.

Does this argument lead to the conclusion that judicial review in general, and section 1 review in particular, should simply be abandoned? The answer to this question is, of course, that it should not. There are good reasons why courts should review the calculus of reasonable limits reflected in legislative enactments. To cite one reason, flaws in the process of representation may mean that in some cases the interests of relevant groups and individuals will be left out of the legislative calculus. In these circumstances, judicial review can alert legislatures and the public to such flaws. However, given the indeterminacy of section 1 review and the formulation of remedies under section 24(1), there is no reason to assume that the judicial calculus of reasonable limits and appropriate remedies is necessarily superior to the decisions reached by legislatures. There is, in other words, no argument that supports judicial supremacy. Consequently, the development of liberal constitutionalism in Canada can be advanced significantly by the so-called "notwithstanding" clause contained in section 33 of the Charter. This is the subject of the final chapter.

CHAPTER 7

Confronting Judicial Supremacy: Section 33 and the Paradox of Liberal Constitutionalism

This book began by suggesting that the entrenchment of the Charter of Rights and Freedoms brings to the surface a central paradox in the political theory of liberal constitutionalism in Canada. This paradox stems from a tension between the fundamental principle of this political theory – constitutional supremacy – and the mechanism by which this principle is enforced – judicial review. Constitutional supremacy requires that political power only be exercised according to the procedural and substantive rules laid down in a constitution; judicial review means that one of the institutions in which political power is located bears principal responsibility for interpreting and applying these rules in specific instances. The tension between these two features of liberal constitutionalism derives from the fact that the power courts possess to define constitutional language makes possible the ascension of judicial supremacy at the expense of constitutional supremacy. As the speed and scope with which courts exercise this power increases, they become constitutional "oracles," and the document itself becomes less relevant as the authoritative source of the rules governing the use of political power.[1] Throughout this book I have argued that this is precisely the role that the Supreme Court of Canada and the lower courts have embraced under the Charter of Rights and Freedoms.

None of this would be particularly worrisome were it not for the ambiguity surrounding the normative legitimacy and institutional capacity of courts undertaking this function in liberal democracies. As expositors of a constitution's meaning, courts exercise a power over specific policy measures and the general political character of the regime that is not subject to the ordinary mechanisms of democratic accountability. As we saw in Chapter Two, one response to this problem is to articulate increasingly sophisticated constitutional theories the purpose of which is to legitimate judicial review by attaching its exercise in specific instances to core principles of liberal democracy. In this chapter, I will examine a second approach to this problem, which is to create tighter bonds between judges and the citizens they govern through changes to the judicial appointments process.

Enhancing the normative legitimacy of constitutional review is not sufficient, however, because judicial power over policy and politics is exercised in an institutional setting that reflects the original, and still important, purpose of adjudication: the resolution of concrete disputes between private parties about specific rights. As we saw in Chapter Six, this institutional setting places certain limitations on the ability of courts to resolve the largely indeterminate policy questions at issue in most Charter cases. I thus explore various proposals intended to remove these institutional impediments to judicial policy-making. Some of these proposals, such as those concerning oral arguments and interveners, concern problems unique to Canada; others are more generic in their nature. These proposals, however, contain a paradox of their own: changing the judicial process to enhance institutional capacity may undermine its legitimacy even further.

In the final analysis, none of the conventional proposals for enhancing either the democratic accountability or institutional capacity of the judicial process is adequate to overcome the tension between the ideal of constitutional supremacy and the reality of judicial supremacy. Most of the proposals for enhancing democratic accountability, for example, do not provide any mechanism for effective, continuous supervision of the manner in which judicial power is exercised. Similarly, the major proposals for enhancing institutional capacity can improve judicial policy-making only at the expense of making courts resemble the very institutions whose decisions they are supposed to review. Consequently, I will argue in this chapter that the "notwithstanding" clause contained in section 33 of the Charter is both a legitimate and effective means within liberal democratic theory of preventing the slide from constitutional supremacy into judicial supremacy. This is not to say, however, that section 33 as it currently exists is perfect, and I will propose amendments to enhance *its* legitimacy and effectiveness.

Enhancing Normative Legitimacy and Institutional Capacity

Chapter Two, and to a lesser extent Chapter Six, canvassed various efforts to ground the legitimacy of judicial review in constitutional theory. At the risk of being repetitive, it is useful to summarize the two principal approaches and their weaknesses. On the one hand, interpretivist theories of judicial review attempt to hold courts democratically accountable through the interpretive convention that judicial decisions must be grounded in specific constitutional provisions or in an interpretation of those provisions that is faithful (or at least not contradictory) to the meaning intended by their framers. The principal weakness of this approach is that it collapses into an argument for judicial self-restraint, which is inconsistent with the basic assumption of liberal constitutionalism that structural restraints are necessary to control political power. Non-interpretivist theories, on the other hand, assert that the abstract and general language of constitutions symbolically represents a set of liberal democratic values that judges must translate into rights against which government action should be measured. The problem with this approach is that reasonable people may disagree about the precise nature of these values and the concrete rights to which they lead. The "right to privacy," for example, can be invoked to support constitutional protection for both private economic transactions and reproductive choice. The choice between these two applications of this right largely depends on the decision-maker's moral vision of a just society. There is no reason to believe, however, that the moral insights of judges are sufficiently superior to those of other political actors to make judicial supremacy tolerable.

Recognizing the insufficiency of constitutional theory alone to justify the active exercise of judicial review, some commentators have suggested the implementation of structural reform designed to introduce greater democratic accountability into the judicial decision-making process, particularly at the Supreme Court level. David Beatty has argued that the democratic integrity of the Supreme Court's constitutional review function can be enhanced by changing the appointments process, the nature of judicial tenure, and the judicial decision-making process. According to Beatty, the most important measure is to shift responsibility for appointing Supreme Court justices from the executive to the legislature. In his view, legislative participation in the appointments process "forges a link through which those who are given authority to rule on the constitutionality of law are made accountable to those who will be governed by the decisions which result."[2] Surveying the methods that various countries employ to achieve this participation, Beatty rejects the American system of executive nomination and legislative ratification on the grounds that "it denies the legislative branch any power to initiate"; in the American model, legislatures can only resist temporarily the executive's intentions.[3] Beatty's concern is that the executive nomination of federal judges in the United States operates at cross-purposes with the public control over the process that underlies legislative ratification. This concern is somewhat misplaced, however, since the U.S. President is electorally accountable to the population as a whole in a way that Canadian executives are not.[4]

Nevertheless, having rejected the U.S. arrangement, Beatty favours the German model, in which the legislative branch has sole authority to select the members of the Federal Constitutional Court. The German Constitutional Court consists of sixteen judges, sitting in two separate eight-judge senates. Each house of the German Parliament appoints four of the judges to each of the two senates. The Bundestag, or lower house, exercises this power through a special parliamentary committee that must approve appointments by a two-thirds majority vote. Similarly, appointments to the Court by the Bundesrat, or upper house, must be approved by a two-thirds majority of the body as a whole.[5] What commends the German model to Beatty is the fact that the legislature is involved throughout the entire process of recruitment, screening, selection, and appointment. According to Beatty, adapting this model for use in the Canadian context, and supplementing it with a process of public hearings, would ensure the "democratic legitimacy of constitutional review" by enabling the groups most interested in judicial appointments – that is, citizens, provincial governments, and the federal government – to influence the appointments process through legislative representatives.[6]

The ultimate purpose of Beatty's proposal is to democratize the appointments process and thereby enhance the legitimacy of the judicial power exercised by the members of the Supreme Court. Although the proposal clearly achieves the first part of this objective, it falls short in its pursuit of the second goal. The principal reason for this is that the *accountability* provided by this appointments process is discrete rather than continuous. While individuals generally tend to behave rather predictably after appointment to the bench, there are sufficient counter-examples from the United States to suggest that democratic control over the appointments process does not alone ensure democratic control over judicial behaviour. The most famous example, of course, is Earl Warren, who, despite his background as a conservative Republican Attorney-General and Governor of California, used his position as Chief Justice of the U.S. Supreme Court to move constitutional law in an unexpectedly liberal direction. A more recent example is Justice Harry Blackmun, who authored the U.S. Court's abortion decision in *Roe v. Wade* (1973). Blackmun's behaviour in *Roe* was obviously contrary to the expectations of Richard Nixon, who appointed Blackmun to the Court on the basis of his supposed "strict constructionist" approach to constitutional interpretation. These are, to be sure, dramatic examples; nevertheless, it is only natural that the influence of colleagues and the changing nature of constitutional issues over time might eventually render judgments about judicial behaviour made during the appointments process irrelevant. Moreover, political shifts in society as a whole are bound to be reflected in changes in the composition of the appointing body, and this means an erosion in the legitimacy initially conferred on Supreme Court justices by a more democratic appointments process.[7] A democratized appointments process requires a more democratic system of judicial tenure.

To his credit, Beatty recognizes this fact and argues that democratic legitimacy requires greater judicial turnover. There is nothing novel, of course, in the proposition that removal powers be used to hold the judges sitting on constitutional courts accountable. As we saw in Chapter One, Alexander Hamilton argued that U.S. Supreme Court justices who usurp the "authority of the legislature" could be legitimately impeached.[8] Beatty's proposal is both simpler and less politically charged. In his view, Supreme Court appointments should be granted for a fixed term only. Although the Canadian requirement of mandatory retirement at age seventy-five provides greater turnover than the constitutional guarantee of life tenure in the United States, it still means that the members of the Court can remain in their positions for substantially long periods.[9] The German case again provides Beatty with a model solution to this problem, since appointments to the Federal Constitutional Court are for non-renewable twelve-year terms.[10]

To summarize Beatty's proposal, he envisions a Canadian Supreme Court in which the democratic legitimacy and accountability of constitutional review are achieved through a system of publicly visible legislative appointments of judges for non-renewable fixed terms. It is not simply coincidence that the models underlying this proposal are found in countries with judicial systems that are not based on the common law, since Beatty's proposal would change the nature of the Supreme Court in a manner that would leave it a common-law judicial institution in name only. Indeed, consistent with his theory of judicial review (discussed in Chapter Six), what Beatty implicitly suggests is the creation of an additional legislative chamber. This would give Canada three such bodies, each accountable to the public in a different way. One chamber, the House of Commons, would be accountable to the population directly; the public accountability of a second chamber (perhaps a reformed Senate) would be moderated by its responsibility to the interests of provincial governments or regions; and a third chamber, to be styled the Supreme Court, would be indirectly accountable to the public through the appointments process controlled by the other legislative bodies. This would provide the third chamber with democratic legitimacy, as well as with the insulation from the momentary passions of majoritarian politics necessary to subject the decisions of the other legislative chambers to constitutional review.

At one level, Beatty's proposal appears to address the basic elements of the paradox of liberal constitutionalism. It allows for judicial review to enforce constitutional norms against legislative behaviour while subjecting the Supreme Court to greater democratic scrutiny. At another level, however, it suffers from an affliction common to many institutional reform proposals: it raises as many problems as it purports to solve. In particular, Beatty's proposal does not explain why the constitutional opinions of this new quasi-legislative chamber in judicial guise should prevail over the constitutional judgments of other legislative bodies. One reason might be that the members of this newly constituted body are more expert in analysing constitutional questions and exercising constitutional review. Yet Beatty himself asserts that politicians are intellectually capable "of understanding the basic principles and methods of constitutional law."[11] A second reason might be that this chamber's isolation from majoritarian politics makes its constitutional judgments more reliable. While this argument clearly supports the prudence of seeking the Court's constitutional advice, it does not, in itself, explain why that advice is necessarily authoritative or should be final. Changes to the method by which Supreme Court appointments are made and terminated may enhance the legitimacy of judicial *review,* but they cannot legitimate judicial *supremacy.* There is the further possibility, moreover, that any radical transformation in the Supreme Court's institutional character may, in fact, be self-defeating.

What gives the constitutional decisions of the Supreme Court and other courts their unique normative status is in large measure the very distinctiveness of the judicial process. Any erosion in this distinctiveness risks undermining whatever normative legitimacy those decisions currently enjoy. This risk is especially acute when considering the institutional capacity question, since it is precisely the distinctiveness of the judicial process that limits the institutional capacity of courts to decide complex and indeterminate policy issues. Consequently, changes to the judicial process designed to enhance the decision-making capacity of courts, like changes designed to enhance the democratic legitimacy of judicial decisions, may actually undermine legitimacy. This is not to say, of course, that all changes to the Supreme Court's decision-making processes fall into this category. For example, Beatty's own proposal to enhance the collegial nature of the Court's decision-making by moving away from the practice of having each justice write separate reasons for judgment in every case would likely have little negative impact on the normative legitimacy of the Court's decisions.[12] Indeed, he is probably correct in asserting that this change would enhance the authoritativeness of the Court's decisions, as well as reduce potential confusion at the implementation stage. That the Court already recognizes this fact is evident in its practice of speaking in a single, anonymous voice in its most controversial decisions, such as those concerning language rights.[13]

Other proposed changes to the Court's decision-making process would have similarly positive consequences without affecting the nature of the Court as a judicial institution. One such change would be to adopt the practice of deciding all cases as a full nine-judge panel. Between 1983 and 1989, less than 8 per cent of the Court's Charter cases were decided by the full panel of nine justices; and more than 85 per cent of Charter cases were decided by panels consisting of seven or fewer justices. The obvious importance of this is that, given differing judicial attitudes toward Charter claims, reliance on panels of fewer than nine judges can mean that outcomes in these cases may depend entirely on the random variable of which judges are assigned to the panel in any particular instance.[14] This may be only a matter of perception, but it is an easily corrected impediment to the complete legitimacy of Charter decisions. Indeed, the U.S. Supreme Court manages a much heavier caseload while always sitting as a full panel.

The Supreme Court could also enhance its decision-making capacity by taking the relatively simple step of reducing its reliance on oral arguments. In contrast to U.S. practice, where each side in a dispute is limited to thirty minutes of oral argument, there are no time limits on oral arguments before the Canadian Supreme Court. In addition, interested parties granted *amicus curiae* ("friend of the court") status in the United States may only participate in oral arguments before the Supreme Court if one of the principal parties agrees to share its thirty-minute allotment with the *amicus* participant. By contrast, groups granted status as interveners in Canada are also granted additional oral argument time. The Canadian Court thus spends a significant amount of time listening to lawyers repeat material found in their written submissions. By contrast, the restrictions on oral argument found in the U.S. Court tend to produce sharper and more dynamic exchanges between the justices and counsel.

Unfortunately, the Canadian Court appears to have dealt with this problem not by reducing the time allotted for oral arguments but by limiting the participation of interveners. As we saw in Chapter Six, however, the varied interests affected by policy-laden Charter decisions require that access to the decision-making process by interested third parties be increased rather than reduced. The reason for this is twofold. First, these groups can provide the Court with information and a perspective on issues that are unavailable from the principal parties. Second, as Donald Horowitz has argued, groups excluded from the decision-making process can reappear later to impede the implementation of constitutional decisions, making it advisable to include them at the outset. An optimal solution to this problem might be to reduce the oral argument time available to disputing parties, virtually eliminate oral participation by interveners, and provide for almost unlimited intervener participation through written submissions.

The proposed reforms canvassed above are designed to permit the Supreme Court to perform its traditional adjudicative functions more efficiently.[15] Other reform proposals developed in the U.S. context would go further toward altering the information-gathering and -processing techniques of courts, as well as their methods of communicating decisions and ensuring compliance. Arthur Selwyn Miller and Jerome Barron, for example, have argued that U.S. courts must adopt several decision-making reforms to ensure that they do not "resort to blind guesses about the effect of their decisions or to an uncritical acceptance of data." In particular, Miller and Barron suggest that the U.S. Supreme Court should appoint a panel of social scientists to assist in its evaluation of legislative facts, should remand complicated cases to trial courts for proper adjudication of legislative fact assertions, and should promulgate specific rules to govern the practice of taking judicial notice of social facts not contained in case materials.[16] Other American commentators, along with most judges, have embraced the idea of relying on "special masters" as expert advisers in formulating complex remedial decrees, as well as in providing ongoing supervision of the implementation of these decrees.[17]

Each of these suggestions could be transplanted into the Canadian context. Indeed, former Justice Bertha Wilson advocated similar types of reforms while serving on the Supreme Court.[18] In her view, two changes were particularly necessary: expanding the number of parties involved in Charter litigation by liberalizing intervention rules, and resolving important problems of proof by enlarging the base of admissible evidence in Charter cases. Dale Gibson has also made reform proposals in this vein, arguing that there should be greater reliance on social science experts and public opinion polls, that the size of the Court be increased, that the justices be provided better research staffs, and that the Law Reform Commission shift its energies toward the development of reform proposals that can be implemented by courts without legislative action.[19]

The types of decision-making reforms advocated by Miller and Barron in the United States, and by Gibson and Wilson in the Canadian context, would undoubtedly enhance the policy-making capacity of judicial institutions. Like

Beatty's proposals, however, these reforms would significantly transform the institutional character of courts as these bodies are understood in the common-law world. To be more precise, they would further erode the institutional differences between courts and the legislative and executive bodies whose decisions judges are charged with reviewing.[20] This consequence of major institutional reform points to the difficulty of simultaneously enhancing normative legitimacy and institutional capacity. It is unrealistic, and indeed undesirable, to expect the Supreme Court to discontinue exercising rights-based constitutional review, or even to expunge policy considerations from its decision-making process and judgments in such cases. At the same time, the Court's capacity to perform this function effectively can only be enhanced through structural reforms that would create a new institution that would no longer be in any meaningful sense a court whose constitutional decisions should carry special weight. The way out of this particular paradox of liberal constitutionalism is to shift the focus of attention from the institutional structure of courts to their decision outputs.

Controlling Judicial Supremacy: Lessons from the American Experience

Scholars of the U.S. Supreme Court's constitutional decision-making have often reflected on the measures available to restrain judicial supremacy or to reverse unpopular decisions in particular cases.[21] Some of these measures, such as the impeachment process advocated by Alexander Hamilton or the Civil War that followed the U.S. Court's *Dred Scott v. Sandford* (1857) decision, are clearly solutions to avoid. Others, however, are worth exploring as possible answers to similar questions in Canada. The most frequently discussed measure for restraining judicial supremacy or reversing judicial error in constitutional decision-making in the United States has been the constitutional amendment process. This method has intuitive appeal, since it parallels the process for correcting judicial error in non-constitutional adjudication. If courts misconstrue statutes or develop unpalatable common-law doctrines, legislatures can respond simply by rewriting those statutes or by enacting legislation to overturn those doctrines. By analogy, if courts misinterpret the constitution, the document should be amended to reverse that misinterpretation or to make the constitution's meaning clearer. Indeed, the Constitution Act, 1867 has been amended twice to reverse judicial decisions.[22]

The major difficulty with this line of argument is that constitutional amendment is in general a cumbersome process that can be derailed by small minorities.[23] While Germany has a rather simple amendment process (amendments must be approved by a two-thirds majority in each legislative chamber), the amendment procedure most often employed in the United States requires an amendment proposal approved by a two-thirds majority in both houses of Congress and ratification of that proposal by three-fourths of the states. Amendments to the Charter of Rights and Freedoms require resolutions of the Senate and House of Commons and of the legislative assemblies of two-thirds of the provinces that contain at least 50 per cent of Canada's population.[24] These requirements are complex for a good reason: a nation's fundamental document should be capable of amendment only when the change is supported by a broad and deep political consensus. If the Supreme Court were rendering decisions in Charter cases about the fundamental core principles of Canada's constitution, then formal amendment would be the only appropriate response to perceived judicial error. However, to rely on a process this cumbersome as the primary response to Supreme Court Charter decisions is questionable when most of those decisions involve policy-oriented disputes decided in the context of the least-restrictive-means branch of the *Oakes* test.

The U.S. experience with the amendment process as a response to perceived judicial misinterpretations of the constitution also suggests that this measure is as impractical as it is cumbersome. Although Congress has initiated numerous amendments to reverse Supreme Court decisions, the process has been successful on only four occasions (producing six amendments). In 1798, the Eleventh Amendment overturned *Chisholm v. Georgia* (1793), in which the Court had held that citizens of one state could sue another state in federal courts. The Thirteenth (1865), Fourteenth (1868), and Fifteenth (1870) Amendments were enacted in the aftermath of the Civil War to reverse *Dred Scott*. Ratification of the Sixteenth Amendment in 1913 reversed the Court's invalidation of a federal income tax in *Pollock v. Farmer's Loan and Trust Company* (1895). Finally, the Twenty-sixth Amendment ratified in 1971 established a uniform voting age of eighteen, which the Court had denied Congress the power to establish on its own in *Oregon v. Mitchell* (1970).[25] Even when employed successfully, however, the amendments produced by this process themselves become subject to constitutional interpretation. As we saw in Chapter One, the U.S. Supreme Court's interpretation of the Fourteenth Amendment significantly weakened its effectiveness.

American presidents also have attempted to reverse long-standing judicial interpretations of the U.S. Constitution through their power over Supreme Court nominations. The most famous example is Franklin Roosevelt's "Court-packing" plan, launched after his landslide re-election in 1936 to reverse the Court's rejection of his early New Deal policies. Roosevelt proposed that Congress pass legislation permitting him to increase the Court's size from nine to fifteen justices by appointing a new justice for every member of the Court over the age of seventy. Roosevelt would have used this power to appoint justices who shared his views about the constitutionality of the New Deal program. Although the plan never became law, it had its intended effect: while the Senate Judiciary Committee debated it in 1937, a single justice changed his mind and voted to uphold Washington state's minimum wage law.[26] The U.S. experience with this approach to "undesirable" constitutional decision-making should be instructive to Canadian policy-makers. Roosevelt's plan ultimately achieved its objective, but it did so at the cost of attacking the institutional integrity of the Court. Indeed, despite Roosevelt's own popularity, the Court-packing plan had little public support. Consequently, it may be the case that plans such as Beatty's, the effect of which is to transform the nature of the Supreme Court, may be difficult to implement.

In addition to the constitutional amendment and judicial appointments process, the U.S. Congress has also attempted to respond to Court decisions by rewriting legislation, by enacting statutes designed to blunt the impact of those decisions, or by simply waiting for the Court to change its mind. For example, Congress responded to the Court's abortion decision in *Roe v. Wade* (1973) by passing legislation that restricts public funding of abortions. Often, however, this option is not entirely satisfactory. Perhaps the best example of the inadequacy of relying on legislative re-enactments concerns the Supreme Court's nullification of the Civil Rights Act of 1875, which Congress had enacted to prohibit private discrimination under its Fourteenth Amendment enforcement powers. The Court held that this statute exceeded those powers because it did not directly apply to state action. It took Congress until 1964 to achieve the same goal through almost identical legislation enacted under its power to regulate interstate commerce. The political opportunity lost in 1875, however, meant four generations of misery for the earlier statute's potential beneficiaries.[27] Similarly, although the Court eventually changed its mind and upheld the constitutionality of child labour legislation, it did so only after a generation of children had suffered from the absence of regulation.[28]

In Canada, the federal Parliament has generally reacted to Charter decisions by attempting to rewrite legislation. Among the best examples are the revised refugee determination procedures enacted in response to *Singh,* the various attempts to enact new abortion legislation after *Morgentaler, Smoling and Scott,* the effort to revise the rules governing commitment of insane offenders after *Swain v. The Queen* (1991),[29] and the attempt to formulate a legislative response to the decision in *Seaboyer.* In addition to the time-lag inherent in the process of rewriting legislation, there is no guarantee that new legislation will achieve Parliament's objectives as effectively as what it is intended to replace. Moreover, the failure to enact new legislation may produce unintended consequences. For example, the absence of a national abortion policy arguably has led to greater provincial diversity than that which existed under the old policy regime. Finally, the new legislation itself is subject to additional constitutional challenge, as Parliament discovered with respect to its new immigration procedures, and will probably discover with respect to the new sexual assault provisions of the Criminal Code.[30]

The U.S. Constitution provides one final option for imposing political restraints on the U.S. Supreme Court's exercise of judicial review: Article III, Section 2 gives Congress the power to regulate and make exceptions to the Court's appellate jurisdiction.[31] The Court upheld Congress's authority to exercise this power in *Ex parte McCardle* (1869), an instance in which Congress took the extraordinary step of removing a case from the Court's appellate jurisdiction while it was still under consideration by the justices.[32] Despite this blatant interference with the outcome of a live controversy, the eight justices then on the bench unanimously held that Congress's plenary power over the Court's appellate jurisdiction forced them to dismiss the case for lack of jurisdiction. Although some scholars have argued that Congress may not exercise this power in a manner "inconsistent with the essential functions of the Supreme Court,"[33] this has not been the position taken by the Court itself since *McCardle*. At most, some justices have suggested that the contemporary Court would not accept congressional restrictions on its appellate jurisdiction over a case already before the Court.[34] Consequently, Congress's authority to alter the Court's appellate jurisdiction has been invoked (largely unsuccessfully) in statutes designed to restrict the Court's power over controversial policy matters like abortion, school prayer, and school busing aimed at racial integration.[35]

The Article III option has four clear advantages over other political responses to judicial review. First, it is grounded in explicit constitutional language. Second, its use has been clearly sanctioned by the Supreme Court. Third, unlike the constitutional amendment process, it can be invoked through the ordinary legislative process. Finally, it does not necessarily strike at the Court's basic institutional character. At the same time, however, this approach does suffer from at least two major disadvantages. The first is that it would be necessary to amend the Judiciary Act each time Congress wished to exercise this option. This raises the possibility that a relatively simple statute would simply collapse under the weight of numerous amendments designed to respond to specific judicial decisions. The second disadvantage is that the Article III option is not statute specific. It might thus operate more like a cleaver than a scalpel, carving out broad exceptions to the Supreme Court's appellate jurisdiction that might exclude the possibility of judicial review in cases where it would otherwise be desirable. To be more precise, the Article III option might substitute legislative supremacy for judicial supremacy, which would be a clear case of a cure being worse than the disease.[36]

The weaknesses inherent in this option, as well as in the other options surveyed above, have led John Agresto to suggest that the most effective institutional check on judicial supremacy in the United States would be to establish the same relationship between Congress and the judiciary as that which exists between Congress and the executive.[37] According to Agresto, it would be perfectly consistent with the constitutional theory of checks and balances to allow Congress to override judicial vetoes by an extraordinary majority in the same way that it can override presidential vetoes by a two-thirds majority of both the Senate and House of Representatives. In Agresto's view, such a process "would have been the perfect balancing of the principle of constitutionalism with active popular sovereignty."[38] Agresto's suggestion can even be taken a step further: this congressional review of judicial review could also be subject to executive veto, which would again then be subject to congressional override. It would take an extraordinary combination of political circumstances for a wholly illegitimate statute to survive the obstacle course established by the initial legislative process, executive review of that process, judicial review of the statute, congressional override of a judicial decision, and executive review of this congressional override.

While Agresto is pessimistic that history can be reversed to add such a process to the U.S. Constitution by amendment, his observation contains an important lesson for Canadian scholars and jurists: legislative control of judicial review is not inherently inconsistent with liberal constitutionalism. Indeed, as Agresto points out, the inspiration for the process he favours comes from no less an advocate and theoretician of liberal constitutionalism than James Madison.[39] What is inconsistent with liberal constitutionalism is the supremacy of any branch of government, as well as the reliance on self-restraint to ensure that the legislature, executive, and judiciary resist the temptation toward supremacy. Whether through theoretical foresight or short-term political trade-offs, the Charter of Rights and Freedoms contains a provision that responds to these two threats to liberal constitutionalism: the so-called "notwithstanding" clause contained in section 33. As I argue below, section 33 is neither an aberration in Canada's new constitutional order nor a fatal capitulation to the doctrine of parliamentary supremacy. At the same time, both its legitimacy and effectiveness can be enhanced.

The Origins and Politics of Section 33

Section 33 of the Charter provides that both Parliament and the provincial legislatures may expressly declare that legislation shall operate "notwithstanding" the Charter's constitutional protection of fundamental freedoms (section 2), legal rights (sections 7 to 14), and equality rights (section 15). Although legislative declarations to this effect automatically expire after five years, they may be renewed indefinitely. Allowing legislative bodies to override protected rights is nothing new in Canada. A similar notwithstanding clause appears in the 1960 Bill of Rights, as well as in the Alberta Individual Rights Protection Act, the Saskatchewan Bill of Rights, and the Quebec Charter of Rights. The crucial difference, of course, is that each of these declarations of rights is a statutory instrument; even without their notwithstanding clauses, they could be altered through ordinary legislation to serve governmental interests. What makes section 33 so controversial is the express declaration in section 52 of the Constitution Act, 1982 that the constitution, including the Charter, is the "supreme law of Canada." Granting legislative bodies the power to override the Charter through ordinary legislation appears to contradict blatantly both the letter and spirit of section 52.

Section 33 is also controversial because of the political circumstances out of which it emerged. Although various scholars and (primarily provincial) politicians had opposed the constitutional entrenchment of rights on both theoretical and practical grounds throughout the period of constitutional development leading to the agreement of November, 1981,[40] section 33 was the immediate and direct product of hard political bargaining and compromise. When the first ministers met on November 2, 1981, for a final round of constitutional negotiations, eight provinces still opposed the federal government's patriation plan. During the course of these negotiations, Saskatchewan Premier Allan Blakeney argued forcefully for a legislative override provision that would apply to everything in the Charter except language rights, democratic rights, and fundamental freedoms.[41] This proposal attracted the attention of the other dissentient provinces, who also pushed for the extension of the override provision to include fundamental freedoms. Sensing the opportunity for agreement, Prime Minister Trudeau indicated his willingness to accept this proposal subject to the premiers' agreeing to attach a five-year time limit on any specific override clause. In what three observers have described as a "classic example of raw bargaining," the federal government and nine provincial governments agreed to this provision without which the negotiations might never have succeeded.[42]

The circumstances that produced section 33 inhibited the public development of a coherent theoretical justification for the legislative override. On the one hand, since section 33 became part of the Charter after the Joint Committee on the Constitution had finished its work, it was not subject to the same searching public inquiry that characterized other key sections of the Charter. On the other hand, since section 33 reflected a complex political compromise, the parties to that compromise had no special incentive to threaten their agreement by raising complicated theoretical questions about the notwithstanding clause: silence was the best policy. The most extensive public discussion of this provision thus occurred on November 20, 1981, when Justice Minister Jean Chrétien introduced the constitutional resolution containing the Charter into the House of Commons. Even then, Chrétien's remarks on section 33 covered only eleven paragraphs and were aimed primarily at assuring the House that it did not "emasculate" the Charter. The only theoretical point that Chrétien stressed in these remarks was that section 33 would be an infrequently used "safety valve" to ensure "that legislatures rather than judges would have the final say on important matters of public policy." Section 33, Chrétien argued, would allow legislatures "to correct absurd situations without going through the difficulty of obtaining constitutional amendments."[43]

Despite Chrétien's explanation of the circumstances that might lead to the use of section 33, the first government to invoke the notwithstanding clause did so with quite different purposes in mind. On June 23, 1982 – nine weeks after the official proclamation of Canada's new constitutional order – the Quebec National Assembly passed legislation (Bill 62) amending all existing Quebec statutes to include a notwithstanding clause.[44] The Quebec law accomplished this blanket override by replacing the text of all provincial Acts adopted before April 17, 1982, and between April 17 and June 23, 1982, with their existing text as amended by the addition of a separate section declaring that each Act "shall operate notwithstanding the provisions of sections 2 and 7 to 15 of the Constitution Act, 1982." If there was still any doubt about the matter, Bill 62 forcefully confirmed Quebec's continued opposition both to the process that produced the Constitution Act, 1982 and to the substance of the new constitution. The Quebec government thus used section 33 to make a pre-emptive strike against a document to which it had refused to give its assent.

The enactment of Bill 62 belied Jean Chrétien's assurances that the impact of section 33 would be limited to instances where legislatures disagreed with the substantive policy choices implicit in judicial interpretation and application of the Charter. Instead, by severely limiting the possibilities for Charter review of Quebec legislation, Bill 62 confirmed many of the worst fears of those who objected to section 33. The second use of the override by a provincial legislature did nothing to alleviate these fears, as the government of Saskatchewan used section 33 to pre-empt a constitutional challenge by provincial government employees to back-to-work legislation.[45] Enacted on January 31, 1986, Saskatchewan's SGEU Dispute Settlement Act ordered government employees to end rotating strikes and resume their duties under the terms of a contract recommended by a conciliator. Fearing that the Act might be found to violate the Charter's guaranteed right to freedom of association, the government used the notwithstanding clause to insulate it from judicial review on these grounds. Although much narrower than Quebec's action – Saskatchewan's notwithstanding clause applied to only one statute and overrode only one sub-section (2[d]) of the Charter – this was another instance of the override provision being employed in circumstances unanticipated by the Justice Minister.

These actions by Quebec and Saskatchewan increased the number of voices calling for the repeal of section 33 through constitutional amendment and also stimulated other proposals to lessen its impact on the Charter. For example, following Quebec's enactment of Bill 62, Stephen Scott argued that the powers of the lieutenant-governors and the Governor General be amended to curtail the ability of these officials to grant royal assent to federal and provincial bills containing override clauses.[46] Although intriguing, Scott's proposal faced the obvious criticism that reverting to monarchy was too high a price to pay for avoiding legislative violations of guaranteed rights.[47] A more common response was to suggest that the use of section 33 might itself be subject to judicial review. According to this position, there were both procedural and substantive grounds on which courts could review any use of section 33.[48]

The procedural argument for judicial review of legislative overrides is that section 33 itself establishes "manner and form" requirements for its use. The most obvious of these requirements are that overrides must be enacted by legislatures rather than executives, must pertain to statutes rather than regulations, and must expire after five years.[49] In addition to these requirements, opponents of Quebec's Bill 62 argued that it was insufficient merely to refer by number to the Charter sections being overridden. In *Alliance des Professeurs de Montréal v. A.-G. Quebec* (1985) they persuaded the Quebec Court of Appeal that it was necessary to include the full text of each relevant Charter section in a notwithstanding clause, thus rendering Bill 62 inoperative.[50] However, in *Ford v. A.-G. Quebec* (1988) the Supreme Court of Canada rejected this argument and held that blanket override provisions containing only section numbers of the Charter constitute a valid exercise of legislative authority under section 33.[51]

The Court also used *Ford* as an occasion for rejecting another possible avenue for judicial review of notwithstanding clauses, declaring that "there is no warrant for importing into [section 33] grounds for substantive review of the legislative policy in exercising the override authority in a particular case."[52] In the aftermath of the Quebec and Saskatchewan actions, commentators had argued that section 33 is subject to substantive review under section 1 of the Charter.[53] Proponents of this argument bolstered their case by highlighting the fact that nothing in the text of section 33 suggests that it should operate notwithstanding section 1. Consequently, their argument took the following form: section 1 permits Charter rights to be subject only to "such reasonable limits" as can be "demonstrably justified in a free and democratic society"; legislative overrides under section 33 represent a limitation of rights; therefore, such overrides must themselves be reasonable and demonstrably justified. According to this argument, a notwithstanding clause would not insulate legislation from Charter review but would simply alter the type of analysis undertaken under section 1. In one version of the argument, legislation containing a notwithstanding clause would be subject to minimal scrutiny, with the burden of proving the override's unreasonableness falling on the statute's challenger.[54]

The Court's decision in *Ford* signalled to governments that the use of section 33 would only be subject to minimal judicial scrutiny according to narrow standards of formal procedure. The immediate result of this decision was to open the door to the third, and most politically explosive, use of section 33 by a provincial government. Three days after the Supreme Court struck down the commercial signs provisions of Bill 101 in the *Ford* decision (December 15, 1988), Quebec Premier Robert Bourassa announced his intention to enact new language legislation (Bill 178) that would be insulated from judicial review by a notwithstanding clause. The new legislation permitted the use of English on interior commercial signs but continued Bill 101's prohibition against English on exterior signs. The negative reaction against Bourassa's decision to override the Supreme Court and invoke section 33 was immediate among Quebec's Anglophone minority and in the rest of Canada. Three Anglophone ministers resigned from Bourassa's cabinet, and Manitoba Premier Gary Filmon reacted by withdrawing from consideration by his province's legislature a resolution to ratify the Meech Lake Constitutional Accord. Bourassa's decision on December 18, 1988, to invoke section 33 undermined political support for the Meech Lake Accord outside Quebec, dealing a fatal blow to its chances for ratification.[55]

Prime Minister Mulroney attempted to salvage the Accord by deflecting the blame for Bourassa's action from the Quebec Premier to the political leaders who had initially agreed to the inclusion of section 33 in the Charter. Speaking before the House of Commons, the Prime Minister called section 33 "that major fatal flaw of 1981, which reduces your individual rights and mine." Section 33, Mulroney continued, "holds rights hostage" and renders the entire constitution suspect. Any constitution, he concluded, "that does not protect the inalienable and imprescriptible individual rights of individual Canadians is not worth the paper it is written on."[56] Despite his condemnation of section 33, however, the Prime Minister did not take the obvious and logical step of introducing a resolution to remove the override power from the Charter. His sole objective appears to have been to sever any connection between the Meech Lake Accord (especially its "distinct society" clause) and Quebec's decision to override the right to free-dom of expression in commercial signs as articulated by the Supreme Court.

The *Ford* decision and its aftermath affected section 33 in two contradictory ways. On the one hand, the decision constitutionally legitimized broad legisla-tive power to use the notwithstanding clause to override certain Charter rights. On the other hand, Quebec's decision to exercise this power to protect the restrictive language provisions of Bill 178 severely undermined the political legitimacy of section 33. As in the case of the *Patriation Reference* (1980), polit-ical reality would prove to be more powerful than constitutional formality. After the events of December, 1988, it became virtually impossible to defend the exis-tence of section 33 outside of Quebec.

Even such astute Charter analysts as Patrick Monahan changed their attitude toward section 33 after Bill 178 and the subsequent demise of the Meech Lake Accord. In his 1987 book on the Charter, Monahan challenged the position advanced by critics of section 33 who argued that it was a "constitutional anom-aly" whose presence in the Charter trivialized rights. Monahan argued instead that section 33 was simply a "powerful and blunt expression" of certain funda-mental ideas found throughout the Charter, including confidence in the political process and belief in the principle that government action is not necessarily a threat to individual liberty. Section 33, Monahan argued in 1987, does not "legit-imate tyranny" but merely ensures "that the political process will not be subject to unreasonable or perverse judicial interpretations."[57] However, writing about the downfall of the Meech Lake Accord four years later, Monahan concluded that "the inclusion of the notwithstanding clause in the 1982 constitution was clearly a very serious mistake." Reflecting on events between 1988 and 1990, Monahan now argued that section 33 had created an unforeseen political dynamic that would eventually divide Quebec and the rest of Canada. In contrast to his relatively strong support for section 33 in his 1987 book, Monahan's 1991 study of the Meech Lake process lamented as unfortunate the fact that "the not-withstanding clause has become truly embedded in the charter in a permanent way."[58]

This change in Monahan's view of section 33 hints at two reasons why the political legitimacy of section 33 is now so weak that Andrew Heard has sug-gested that, outside of Quebec, a binding constitutional convention is emerging against using the notwithstanding clause.[59] One reason is that there was never any coherent articulation of the theoretical consistency of liberal constitution-alism with the presence of a legislative override provision. As Monahan pointed out in his 1987 book, commentators tended to view section 33 as the anomalous product of raw political bargaining. In addition, there was also a tendency to equate constitutional supremacy with judicial supremacy. However, as Agresto has argued, and as I have also attempted to demonstrate, the essence of liberal constitutionalism is the presence of checks on political power, including checks on the political power exercised by courts. A legislative override like section 33 is clearly consistent with this understanding of constitutionalism.

The second reason for the current lack of legitimacy surrounding section 33 is an accident of history. To be more precise, Canadians experienced a use of the notwithstanding clause that they found outrageous before they experienced a Supreme Court decision of equivalent political unpopularity. Even the Court's 1988 abortion decision did not have the same political effect as the U.S. Court's abortion ruling, largely because the Canadian Court did not step fully into the arena of moral decision-making. One wonders, however, what might have happened had the Court issued its politically unpopular *Seaboyer* decision on the Criminal Code's rape shield law, or even its *Askov* decision on unreasonable trial delays, before December 18, 1988.

Both the *Seaboyer* and *Askov* decisions can be marshalled to support the proposition that section 33 can have an important and positive role to play in the development of liberal constitutionalism in Canada. The Criminal Code provisions struck down in *Seaboyer* were not the ill-considered products of a tyrannical majority operating under the influence of momentary hysteria. Quite to the contrary, they were a thoughtful and serious attempt to deal with what informed observers had identified as a considerable weakness in the administration of criminal justice. Responding to criticism of the common-law rules governing sexual history evidence, Parliament amended the Criminal Code in 1976 to limit the permissible scope of inquiry into a complainant's previous sexual conduct. Ironically, the Supreme Court interpreted this provision in a manner that actually provided less protection to the complainant from this type of inquiry.[60] Consequently, Parliament undertook further reforms in 1982, generating the Code provisions nullified in *Seaboyer.* The government has now been forced to repeat this complicated exercise in a possibly futile attempt to satisfy requirements imposed by seven justices of the Supreme Court. Indeed, the legislation proposed by the government to replace the nullified provisions will undoubtedly raise constitutional challenges, since it redefines both the nature of consent and the defences available to the accused in sexual assault proceedings.[61] By invoking section 33 to uphold the existing legislation, however, Parliament could have simultaneously accomplished two important objectives: reinstate an important policy measure, and assert its equal authority to interpret the Charter.

The *Askov* decision presents a similar opportunity. By amending the Criminal Code to define its understanding of what constitutes "unreasonable" trial delays, Parliament could have removed from the Supreme Court the burden of correcting the unintended, and unanticipated, consequences of the *Askov* decision. Legislative action would be doubly useful, since the Court's only recourse was to clarify its original intent through another decision that is just as susceptible of misunderstanding or miscommunication as *Askov.* Since the Court has never passed judgment on such a legislative provision (which might, for example, define delays of more than fourteen months as unreasonable), lower courts and provincial attorneys-general should adhere to it. For reasons that will become evident below, judicial review of this amendment should not be preempted by immediate use of the legislative override. However, if the Court were to nullify this definition of unreasonableness, and if the consequences were as negative as those that followed *Askov* (i.e., the termination of tens of thousands of prosecutions), Parliament would be justified in invoking section 33.

As Patrick Monahan's conversion on the section 33 issue indicates, to suggest in the post-Bill 178 era that any use of the legislative override might be justified amounts to political heresy. Indeed, one might criticize the above analysis as somewhat misleading, since it relies on federal legislative examples to defend the use of section 33 at a time when only provincial governments have invoked this provision. In modern federal systems, sub-national governments have come to be perceived as the principal threat to rights and liberties, and analysts who might be willing to concede the legitimacy of section 33 to respond to decisions like *Askov* and *Seaboyer* would not accept the legitimacy of provincial overrides. Nevertheless, in the next section of this chapter I intend to tread on this controversial ground in an attempt to reclaim the theoretical and constitutional legitimacy of section 33 in both the federal and provincial contexts. In the process, I also intend to suggest some possible changes in the structure of this provision that might contribute to its legitimacy.

The Legitimacy of a Legislative Override

To say that section 33 currently lacks a strong theoretical justification is not to imply that such a justification is totally absent. The legislative override has, for the most part, been rationalized as a "major concession to the traditional British principle of parliamentary supremacy."[62] However, as Samuel LaSelva has pointed out, parliamentary (or legislative) supremacy is "the very antithesis of constitutionalism."[63] Consequently, critics of the legislative override are correct to attack it on these grounds. To the extent that section 33 perpetuates the vestiges of legislative supremacy, it is indeed indefensible within the constitutional framework created by section 52 of the Constitution Act, 1982. As I have suggested throughout this chapter, if there is any theoretical justification for a legislative override, it lies in what section 33 contributes to the doctrine of constitutional supremacy. The key to making the case that section 33 does indeed contribute to this doctrine is to demonstrate that the legislative and executive branches of government possess *equal* responsibility and authority to inject meaning into the indeterminate words and phrases of the Charter.

The principal obstacle to achieving this objective is the almost universal belief – reflected in the Supreme Court's own Charter jurisprudence – in the modern understanding of the relationship between courts and constitutions. This modern understanding can be summarized in the following syllogism: the constitution is the supreme law; the judiciary is the authoritative voice of the constitution's meaning; therefore, the judiciary is the authoritative source of supreme law. The modern approach to judicial review consists in the widespread acceptance of the minor premise, and it is perhaps best illustrated by the Supreme Court's *Dolphin Delivery* (1986) and *British Columbia Government Employees' Union* (1988) decisions. In *Dolphin Delivery,* the line that the Court drew between governmental and non-governmental action did not serve private economic interests so much as it served the Court's own institutional interests. By denying that courts are governmental actors, the Supreme Court articulated the premise that courts enjoy a privileged position in relation to the Charter. Similarly, in the *British Columbia Government Employees' Union* decision, the Court refused to allow freedom of expression and association to inhibit access to courts because of their important role under the Charter. Indeed, the Court argued that the Charter could not be used to close British Columbia courts because without operating courts the Charter would be meaningless, and if the Charter is meaningless, democracy ceases to exist.[64]

This formulation is only accurate, however, if one assumes that legislatures are normally in the business of denying rights. While it is impossible to deny that every state is capable of engaging in acts of tyranny, the corruption of any state that did so with regularity would be so complete as to permeate every institution, including the courts. By contrast, the very operation of liberal democratic states requires that their citizens and officials share a basic commitment to the fundamental tenets of liberal constitutionalism. Where this commitment exists, legislators do not seek to deny rights as an end in itself. Instead, they seek to achieve important policy objectives consistent with their understanding of the public good, which often entails limiting the rights and liberties of citizens generally, or of specific groups of citizens. Indeed, these policy objectives often confer rights and benefits on individuals and groups, which also requires limiting the rights of others. The actual dynamics of legislative and judicial action are thus more complex than the simplistic view that legislatures violate rights while courts protect (or extend) rights and liberties.

This more benign understanding of the role of legislatures in liberal democracies provides only minimal support for their equal authority as constitutional interpreters, however. A more important case for this authority can be constructed by recalling Alexander Hamilton's discussion of judicial power that was examined in Chapter One.[65] Hamilton clearly agreed with the proposition that courts should nullify statutes found to be in conflict with the constitution, and that courts pose a lesser threat to liberty than legislatures or executives. Nevertheless, he attached two significant qualifications to these statements. Hamilton defined constitutional conflicts very narrowly to include blatant violations of specific constitutional provisions, as well as violations of the constitution's "*manifest* tenor" (emphasis added). Although this latter term might imply some room for judicial creativity, it should again be remembered that Hamilton considered judicial usurpation of legislative power sufficient grounds for the impeachment of judges. In a similar fashion, he stressed that judicial power would remain a minor threat to liberty only so long as it did not combine with legislative or executive power. Denying any branch of government a monopoly over constitutional interpretation thus contributes to the overlapping separation of powers that serves to prevent tyranny.[66]

Fortunately, it is not necessary to rely solely on this American formulation of constitutionalism to conclude that legislatures may legitimately engage in constitutional interpretation. Indeed, a similar view is implicit in the initial formulation of Lord Sankey's famous "living tree" metaphor, which now serves as the justification for broad judicial interpretation of the Charter. Sankey's original point, however, was that courts should avoid overly narrow interpretations of constitutional language in order not to restrict legislative innovativeness. In the *Edwards* case, for example, Sankey asserted that, if it so chose, the government of Canada could interpret the term "persons" in section 24 of the BNA Act to include women, thereby allowing for the appointment of women to the Senate.[67] Similarly, provincial legislatures employed a then novel interpretation of the term "civil rights" to justify legislation that protected individuals against discrimination in employment and accommodation. The provinces continuously expanded this interpretation at each step in the process that eventually led to modern human rights legislation. Had courts ignored Sankey's advice, this progressive development might have foundered on the originally narrow meaning of civil rights that existed at Confederation.

This analysis suggests that, in its original formulation, the living tree doctrine had two principal elements. First, it acknowledged that legislatures may interpret constitutional language in ways that depart from its original meaning. Second, it instructed courts to be circumspect in reviewing these legislative re-interpretations, lest they interfere with progressive policy developments. This reading of the living tree doctrine is not conclusive, however, since critics of the legislative override could concede these points yet argue that the doctrine simply grants legislatures the authority to expand rights but not to contract them. There are at least two responses to this criticism. One is that there is no logically necessary reason why legislative power to interpret constitutional language should function in only one direction. The second reason is that it is virtually impossible to expand the interpretation of some rights without simultaneously contracting the interpretation of other rights. For example, the expansion of civil rights inherent in human rights legislation has been achieved primarily by narrowing the scope of property rights. If legislatures may contract property rights, there is no reason in principle why they may not contract other rights.

This returns the discussion to an earlier point: the principal issue in an overwhelming majority of Charter cases is not legislative abrogation of rights, but the constitutional validity of a shifting balance in the relative importance attached to competing rights. What this suggests is that constitutional review under the Charter serves a useful purpose by forcing legislators to give coherent reasons for their policy choices and to consider whether the *identical* goal might be achieved *as effectively* through other means. It also suggests, however, that section 33 does not permit legislatures to override rights, but to override the judicial interpretation of what constitutes a reasonable balance between competing rights.[68] The value of section 33 thus lies in the power it grants legislatures to re-assert the democratic will against judicial will. More importantly, section 33 can have a positive impact by encouraging a more politically vital discourse on the meaning of rights and their relationship to competing constitutional visions than what emanates from the judicial monologue that results from a regime of judicial supremacy.

It almost goes without saying that none of this means that section 33 is perfect in its current form. Although post-Bill 178 defenders of the legislative override were difficult to find, there was at least one who offered concrete suggestions for improving this constitutional provision. According to Peter Russell, the legislative override should be subject to two separate enactments, the first coming before and the second after an election.[69] Russell's proposal could be met in the following fashion: in addition to the current stipulation that overrides expire automatically after five years, legislative overrides could also expire with the dissolution of the Parliament or legislature responsible for invoking the override. This would force incoming governments and legislative majorities to reconsider all existing notwithstanding clauses contained in legislation. For example, the notwithstanding clause contained in Bill 178 would have expired with the Quebec election held in the autumn of 1989. One possible danger in this proposal is that, since overrides would be constantly before a legislature, their re-enactment might simply become routine.

In addition to the concerns expressed by Russell, section 33 suffers from two additional formal weaknesses, both of which can be addressed through rather simple amendments to the override provision. The first weakness is that, as the Supreme Court has confirmed, there is currently nothing that prohibits legislatures from using the legislative override to pre-empt judicial review. This should be prevented, however, because it is precisely under these circumstances that section 33 becomes an instrument of legislative supremacy. The doctrine of constitutional supremacy includes an important review function for courts, and the legislative override should not be used to undercut that function. Consequently, it is necessary to amend section 33 in a manner that avoids this problem. The second weakness concerns the ability of legislatures to invoke section 33 by a simple majority vote. Just as constitutional amendments (or legislative overrides of executive vetos in the United States) require extraordinary majorities to become law, legislative overrides of constitutional decisions should also require an extraordinary majority before becoming effective. This was recognized in the federal government's 1991 constitutional reform proposals, which advocated abandoning the simple majority rule in favour of a three-fifths majority requirement.[70]

All of these proposed reforms could be accommodated through amendments to sections 33(1) and 33(3) of the Charter. Once these amendments are in place, the relevant Charter sections might read as follows (changes in italics):

33.(1) Parliament or the legislature of a province may expressly declare in an Act of Parliament or of the legislature, as the case may be, that the Act or a provision thereof shall operate notwithstanding *a final judicial decision that the legislation or a provision thereof abrogates or unreasonably limits* a provision included in section 2 or sections 7 to 15 of this Charter. *A declaration under this subsection becomes effective upon the agreement of three-fifths of the House of Commons and Senate or three-fifths of the provincial legislature, as the case may be.*

(3) A declaration made under subsection (1) shall cease to have effect *upon the dissolution of the Parliament or legislature making the declaration* or five years after it comes into force or on such earlier date as may be specified in the declaration.

The purpose of the first amendment to section 33(1) is to prevent pre-emptive use of the legislative override, thus allowing courts at least an opportunity to offer their judgment as to the constitutionality of legislation. This amendment also emphasizes the fact that, in invoking the notwithstanding clause, legislatures would not be overriding Charter rights *per se,* but judicial interpretations of those rights. The second amendment to section 33(1) simply establishes the three-fifths majority requirement. Although this amendment requires acceptance by a three-fifths majority of the Senate, the current structure and role of the Senate might mean that a simple majority vote would suffice in that body, whatever the requirement in the House of Commons. Finally, the change to section 33(3) operationalizes the principle that one consequence of an election should be the automatic reconsideration of existing legislative overrides in federal or provincial legislation. This amendment would also guarantee that existing notwithstanding clauses would become election issues.[71]

Although none of these changes is likely to satisfy the most adamant opponents of section 33, they represent one strategy for making the legislative override even more compatible with liberal constitutional theory. The core principle of that theory is the subordination of all political power, including judicial power, to procedural and substantive constitutional rules. While it is true that no constitution can long survive if its meaning "is frozen in time to the moment of adoption,"[72] liberal constitutionalism does not establish a judicial monopoly over the process of adapting constitutional language to changing social circumstances. In addition to changes enacted through formal amending procedures, both legislatures and executives must play an important role in the continuous process of adaptation. In Canada, the procedural rules of the constitution have been kept flexible with relatively little judicial assistance through the evolution of various constitutional conventions.[73] Moreover, the original formulation of the living tree doctrine allowed Canadian governments to pursue innovative policy choices consistent with novel interpretations of constitutional language. Contrary to the assertions of most opponents of section 33, who would prefer a judicial monopoly over constitutional interpretation, such a monopoly may actually produce more rigidity than flexibility.

There is one further objection to the override power conferred on legislatures by section 33: it makes legislatures – and hence the majorities they represent – judges in their own cause with respect to the constitutionality of their actions. Legislatures, in other words, are bound to be biased when considering the constitutionality of their own enactments. The principal weakness of this objection is that it assumes the existence of a monolithic and homogeneous majority able to assert its will through a government whose decisions constitute rational choices made by a unitary actor. To be sure, while a parliamentary system of government does lend itself more easily to systematic majority rule, it is also true that a parliamentary majority's future electoral fortunes depend on its being sensitive to diverse political demands. For practical reasons, therefore, the majority's own cause must accommodate the minority's cause to some extent. Moreover, the legislature that overrides a judicial interpretation of rights may reflect a different majority coalition than that which originally enacted the statute in question. Finally, a "bureaucratic politics" analysis of policy formation suggests that no single actor, or even set of actors, completely controls the policy process.[74] All of this indicates that the reality of liberal democratic politics is more complex than opponents of section 33 assume.

Conclusion

The current strong opposition to any use of the notwithstanding clause to override unacceptable judicial interpretation and application of Charter rights is the product of an historical accident and three conceptual errors. The historical accident is that Canadians experienced a use of section 33 that they found objectionable before the Supreme Court rendered a politically unpopular Charter decision. Until the *Askov* and *Seaboyer* decisions, none of the Court's decisions provoked broad public disapproval. Unfortunately, the political leaders who took advantage of Quebec's inclusion of a notwithstanding clause in Bill 178 to condemn section 33 cannot now rely on the legislative override in circumstances where it might be beneficial.

One of the conceptual errors underlying opposition to the legislative override involves a misunderstanding of the constitutional role of legislatures and courts in liberal constitutional theory. Nothing in that theory assigns the task of constitutional interpretation exclusively to courts: legislatures also have a legitimate and important role to play. The second conceptual error stems from a basic misunderstanding of the legislative process as being characterized by the haphazard adoption of measures motivated by majority tyranny. To be sure, legislatures can act both irrationally and arbitrarily; and judicial review provides an important check on these pathologies of legislative behaviour. Nevertheless, judicial supremacy may be a cure worse than the disease, since courts suffer from their own institutional pathologies when it comes to evaluating complex policy choices. Finally, the opposition to section 33 is fuelled by a basic misunderstanding of the nature of Charter adjudication. As I have argued throughout this book, Charter cases only rarely resolve disputes about fundamental rights and almost never resolve disputes about fundamental moral principles. To be sure, although many Charter cases involve fundamental questions about rights or moral principles (for example, abortion), the outcome in these cases almost never hinges on the resolution of these questions. In most cases, the dispute is

reduced to a conflict over the application of the least-restrictive-means component of the *Oakes* test. However, even if Charter cases did involve serious disputes about fundamental moral principles on a regular basis, there would be no
reason to leave the resolution of these disputes in the exclusive hands of
Supreme Court justices. Elevation to a nation's highest court does not transform
an individual into a moral philosopher. Indeed, there is nothing in legal training
or in the practice of law that imparts superior judgment in such matters.

The paradox of liberal constitutionalism is that its main enforcement mechanism poses a significant threat to the political principles that this mechanism
exists to protect. Moreover, it is both unrealistic and inconsistent with liberal
constitutionalism to expect judges to be self-restrained in their exercise of political power in the context of constitutional review. What is necessary is a structural check on judicial power that better balances "the principle of constitutionalism with active popular sovereignty."[75] The doctrine of judicial supremacy
cannot be a substitute for the principle of constitutional supremacy.

Conclusion

This book has examined the manner in which the Supreme Court of Canada has mobilized the new forms of judicial power made available by the Charter of Rights and Freedoms. In brief, the pattern of decision-making exhibited by the Supreme Court in the key areas of fundamental freedoms, legal rights, and equality rights suggests that the paradox of liberal constitutionalism – that is, the transformation of constitutional supremacy into judicial supremacy in the very process of enforcing the former – has become an important feature of Canadian politics. Although the Court has deferred to legislative policy choices in specific instances, it has shown little restraint in building up its own powers of judicial review or in asserting its own pre-eminent authority over the development of Charter-related constitutional principles. In the area of fundamental freedoms it has, with some notable exceptions, refrained from placing definitional limits on the scope of the freedoms protected under section 2. With legal rights, the Court has rejected the utilitarian, crime-control approach to fair procedure in favour of the dignity-enhancement, due process approach. In addition, it has asserted constitutional control over the *substance* of the criminal law, as well as criminal procedure. Moreover, the Court has accepted the results-oriented substantive interpretation of equality rights, as well as a relatively open-ended interpretation of the groups protected under section 15. Finally, by disassociating the Charter's text from the meaning intended by those who wrote it (again, with some notable exceptions), the Court has provided itself with maximum flexibility to define the text as it wishes.

This tendency toward judicial supremacy is a particularly important development in view of the Court's explicit engagement in policy analysis in the application of sections 1 and 24(1) of the Charter. Much of what is most important about the Court's Charter jurisprudence takes place within the context of these two sections, in which the Court balances interests and reallocates public

resources. While it may be appropriate for the Court to be final in defining fundamental constitutional principles (a proposition that nevertheless is debatable), it
is less clear that it should be the final arbiter in determining the political and policy consequences that flow from those principles. Reasonable people may share
identical principles while sharply disagreeing about how they apply to specific
policy questions. When applied to the jurisprudence of reasonable limits and
appropriate remedies, judicial supremacy can mean the elevation of particular
policy agendas to constitutional status.

What has occurred during the Charter era is not so much the "political seduction of the law"[1] as the legal seduction of politics. The willingness of interest
groups to pursue their political agendas through Charter litigation and the general acquiescence of both the public and government to Supreme Court Charter
decisions reflect the relatively new assumption that almost every issue, and certainly the most divisive moral issues, is better resolved through the judicial process than through the conventional political process. Underlying this assumption is a significant transformation in the perception of politics and litigation. In
the traditional understanding, the essence of politics was the search for that compromise among private interests that best coincided with the public good. Litigation, by contrast, was a process for resolving indivisible conflicts between private interests. The emerging view, reflected in current attitudes toward the Charter, is that politics is a process whereby private groups capture public resources
to promote their own interests; and litigation is perceived as the principal way of
reasserting a public interest that is ignored by the political process. Moreover, in
the current celebration of constitutional adjudication there is a denigration of
incremental approaches to resolving social conflict. The irony, of course, is that
constitutional adjudication takes place in perhaps the most incrementally oriented decision-making institution in our political system.

This transformation in the conventional understanding of politics and litigation is tied to broader themes in the theory of liberal democracy. The founders of liberal democracy shared a view of human nature in which autonomous
and free individuals are assumed to act in their self-interest, a characteristic
that contributed to social and political divisiveness, as well as to the tendency
for political officials to abuse their power. Although liberal democratic theorists recognized that any society could mitigate these defects by imposing a collective interest on its members, they insisted that this solution could only be
implemented at the cost of the very principles that liberal democracy was
designed to protect, and at the cost of the energy and creativity to which the
pursuit of self-interest contributes. The modern advocates of constitutional
adjudication seem to reject this component of liberal democratic theory, asserting instead that it is possible to eliminate the "causes of faction" by replacing
the partisan and fallible reason of conventional policy-makers with the dispassionate and principled reasoning of judges.[2] In even broader terms, this attitude is part of the modern faith in the ability of technology to solve human
problems, in this case to solve moral-political dilemmas through the technology of adjudication.[3] However, as Chapter Six argued, several outstanding

questions remain about the appropriateness of this technology for the task that it now attempts to undertake.

To many Charter sceptics who have criticized its impact on Canadian political life, the phenomenon described in this book is an inevitable outcome of liberalism and its emphasis on individual rights. From their perspective, the solution is to abandon liberal individualism in favour of communitarianism and collective rights. Nor do they view this as a particularly radical solution: its roots already exist in both Canadian political culture and the Charter. One should think carefully, however, about transforming this cultural tendency into an overarching constitutional principle, since the application of the communitarian principle might lead to unexpected, and undesired, results. Take, for example, the abortion law struck down in *Morgentaler, Smoling and Scott.* In this instance, the federal government designed an abortion policy that allowed local, or at least provincial, communities to provide a level of access to abortion consistent with community moral standards. The predictable result was that access to abortion varied both across and within provinces. From a communitarian perspective, however, there seems to be little that can be said against this decision to devolve the implementation of abortion policy to local communities. Indeed, a coherent communitarian theory might require this approach to issues on which a national consensus is difficult to reach.

Or would it? One communitarian response might be that women as a group possess a special collective right to reproductive choice, which allows them to claim an exemption from community moral standards in this area. This response works well until the collective rights of women clash with the collective rights of other groups. This was precisely the case in *Casagrande v. Hinton Roman Catholic Separate School District* (1987), in which an unmarried, female teacher brought an unsuccessful section 15 challenge to the school district's decision to dismiss her after she became pregnant.[4] In upholding the school district's decision, the trial court held that the collective right of denominational schools to police the moral comportment of their employees (guaranteed, the court said, by section 29 of the Charter[5]) overrides at least some equality claims. Whether the right to reproductive choice (in this case, the right to become pregnant) belongs to women individually or collectively, it is clear that the court believed that another group enjoyed a collective right to claim protection from the requirements that flow from the broader community's understanding of equal treatment.

The point of this example – in which the religious freedom of one group came into direct conflict with the equality rights of another – is that the substitution of collective rights for individual rights does not really solve anything. One can speak of the collective right of communities, or of the collective rights of specific groups within a community, but it will always be necessary in a heterogeneous, pluralist society to resolve disputes among these equally strong competing claims. Moreover, in most instances there will be more than one principled way to resolve a particular dispute. What occurs in Charter adjudication is that the Supreme Court uses its considerable discretion to employ one principle rather than another, thereby conferring constitutional status on the privileged principle. The particular choice may aim at advancing the public good or human dignity, but it inevitably reflects a *judicial* vision of those two values. Automatic deference to that vision rests on the assumption that the legislative vision reflected in statutes or other government action is the product of self-interested majorities who act without regard to the interests of the minority. This assumption can only be true, however, if the majority is permanent; otherwise, the self-interest of those *temporarily* in the majority dictates that the interests of their opponents *temporarily* in the minority not be absolutely excluded from consideration. Majorities tend to dissolve and must be reconstructed on every issue: today's foe on employment equity policy may be tomorrow's friend on anti-pornography policy. Judicial supremacy cannot be defended by characterizing the legislative process as a continuous attempt by the majority to oppress the minority. To be sure, any particular outcome of the legislative process will give one interest (or set of interests) more of what it wants than it gives others, but the process as a whole is not a zero-sum game. However, if the process does become a zero-sum game for some groups or individuals, then it indicates a fundamental breakdown in the principles and practice of liberal democratic politics. To believe that courts could preserve those principles and practices after the public foundation that supports them has disintegrated seems to me overly optimistic.

It is possible, of course, that a social consensus eventually will emerge that indicates which competing principle best promotes the public good. There is then considerable value in elevating that principle to a permanently privileged position by entrenching it in the constitution through the amending process. There are two signs that such a social consensus has clearly coalesced around a particular principle. First, it will be possible to articulate the principle in sufficiently specific terms that its impact on future legislation and government policy is clear. This, in fact, is true of every post-Bill of Rights amendment to the U.S. Constitution except the Fourteenth and Fifteenth amendments. Consequently, most post-Bill of Rights amendments are almost never the focus of legal disputes because their meaning is so clear that legislatures simply do not contravene the principles they contain. The second indicator of true social consensus is that it will be relatively easy to build the extraordinary majority necessary to enact the relevant constitutional amendments. As Jane Mansbridge has said about the failure to secure the Equal Rights Amendment in the United States, "[n]o really controversial amendment has passed since Prohibition was repealed."[6] Both the initial opposition to the Charter and the amount of litigation it has engendered suggest that there is no social consensus about the meaning of its terms; and judicial decisions that accept one interpretation of their meaning rather than another simply cannot be taken as indicating that such a social consensus has subsequently emerged. Judicial review serves a useful purpose by adding another thoughtful voice to the continuing public debate about the principles by which we should be governed, but it is no substitute for that debate. That is, I fear, the direction that Charter review is taking.

The ascendency of justiciable rights over bargainable interests has made the

Charter the touchstone not only of ordinary political debates but of the process of constitutional change as well. The most obvious example is the Charter's role in the demise of the 1987 Meech Lake Constitutional Accord. The Meech Lake agreement was the product of the same traditional approach to constitutional change that produced the 1981 agreement: a (relatively) private round of negotiations among first ministers. However, as Alan Cairns has pointed out, the Charter radically transformed the terrain of constitutional discourse between 1981 and 1987.[7] In providing special constitutional protection for various groups (all numerical minorities, except women), the Charter conferred explicit constitutional status on those groups; and they demanded the right to have their voices heard in the process of constitutional change. Consequently, no proposal for constitutional reform that did not explicitly solicit their contribution could enjoy full legitimacy. These groups legitimately claimed not only access to the process but also guardianship over the substance of constitutional change. Thus, their resistance to the Meech Lake Accord rose substantially as arguments mounted that the Accord's "distinct society" clause might weaken the Charter's force in Quebec. The enactment of Bill 178 appeared to confirm this fear, and the agreement lost most of its legitimacy outside of Quebec.

The Meech Lake episode is very revealing about how the Charter has come to be viewed by those groups with a direct stake in it. In their view, the Charter is not simply one part of the "supreme law of Canada," it is the supreme law itself; and any government action, including formal constitutional amendment, that threatens to weaken the Charter is considered constitutionally – not simply politically – illegitimate. The stakes of the game are considerably elevated when interest group competition moves from the parliamentary to the constitutional arena, and this explains the strong incentive that groups have to safeguard their constitutional positions. The federal government recognized this in its post-Meech Lake proposals for constitutional reform.[8] First, the government proposed to define the nature of Quebec's distinct society more clearly and, more importantly, to place the new distinct society clause within the Charter itself. This would transform the clause from an overarching constitutional principle superior to the Charter – as critics argued was the case with the Meech Lake Accord – into merely one interpretive clause among several others. Second, the government proposed to amend section 33 of the Charter to provide that legislative overrides could only be invoked with the approval of 60 per cent of the members of Parliament or the provincial legislature. The obvious aim of this proposal was to make the notwithstanding clause more difficult to enact. Both of these proposals sought to assuage concerns that the Charter might be weakened.

The desire to constitutionalize policy matters covered by political rights, which underlies the pre-eminence now enjoyed by the Charter in constitutional debates, has been extended into the area of economic and social policy. Although the enforcement of the Charter's fundamental freedoms, legal rights, and equality rights has an obvious impact on economic and social policy, the proposal to entrench a charter of social and economic rights in the constitution would make this more explicit. This proposal first took concrete form in September, 1991 at the initiative of the NDP government of Ontario. Responding partly to the federal government's proposal to entrench traditional property rights,[9] and partly to concerns about the fate of disadvantaged social and economic groups under ordinary Charter litigation, the Ontario government urged the adoption of a social charter "that would entrench our commitment to social justice more explicitly, and would make governments more accountable, either in the courts or some other adjudicative body, for the obligations raised by that commitment."[10] This proposal generated extensive debate about the desirability of entrenching such rights, the nature of the rights themselves, and the appropriate mechanism for enforcing constitutionally entrenched social and economic rights.

There is an important parallel between some of the principal arguments marshalled in support of a social charter and the objectives underlying the Trudeau government's push for the Charter of Rights and Freedoms. Just as the 1982 Charter was designed in part to mute the centrifugal forces at work in Canada, many proponents of a social charter perceive it as helping to shape the still elusive Canadian national identity. Thus, the government of Ontario argues that the constitutional entrenchment of social rights would protect the "institutions of social policy" through which our common identity is now expressed.[11] Moreover, it is clear that one important purpose of a social charter would be to obligate the federal government to continue, and probably augment, its financial participation in social programs administered by the provinces. This participation would take the form of national standards for social programs and would aim at harmonizing social policy across provinces.[12]

The relationship between the Charter of Rights and Freedoms and national unity ought to be the cause for sober reflection by proponents of this argument, however. From the moment that the federal government and nine provinces agreed to the Charter's entrenchment without Quebec's consent, to the death of the Meech Lake Accord, the Charter has exacerbated political conflict and divisions in Canada. At the level of macro-politics, the phenomenon that Alan Cairns calls "constitutional minoritarianism" has made agreement on fundamentals even more difficult. At the level of micro-politics, constitutional minoritarianism encourages the use of litigation to resolve disputes, pushing those disputes into an adversarial forum where the stakes are high. In retrospect, there is no reason to believe that such a process will reduce conflict. A social charter may articulate a set of goals with which all Canadians can agree, but that is perhaps the easiest task in politics: real conflict emerges when the discussion turns to setting priorities among those goals and to designing specific strategies and tactics for achieving them. Canadians now seem to expect more from their constitution – that it can "guarantee" liberty, equality, social justice, and national unity, for example – than the document can deliver. We might be better off rediscovering the value of the public realm of politics, as well as the value of constitutional parsimony.

APPENDIX

The Canadian Charter of Rights and Freedoms

Whereas Canada is founded upon principles that recognize the supremacy of God and the rule of law:

Guarantee of Rights and Freedoms

1. The *Canadian Charter of Rights and Freedoms* guarantees the rights and freedoms set out in it subject only to such reasonable limits prescribed by law as can be demonstrably justified in a free and democratic society.

Fundamental Freedoms

2. Everyone has the following fundamental freedoms:
   (a) freedom of conscience and religion;
   (b) freedom of thought, belief, opinion and expression, including freedom of the press and other media of communication;
   (c) freedom of peaceful assembly; and
   (d) freedom of association.

Democratic Rights

3. Every citizen of Canada has the right to vote in an election of members of the House of Commons or of a legislative assembly and to be qualified for membership therein.

4. (1) No House of Commons and no legislative assembly shall continue for longer than five years from the date fixed for the return of the writs at a general election of its members.
   (2) In time of real or apprehended war, invasion or insurrection, a

House of Commons may be continued by Parliament and a legislative assembly may be continued by the legislature beyond five years if such continuation is not opposed by the votes of more than one-third of the members of the House of Commons or the legislative assembly, as the case may be.

5. There shall be a sitting of Parliament and of each legislature at least once every twelve months.

Mobility Rights

6.   (1) Every citizen of Canada has the right to enter, remain in and leave Canada.

    (2) Every citizen of Canada and every person who has the status of a permanent resident of Canada has the right
       (a) to move to and take up residence in any province; and
       (b) to pursue the gaining of a livelihood in any province.

    (3) The rights specified in subsection (2) are subject to
       (a) any laws or practices of general application in force in a province other than those that discriminate among persons primarily on the basis of province of present or previous residence; and
       (b) any laws providing for reasonable residency requirements as a qualification for the receipt of publicly provided social services.

    (4) Subsections (2) and (3) do not preclude any law, program or activity that has as its object the amelioration in a province of conditions of individuals in that province who are socially or economically disadvantaged if the rate of employment in that province is below the rate of employment in Canada.

Legal Rights

7. Everyone has the right to life, liberty and security of the person and the right not to be deprived thereof except in accordance with the principles of fundamental justice.

8. Everyone has the right to be secure against unreasonable search or seizure.

9. Everyone has the right not to be arbitrarily detained or imprisoned.

10. Everyone has the right on arrest or detention
    (a) to be informed promptly of the reasons therefor;
    (b) to retain and instruct counsel without delay and to be informed of that right; and
    (c) to have the validity of the detention determined by way of *habeas corpus* and to be released if the detention is not lawful.

11. Any person charged with an offence has the right
    (a) to be informed without unreasonable delay of the specific offence;
    (b) to be tried within a reasonable time;
    (c) not to be compelled to be a witness in proceedings against that person, in respect of the offence;
    (d) to be presumed innocent until proven guilty according to law in a fair and public hearing by an independent and impartial tribunal;
    (e) not to be denied reasonable bail without just cause;
    (f) except in the case of an offence under military law tried before a military tribunal, to the benefit of trial by jury where the maximum punishment for the offence is imprisonment for five years or a more severe punishment;
    (g) not to be found guilty on account of any act or omission unless, at the time of the act or omission, it constituted an offence under Canadian or international law or was criminal according to the general principles of law recognized by the community of nations;
    (h) if finally acquitted of the offence, not to be tried for it again and, if finally found guilty and punished for the offence, not to be tried or punished for it again; and
    (i) if found guilty of the offence and if the punishment for the offence has been varied between the time of commission and the time of sentencing, to the benefit of the lesser punishment.

12. Everyone has the right not to be subjected to any cruel and unusual treatment or punishment.

13. A witness who testifies in any proceedings has the right not to have any incriminating evidence so given used to incriminate that witness in any other proceedings, except in a prosecution for perjury or for the giving of contradictory evidence.

14. A party or witness in any proceedings who does not understand or speak the language in which the proceedings are conducted or who is deaf has the right to the assistance of an interpreter.

Equality Rights

15. (1) Every individual is equal before and under the law and has the right to the equal protection and equal benefit of the law without discrimination and, in particular, without discrimination based on race, national or ethnic origin, colour, religion, sex, age or mental or physical disability.
    (2) Subsection (1) does not preclude any law, program or activity that has as its object the amelioration of conditions of disadvantaged individuals or groups including those that are disadvantaged

because of race, national or ethnic origin, colour, religion, sex, age
or mental or physical disability.

Official Languages of Canada

16. (1) English and French are the official languages of Canada and have
equality of status and equal rights and privileges as to their use in all
institutions of the Parliament and government of Canada.

    (2) English and French are the official languages of New Brunswick
and have equality of status and equal rights and privileges as to their
use in all institutions of the legislature and government of New
Brunswick.

    (3) Nothing in this Charter limits the authority of Parliament or a legis-
lature to advance the equality of status or use of English or French.

17. (1) Everyone has the right to use English or French in any debates and
other proceedings of Parliament.

    (2) Everyone has the right to use English or French in any debates and
other proceedings of the legislature of New Brunswick.

18. (1) The statutes, records and journals of Parliament shall be printed and
published in English and French and both language versions are
equally authoritative.

    (2) The statutes, records and journals of the legislature of New
Brunswick shall be printed and published in English and French and
both language versions are equally authoritative.

19. (1) Either English or French may be used by any person in, or in any
pleading in or process issuing from, any court established by Parliament.

    (2) Either English or French may be used by any person in, or in any
pleading in or process issuing from, any court of New Brunswick.

20. (1) Any member of the public in Canada has the right to communicate
with, and to receive available services from, any head or central
office of an institution of the Parliament of Canada or government
of Canada in English or French, and has the same right with respect
to any other office of any such institution where
    (a) there is a significant demand for communications with and
services from that office in such language; or
    (b) due to the nature of the office, it is reasonable that commu-
nications with and services from that office be available in
both English and French.

    (2) Any member of the public in New Brunswick has the right to com-
municate with, and to receive available services from, any office of

an institution of the legislature or government of New Brunswick in English or French.

21. Nothing in sections 16 to 20 abrogates or derogates from any right, privilege or obligation with respect to the English and French languages, or either of them, that exists or is continued by virtue of any other provision of the Constitution of Canada.

22. Nothing in sections 16 to 20 abrogates or derogates from any legal or customary right or privilege acquired or enjoyed either before or after the coming into force of this Charter with respect to any language that is not English or French.

Minority Language Educational Rights

23.   (1) Citizens of Canada
    (a) whose first language learned and still understood is that of the English or French linguistic minority population of the province in which they reside, or
    (b) who have received their primary school instruction in Canada in English or French and reside in a province where the language in which they received that instruction is the language of the English or French linguistic minority population of the province,

have the right to receive primary and secondary school instruction in that language in that province.

   (2) Citizens of Canada of whom any child has received or is receiving primary or secondary school instruction in English or French in Canada, have the right to have all their children receive primary and secondary school instruction in the same language.

   (3) The right of citizens of Canada under subsections (1) and (2) to have their children receive primary and secondary school instruction in the language of the English or French linguistic minority population of a province
    (a) applies wherever in the province the number of children of citizens who have such a right is sufficient to warrant the provision to them out of public funds of minority language instruction; and
    (b) includes, where the number of those children so warrants, the right to have them receive that instruction in minority language educational facilities provided out of public funds.

Enforcement

24.   (1) Anyone whose rights or freedoms, as guaranteed by this Charter, have been infringed or denied may apply to a court of competent

jurisdiction to obtain such remedy as the court considers appropriate and just in the circumstances.

(2) Where, in proceedings under subsection (1), a court concludes that evidence was obtained in a manner that infringed or denied any rights or freedoms guaranteed by this Charter, the evidence shall be excluded if it is established that, having regard to all the circumstances, the admission of it in the proceedings would bring the administration of justice into disrepute.

General

25. The guarantee in this Charter of certain rights and freedoms shall not be construed so as to abrogate or derogate from any aboriginal, treaty or other rights or freedoms that pertain to the aboriginal peoples of Canada including

    (a) any rights or freedoms that have been recognized by the Royal Proclamation of October 7, 1763; and

    (b) any rights or freedoms that now exist by way of land claims agreements or may be so acquired. [As amended by the Constitution Amendment Proclamation, 1983]

26. The guarantee in this Charter of certain rights and freedoms shall not be construed as denying the existence of any other rights or freedoms that exist in Canada.

27. This Charter shall be interpreted in a manner consistent with the preservation and enhancement of the multicultural heritage of Canadians.

28. Notwithstanding anything in this Charter, the rights and freedoms referred to in it are guaranteed equally to male and female persons.

29. Nothing in this Charter abrogates or derogates from any rights or privileges guaranteed by or under the Constitution of Canada in respect of denominational, separate or dissentient schools.

30. A reference in this Charter to a province or to the legislative assembly or legislature of a province shall be deemed to include a reference to the Yukon Territory and the Northwest Territories, or to the appropriate legislative authority thereof, as the case may be.

31. Nothing in this Charter extends the legislative powers of any body or authority.

Application of Charter

32. (1) This Charter applies

    (a) to the Parliament and government of Canada in respect of all matters within the authority of Parliament including all matters relating to the Yukon and Northwest Territories; and

(b) to the legislature and government of each province in respect of all matters within the authority of the legislature of each province.

(2) Notwithstanding subsection (1), section 15 shall not have effect until three years after this section comes into force.

33. (1) Parliament or the legislature of a province may expressly declare in an Act of Parliament or of the legislature, as the case may be, that the Act or a provision thereof shall operate notwithstanding a provision included in section 2 or sections 7 to 15 of this Charter.

(2) An Act or a provision of an Act in respect of which a declaration made under this section is in effect shall have such operation as it would have but for the provision of this Charter referred to in the declaration.

(3) A declaration made under subsection (1) shall cease to have effect five years after it comes into force or on such earlier date as may be specified in the declaration.

(4) Parliament or the legislature of a province may re-enact a declaration made under subsection (1).

(5) Subsection (3) applies in respect of a re-enactment made under subsection (4).

Citation

34. This Part may be cited as the *Canadian Charter of Rights and Freedoms*.

Notes

Introduction

1. Alexander Hamilton, James Madison, and John Jay, *The Federalist Papers,* ed. Clinton Rossiter (New York: New American Library, 1961), No. 51, 322.
2. John Agresto, *The Supreme Court and Constitutional Democracy* (Ithaca, N.Y.: Cornell University Press, 1984), 11. Other studies of the relationship between judicial power and constitutional democracy include Edward McWhinney, *Judicial Review in the English-Speaking World,* 2nd ed. (Toronto: University of Toronto Press, 1960); Philip M. Blair, *Federalism and Judicial Review in West Germany* (New York: Oxford University Press, 1981); Jerold L. Waltman and Kenneth M. Holland eds., *The Political Role of Law Courts in Modern Democracies* (New York: St. Martin's Press, 1988); Kenneth M. Holland, ed., *Judicial Activism in Comparative Perspective* (New York: St. Martin's Press, 1991).
3. See, e.g., Patrick Monahan, *Politics and the Constitution: The Charter, Federalism and the Supreme Court of Canada* (Toronto: Carswell/Methuen, 1987); Allan C. Hutchinson and Andrew Petter, "Private Rights/Public Wrongs: The Liberal Lie of the Charter," *University of Toronto Law Journal,* 38 (1988), 278-97; Michael Mandel, *The Charter of Rights and the Legalization of Politics in Canada* (Toronto: Wall & Thompson, 1989).
4. Mandel, *The Charter of Rights and the Legalization of Politics in Canada,* 71.
5. *Ibid.,* 311.
6. David M. Beatty, *Talking Heads and the Supremes: The Canadian Production of Constitutional Review* (Toronto: Carswell, 1990), 118.
7. Dale Gibson, "Judges As Legislators: Not Whether But How," *Alberta Law Review,* 25 (1987), 252.
8. M. Elizabeth Atcheson, Mary Eberts, and Beth Symes, *Women and Legal Action: Precedents, Resources and Strategies for the Future* (Ottawa: Canadian Advisory Council on the Status of Women, 1984). According to this report, the Charter gives women a unique opportunity "to stress litigation as a vehicle for social change."

9. Leonard W. Levy, *Original Intent and the Framers' Constitution* (New York: Macmillan, 1988), 362-63.

10. Peter H. Russell, "The Effect of a Charter of Rights on the Policy-Making Role of Canadian Courts," *Canadian Public Administration*, 25 (1982), 15, 32.

11. Robert Bork, *The Tempting of America: The Political Seduction of the Law* (New York: Simon and Schuster, 1990), 139-43.

12. *The Federalist Papers*, No. 10, 77-84; No. 51, 320-25.

13. Section 93(1) protects the rights of denominational schools, while section 133 gives equal standing to French and English in the legislatures and courts of Canada and Quebec.

14. The following summary of the Charter's origin and structure relies extensively on Ian Greene, *The Charter of Rights* (Toronto: Lorimer, 1989), 37-69. Useful summaries can also be found in Mandel, *The Charter of Rights and the Legalization of Politics in Canada*, 4-32; and in Dale Gibson, *The Law of the Charter: Equality Rights* (Toronto: Carswell, 1990), 36-45.

15. Government of Canada, *A Time For Action: Toward the Renewal of the Canadian Federation* (Ottawa, 1978), 8.

16. A history of these negotiations is provided in Roy Romanow, John Whyte, and Howard Leeson, *Canada Notwithstanding: The Making of the Constitution, 1976-1982* (Toronto: Carswell/Methuen, 1984). The Supreme Court decision was *Reference re Resolution to Amend the Constitution*, [1981] 1 S.C.R. 753.

17. See Peter H. Russell, "The Political Purposes of the Canadian Charter of Rights and Freedoms," *Canadian Bar Review,* 61 (1983), 33.

18. The Fifth Amendment to the U.S. Constitution provides that "[n]o person shall be . . . deprived of . . . property without due process of law; nor shall private property be taken for public use, without just compensation." For a discussion of the "takings" clause, see Richard A. Epstein, *Takings: Property and the Power of Eminent Domain* (Cambridge, Mass.: Harvard University Press, 1985).

19. See, e.g., Dennis Stone and F. Kim Walpole, "The Canadian Constitution Act and the Constitution of the United States: A Comparative Analysis," *Canadian-American Law Journal*, 2 (1983), 1-36; Walter S. Tarnopolsky, "The New Canadian Charter of Rights and Freedoms as Compared and Contrasted with the American Bill of Rights," *Human Rights Quarterly,* 5 (1983), 227-74; Paul Bender, "The Canadian Charter of Rights and Freedoms and the United States Bill of Rights: A Comparison," *McGill Law Journal*, 28 (1983), 811-66; Drew S. Days, III, "Civil Rights in Canada: An American Perspective," *American Journal of Comparative Law,* 32 (1984), 328-38; David Rosenberg, "Litigating Civil Rights and Liberties in the United States: A Vital But Flawed Enterprise," and Stephen L. Spitz, "Litigation Strategy in Equality Rights: The American Experience," in J.M. Weiler and R.M. Elliot, eds., *Litigating The Values of a Nation: The Canadian Charter of Rights and Freedoms* (Toronto: Carswell, 1986), 357-77, 385-410.

20. Peter W. Hogg, *Constitutional Law of Canada,* 2nd ed. (Toronto: Carswell, 1985), 679 n149.

21. Romanow, Whyte, and Leeson, *Canada Notwithstanding*, 245-46.

22. Alan D. Gold, "The Legal Rights Provisions – A New Vision or Déjà Vu," *Supreme Court Law Review,* 4 (1982), 108.

23. F.L. Morton, "The Politics of Rights: What Canadians Should Know About the American Bill of Rights," *Windsor Review of Legal and Social Issues,* 1 (1989), 61-96; Peter W. Hogg, "The Charter of Rights and American Theories of Interpretation," *Osgoode Hall Law Journal,* 25 (1987), 87-113.

24. *Law Society of Upper Canada v. Skapinker,* [1984] 1 S.C.R. 357, 9 D.L.R. (4th) 161 at 168.

25. *Reference re s.94(2) of the Motor Vehicle Act,* [1985] 2 S.C.R. 486, 24 D.L.R. (4th) 536 at 546.

26. [1987] 1 S.C.R. 588 at 639.

27. *Simmons v. The Queen* (1988), 55 D.L.R. (4th) 673 at 689.

Chapter One

1. [1988] 1 S.C.R 30.

2. *Morgentaler v. The Queen,* [1976] 1 S.C.R. 616 at 671 (accepting Parliament's judgment that "the desire of a woman to be relieved of her pregnancy is not, of itself, justification for performing an abortion").

3. [1988] 1 S.C.R. 30 at 46.

4. The justices of the Canadian Supreme Court and other federally appointed judges hold their positions until age seventy-five; U.S. federal judges, including Supreme Court justices, have life tenure.

5. *Dr. Bonham's Case,* 8 Rep. 118a (C.P. 1610).

6. For a discussion, see John Agresto, *The Supreme Court and Constitutional Democracy* (Ithaca, N.Y.: Cornell University Press, 1985), 41.

7. A.V. Dicey, *Introduction to the Study of the Law of the Constitution* (Indianapolis: Liberty Classics, 1982), 3-4, 371-72. This edition is a reprint of the 8th edition of Dicey's classic work, published by Macmillan of London in 1915.

8. M.H. Smith, *The Writs of Assistance Case* (Berkeley: University of California Press, 1978), 544.

9. Raoul Berger, *Congress v. The Supreme Court* (Cambridge, Mass.: Harvard University Press, 1969), 36-46.

10. *Ibid.,* 49.

11. Max Farrand, ed., *The Records of the Federal Convention of 1787,* 4 Vols. (New Haven: Yale University Press, 1966), 1:97 (Gerry); 2:76 (Martin); 1:98 (King); 2:73 (Wilson); 2:78 (Mason); 2:92 (Morris).

12. Ralph A. Rossum, "The Courts and the Judicial Power," in Leonard W. Levy and Dennis J. Mahoney, eds., *The Framing and Ratification of the Constitution* (New York: Macmillan, 1987), 222-41.

13. Berger, *Congress v. The Supreme Court,* 335, 339-46.

14. The two quotes are from the Anti-Federalists Brutus and The Federal Farmer. They are cited in Herbert J. Storing, *What The Anti-Federalists Were For* (Chicago: University of Chicago Press, 1981), 50.

15. Alexander Hamilton, James Madison, and John Jay, *The Federalist Papers,* ed. Clinton Rossiter (New York: New American Library, 1961), No. 78, 465, 466.

16. The logic underlying Hamilton's argument can be traced back to the Act of Settlement (1701), which established judicial independence in England.

17. *The Federalist Papers,* No. 78, 467, 466, 469.

18. 1 Cranch (5 U.S.) 137 (1803).

19. This narrative of the events surrounding *Marbury v. Madison* is taken from Ralph A. Rossum and G. Alan Tarr, *American Constitutional Law: Cases and Interpretation,* 2nd ed. (New York: St. Martin's, 1987), 64.

20. *The Federalist Papers,* No. 78, 466; No. 81, 485; No. 84, 515.

21. William W. Van Alstyne, "A Critical Guide to *Marbury v. Madison,*" *Duke Law Journal* (1969), 14-16.

22. See *Fletcher v. Peck,* 6 Cranch 87 (1810); *Martin v. Hunter's Lessee,* 1 Wheaton 304 (1816); *Cohens v. Virginia,* 6 Wheaton 264 (1821).

23. Robert G. McCloskey, *The American Supreme Court* (Chicago: University of Chicago Press, 1960), 231.

24. Christopher Wolfe, "A Theory of U.S. Constitutional History," *Journal of Politics,* 43 (1981), 292-316.

25. See, e.g., Henry Steele Commager, "Judicial Review and Democracy," in Leonard Levy, ed., *Judicial Review and the Supreme Court* (New York: Harper and Row, 1967), 73; Commager, *Majority Rule and Minority Rights* (New York: Oxford University Press, 1943).

26. 60 U.S. 393 (1857).

27. Harry V. Jaffa, *Crisis of the House Divided: An Interpretation of the Issues in the Lincoln-Douglas Debates,* Phoenix edition reprint (Chicago: University of Chicago Press, 1982), 284.

28. *The Slaughterhouse Cases,* 83 U.S. 36 (1873); *Civil Rights Cases,* 109 U.S. 3 (1883); *Plessy v. Ferguson,* 163 U.S. 537 (1896).

29. See, e.g., *Lochner v. New York,* 198 U.S. 45 (1905); *Hammer v. Dagenhart,* 247 U.S. 251 (1918); *Bailey v. Drexel Furniture Co.,* 259 U.S. 20 (1922); *Adkins v. Children's Hospital,* 261 U.S. 525 (1923).

30. *Schecter Poultry Corp. v. United States,* 295 U.S. 495 (1935); *United States v. Butler,* 297 U.S. 1 (1936); *Carter v. Carter Coal Co.,* 298 U.S. 238 (1936).

31. 347 U.S. 483 (1954).

32. Robert M. Cover, "The Origins of Judicial Activism in the Protection of Minorities," *Yale Law Journal,* 91 (1982), 1287-1316. *Brown*'s constitutional soundness is less clear. See Raoul Berger, *Government By Judiciary: The Transformation of the Fourteenth Amendment* (Cambridge, Mass.: Harvard University Press, 1977), 117-33.

33. Alan D. Gold, "The Legal Rights Provisions – A New Vision or Déjà Vu," *Supreme Court Law Review,* 4 (1982), 108.

34. 410 U.S. 113 (1973).

35. 381 U.S. 479 (1965).

36. These amendments included the First (freedom of speech and religion), Third (prohibition on the quartering of soldiers in private homes during peacetime), Fourth

(prohibition against unreasonable searches and seizures), Fifth (right against self-incrimination), and Ninth (unenumerated rights).

37. *Roe v. Wade,* 410 U.S. 113, 174 (1973) (Rehnquist, J., dissenting); *Doe v. Bolton,* 410 U.S. 179, 222 (1973) (White, J., dissenting).

38. Richard A. Epstein, "Substantive Due Process By Any Other Name: The Abortion Cases," *Supreme Court Review* (1973), 159-85.

39. John Hart Ely, "The Wages of Crying Wolf: A Comment on *Roe v. Wade,*" *Yale Law Journal,* 82 (1973), 920-44.

40. See, e.g., Jennifer Smith, "The Origins of Judicial Review in Canada," *Canadian Journal of Political Science,* 16 (1983), 115-34.

41. Peter H. Russell, *The Judiciary in Canada: The Third Branch of Government* (Toronto: McGraw-Hill Ryerson, 1987), 93.

42. The reference procedure allows both the federal and provincial governments to refer statutes to the Supreme Court or the provincial courts of appeal for an advisory opinion on their constitutionality. It was included in the Supreme Court Act of 1875, and its constitutionality was upheld in *A.-G. Ont. v. A.-G. Canada,* [1910] 43 S.C.R. 536.

43. Peter W. Hogg, *Constitutional Law of Canada,* 2nd ed. (Toronto: Carswell, 1985), 37-40.

44. Other substantive limitations of parliamentary sovereignty imposed by the Constitution Act, 1867 include those pertaining to denominational schools (section 93) and language rights (section 133).

45. B.L. Strayer, *Judicial Review of Legislation in Canada* (Toronto: University of Toronto Press, 1968), 15-16.

46. Hogg, *Constitutional Law of Canada,* 94-95.

47. *Ibid.,* 86-89. The "quasi-federal" nature of Canada's original design is evident in several provisions. In contrast to the United States, provinces were granted enumerated powers, while the national government retained all residual powers. More specifically, the division of powers gave the national government significant control over provincial matters. For example, section 90 permitted the federal government to disallow provincial legislation, and section 96 gave the federal government the exclusive power to appoint judges to the provincial superior and district courts.

48. See, e.g., *Citizens Insurance Co. v. Parsons* (1881), 7 App. Cas. 96; *A.-G. Ontario v. A.-G. Canada (Local Prohibition Case),* [1896] A.C. 348; *In re Board of Commerce Act and Combines and Fair Practices Act,* [1922] 1 A.C. 191; *Toronto Electric Commissioners v. Snider,* [1925] A.C. 396; *A.-G. Canada v. A.-G. Ontario (Employment and Social Insurance Act Reference),* [1937] A.C. 355; *A.-G. British Columbia v. A.-G. Canada (Natural Products Marketing Act Reference),* [1937] A.C. 377.

49. For a discussion, see Robert C. Vipond, "Constitutional Politics and the Legacy of the Provincial Rights Movement in Canada," *Canadian Journal of Political Science,* 18 (1985), 267-94.

50. The major critics and their arguments are surveyed in Alan C. Cairns, "The Judicial Committee and Its Critics," *Canadian Journal of Political Science,* 4 (1971), 302-12. Cairns points out, however, that the Judicial Committee's decisions also enjoyed support from some analysts. Cairns also challenges the assertion by critics of the

Judicial Committee that this body could have unilaterally effected significant changes in Canadian federalism. In his view, the Committee's decisions reflected to a significant degree important aspects of Canada's social and political fabric.

51. Frank R. Scott, "The Development of Canadian Federalism," in Scott, *Essays on the Constitution* (Toronto: University of Toronto Press, 1977), 47-48.

52. Scott, "The Privy Council and Mr. Bennett's 'New Deal' Legislation," *ibid.*, 101.

53. Bora Laskin, " 'Peace, Order and Good Government' Re-Examined," *Canadian Bar Review,* 25 (1947), 1060, 1085.

54. See Frederick Vaughan, "Critics of the Judicial Committee of the Privy Council: The New Orthodoxy and an Alternative Explanation," *Canadian Journal of Political Science,* 19 (1986), 495-519.

55. See, e.g., *Severn v. The Queen,* [1878] 2 S.C.R. 70. In the *Local Prohibition Case* (1896), the Judicial Committee reversed a decision of the Supreme Court in order to uphold a broader view of provincial power.

56. *A.-G. Ontario v. A.-G. Canada,* [1947] A.C. 128, 153.

57. James G. Snell and Frederick Vaughan, *The Supreme Court of Canada: History of the Institution* (Toronto: University of Toronto Press, 1985), 171-95.

58. *A.-G. Ontario v. Canada Temperance Federation,* [1946] A.C. 193.

59. *Johannesson v. West St. Paul,* [1952] 1 S.C.R. 292.

60. See, e.g., *Reference re The Offshore Mineral Rights of British Columbia,* [1967] S.C.R. 792; *A.-G. Manitoba v. Manitoba Egg and Poultry Association et al.,* [1971] S.C.R. 689; *Reference re the Anti-Inflation Act,* [1976] 2 S.C.R. 373; *Public Service Board v. Dionne,* [1978] 2 S.C.R. 191; *Canadian Industrial Gas & Oil Ltd. v. Saskatchewan,* [1978] 2 S.C.R. 545; *Central Canada Potash Co. Ltd. and A.-G. Canada v. Saskatchewan,* [1979] 1 S.C.R. 42.

61. *Reference re the Anti-Inflation Act,* [1976] 2 S.C.R. 373.

62. *Ibid.,* 451.

63. Russell, *The Judiciary in Canada,* 342; Donald Smiley, *Constitutional Adaptation and Canadian Federalism Since 1945* (Royal Commission on Bilingualism and Biculturalism, 1970), 40.

64. Patrick Monahan, *Politics and the Constitution: The Charter, Federalism and the Supreme Court of Canada* (Toronto: Carswell/Methuen, 1987), 150-59.

65. *Reference re Legislative Authority of Parliament to Alter or Replace the Senate,* [1980] 1 S.C.R. 54; *A.-G. Manitoba et al. v. A.-G. Canada et al. (Patriation Reference),* [1981] 1 S.C.R. 753; *A.-G. Quebec v. A.-G. Canada (Quebec Veto Reference),* [1982] 2 S.C.R. 793.

66. J.R. Mallory, *Social Credit and the Federal Power in Canada* (Toronto: University of Toronto Press, 1954), 173, 177-78.

67. *Saumur v. Quebec and A.-G. Quebec,* [1953] 2 S.C.R. 299; *Johnson v. A.-G. Alberta,* [1954] S.C.R. 127; *Switzman v. Elbling,* [1957] S.C.R. 285.

68. Hogg, *Constitutional Law of Canada,* 635.

69. *Ibid.,* 636-38.

70. *Reference re Alberta Statutes,* [1938] 2 S.C.R. 100 at 133-34; *Switzman v. Elbling,* [1957] S.C.R. 285 at 328.

71. *A.-G. Canada and Dupond v. Montreal,* [1978] 2 S.C.R. 770 at 796.

72. *Re Ontario Public Service Employees' Union and A.-G. Ontario* (1987), 41 D.L.R. (4th) 1 at 40.

73. For the Bill's legislative history, see Walter S. Tarnopolsky, *The Canadian Bill of Rights,* 2nd rev. ed. (Toronto: Macmillan of Canada, 1978), 11-14.

74. [1963] S.C.R. 652.

75. *Ibid.,* 654.

76. *Lavell v. A.-G. Canada,* [1974] S.C.R. 1349; *Bliss v. A.-G. Canada,* [1979] 1 S.C.R. 183.

77. [1974] S.C.R. 1349, 1366.

78. [1979] 1 S.C.R. 183, 190.

79. Russell, *The Judiciary in Canada,* 343. Thirty-four cases reached the Court, of which only five were successful.

80. *R. v. Drybones,* [1970] S.C.R. 282.

81. *Hogan v. The Queen,* [1975] 2 S.C.R. 574, 579.

82. S.I. Bushnell, "The Use of American Cases," *University of New Brunswick Law Journal,* 35 (1986), 164.

83. *R. v. Appleby,* [1972] S.C.R. 303; *Curr v. The Queen,* [1972] S.C.R. 889; *Morgentaler v. The Queen,* [1976] 1 S.C.R. 616; *Côté v. The Queen,* [1975] 1 S.C.R. 303; *R. v. Burnshine,* [1975] 1 S.C.R. 693; *Adgey v. The Queen,* [1975] 2 S.C.R. 426; *Hogan v. The Queen,* [1975] 2 S.C.R. 574.

84. 156 U.S. 432 (1895); 343 U.S. 790 (1952).

85. *Salsburg v. Maryland,* 346 U.S. 545 (1954); *Cunningham v. United States,* 256 F.2d 467 (5th Cir. 1958); *State v. Meyer,* 37 N.W. 2d 3 (Minn. Sup. Ct. 1947). See Hogg, *Constitutional Law of Canada,* 789-90.

86. *Roe v. Wade,* 410 U.S. 113 (1973); *People v. Barksdale,* 503 P.2d 257 (Cal. Sup. Ct. 1972).

87. *Gideon v. Wainwright,* 372 U.S. 335 (1963); *Malloy v. Hogan,* 378 U.S. 1 (1964); *Mapp v. Ohio,* 367 U.S. 643 (1961); *Miranda v. Arizona,* 384 U.S. 430 (1966); *Schmerber v. California,* 384 U.S. 757 (1966).

88. *West Coast Hotel Co. v. Parrish,* 300 U.S. 379 (1937).

89. Hogg, *Constitutional Law of Canada,* 748, n38.

90. *Thorson v. A.-G. Canada,* [1975] 1 S.C.R. 138.

91. See Dale Gibson and Scott Gibson, "Enforcement of the Canadian Charter of Rights and Freedoms," in Gérald-A. Beaudoin and Ed Ratushny, eds., *The Canadian Charter of Rights and Freedoms,* 2nd ed. (Toronto: Carswell, 1989), 791-92.

92. 392 U.S. 83 (1968). Cited by Laskin at [1975] 1 S.C.R. 138, 159. In this decision, the U.S. Court modified the unequivocal rejection of ordinary taxpayer standing that it had articulated in *Frothingham v. Mellon,* 262 U.S. 447 (1923).

93. See Rossum and Tarr, *American Constitutional Law,* 51.

94. *Min. of Justice (Can.) v. Borowski,* [1981] 2 S.C.R. 575, 598.

95. *United States v. Richardson,* 418 U.S. 166, 188 (1974) (Powell, J., concurring).

96. Peter W. Hogg, "Is The Supreme Court Biased in Constitutional Cases?" *Canadian Bar Review,* 57 (1979), 721.

97. *Garcia v. San Antonio Metropolitan Transit Authority,* 469 U.S. 528 (1985). See Roger Brooks, "*Garcia,* The Seventeenth Amendment, and the Role of the Supreme

Court in Defending Federalism," *Harvard Journal of Law and Public Policy,* 10 (1987), 189-211.

98. Monahan, *Politics and the Constitution,* 224.

99. Roy Romanow, John Whyte, and Howard Leeson, *Canada Notwithstanding: The Making of the Constitution, 1976-1982* (Toronto: Carswell/Methuen, 1984), 248.

100. Christopher P. Manfredi, "The Use of United States Decisions By The Supreme Court of Canada Under The Charter of Rights and Freedoms," *Canadian Journal of Political Science,* 23 (1990), 507.

101. Ian Greene has argued that it is misleading to analyse the Canadian political system according to the concepts of legislative and constitutional supremacy. According to Greene, the fact that Canadian legislatures are dominated by executives who exercise considerable control over constitutional development and amendment makes executive federalism a more accurate and useful concept. See Ian Greene, "The Myths of Legislative and Constitutional Supremacy," in David P. Shugarman and Reg Whitaker, eds., *Federalism and Political Community: Essays in Honour of Donald Smiley* (Peterborough, Ont.: Broadview Press, 1989), 267-90. The ultimate failure of executive federalism in the Meech Lake Accord episode of Canadian constitutional history renders this argument less persuasive, however.

102. F.L. Morton, "The Political Impact of the Canadian Charter of Rights and Freedoms," *Canadian Journal of Political Science,* 20 (1987), 55; Agresto, *The Supreme Court and Constitutional Democracy,* 77-138. The assertion that the U.S. Constitution is "what the Court says it is" was made by Chief Justice Charles Evans Hughes while he was governor of New York. In *Cooper v. Aaron,* 358 U.S. 1, 17 (1958), the U.S. Supreme Court declared that "the federal judiciary is supreme in the exposition of the law of the Constitution."

103. Arthur Brooks Lapsley, ed., *The Writings of Abraham Lincoln,* 8 vols. (New York: Lamb Publishing Co., 1906), 5:262.

104. *Ibid.*

105. Jeremy Rabkin, *Judicial Compulsions: How Public Law Distorts Public Policy* (New York: Basic Books, 1989), 141.

106. F.L. Morton and Peter H. Russell, "The Supreme Court of Canada's First 100 Charter of Rights Decisions: A Quantitative Analysis," paper presented to the annual meeting of the Canadian Political Science Association, May 27-29, 1990.

107. *McKinney v. University of Guelph* (1990), 76 D.L.R. (4th) 545; *Harrison v. University of British Columbia* (1990), 77 D.L.R. (4th) 55.

108. *R. v. Keegstra,* [1990] 3 S.C.R. 697; *Reference re ss. 193 and 195 of the Criminal Code,* [1990] 1 S.C.R. 1123.

109. David M. O'Brien, *Storm Center: The Supreme Court in American Politics,* 2nd ed. (New York: W.W. Norton, 1990), 60.

110. Morton and Russell, "The Supreme Court of Canada's First 100 Charter Decisions."

111. Andrew Heard has argued that "the present reluctance of most governments to utilize the notwithstanding clause . . . may develop into a binding convention." Andrew Heard, *Canadian Constitutional Conventions: The Marriage of Law and Politics* (Toronto: Oxford, 1991), 147.

112. Robert Dahl, "Decision Making in a Democracy: The Supreme Court as National Policy Maker," *Journal of Public Law,* 6 (1958), 279-95.

Chapter Two

1. Andrew Heard, "The Charter in the Supreme Court of Canada: The Importance of Which Judges Hear an Appeal," *Canadian Journal of Political Science,* 24 (1991), 293.
2. John Hart Ely, *Democracy and Distrust: A Theory of Judicial Review* (Cambridge, Mass.: Harvard University Press, 1980), 1.
3. Patrick Monahan, *Politics and the Constitution: The Charter, Federalism and the Supreme Court of Canada* (Toronto: Carswell/Methuen, 1987), 95.
4. David J. Elkins, "Facing Our Destiny: Rights and Canadian Distinctiveness," *Canadian Journal of Political Science,* 22 (1989), 703-04.
5. Monahan, *Politics and the Constitution,* 96.
6. Edwin Meese III, Speech before the American Bar Association, July 9, 1985, Washington, D.C., in *The Great Debate: Interpreting Our Written Constitution,* booklet published by The Federalist Society (Washington, D.C., 1986), 1-10.
7. William J. Brennan, Jr., Address to the Text and Teaching Symposium, Georgetown University, October 12, 1985, Washington, D.C., in *The Great Debate,* 11-25; John Paul Stevens, Speech before the Federal Bar Association, October 23, 1985, Chicago, in *The Great Debate,* 27-30.
8. Edwin Meese III, Speech before the D.C. Chapter of the Federalist Society Lawyers Division, November 15, 1985, Washington, D.C., in *The Great Debate,* 36.
9. Robert H. Bork, Speech before the University of San Diego Law School, November 18, 1985, San Diego, in *The Great Debate,* 46, 44.
10. On the Bork nomination, see Ethan Bonner, *Battle For Justice: How The Bork Nomination Shook America* (New York: W.W. Norton, 1989).
11. Arthur Selwyn Miller, *Toward Increased Judicial Activism* (Westport, Conn.: Greenwood Press, 1982), 249. Miller argued that strict judicial adherence to the Constitution as understood by its framers is tantamount to "rule from the grave."
12. Paul Brest, "The Misconceived Quest For The Original Understanding," *Boston University Law Review,* 60 (1980), 204-54; H. Jefferson Powell, "The Original Understanding of Original Intent," *Harvard Law Review,* 98 (1985), 885-948. The best book-length articulation of this view is Leonard W. Levy, *Original Intent and the Framers' Constitution* (New York: Macmillan, 1988). In fairness to Levy, he would prefer that constitutional law be grounded in the principles and purposes of the text as revealed by conventional rules of construction. However, Levy doubts whether any set of legal rules can prevent judges from pouring whatever meaning they like into the Constitution's open-ended phrases.
13. Ely, *Democracy and Distrust,* 2-3; *Roe v. Wade,* 410 U.S. 113 (1973).
14. John Hart Ely, "The Wages of Crying Wolf: A Comment on *Roe v. Wade*," *Yale Law Journal,* 82 (1973), 949, 947.

15. *Ibid.*, 926.
16. Ely, *Democracy and Distrust,* 11-41. The Ninth Amendment provides that the "enumeration in the Constitution, of certain rights, shall not be construed to deny or disparage others retained by the people." Section 26 of the Charter of Rights and Freedoms is similarly worded.
17. *Ibid.*, 92, 102.
18. See Michael J. Perry, *The Constitution, The Courts, and Human Rights* (New Haven: Yale University Press, 1982).
19. Miller, *Toward Increased Judicial Activism,* 6.
20. Perry, *The Constitution, The Courts, and Human Rights,* 2.
21. *Ibid.*, 101, 102, 112-13, 115.
22. *Ibid.*, 103-07. See Levy, *Original Intent and the Framers' Constitution,* 378; Harry V. Jaffa, "What Were the 'Original Intentions' of the Framers of the Constitution of the United States?" *University of Puget Sound Law Review,* 10 (1987), 343-448.
23. Miller, *Toward Increased Judicial Activism,* 247. A good example of this theory of judicial review is Justice Thurgood Marshall's argument against capital punishment in *Gregg v. Georgia,* 428 U.S. 153, 231-241 (1976) (Marshall, J., dissenting).
24. Rainer Knopff, *Human Rights and Social Technology: The New War on Discrimination* (Ottawa: Carleton University Press, 1989), 35-70.
25. Perry, *The Constitution, The Courts and Human Rights,* 125-45. This constitutional provision allows Congress to regulate the U.S. Supreme Court's appellate jurisdiction. The meaning and implication of this provision are explored more fully in Chapter 7.
26. John Agresto, *The Supreme Court and Constitutional Democracy* (Ithaca, N.Y.: Cornell University Press, 1984), 107-11, 116-25.
27. Alexander Hamilton, James Madison, and John Jay, *The Federalist Papers,* ed. Clinton Rossiter (New York: New American Library, 1961), No. 51, 322, 321; No. 10, 84.
28. Agresto, *The Supreme Court and Constitutional Democracy,* 112-16.
29. Mark Tushnet, *Red, White, and Blue: A Critical Analysis of Constitutional Law* (Cambridge, Mass.: Harvard University Press, 1988), 1.
30. *The Federalist Papers,* No. 51, 322.
31. See, e.g., John D. Whyte, "Fundamental Justice: The Scope and Application of Section 7 of the Charter," *Manitoba Law Journal,* 13 (1983), 455; H. Scott Fairley, "Enforcing The Charter: Some Thoughts on an Appropriate and Just Standard for Judicial Review," *Supreme Court Law Review,* 4 (Special Issue, 1982), 234-38. In fact, the argument may even be stronger in Canada, where the legislative process lacks the formal and informal institutional checks on majority will found in the United States.
32. Monahan, *Politics and the Constitution,* 7-8.
33. *Ibid.*, 68, 98, 105.
34. See, e.g., Gad Horowitz, "Conservatism, Liberalism and Socialism in Canada: An Interpretation," *Canadian Journal of Economics and Political Science,* 32 (1966), 143-71. According to Horowitz, the principal reason for this cultural difference between Canada and the United States is the persistence of "toryism" in Canada,

which profoundly influenced the development of conservatism, liberalism, and socialism in at least English-speaking Canada.

35. Monahan, *Politics and the Constitution,* 92. The general debate between liberalism and communitarianism has become a dominant feature of political science scholarship. For communitarian critiques of liberalism, see Alasdair MacIntyre, *After Virtue* (South Bend, Indiana: University of Notre Dame Press, 1981); Michael Sandel, *Liberalism and the Limits of Justice* (Cambridge: Cambridge University Press, 1982). For liberal responses, see Amy Gutmann, "Communitarian Critics of Liberalism," *Philosophy and Public Affairs,* 14 (1985), 308-22; Robert Thigpen and Lyle Downing, "Liberalism and the Communitarian Critique," *American Journal of Political Science,* 31 (1987), 637-55; Stephen Holmes, "The Permanent Structure of Antiliberal Thought," in Nancy L. Rosenblum, ed., *Liberalism and the Moral Life* (Cambridge, Mass.: Harvard University Press, 1989), 227-53. The entire debate is summarized in Patrick Neal and David Paris, "Liberalism and the Communitarian Critique: A Guide for the Perplexed," *Canadian Journal of Political Science,* 23 (1990), 419-39.

36. Monahan, *Politics and the Constitution,* 109.

37. Charles Taylor, "Alternative Futures: Legitimacy, Identity and Alienation in Late Twentieth Century Canada," in Alan Cairns and Cynthia Williams, eds., *Constitutionalism, Citizenship and Society in Canada* (Toronto: University of Toronto Press, 1985), 190, 194.

38. Monahan, *Politics and the Constitution,* 96, 98, 104, 111-20.

39. See, generally, Robert C. Vipond, *Liberty and Community: Canadian Federalism and the Failure of the Constitution* (Albany, N.Y.: SUNY Press, 1991).

40. This discussion of Social Credit in Alberta relies extensively on J.R. Mallory, *Social Credit and the Federal Power in Canada* (Toronto: University of Toronto Press, 1954), 57-90.

41. *Ibid.,* 77.

42. *Ibid.,* 13-14. Mallory agrees with the interpretation offered by E.A. Forsey, "Disallowance of Provincial Acts, Reservation of Provincial Bills, and Refusal of Assent by Lieutenant-Governors since 1867," *Canadian Journal of Economics and Political Science,* 4 (1938), 47.

43. *Reference re Alberta Statutes,* [1938] 2 S.C.R. 100.

44. Mallory, *Social Credit and the Federal Power in Canada,* 60.

45. These episodes are reported in Thomas R. Berger, *Fragile Freedoms: Human Rights and Dissent in Canada* (Toronto: Clarke, Irwin & Company, 1981), 141, 163-89.

46. *Saumur v. Quebec,* [1953] 2 S.C.R. 299; *Switzman v. Elbling* [1957] S.C.R. 285.

47. Peter H. Russell, Rainer Knopff, and F.L. Morton, eds., *Federalism and the Charter: Leading Constitutional Decisions,* new ed. (Ottawa: Carleton University Press, 1989), 300.

48. Monahan, *Politics and the Constitution,* 113.

49. The problems of a purely communitarian theory of politics from this perspective are discussed by Will Kymlicka, *Liberalism, Community and Culture* (Oxford: Clarendon Press, 1991), 47-99.

50. Allan C. Hutchinson and Andrew Petter, "Private Rights/Public Wrongs: The Liberal Lie of the Charter," *University of Toronto Law Journal,* 38 (1988), 278-97.

51. *Retail, Wholesale and Department Store Union, Local 580 et al. v. Dolphin Delivery Ltd.,* [1986] 2 S.C.R. 573.

52. Hutchinson and Petter, "Private Rights/Public Wrongs," 286, 296.

53. See Harry V. Jaffa, *The Conditions of Freedom: Essays in Political Philosophy* (Baltimore: Johns Hopkins University Press, 1975), 149-60.

54. [1986] 2 S.C.R. 573 at 598-99.

55. *Law Society of Upper Canada v. Skapinker* (1984), 9 D.L.R. (4th) 161 at 169; *McCulloch v. Maryland,* 17 U.S. 316 (1819).

56. 17 U.S. at 407. Cited in 9 D.L.R. (4th) at 169-70.

57. 9 D.L.R. (4th) at 170.

58. *Hunter v. Southam* (1984), 11 D.L.R. (4th) 641 at 650.

59. *R. v. Big M Drug Mart* (1985), 18 D.L.R. (4th) 321 at 359-60.

60. *Reference re s.94(2) of the Motor Vehicle Act (B.C.)* (1985), 24 D.L.R. (4th) 536; *Edwards v. A.-G. Canada,* [1930] A.C. 124 at 136. According to Lord Sankey, "the B.N.A. Act planted in Canada a living tree capable of growth and expansion within its natural limits."

61. 24 D.L.R. (4th) at 554-55.

62. *Morgentaler, Smoling and Scott v. The Queen* (1988), 44 D.L.R. (4th) 385 at 394.

63. F.L. Morton and Rainer Knopff, "Permanence and Change in a Written Constitution: The 'Living Tree' Doctrine and the Charter of Rights," 2 *Supreme Court Law Review,* 1 (1990), 545.

64. The discussion that follows draws significantly on Ralph A. Rossum and G. Alan Tarr, *American Constitutional Law: Cases and Interpretation,* 2nd ed. (New York: St. Martin's, 1987), 88-89.

65. 17 U.S. 316, 421 (1819).

66. This appears to have been Marshall's understanding of his decision. See Gerald Gunther, ed., *John Marshall's Defense of McCulloch v. Maryland* (Palo Alto, Calif.: Stanford University Press, 1969).

67. *R. v. Oakes,* [1986] 1 S.C.R. 103, 26 D.L.R. (4th) 200 at 227. Section 1 is discussed in more detail later in the chapter.

68. See Christopher Wolfe, "A Theory of U.S. Constitutional History," *Journal of Politics,* 43 (1981), 292-316.

69. *R. v. Big M Drug Mart* (1985), 18 D.L.R. (4th) 321 at 371-72; *Griggs v. Duke Power Co.,* 401 U.S. 424 (1970).

70. 18 D.L.R. (4th) 321 at 371 (citing 401 U.S. at 432).

71. See Knopff, *Human Rights and Social Technology,* 57-58.

72. *Ibid.,* 58.

73. Laurence Tribe, *American Constitutional Law* (Mineola, N.Y.: Foundation Press, 1978), 1031-32.

74. *Operation Dismantle v. The Queen,* [1985] 1 S.C.R. 441, 18 D.L.R. (4th) 481 at 500-05.

75. *Ibid.,* 500. Wilson summarized the doctrine by citing Justice William Brennan's opinion in *Baker v. Carr,* 369 U.S. 186, 210-211, 217 (1962). She also noted that U.S.

courts were especially deferential to the executive in foreign policy matters [citing *Atlee v. Laird,* 347 F.Supp. 689 (E.D. Pa. 1972)].

76. *Ibid.,* 501. These exceptions included *Marbury v. Madison,* 5 U.S. (1 Cranch) 137 (1803); *Brown v. Board of Education,* 347 U.S. 483 (1954); and *United States v. Nixon,* 418 U.S. 583 (1974).

77. 18 D.L.R. (4th) at 503.

78. See F.L. Morton, "The Political Impact of the Canadian Charter of Rights and Freedoms," *Canadian Journal of Political Science,* 20 (1987), 35. According to one analysis, the Canadian Court has even gone further than the Warren Court in certain areas of criminal procedure. See Robert Harvie and Hamar Foster, "Ties That Bind? The Supreme Court of Canada, American Jurisprudence, and the Revision of Canadian Criminal Law Under the Charter," *Osgoode Hall Law Journal,* 28 (1990), 729-87.

79. Ely, *Democracy and Distrust,* 43-72.

80. 24 D.L.R. (4th) at 550.

81. *Reference re s.94(2) of the British Columbia Motor Vehicle Act,* [1985] 2 S.C.R. 486; 24 D.L.R. (4th) 536.

82. 24 D.L.R. (4th) at 561.

83. Chief Justice Dickson and Justices Beetz, Chouinard, and Le Dain all concurred with Justice Lamer's reasons for judgment. Justices McIntyre and Wilson wrote separate reasons, but both agreed that "fundamental justice" includes a substantive element in addition to procedural guarantees.

84. 24 D.L.R. (4th) at 545.

85. *Ibid.,* 545-46.

86. *Ibid.,* 546. Lamer cited *R. v. Big M Drug Mart Ltd.* (1985), 18 D.L.R. (4th) 321, 360 ("full benefit of the *Charter*'s protection," *per* Dickson, C.J.C) and *Curr v. The Queen* (1972), 26 D.L.R. (3d) 603, 614 ("objective and manageable standards," *per* Laskin, J.).

87. *Ibid.,* 548.

88. Roy Romanow, John Whyte, and Howard Leeson, *Canada Notwithstanding: The Making of the Constitution, 1976-1982* (Toronto: Carswell/Methuen, 1984), 245-46.

89. Rossum and Tarr, *American Constitutional Law,* 305.

90. 60 U.S. 393 (1857); 156 U.S. 578 (1897).

91. *Duke v. The Queen* (1972), 28 D.L.R. (3d) 129, 134 (Fauteux, C.J.C.).

92. *Minutes of Proceedings and Evidence of the Special Joint Committee of the Senate and House of Commons on the Constitution of Canada,* 32nd Parliament, 1st Session, 46:32 (27 January 1981).

93. *Ibid.*

94. *Ibid.,* 46:41. One could infer from Chrétien's testimony, however, that "principles of fundamental justice" gives *some* power to courts over the substance of legislation.

95. *Re Latham and Solicitor-General of Canada et al.* (1984), 9 D.L.R. (4th) 393, 405 (F.C.T.D).

96. See, e.g., *Re Potma and R.* (1983), 41 O.R. (2d) 43, 52 (C.A.); *R. v. Hayden* (1983), 3 D.L.R. (4th) 361, 363 (Man. C.A.); *R. v. Swain* (1986), 53 O.R. (2d) 609 (C.A.).

97. 24 D.L.R. (4th) 536, 550.

98. For an analysis of this development, see David J. Mullan, "Natural Justice and

Fairness – Substantive as well as Procedural Standards for the Review of Administrative Decision-Making," *McGill Law Journal,* 27 (1982), 250-98.

99. *Proceedings of the Joint Committee,* 46:49 (testimony of Roger Tassé). Ironically, Tassé's comments were in response to a Committee member who could not "see how [s.7] is going to interfere with the administration of the Motor Vehicles Branch in the province of British Columbia."

100. 24 D.L.R. (4th) 536, 556.

101. *Ibid.,* 554.

102. *Ibid.,* 550.

103. See Peter W. Hogg, *Constitutional Law of Canada,* 2nd ed. (Toronto: Carswell, 1985), 679 n149. Section 1 originally guaranteed the rights and freedoms set out in the Charter "subject only to such reasonable limits *as are generally accepted* in a free and democratic society *with a parliamentary system of government.*" (Emphasis added.)

104. *Ibid.,* 682-89.

105. *R. v. Oakes* (1986), 26 D.L.R. (4th) 200, at 227-28.

106. T. Alexander Aleinikoff, "Constitutional Law in the Age of Balancing," *Yale Law Journal,* 96 (1987), 945, 948, 966-72, 984-85.

107. Hutchinson and Petter, "Private Rights/Public Wrongs," 296.

108. For a similar view of U.S. constitutional commentators, see Charles R. Kesler, "The Founders and the Classics," in James W. Muller, ed., *The Revival of Constitutionalism* (Lincoln: University of Nebraska Press, 1988), 43-44.

Chapter Three

1. *R. v. Big M Drug Mart* (1985), 18 D.L.R. (4th) 321.

2. *R.W.D.S.U. v. Dolphin Delivery* (1986), 33 D.L.R. (4th) 174.

3. *R. v. Big M Drug Mart* (1985), 18 D.L.R. (4th) 321; *Edwards Books and Art v. The Queen,* [1986] 2 S.C.R. 713, 35 D.L.R. (4th) 1.

4. R.S.C. 1970, c. L-13.

5. *Big M Drug Mart* raised a series of constitutional questions, including whether the Lord's Day Act properly fell within the federal government's criminal law power; whether corporations have standing to challenge the validity of legislation under section 2; and whether a provincial court has the jurisdiction to declare legislation contrary to the Charter invalid and to dismiss charges brought under the impugned statute. The Court answered all of these questions in the affirmative.

6. *A.-G. Ontario v. Hamilton Street Railway,* [1903] A.C. 524.

7. *Reference re Legislation Respecting Abstention from Labour on Sunday* (1905), 35 S.C.R. 581.

8. *Robertson and Rosetanni v. The Queen,* [1963] S.C.R. 651.

9. *Ibid.,* 657

10. 18 D.L.R. (4th) at 359.

11. *Ibid.,* 362, 361.

12. *Ibid.,* 362.

13. *Ibid.,* 361.

14. See Richard E. Morgan, *Disabling America: The "Rights Industry" in Our Time* (New York: Basic Books, 1984), 23. Interestingly, in 1992 one of these amendments (dealing with Congressional pay raises) was finally ratified, becoming the Twenty-seventh Amendment to the U.S. Constitution.

15. 18 D.L.R. (4th) at 348. These U.S. decisions included *McGowan v. Maryland,* 366 U.S. 420 (1961); *Braunfield v. Brown,* 366 U.S. 599 (1961); *Gallagher v. Crown Kosher Supermarket,* 366 U.S. 617 (1961); and *Two Guys from Harrison-Allentown v. McGinley,* 366 U.S. 582 (1961).

16. 18 D.L.R. (4th) at 348.

17. *Ibid.,* 356.

18. *Ibid.,* 353.

19. *Ibid.,* 352.

20. *Ibid.,* 353.

21. *Ibid.,* 352 (Dickson), 372 (Wilson, J., concurring).

22. R.S.O. 1980, c. 453.

23. 35 D.L.R. (4th) at 21.

24. *Ibid.,* 37-41. Dickson found the evidence with respect to observers of another day of the week insufficient to measure the statute's impact on them.

25. See the U.S. cases cited at note 15.

26. 35 D.L.R. (4th) at 51.

27. *Ibid.,* 46-48.

28. *Ibid.,* 33.

29. *Ibid.,* 41-52.

30. *Jones v. The Queen* (1986), 31 D.L.R. (4th) 569.

31. R.S.A. 1980, c. S-3, ss. 142, 143, 180.

32. The trial judge agreed with Jones that the Act offended his right to liberty in both a narrow (by imposing imprisonment as a sanction for the offence) and broad sense (by denying him the right to raise his children as he saw fit). The judge found these infringements of liberty inconsistent with procedural fundamental justice because the Act allowed for only one means of proving efficient home instruction (a certificate from a provincial education inspector).

33. 31 D.L.R. (4th) at 591.

34. *Ibid.* Emphasis in original.

35. *Ibid.,* 592. *Brown v. Board of Education,* 347 U.S. 483, 493 (1954).

36. 31 D.L.R. (4th) at 594-95. Citing *Sheridan Road Baptist Church v. Department of Education,* 348 N.W. 2d 263 (Mich. Ct. App. 1984) and *New Jersey State Board of Higher Education v. Board of Directors of Shelton College,* 448 A.2d 988 (N.J. Sup. Ct. 1982).

37. 31 D.L.R. (4th) at 599. Citing *New Jersey-Philadelphia Presbytery of the Bible Presbyterian Church v. New Jersey State Board of Higher Education,* 740 F.2d. 957 (3d Cir. 1984).

38. 31 D.L.R. (4th) at 576. Citing *Committee for Public Education and Religious Liberty v. Regan,* 444 U.S. 646, 653 (1980).

39. 31 D.L.R. (4th) at 576. Citing *Everson v. Board of Education,* 330 U.S. 1 (1947);

Board of Education v. Allen, 392 U.S. 236 (1968); *Wolman v. Walter,* 433 U.S. 229 (1977).

40. 31 D.L.R. (4th) at 577.

41. *Ibid.,* 578. Counsel for appellants in *Jack and Charlie v. The Queen,* [1985] 2 S.C.R. 332 advanced a similar argument. The issue in *Jack and Charlie* was whether provisions of the Wildlife Act, 1966 (B.C.) infringed the appellants' freedom of religion. Section 2(a) of the Charter did not apply, however, since the Charter had not been enacted when the offence in question was committed.

42. 31 D.L.R. (4th) at 579. Citing *Braunfield v. Brown,* 366 U.S. 599, 606 (1961).

43. 31 D.L.R. (4th) at 579.

44. *Reference re An Act to Amend the Education Act (Ontario)* (1987), 40 D.L.R. (4th) 18.

45. *Ibid.,* 37.

46. *Ibid.,* 27.

47. Peter W. Hogg, *Constitutional Law of Canada,* 2nd ed. (Toronto: Carswell, 1985), 825.

48. *Tiny Township Catholic Separate School Trustees v. The Queen* (1928), A.C. 363.

49. Section 29 provides that "[n]othing in this Charter abrogates or derogates from any rights or privileges guaranteed by or under the Constitution of Canada in respect of denominational, separate or dissentient schools." The Ontario court ruled that in exercising its legitimate s.93 powers, the province was creating a right "under the Constitution of Canada" that could not be abrogated by another section of the Charter. For a succinct discussion of the Bill 30 reference, see Peter H. Russell, Rainer Knopff, and F.L. Morton eds., *Federalism and the Charter: Leading Constitutional Decisions,* new ed. (Ottawa: Carleton University Press, 1989), 660-61.

50. 40 D.L.R. (4th) at 59.

51. *Ibid.,* 60.

52. Alexis de Tocqueville, *Democracy in America,* tr. George Lawrence, ed. J.P. Mayer (New York: Doubleday, 1969), II, 525-30, 544.

53. *Retail, Wholesale and Dept. Store Union v. Dolphin Delivery Ltd.,* [1986] 2 S.C.R. 573, 33 D.L.R. (4th) 174. For a critical analysis of this decision, see Brian Slattery, "The *Charter*'s Relevance To Private Litigation: Does *Dolphin* Deliver?" *McGill Law Journal,* 32 (1987), 905-23; Allan Hutchinson and Andrew Petter, "Private Rights/Public Wrongs: The Liberal Lie of the Charter," *University of Toronto Law Journal,* 38 (1988), 278-97.

54. 33 D.L.R. (4th) at 191.

55. *Ibid.,* 191-94. Among the literature supporting this conclusion, McIntyre cited Hogg, *Constitutional Law of Canada,* 674-75; Katherine Swinton, "Application of the Canadian Charter of Rights and Freedoms," in Walter Tarnopolsky and Gérald-A. Beaudoin, eds., *The Canadian Charter of Rights and Freedoms: Commentary* (Toronto: Carswell, 1982), 47-48; and Anne McLellan and Bruce P. Elman, "To Whom Does the Charter Apply?: Some Recent Cases on s.32," *Alberta Law Review,* 24 (1986), 367. On the other side of the issue, McIntyre cited Dale Gibson, "The Charter of Rights and the Private Sector," *Manitoba Law Journal,* 12 (1982), 213-19; and Gibson, "Distinguishing the Governors from the Governed: The Meaning of

'Government' under Section 32(1) of the Charter," *Manitoba Law Journal*, 13 (1983), 505-22.

56. 33 D.L.R. (4th) at 195.

57. *Ibid.*

58. *Ibid.,* 196.

59. *Shelley v. Kraemer,* 334 U.S. 1 (1948). For an overview of the state action doctrine and racial discrimination, see David M. O'Brien, *Constitutional Law and Politics: Civil Rights and Liberties* (New York: W.W. Norton, 1991), 1254-70.

60. *Civil Rights Cases,* 109 U.S. 3 (1883).

61. 334 U.S. at 14.

62. *Runyon v. McCrary,* 427 U.S. 160 (1976). The Court avoided the state action doctrine in this instance by relying on the Thirteenth Amendment. For a critical discussion of *Shelley,* see Robert H. Bork, *The Tempting of America: The Political Seduction of the Law* (New York: Simon & Schuster, 1990), 151-53.

63. 33 D.L.R. (4th) at 196.

64. *British Columbia Government Employees' Union v. A.-G. British Columbia,* [1988] 2 S.C.R. 214.

65. 33 D.L.R. (4th) at 184. McIntyre included among his examples of judicial recognition of this principle the dissenting opinion of Justice Oliver Wendell Holmes in *Abrams v. United States,* 250 U.S. 616, 630 (1919).

66. 33 D.L.R. (4th) at 186.

67. *Thornhill v. Alabama,* 310 U.S. 88 (1940).

68. 33 D.L.R. (4th) at 187.

69. *Ibid.,* 189-90.

70. [1988] 2 S.C.R. at 229.

71. *Ibid.,* 237.

72. *Ibid.,* 244.

73. *Ibid.,* 247-48.

74. *Ibid.,* 250-52 (McIntyre, J., concurring).

75. *Rio Hotel Ltd. v. New Brunswick (Liquor Licence Board)* (1987), 44 D.L.R. (4th) 663, 679 (*per* Estey, J.). The Court rejected another freedom of expression claim on similar grounds in *McKay et al. v. Manitoba* (1989), 61 D.L.R. (4th) 385. In this instance, the Court declined to resolve Charter issues in a "factual vacuum."

76. *Ford v. Quebec (Attorney-General)* (1988), 54 D.L.R. (4th) 577.

77. Robert J. Sharpe, "Commercial Expression and the Charter," *University of Toronto Law Journal,* 37 (1987), 229-59.

78. See, e.g., *Re Law Society of Manitoba and Savino* (1983), 1 D.L.R. (4th) 285 (Man. C.A.) (holding that commercial expression is protected by the Charter); *Re Klein and Law Society of Upper Canada* (1985), 50 O.R. (2d) 118 (Div. Ct.) (holding that commercial expression is not protected by the Charter).

79. *Virginia State Board of Pharmacy v. Virginia Citizens Consumer Council Inc.,* 425 U.S. 748 (1976).

80. 54 D.L.R. (4th) at 610-613. The American cases cited included *Valentine v. Chrestenson,* 316 U.S. 52 (1942); *Virginia State Board of Pharmacy v. Virginia Citizens Consumer Council Inc.,* 425 U.S. 748 (1976); *Central Hudson Gas & Electric v.*

Public Service Commission of New York, 447 U.S. 557 (1980); *Posados de Puerto Rico Associates v. Tourism Co. of Puerto Rico,* 106 S.Ct. 2968 (1986). The Court also cited five articles from leading U.S. law reviews.

81. 54 D.L.R. (4th) at 628.

82. *A.-G. Quebec v. Irwin Toy Ltd.,* [1989] 1 S.C.R. 927. This case is also important because the Court held that corporations could not claim section 7 rights.

83. *Ibid.,* 1008 (McIntyre, J., dissenting).

84. *Royal College of Dental Surgeons of Ontario v. Rocket and Price* (1990), 71 D.L.R. (4th) 68.

85. *Ibid.,* 76. Citing *Semler v. Oregon State Board of Dental Examiners,* 294 U.S. 608, 612 (1935); *Virginia State Board of Pharmacy v. Virginia Citizens Consumer Council Inc.,* 425 U.S. 748, 773 n25 (1976); and *Bates v. State Bar of Arizona,* 433 U.S. 350, 366 (1977).

86. 71 D.L.R. (4th) at 77.

87. *Ibid.,* 80-83.

88. *Reference re ss. 193 and 195 of the Criminal Code,* [1990] 1 S.C.R. 1123. This case also raised "economic liberty" issues under section 7 of the Charter.

89. *Ibid.,* 1136.

90. *Ibid.,* 1206.

91. *Ibid.,* 1214-15.

92. See, e.g., *R. v. Canadian Newspapers Company Ltd.,* [1988] 2 S.C.R. 122 (upholding as a reasonable limit on freedom of the press Criminal Code provisions banning publication of the complainant's name in sexual assault proceedings); *Slaight Communications v. Davidson* (1989), 59 D.L.R. (4th) 416 (upholding as a reasonable limit on freedom of expression an adjudicator's order concerning what an employer must include in letters of reference for an employee wrongfully dismissed); *Edmonton Journal v. A.-G. Alberta* (1989), 64 D.L.R. (4th) 577 (striking down legislation limiting matters that may be published about court proceedings involving matrimonial disputes and pre-trial civil proceedings generally).

93. The freedom of the press case is *Moysa v. Labour Relations Board* (1989), 60 D.L.R. (4th) 1. In this decision, the Court unanimously held that section 2(b) does not protect journalists from orders compelling them to testify before regulatory bodies.

94. T. Alexander Aleinikoff, "Constitutional Law in the Age of Balancing," *Yale Law Journal,* 96 (1987), 984-86.

95. *R. v. Keegstra,* [1990] 3 S.C.R. 697.

96. As defined by s.318(4) of the Criminal Code, "identifiable group" means "any section of the public distinguished by colour, race, religion or ethnic origin."

97. [1990] 3 S.C.R. at 732.

98. *Ibid.,* 778-79.

99. These defences permit individuals to avoid conviction if: (a) they establish that the statements communicated were true; (b) they express or attempt to establish by argument an opinion on a religious subject; (c) the statements were relevant to the public interest and contributed to a discussion for the public benefit; or (d) they intended to point out matters producing or intending to produce feelings of hatred toward an identifiable group in Canada.

100. [1990] 3 S.C.R. at 779-83.
101. *Ibid.,* 855.
102. *Ibid.,* 857. Justice McLachlin conceded that, although this "harm principle" was relevant, it was not constitutionally determinative. In her view, "harm" could be defined relatively broadly to include not only the incitement of others to hatred, but also the less visible impact of such expression on members of the groups identified in it. This caveat may have come at the urging of the Women's Legal Education and Action Fund (LEAF), which intervened on behalf of the Crown because of its interest in using section 319(2) against pornography. The difficulty of demonstrating any direct link between pornography and specific acts of violence against women means that a narrow harm principle would weaken the impact of section 319(2) on pornography.
103. *Ibid.,* 860.
104. Lily Harmer, "The Right To Strike: Charter Implications and Interpretations," *University of Toronto Faculty of Law Review,* 47 (1989), 427, 441; Patrick Monahan and Andrew Petter, "Developments in Constitutional Law: 1986-1987," *Supreme Court Law Review,* 10 (1988), 116.
105. *Reference re Public Service Employee Relations Act (Alberta)* (1987), 38 D.L.R. (4th) 161; *Public Service Alliance of Canada v. The Queen* (1987), 38 D.L.R. (4th) 249; *Retail, Wholesale and Department Store Union (Saskatchewan Dairy Workers) v. Saskatchewan* (1987), 38 D.L.R. (4th) 277.
106. 38 D.L.R. (4th) at 239 (*per* Le Dain, J.). Another consequence might be to grant constitutional status to the civil disobedience carried out by anti-abortion associations for whom blocking access to, and indeed closing, abortion clinics is a central aim.
107. *Ibid.,* 240.
108. *Ibid.,* 173-74 (*per* Dickson, C.J.C.).
109. *Collymore v. Attorney-General,* [1970] A.C. 538.
110. *Collymore v. Attorney-General* (1967), 12 W.I.R. 5, 15.
111. *Dolphin Delivery v. Retail, Wholesale & Dept. Store Union, Loc. 580* (1984), 10 D.L.R. (4th) 198 (B.C.C.A.); *Public Service Alliance of Canada v. The Queen* (1984), 11 D.L.R. (4th) 387 (F.C.A.); *Nfld. Ass'n of Public Employees v. The Queen* (1985), 53 Nfld. & P.E.I.R. 1 (S.C.T.D.); *Re Prime and Manitoba Labour Board* (1983), 3 D.L.R. (4th) 74 (Man. Q.B.); *Halifax Police Officers & N.C.O's Ass'n v. City of Halifax* (1984), 64 N.S.R. (2d) 368 (S.C.T.D.).
112. 38 D.L.R. (4th) at 176.
113. *Re Service Employees' Int'l Union, Loc. 204 and Broadway Manor Nursing Home* (1983), 4 D.L.R. (4th) 231 (Ont. Div. Ct.).
114. 38 D.L.R. (4th) at 183.
115. *Ibid.,* 195.
116. *Ibid.,* 197.
117. *Ibid.,* 198-201.
118. *Ibid.,* 197. Citing Alexis de Tocqueville, *Democracy in America,* 2 vols., edited by P. Bradley (New York: Knopf, 1945), I:196.
119. 38 D.L.R. (4th) at 217 (*per* McIntyre).
120. *Ibid.,* 218-19.

121. *Ibid.,* 219-20.

122. *Ibid.,* 221-23.

123. *Ibid.,* 225-26. McIntyre's reliance on "framers' intent" in this context should be noted, since the Court as a whole appeared to have rejected this as a method for determining the meaning of Charter rights in the British Columbia *Motor Vehicle Reference.*

124. *Ibid.,* 227.

125. *Ibid.,* 228.

126. *Ibid.,* 229.

127. *Ibid.,* 229-31.

128. A four-to-three majority of the Court also relied on the *Alberta Labour Reference* to uphold a provision of the Northwest Territories Public Service Act, 1974, which stipulated that the territorial government would only bargain collectively with public service employees' associations incorporated by a statute for that purpose. Opponents of this provision argued that it prohibited public-sector employees from joining the association of their choice. The Court majority countered that, according to the *Labour Trilogy,* the right to collective bargaining was not an essential component of the constitutional status of associations. See *Professional Institute of the Public Service of Canada v. Commissioner of the Northwest Territories* (1990), 72 D.L.R. (4th) 1.

129. *Law Society of Alberta v. Black,* [1989] 1 S.C.R. 591 at 635-40 (McIntyre, J., dissenting in part).

130. See *Re Lavigne and Ontario Public Service Employees Union et al.* (1986), 29 D.L.R. (4th) 327 (Ont. Sup. Ct.) At issue in *Lavigne* was whether compulsory union dues could be used to support political causes with which individual union members disagreed. The Ontario Supreme Court found this use of dues to be contrary to freedom of association. Its decision was overturned on other grounds in *Re Lavigne and Ontario Public Service Employees Union et al.* (1989), 56 D.L.R. (4th) 474 (Ont. C.A.). For a discussion of this issue, see Christopher P. Manfredi, *"Re Lavigne and Ontario Public Service Employees Union*: Remedial Decree Litigation and Public Administration Under the Charter of Rights and Freedoms," *Canadian Public Administration,* 34 (1991), 395-416.

Chapter Four

1. F.L. Morton, "The Political Impact of the Canadian Charter of Rights and Freedoms," *Canadian Journal of Political Science,* 20 (1987), 53. See also Patrick Monahan, *Politics and the Constitution: The Charter, Federalism and the Supreme Court of Canada* (Toronto: Carswell, 1987), 37-38.

2. See Bruce C. Hafen, "Exploring Test Cases in Child Advocacy," *Harvard Law Review,* 100 (1986), 441.

3. For an overview of these interpretive questions, see Peter W. Hogg, *Constitutional Law of Canada,* 2nd ed. (Toronto: Carswell, 1985), 743-49. For other general discussions of s.7, see David C. McDonald, *Legal Rights in the Canadian Charter of Rights and Freedoms,* 2nd ed. (Toronto: Carswell, 1989), 105-225; Morris Manning,

Rights, Freedoms, and the Courts: A Practical Analysis of the Constitution Act, 1982 (Toronto: Emond-Montgomery, 1983), 1227-74.

4. On the meaning of fundamental justice, see Alan D. Gold, "The Legal Rights Provisions – A New Vision or Déjà Vu," *Supreme Court Law Review,* 4 (Special Issue 1982), 107-30; Patrice Garant, "Fundamental Rights and Fundamental Justice," in Gérald-A. Beaudoin and Ed Ratushny, eds., *The Canadian Charter of Rights and Freedoms,* 2nd ed. (Toronto: Carswell, 1989), 369-83; John D. Whyte, "Fundamental Justice: The Scope and Application of Section 7 of the Charter," *Manitoba Law Journal,* 13 (1983), 455-75; Luc Tremblay, "Section 7 of the Charter: Substantive Due Process," *University of British Columbia Law Review,* 18 (1984), 201-53; Timothy J. Christian, "Section 7 of the *Charter of Rights and Freedoms*: Constraints on State Action," *Alberta Law Review,* 22 (1984), 222-46; A. Wayne MacKay, "Fairness After The Charter: A Rose By Any Other Name?" *Queen's Law Journal,* 10 (1985), 263-335; Tom Cumming, "Fundamental Justice in the Charter," *Queen's Law Journal,* 11 (1986), 134-65; Bruce Chapman, "Criminal Law Liability and Fundamental Justice: Toward A Theory of Substantive Judicial Review," *University of Toronto Faculty of Law Review,* 44 (1986), 153-78.

On the meaning of "liberty" and "security of the person," see Tanya Lee, "Section 7 of the *Charter*: An Overview," *University of Toronto Law Review,* 43 (1985), 1-15 (arguing for a broad definition of liberty); Jean McBean, "The Implications of Entrenching Property Rights in Section 7 of the *Charter of Rights,*" *Alberta Law Review,* 26 (1988), 548-83 (examining, *inter alia,* "judicial amendment" of s.7 to encompass the protection of economic rights); and Ian Johnstone, "Section 7 of the *Charter* and Constitutionally Protected Welfare," *University of Toronto Faculty of Law Review,* 46 (1988), 1-47 (interpreting "security of the person" as protecting welfare benefits).

5. *Morgentaler, Smoling and Scott v. The Queen,* [1988] 1 S.C.R. 30.

6. *Reference re s.94(2) of the Motor Vehicle Act,* [1985] 2 S.C.R. 486, 24 D.L.R. (4th) 536, 560.

7. Decisions involving procedural fundamental justice include *Re Singh and Minister of Employment and Immigration,* [1985] 1 S.C.R. 177, 17 D.L.R. (4th) 422; *Spencer v. The Queen,* [1985] 2 S.C.R. 278, 21 D.L.R. (4th) 756; *Albright v. The Queen,* [1987] 2 S.C.R. 383, 45 D.L.R. (4th) 11; *R v. Sieben,* [1987] 1 S.C.R. 295; *R. v. Hamill,* [1987] 1 S.C.R. 301; *R. v. Vermette,* [1988] 1 S.C.R. 985; *Gamble v. The Queen,* [1988] 2 S.C.R. 595; *R. v. Potvin,* [1989] 1 S.C.R. 525; *Dupont v. Watier,* [1989] 1 S.C.R. 1588; *Thomson Newspapers v. Canada* (1990), 67 D.L.R. (4th) 161; *Stelco Inc. v. A.-G. Canada* (1990), 68 D.L.R. (4th) 518; *Swain v. The Queen,* [1991] 1 S.C.R. 933. Cases involving substantive fundamental justice include *Krug v. The Queen,* [1985] 2 S.C.R. 255, 21 D.L.R. (4th) 161; *Reference re s.94(2) of the Motor Vehicle Act,* [1985] 2 S.C.R. 486, 24 D.L.R. (4th) 536; *Republic of Argentina v. Mellino,* [1987] 1 S.C.R. 536, 40 D.L.R. (4th) 74; *United States of America v. Allard and Charette,* [1987] 1 S.C.R. 564, 40 D.L.R. (4th) 102; *Vaillancourt v. The Queen,* [1987] 2 S.C.R. 636, 47 D.L.R. (4th) 399; *Stevens v. The Queen,* [1988] 1 S.C.R. 1153; *Canada v. Schmidt,* [1987] 1 S.C.R. 500; *R. v. Laviolette,* [1987] 2 S.C.R. 667; *Cornell v. The Queen,* [1988] 1 S.C.R. 461; *R v. Beare* (1988), 55 D.L.R. (4th) 481.

Two important decisions have involved both procedural and substantive claims: *Lyons v. The Queen,* [1987] 2 S.C.R. 309, 44 D.L.R. (4th) 193; *R v. Milne,* [1987] 2 S.C.R. 512, 46 D.L.R. (4th) 487. In addition to these "liberty" and "security of the person" cases, the Court has also considered two cases involving the right to life: *Borowski v. A.-G. Canada,* [1989] 1 S.C.R. 342; and *Daigle v. Tremblay* (1989), 62 D.L.R. (4th) 634.

8. In *Sieben* and *Hamill,* the Crown conceded that provisions in the Narcotic Control Act infringed procedural principles of fundamental justice by permitting searches pursuant to writs of assistance as opposed to judicially authorized warrants. In *Gamble,* however, the Court decided by a three-to-two majority that a woman convicted and sentenced before the proclamation of the Charter to life imprisonment without eligibility for parole for twenty-five years under the wrong provisions of the Criminal Code was being denied liberty contrary to fundamental justice by the current operation of the parole ineligibility provision.

9. These cases are the *Motor Vehicle Reference, Vaillancourt,* and *Laviolette.* The two important cases are the *Motor Vehicle Reference* and *Vaillancourt.*

10. Monahan, *Politics and the Constitution,* 40-41; Morton, "The Political Impact of the Canadian Charter of Rights and Freedoms," 37-39.

11. *Spencer v. The Queen,* [1985] 2 S.C.R. 278, 21 D.L.R. (4th) 756; *Albright v. The Queen,* [1987] 2 S.C.R. 383, 45 D.L.R. (4th) 11; *R. v. Vermette,* [1988] 1 S.C.R. 985.

12. 21 D.L.R. (4th) 756, 761.

13. 45 D.L.R. (4th) 11, 20.

14. *Re Singh and Minister of Employment and Immigration,* [1985] 1 S.C.R 177, 17 D.L.R. (4th) 422. The Immigration Act, 1976 defined a Convention refugee as, *inter alia,* "any person who, by reason of a well-founded fear of persecution for reasons of ... political opinion, (a) is outside the country of his nationality and is unable or, by reason of such fear, is unwilling to avail himself of the protection of the country."

15. The legislative scheme of the Immigration Act, 1976 is set out in Justice Wilson's reasons for judgment at 17 D.L.R. (4th) 422, 445-455.

16. *Ibid.,* 465.

17. *Ibid.,* 466.

18. *Ibid.*

19. *Ibid.,* 462.

20. *Ibid.,* 469.

21. *Lyons v. The Queen,* [1987] 2 S.C.R. 309, 44 D.L.R. (4th) 193.

22. R.S.C. 1970, c. C-34, Part XXI, s.688.

23. 44 D.L.R. (4th) 193, 229-45.

24. *Ibid.,* 237.

25. *Ibid.*

26. *Ibid.,* 213-14.

27. *Ibid.,* 214.

28. *Ibid.*

29. *R. v. Milne,* [1987] 2 S.C.R. 512, 46 D.L.R. (4th) 487. The Court decided this case according to the same principle as *Lyons.*

30. *Republic of Argentina v. Mellino,* [1987] 1 S.C.R. 536, 40 D.L.R. (4th) 74; *United*

States of America v. Allard and Charette, [1987] 1 S.C.R. 564, 40 D.L.R. (4th) 102; *Canada v. Schmidt,* [1987] 1 S.C.R. 500. In two of the extradition decisions (*Mellino* and *Allard and Charette*), the Court could not find any violation of fundamental justice directly attributable to Canadian law or the actions of Canadian authorities. In the third extradition case, the Court held that, except under unusual circumstances, it does not violate substantive justice for Canada to extradite individuals to a foreign country for trial in accordance with that country's procedures, even if those procedures are deficient by Canadian constitutional standards.

31. *Cornell v. The Queen,* [1988] 1 S.C.R. 461. In *Cornell* the Court held that fundamental justice does not encompass equality rights, which are protected by section 15 of the Charter.
32. *R. v. Beare* (1988), 55 D.L.R. (4th) 481.
33. *Krug v. The Queen,* [1985] 2 S.C.R. 255, 21 D.L.R. (4th) 161.
34. 21 D.L.R. (4th) 161, 170.
35. *Ibid.,* 171.
36. The Court decided *Krug* two months before the *Motor Vehicle Reference.*
37. *Stevens v. The Queen,* [1988] 1 S.C.R. 1153.
38. *Ibid.,* 1161-74.
39. *Ibid.,* 1177.
40. *R. v. Vaillancourt,* [1987] 2 S.C.R. 636, 47 D.L.R. (4th) 399.
41. 47 D.L.R. (4th) 399, 414.
42. *Ibid.,* 415. The Court granted relief under s.7 on the same grounds in *R. v. Laviolette,* [1987] 2 S.C.R. 667.
43. *Stevens v. The Queen,* [1988] 1 S.C.R. 1153, 1176 (Wilson, J., dissenting).
44. *R. v. Martineau,* [1990] 2 S.C.R. 633.
45. [1991] 1 S.C.R. 933.
46. *Jones v. The Queen,* [1986] 2 S.C.R. 284, 31 D.L.R. (4th) 569; *Re Eve,* [1986] 2 S.C.R. 388, 31 D.L.R. (4th) 1; *Edwards Books and Art Ltd. v. The Queen,* [1986] 2 S.C.R. 713, 35 D.L.R. (4th) 1; *B.C.G.E.U. v. British Columbia,* [1988] 2 S.C.R. 214; *Operation Dismantle Inc. v. The Queen,* [1985] 1 S.C.R. 441, 18 D.L.R. (4th) 481; *Morgentaler, Smoling and Scott v. The Queen,* [1988] 1 S.C.R. 30, 44 D.L.R. (4th) 385.
47. 18 D.L.R. (4th) 481, 500-05 (*per* Wilson, J.). For a discussion of *Operation Dismantle*'s potential impact on legislative and executive decision-making, see J.R. Mallory, "'Beyond Manner and Form': Reading Between the Lines in *Operation Dismantle Inc. v. R.,*" *McGill Law Journal,* 31 (1986), 480-95.
48. 18 D.L.R. (4th) 481, 494 (*per* Dickson, C.J.).
49. *Ibid.,* 487. Emphasis added.
50. *Ibid.,* 490.
51. *Ibid.,* 485.
52. *Ibid.,* 481, 509.
53. *Ibid.,* 518.
54. *Ibid.* Justice Wilson argued that s.7 would apply if the threat were more direct. For example, if the government chose to test the missiles with live warheads, there would be a violation of s.7 that it could attempt to justify under s.1.

55. *Re Eve,* [1986] 2 S.C.R. 388, 31 D.L.R. (4th) 1.

56. 31 D.L.R. (4th) 1, 35.

57. *Parens patriae* is a doctrine in the law of equity according to which courts may exercise protective control over the person and property of children. Justice La Forest also indicated, however, that legislatures could decide that sterilization of the mentally incompetent is desirable for general social purposes. Such legislation, however, would then be subject to review under the Charter.

58. An Alberta Provincial Court judge initially acquitted Jones, but the Alberta Court of Appeal imposed conviction after deciding in favour of the Crown's appeal of the lower court decision.

59. 31 D.L.R. (4th) 569, 596.

60. *Ibid.,* 583.

61. *Edwards Books and Art Ltd. v. The Queen,* [1986] 2 S.C.R. 713, 35 D.L.R. (4th) 1.

62. 35 D.L.R. (4th) 1, 54.

63. *B.C.G.E.U. v. British Columbia,* [1988] 2 S.C.R. 214.

64. *Ibid.,* 245.

65. *Ibid.,* 246.

66. Hogg, *Constitutional Law of Canada,* 742.

67. *Ibid.,* 750.

68. Herbert L. Packer, *The Limits of the Criminal Sanction* (Palo Alto, Calif.: Stanford University Press, 1968), 158, 157.

69. *Ibid.,* 163-64.

70. Robert Harvie and Hamar Foster, "Ties That Bind? The Supreme Court of Canada, American Jurisprudence, and the Revision of Canadian Criminal Law Under The Charter," *Osgoode Hall Law Journal,* 28 (1990), 729-87.

71. Ralph A. Rossum, *The Politics of the Criminal Justice System* (New York: Marcel Dekker, 1978), 185. A good history of this period is found in Fred P. Graham, *The Due Process Revolution: The Warren Court's Impact on Criminal Law* (New York: Hayden Book Co., 1970). The Supreme Court has applied eleven of thirteen procedural guarantees in the Bill of Rights to the states. Two of the eleven were incorporated in 1948: see *In re Oliver,* 333 U.S. 257 (1948) (public trial) and *Cole v. Arkansas,* 333 U.S. 196 (1948) (notice). In 1949, the Court incorporated the Fourth Amendment's guarantee against unreasonable search and seizure (*Wolf v. Colorado,* 338 U.S. 25 (1949)), although it was not until 1961 that it incorporated the exclusionary rule in *Mapp v. Ohio,* 367 U.S. 643 (1961). The remaining eight guarantees were incorporated during the 1960s, including double jeopardy (*Benton v. Maryland,* 395 U.S. 784 (1969)), self-incrimination (*Malloy v. Hogan,* 378 U.S. 1 (1964)), speedy trial (*Klopfer v. North Carolina,* 386 U.S. 213 (1967)), jury trials (*Duncan v. Louisiana,* 391 U.S. 145 (1967)), confrontation (*Pointer v. Texas,* 380 U.S. 400 (1965)), compulsory process (*Washington v. Texas,* 388 U.S. 14 (1967)), right to counsel (*Gideon v. Wainwright,* 372 U.S. 335 (1963)), and cruel and unusual punishment (*Robinson v. California,* 370 U.S. 660 (1962)).

72. *Weeks v. United States,* 232 U.S. 383 (1914); *Wolf v. Colorado,* 338 U.S. 25 (1949).

73. Ralph A. Rossum and G. Alan Tarr, *American Constitutional Law: Cases and Interpretation,* 2nd ed. (New York: St. Martin's, 1987), 434.

74. *Mapp v. Ohio,* 367 U.S. 643 (1961).
75. Donald L. Horowitz, *The Courts and Social Policy* (Washington, D.C.: Brookings, 1977), 222-37; Stephen R. Schlesinger, "Criminal Procedure in the Courtroom," in James Q. Wilson, ed., *Crime and Public Policy* (San Francisco: Institute for Contemporary Studies, 1983), 192-200.
76. Rainer Knopff and F.L. Morton, *Charter Politics* (Toronto: Nelson Canada, 1992), 52.
77. Compare, for example, the outcomes in *R. v. Therens,* [1985] 1 S.C.R. 613 and *Manninen v. The Queen,* [1987] 1 S.C.R. 1233 with *R. v. Wray,* [1971] S.C.R. 272 and *Hogan v. The Queen,* [1975] 2 S.C.R. 574.
78. Morton, "The Political Impact of the Charter of Rights and Freedoms," 37.
79. The data that follow are from F.L. Morton, Peter H. Russell, and M.J. Withey, "The Supreme Court's First One Hundred Charter Decisions: A Statistical Analysis," Research Unit For Socio-Legal Studies, University of Calgary, 1990.
80. This is not surprising, of course, since it would be difficult to show that an otherwise unreasonable search or seizure was somehow a reasonable limit on Charter rights.
81. Contrary to American jurisprudence, it accepted the reasonableness of randomly stopping motor vehicles in *Hufsky v. The Queen,* [1988] 1 S.C.R. 621, 637. Similarly, a majority of the Court held in *Smith v. The Queen* (1989), 61 D.L.R. (4th) 462 that arrested or detained persons who fail to exercise their right to counsel diligently may not require the police to suspend their investigations or questioning. This is in marked contrast to the U.S. Court's decision in *Miranda v. Arizona* (1966), which declared that police must cease questioning at any time the detainee requests them to stop.
82. *Reference re Section 94(2) of the Motor Vehicle Act (B.C.)* (1985), 24 D.L.R. (4th) 536, 557 (noting U.S. recognition of the important relationship between liberty and procedural safeguards); *Vaillancourt v. The Queen,* [1987] 2 S.C.R. 636, 47 D.L.R. (4th) 399, 412-13 (noting decline of felony murder statutes in some U.S. jurisdictions); *Gamble v. The Queen,* [1988] 2 S.C.R. 595, 645-46 (noting the broad scope of the liberty interests served by *habeas corpus* remedies in U.S. jurisprudence).
83. [1985] 1 S.C.R. 177, 17 D.L.R. (4th) 422.
84. 17 D.L.R. (4th), 458, 469. Wilson actually found the U.S. jurisprudence on the specific question at issue too restrictive. *Ibid.,* 462-64.
85. These costs are outlined in Michael Mandel, *The Charter of Rights and the Legalization of Politics* (Toronto: Wall & Thompson, 1988), 172-83.
86. Laurence H. Tribe, *American Constitutional Law* (Mineola, N.Y.: Foundation Press, 1978), 502.
87. Christopher P. Manfredi, "Human Dignity and the Psychology of Interrogation in *Miranda v. Arizona,*" *Canadian Journal of Law and Society,* 1 (1986), 110-12; Packer, *The Limits of the Criminal Sanction,* 165-66.
88. Welsh S. White, "Police Trickery in Inducing Confessions," *University of Pennsylvania Law Review,* 127 (1979), 628; Mark Berger, *Taking The Fifth: The Supreme Court and the Privilege Against Self-Incrimination* (Lexington, Mass.: Lexington Books, 1980), 32.
89. 384 U.S. 436 (1966).

90. *Ibid.*, 448, 445, 455, 467, 460.

91. *In re Gault,* 387 U.S. 1, 47 (1967).

92. *Hunter v. Southam* (1984), 11 D.L.R. (4th) 641, 653.

93. *Katz v. United States,* 389 U.S. 347, 351 (1967).

94. 11 D.L.R (4th), 653 (emphasis in original); 389 U.S. 347, 356-57.

95. 11 D.L.R (4th) at 653. The Court exhibited a more moderate understanding of unreasonable search and seizure than its American counterpart in *Hufsky v. The Queen,* [1988] 1 S.C.R. 621, 637. In this instance, the Court rejected the American view that random stopping of motor vehicles is unreasonable.

96. [1985] 1 S.C.R. 613, 18 D.L.R. (4th) 655.

97. 18 D.L.R. (4th) at 680. Compare this with various statements about the nature of custodial interrogation made by Chief Justice Warren in *Miranda.* Caution is necessary in directly attributing Le Dain's statement to *Miranda,* since he did not cite this case in his reasons for judgment. It did appear, however, in Justice Lamer's reasons. See 18 D.L.R. (4th) at 665.

98. Harvie and Foster, "Ties That Bind?" 752-55.

99. *R. v. Oakes* (1986), 26 D.L.R. (4th) 200. Narcotic Control Act, R.S.C. 1970, c. N-1. Justice Estey, joined by Justice McIntyre, concurred separately in very brief reasons for judgment.

100. 26 D.L.R. (4th) at 212. Emphasis added.

101. The Court would unanimously uphold the principle that reverse onus provisions violate s.11(d) in *Schwartz v. The Queen* (1988), 55 D.L.R. (4th) 1. In this case, however, four justices held that s.106.7(2) of the Criminal Code does not create a reverse onus by requiring individuals charged with certain weapons offences to produce a valid registration certificate. Dickson dissented from this aspect of the decision.

102. 397 U.S. 358 (1970).

103. This was evident in Brennan's presentation to the Text and Teaching Symposium at Georgetown University (October 12, 1985). See *The Great Debate: Interpreting Our Written Constitution* (Washington, D.C.: The Federalist Society, 1986), 23-24.

104. 26 D.L.R. (4th) at 221.

105. 397 U.S. at 363-64.

106. *Ibid.,* 361.

107. See Anthony A. Morano, "A Reexamination of the Development of the Reasonable Doubt Rule," *Boston University Law Review,* 55 (1975), 507-28.

108. The Chief Justice of Saskatchewan, for example, struck down compulsory fingerprinting provisions in the Criminal Code on the grounds that they violated section 7's protection of the "dignity and worth of the person." The Supreme Court agreed with this conclusion in part, although largely for different reasons. See *R. v. Beare* (1988), 55 D.L.R. (4th) 481, 487, 492-93.

109. See, e.g., *R. v. Dyment* (1988), 55 D.L.R. (4th) 503 (holding that transferring blood samples taken by physicians during medical treatment to the police violates s.8), and *Duarte v. The Queen* (1990), 65 D.L.R. (4th) 240 (holding that police recording of conversations with the consent of a participant, but without prior judicial authorization, violates s.8).

110. (1988) 55 D.L.R. (4th) 673 at 706.

111. (1986) 26 D.L.R. (4th) 493 at 503.

112. 26 D.L.R. (4th) at 504-05. Citing *Adams v. United States,* 317 U.S. 269 (1942); *Minor v. United States,* 375 F.2d 170 (8th Cir. 1967); *Von Motke v. Gillies,* 332 U.S. 708 (1947).

113. Harvie and Foster, "Ties That Bind?" 750.

114. Tribe, *American Constitutional Law,* 504.

115. John Rawls, *A Theory of Justice* (Cambridge, Mass.: Harvard University Press, 1971), 440, 180-83.

116. 17 D.L.R. (4th) at 469.

117. *Askov v. The Queen* (1990), 74 D.L.R. (4th) 355.

118. *Ibid.,* 381.

119. *Lochner v. New York,* 198 U.S. 45 (1905); *Hammer v. Dagenhart,* 247 U.S. 251 (1918); *Bailey v. Drexel Furniture Company,* 259 U.S. 20 (1922); *Adkins v. Children's Hospital,* 261 U.S. 525 (1923).

120. See *Minutes of Proceedings and Evidence of the Special Joint Committee of the Senate and House of Commons on the Constitution of Canada,* 32nd Parliament, First Session, 45:9-33 (January 26, 1981); Alexander Alvaro, "Why Property Rights Were Excluded From the Canadian Charter of Rights and Freedoms," *Canadian Journal of Political Science,* 24 (1991), 309-29.

121. McBean, "The Implications of Entrenching Property Rights in Section 7 of the Charter of Rights," 554-59.

122. Section 2: *Reference re Public Service Relations Act (Alberta)* (1987), 38 D.L.R. (4th) 161. Section 7: *Edwards Books and Art Ltd. v. The Queen* (1986), 35 D.L.R. (4th) 1; *Reference re ss. 193 and 195 of the Criminal Code,* [1990] 1 S.C.R. 1123.

123. *Hunter v. Southam* (1984), 11 D.L.R. (4th) 641; *Thomson Newspapers v. Canada* (1990), 67 D.L.R. (4th) 161. The evolution of competition law is surveyed in Hogg, *Constitutional Law of Canada,* 406-09.

124. 67 D.L.R. (4th) at 303.

125. *Ibid.,* 213, 215-16.

126. *Ibid.,* 222-23 (La Forest); 289 (L'Heureux-Dubé).

127. *Ibid.,* 200.

128. *Ibid.,* 244, 246 (La Forest); 280-81 (L'Heureux-Dubé).

129. *Ibid.,* 173.

130. For an overview, see Katherine E. Swinton, *The Supreme Court and Canadian Federalism: The Laskin-Dickson Years* (Toronto: Carswell, 1990), 132-70.

131. *Morgentaler, Smoling and Scott v. The Queen,* [1988] 1 S.C.R. 30, 44 D.L.R. (4th) 385. The other cases are *Borowski v. A.-G. Canada,* [1989] 1 S.C.R. 342 and *Daigle v. Tremblay* (1989), 62 D.L.R. (4th) 634. *Borowski* also involved the constitutionality of section 251, but from the opposite side. At issue was whether the right to life guaranteed by s.7 of the Charter applied to fetuses, and if it did whether s.251 infringed that right. However, by the time the Court heard oral argument in the case, it had struck down s.251 in *Morgentaler, Smoling and Scott.* Consequently, it ruled Borowski's claim moot. At issue in *Daigle* was the validity of an interlocutory injunction granted by the Quebec Superior Court at the request of a woman's former boyfriend prohibiting her from having an abortion. Although counsel for the

boyfriend argued that the injunction was necessary to uphold the fetus's s.7 right to life, the Court found it unnecessary to address this issue because the dispute was a civil action between two private parties in which no government action was involved.

132. *Morgentaler v. The Queen,* [1976] 1 S.C.R. 616.

133. 44 D.L.R. (4th) 385, 397.

134. *Ibid.,* 461.

135. *Ibid.,* 490. Among the American cases cited by Justice Wilson were *Griswold v. Connecticut,* 381 U.S. 479 (1965); *Roe v. Wade,* 410 U.S. 113 (1973); *City of Akron v. Akron Center for Reproductive Health Inc.,* 462 U.S. 416 (1983). These U.S. cases involved several constitutional provisions, including the Fourth (prohibition against unreasonable searches and seizures), Fifth (privilege against self-incrimination), and Fourteenth (due process) Amendments.

136. *Ibid.,* 486.

137. *Ibid.,* 491 (emphasis in original).

138. Justice Wilson also contended that section 251 offended the freedom of conscience and religion guaranteed by section 2(a) of the Charter because it interfered with a decision that "is essentially a moral decision, a matter of conscience." *Ibid.,* 494.

139. *Ibid.,* 397. Justice Lamer concurred in the Chief Justice's reasons for judgment. Justice Beetz wrote a separate opinion along similar lines in which Justice Estey concurred. Justice La Forest concurred in Justice McIntyre's dissenting opinion.

140. *Ibid.,* 399.

141. *Ibid.,* 400.

142. *Ibid.,* 401.

143. *Ibid.,* 402.

144. *Ibid.*

145. *Ibid.,* 407.

146. *Ibid.*

147. These flaws are discussed *ibid.,* 408-12.

148. *Ibid.,* 414.

149. *Ibid.,* 412 (citing *Reference re s.94(2) of the Motor Vehicle Act* (1985), 24 D.L.R. (4th) 536, 550).

150. Rachel F. Moran, "Reflections on the Enigma of Indeterminacy in Child Advocacy Cases," *California Law Review,* 74 (1986), 627.

151. Christopher P. Manfredi, "Adjudication, Policy-Making and the Supreme Court of Canada: Lessons from the Experience of the United States," *Canadian Journal of Political Science,* 22 (1989), 328.

152. 44 D.L.R. (4th) at 474 (McIntyre, J., dissenting).

153. Monahan argues that this is inevitable in Charter adjudication. See Monahan, *Politics and the Constitution,* 68-71.

154. 44 D.L.R. (4th) at 394.

Chapter Five

1. Alexis de Tocqueville, *Democracy in America,* trans. H. Reeve (New York: Knopf, 1945), II:102, 304-05.

2. Alan C. Cairns, "Constitutional Minoritarianism in Canada," in Ronald L. Watts and Douglas M. Brown, eds., *Canada: The State of the Federation, 1990* (Kingston: Queen's University Institute of Intergovernmental Relations, 1990), 77.

3. Aristotle, *Nicomachean Ethics,* 1131a15; *Politics,* 1282b15, in Richard McKeon, ed., *The Basic Works of Aristotle* (New York: Random House, 1941).

4. Democracy, in particular, rests on the assumption that equality in one respect (free birth) implies absolute equality in all respects. See Aristotle, *Politics,* 1301a25.

5. John Locke, *Two Treatises on Government,* ed. Peter Laslett (New York: New American Library, 1960), II:4, 7, 309, 312.

6. *Ibid.,* II:54, 346.

7. Jefferson to Roger C. Weightman, June 26, 1826, in *The Works of Thomas Jefferson,* ed. Paul Leicester Ford (New York: G.P. Putnam's Sons, 1905), XII:477.

8. A.V. Dicey, *The Law of the Constitution,* 8th ed. (London: Macmillan, 1915), 107-22.

9. *Roncarelli v. Duplessis,* [1959] S.C.R. 121.

10. See Peter W. Hogg, *Constitutional Law of Canada,* 2nd ed. (Toronto: Carswell, 1985), 630-31; James G. Snell and Frederick Vaughan, *The Supreme Court of Canada: History of the Institution* (Toronto: University of Toronto Press, 1985), 207 n26.

11. See Dale Gibson, *The Law of the Charter: Equality Rights* (Toronto: Carswell, 1990), 62-63.

12. A summary of these criticisms can be found in Gwen Brodsky and Shelagh Day, *Canadian Charter Equality Rights For Women: One Step Forward or Two Steps Back?* (Ottawa: Canadian Advisory Council on the Status of Women, 1989), 145-83.

13. *Ibid.,* 187-201.

14. Two excellent summaries of policy developments in the human rights field on which I rely extensively are Walter S. Tarnopolsky, *Discrimination and the Law in Canada* (Toronto: Richard De Boo, 1982), 25-37; and Rainer Knopff, *Human Rights and Social Technology: The New War on Discrimination* (Ottawa: Carleton University Press, 1989), 35-70.

15. Fair accommodation legislation dealt with equality of access to "the accommodation, services or facilities available in any place to which the public is customarily admitted," and the provinces later extended this protection to residential and commercial accommodation. Fair employment legislation aimed at the same objective, and included two additional grounds of discrimination: sex and age.

16. Knopff, *Human Rights and Social Technology,* 39-40.

17. *Re Ontario Human Rights Commission et al. and Simpsons-Sears Ltd.* (1985), 23 D.L.R. (4th) 321 at 329.

18. Knopff, *Human Rights and Social Technology,* 39, 75-83.

19. John Rawls, *A Theory of Justice* (Cambridge, Mass.: Harvard University Press, 1971); Ronald Dworkin, *Taking Rights Seriously* (Cambridge, Mass.: Harvard University Press, 1978). The contribution of these two works to liberal conceptions of equality is ably discussed in Rogers M. Smith, *Liberalism and American Constitutional Law* (Cambridge, Mass.: Harvard University Press, 1985), 185-97.

20. For a discussion of systemic discrimination, see Knopff, *Human Rights and Social Technology,* 145-81.

21. For a discussion of affirmative action, see *ibid.*, 183-209; Tarnopolsky, *Discrimination and the Law in Canada*, 83-155.

22. This argument is made forcefully by Knopff, *Human Rights and Social Technology*, 30-31.

23. In particular, the Court's decision in *Saumur v. Quebec and A.-G. Quebec*, [1953] 2 S.C.R. 299 left open the possibility that Quebec could save its restrictions on Jehovah's Witnesses by simply amending the province's 1941 Freedom of Worship Act.

24. *R. v. Drybones*, [1970] S.C.R. 282; *A.-G. Canada v. Lavell* (1973), 38 D.L.R. (3d) 481; *Bliss v. A.-G. Canada* (1978), 92 D.L.R. (3d) 417. A companion case to *Lavell* was *Isaac et al. v. Bedard.*

25. *Law Society of British Columbia v. Andrews*, [1989] 1 S.C.R. 143 at 170.

26. *R. v. Drybones* (1969), 9 D.L.R. (3d) 473.

27. (1963) 41 D.L.R. (2d) 485.

28. *Ibid.*, 489-90 (*per* Cartwright, C.J.C.).

29. 9 D.L.R. (3d) at 476 (*per* Cartwright, C.J.C).

30. *Ibid.*, 477-86 (*per* Ritchie, J.).

31. Brodsky and Day, *Canadian Charter Equality Rights for Women*, 14.

32. 92 D.L.R. (3d) at 422.

33. David Baker, "The Changing Norms of Equality in the Supreme Court of Canada," *Supreme Court Law Review*, 9 (1987), 519.

34. (1981) 124 D.L.R. (3d) 1.

35. *Ibid.*, 8-10.

36. *Regents of University of California v. Bakke*, 438 U.S. 265 (1978); *United Steelworkers of America v. Weber*, 443 U.S. 193 (1979).

37. (1985) 23 D.L.R. (4th) 321; (1985) 23 D.L.R. (4th) 481.

38. (1985) 23 D.L.R. (4th) 321 at 329, 331. McIntyre borrowed this last statement from U.S. Supreme Court Justice Felix Frankfurter's dissent in *Dennis v. United States*, 339 U.S. 162, 184 (1949).

39. (1985) 23 D.L.R. (4th) 481 at 498.

40. (1987) 40 D.L.R. (4th) 193.

41. *Ibid.*, 199.

42. *Ibid.*, 205-09.

43. *Ibid.*, 213-14.

44. *Ibid.*, 215.

45. Interpretation Act, R.S.C. 285, c. I-21.

46. *Brooks v. Canada Safeway Ltd.* (1988), 59 D.L.R. (4th) 321.

47. *Ibid.*, 339.

48. *Ibid.*, 341, 339.

49. *Ibid.*, 344.

50. Hogg, *Constitutional Law of Canada*, 797.

51. The data discussed in this paragraph are drawn from tables prepared by the Special Joint Committee. See *Minutes of Proceedings and Evidence of the Special Joint Committee of the Senate and House of Commons on the Constitution of Canada*, 32nd Parliament, 1st Session, 52:92-96 (February 13, 1981).

52. Section 7 was the subject of 24.8 per cent of the specific submissions, while ss. 8-14 combined to attract 35.5 per cent of these submissions.
53. Roy Romanow, John Whyte, and Howard Leeson, *Canada Notwithstanding: The Making of the Constitution, 1976-1982* (Toronto: Carswell/Methuen, 1984), 253-55.
54. Section 28 provides that "[n]otwithstanding anything in this Charter, the rights and freedoms referred to in it are guaranteed equally to male and female persons." See Penney Kome, *The Taking of Twenty-Eight: Women Challenge the Constitution* (Toronto: Women's Press, 1983).
55. *Minutes and Proceedings of the Special Joint Committee,* 47:88-92 (January 28, 1981); 48:17-48 (January 29, 1981).
56. *Ibid.,* 48:25 (January 29, 1981). Senator Duff Roblin was particularly concerned about the impact this might have on the practice of reserving high-level policy-making positions for members of the governing political party.
57. *Ibid.,* 48:28, 33 (January 29, 1981).
58. Clare F. Beckton, "Section 15 of the *Charter* – Statute Audits and the Search For Equality," *Saskatchewan Law Review,* 50 (1986), 113.
59. *Ibid.,* 119-20.
60. Brodsky and Day, *Canadian Charter Equality Rights For Women,* 217-77.
61. *Re Blainey and Ontario Hockey Association* (1986), 26 D.L.R. (4th) 728 (Ont. C.A.); *Schacter v. The Queen* (1990), 66 D.L.R. (4th) 635 (F.C.A.) affirming (1988), 52 D.L.R. (4th) 525 (F.C.T.D.).
62. 26 D.L.R. (4th) at 735, 747.
63. *R.W.D.S.U v. Dolphin Delivery* (1986), 33 D.L.R. (4th) at 197.
64. See, e.g., Jody Freeman, "Justifying Exclusion: A Feminist Analysis of the Conflict between Equality and Association Rights," *University of Toronto Faculty of Law Review,* 47 (1989), 269-316; *Re Tomen and Federation of Women Teachers' Associations of Ontario* (1989), 61 D.L.R (4th) 565 (Ont. C.A.).
65. (1988) 52 D.L.R. (4th) 525 at 539, 542.
66. *Ibid.,* 548. The Federal Court of Appeal later upheld the trial judge's competence to issue this remedy.
67. Michael Mandel, *The Charter of Rights and the Legalization of Politics in Canada* (Toronto: Wall & Thompson, 1989), 270.
68. Parliament first included maternity benefits in the Act in 1971. Amendments to the Act in 1977, 1982, and 1988 gradually refined and extended the benefits available for child-care leave.
69. This phrase is from Rainer Knopff, "What Do Constitutional Equality Rights Protect Canadians Against?" *Canadian Journal of Political Science,* 20 (1987), 265-86.
70. See, e.g., *R. v. Big M Drug Mart,* [1985] 1 S.C.R. 295; *Morier v. Rivard,* [1985] 2 S.C.R. 716; *City of Brossard v. Pelletier,* [1986] 1 S.C.R. 53; *R. v. Hill,* [1986] 1 S.C.R. 313; *McDonald v. City of Montreal,* [1986] 1 S.C.R. 460; *Re Eve,* [1986] 2 S.C.R. 388; *Edwards Books and Art v. The Queen,* [1986] 2 S.C.R. 713; *A.-G. Manitoba v. Metropolitan Stores,* [1987] 1 S.C.R. 110; *Canada v. Schmidt,* [1987] 1 S.C.R. 500; *Reference re An Act to Amend the Education Act (Ontario),* [1987] 1 S.C.R. 1148; *O.P.S.E.U. v. Ontario (Attorney-General),* [1987] 2 S.C.R. 2; *R.W.D.S.U v. Dolphin Delivery,* [1987] 2 S.C.R. 573.

71. [1989] 1 S.C.R. 143. Andrews, a British subject permanently resident in Canada, brought the original dispute before the British Columbia Supreme Court in 1985. The Supreme Court of Canada added Kinersly, a U.S. citizen permanently resident in Canada and articling in British Columbia, as a co-respondent on January 28, 1987. The Court apparently took this step to avoid the problem of mootness, since Andrews acquired Canadian citizenship before the case was resolved.

72. [1989] 1 S.C.R. at 163-64.

73. *Ibid.,* 163-69.

74. Under this theory, section 1 would only become relevant if the government sought to justify otherwise unreasonable distinctions during periods of national emergency.

75. [1989] 1 S.C.R. at 178-81. See Peter Hogg, *Constitutional Law of Canada,* 2nd ed. (Toronto: Carswell, 1985), 800-01; *Andrews v. Law Society of British Columbia* (1985), 22 D.L.R. (4th) 600 at 610 (*per* McLachlin, J.A.); *Smith, Kline and French Laboratories Ltd. v. Canada (Attorney-General),* [1987] 2 F.C. 359 at 367-69 (*per* Hugessen, J.A.).

76. [1989] 1 S.C.R. at 170-71.

77. *Ibid.,* 174.

78. *Ibid.,* 181-82. McIntyre failed to note that he had also departed from this analytical approach in some cases, most notably the *Alberta Labour Reference.*

79. *Ibid.,* 182.

80. *Ibid.,* 183.

81. *United States v. Carolene Products,* 304 U.S. 144, 152-53 n4 (1938).

82. For a discussion of these "levels of scrutiny," see Ralph A. Rossum and G. Alan Tarr, *American Constitutional Law: Cases and Interpretation,* 2nd ed. (New York: St. Martin's, 1987), 544-64.

83. [1989] 1 S.C.R. at 152-53.

84. *Ibid.,* 184.

85. For a discussion of some laws that might fall into this category, see Knopff, "What Do Constitutional Equality Rights Protect Canadians Against?" 281-84.

86. Gerald Gunther, "The Supreme Court, 1971 Term – Forward: In Search of Evolving Doctrine on a Changing Court: A Model for a Newer Equal Protection," *Harvard Law Review,* 86 (1972), 8.

87. *R. v. Turpin,* [1989] 1 S.C.R. 1296.

88. *Ibid.,* 1329-30.

89. *Ibid.,* 1332.

90. *McKinney v. University of Guelph* (1990), 76 D.L.R. (4th) 545. The other cases include *Harrison v. University of British Columbia* (1990), 77 D.L.R. (4th) 55 and *Stoffman v. Vancouver General Hospital,* [1990] 3 S.C.R. 483.

91. 76 D.L.R. (4th) at 644-47 (*per* La Forest, J.); 76 D.L.R. (4th) at 600-10 (*per* Wilson, J.).

92. *Ibid.,* 654-60 (*per* La Forest, J.); 623-25 (*per* Wilson, J.).

93. *Ibid.,* 634 (*per* La Forest, J.).

94. *Ibid.,* 634-35.

95. *Ibid.,* 638-43.

96. *Ibid.,* 572-73 (*per* Wilson, J.).

97. *Ibid.,* 581-82.
98. *Ibid.,* 579-80.
99. *Ibid.,* 583-84.
100. *Ibid.,* 584-93.
101. *Ibid.,* 643-44.
102. Further evidence of this ascendancy can be found in the Abella Commission Report and the report of the Parliamentary Committee on Equality Rights. See Canada, Royal Commission on Equality in Employment, *Report of the Commission on Equality in Employment* (Ottawa, 1984); Standing Committee on Justice and Legal Affairs, Sub-Committee on Equality Rights, *Equality For All: Report of the Parliamentary Committee on Equality Rights* (Ottawa, 1985).
103. *Re Tomen and Federation of Women Teachers' Associations of Ontario* (1989), 61 D.L.R (4th) 565 (Ont. C.A.); *R. v. Keegstra,* [1990] 3 S.C.R. 697.
104. [1990] 3 S.C.R. 697 at 733, 755-57 (*per* Dickson, C.J.); 833-35, 847 (*per* McLachlin, J.).

Chapter Six

1. Katherine E. Swinton, *The Supreme Court and Canadian Federalism: The Laskin-Dickson Years* (Toronto: Carswell, 1990), 137-58.
2. Abram Chayes, "The Role of the Judge in Public Law Litigation," *Harvard Law Review,* 89 (1976), 1282-83, 1302.
3. On the incompatibility of traditional adjudication with public law litigation, see Donald L. Horowitz, *The Courts and Social Policy* (Washington, D.C.: Brookings, 1977); Colin S. Diver, "The Judge as Political Powerbroker: Superintending Structural Change in Public Institutions," *Virginia Law Review,* 65 (1979), 43-106; Eleanor Wolf, *Trial and Error: The Detroit School Segregation Case* (Detroit: Wayne State University Press, 1981); and Rogers Elliott, *Litigating Intelligence: IQ Tests, Special Education, and Social Science in the Courtroom* (Dover, Mass.: Auburn House, 1987).

   On the possibility of restructuring traditional adjudication, see Aryeh Neier, *Only Judgment: The Limits of Litigation in Social Change* (Middletown, Conn.: Wesleyan University Press, 1982), 170-93; Arthur Selwyn Miller and Jerome A. Barron, "The Supreme Court, the Adversary System, and the Flow of Information to the Justices: A Preliminary Inquiry," *Virginia Law Review,* 61 (1975), 1187-1245; Leif H. Carter, "When Courts Should Make Policy: An Institutional Approach," in John Gardner, ed., *Public Law and Public Policy* (New York: Praeger, 1977), 141-57; Ralph Cavanagh and Austin Sarat, "Thinking About Courts: Toward and Beyond a Jurisprudence of Judicial Competence," *Law and Society Review,* 14 (1980), 371-420.
4. For a review of the early jurisprudence interpreting section 1, see Peter W. Hogg, *Constitutional Law of Canada,* 2nd ed. (Toronto: Carswell, 1985), 678-90.
5. Lorraine Eisenstat Weinrib, "The Supreme Court of Canada and Section One of the Charter," *Supreme Court Law Review,* 10 (1988), 476.
6. *R. v. Oakes* (1986), 26 D.L.R. (4th) 200 at 225.
7. [1984] 2 S.C.R. 66.

8. Peter H. Russell, Rainer Knopff, and F.L. Morton, *Federalism and the Charter: Leading Constitutional Decisions* (Ottawa: Carleton University Press, 1989), 619.

9. [1984] 2 S.C.R. at 88. It would seem, however, that the establishment of an official state religion would not, in itself, constitute a total abrogation of freedom of religion. It would also be necessary to prohibit individuals from practising any other religion, perhaps under threat of criminal sanction.

10. Rainer Knopff, "What Do Constitutional Equality Rights Protect Canadians Against?" *Canadian Journal of Political Science,* 20 (1987), 279-80.

11. (1986) 26 D.L.R. (4th) 200.

12. *Ibid.,* 227-28.

13. Bernard H. Siegan, *Economic Liberties and the Constitution* (Chicago: University of Chicago Press, 1980), 324. According to Siegan, governments could defend constraints on liberty only by persuading a court that "the legislation serves important governmental objectives; . . . that the restraint imposed by government is substantially related to achievement of those objectives, that is, . . . the fit between means and ends must be close; and . . . that a similar result cannot be achieved by a less drastic means." For a criticism of Siegan's approach from an ideologically like-minded commentator, see Robert Bork, *The Tempting of America: The Political Seduction of the Law* (New York: Simon and Schuster, 1990), 224-29.

14. The most forceful critic of the view that the *Oakes* test endorses a balancing approach to constitutional rights is Weinrib, "The Supreme Court of Canada and Section One of the Charter," 470, 486.

15. T. Alexander Aleinikoff, "Constitutional Law in the Age of Balancing," *Yale Law Journal,* 96 (1987), 945-46; *Roe v. Wade,* 410 U.S. 113 (1973).

16. Patrick Monahan and Andrew Petter, "Developments in Constitutional Law: The 1985-86 Term," *Supreme Court Law Review,* 9 (1987), 103. Chief Justice Dickson's affinity for a "balancing" approach to section 1 is consistent with his view of constitutional interpretation in federalism cases. See Swinton, *The Supreme Court and Canadian Federalism,* 293-317.

17. *Re Singh and Minister of Employment and Immigration,* [1985] 1 S.C.R. 177 at 218-19.

18. *Edwards Books and Art v. The Queen* (1986), 35 D.L.R. (4th) 1; *Irwin Toy v. A.-G. Quebec* (1989), 58 D.L.R. (4th) 577 at 623-26.

19. *Ford v. Quebec (Attorney-General)* (1988), 54 D.L.R. (4th) 577; *A.-G. Quebec v. Irwin Toy Ltd.,* [1989] 1 S.C.R. 927.

20. David Beatty, *Talking Heads and the Supremes: The Canadian Production of Constitutional Review* (Toronto: Carswell, 1990), 116.

21. Max Farrand, ed., *The Records of the Federal Convention of 1787,* 4 vols. (New Haven: Yale University Press, 1966), 1:97. The quote is from Elbridge Gerry of Massachusetts.

22. *Morgentaler, Smoling and Scott v. The Queen,* [1988] 1 S.C.R. 30.

23. For a discussion of diversity as a value to be protected under section 1, see Swinton, *The Supreme Court and Canadian Federalism,* 340-42. Ironically, the absence of a national abortion law since the Court's decision in *Morgentaler, Smoling and Scott* has resulted in even greater diversity, with the provinces regulating access to

abortion under their health care laws. How long the courts will allow this situation to continue is uncertain.

24. *Seaboyer v. The Queen* (1991), 83 D.L.R. (4th) 193. Criminal Code, ss. 276, 277. The Court upheld section 277, but struck down section 276.

25. John Hart Ely, *Democracy and Distrust: A Theory of Judicial Review* (Cambridge, Mass.: Harvard University Press, 1980); Patrick Monahan, *Politics and the Constitution: The Charter, Federalism and the Supreme Court of Canada* (Toronto: Carswell/Methuen, 1987).

26. Diver, "The Judge as Political Powerbroker," 77-88, 90-103.

27. *Ibid.*, 46-48. See also Peter H. Russell, *The Judiciary in Canada: The Third Branch of Government* (Toronto: McGraw-Hill Ryerson, 1987), 5-10.

28. Alexander M. Bickel, *The Supreme Court and the Idea of Progress* (New York: Harper and Row, 1970), 175.

29. Horowitz, *The Courts and Social Policy,* 33.

30. *Ibid.*, 34-56. According to Horowitz, the five principal attributes of adjudication are that it is focused, piecemeal, passive, ill-adapted to ascertaining social facts, and fails to provide adequately for policy review. The best-known Canadian discussion of the impact of traditional adjudicative attributes on judicial policy-making is Paul Weiler, *In the Last Resort* (Toronto: Carswell, 1974). Potential problems of judicial incapacity under the Charter were also noted in its early implementation. See A. Wayne MacKay, "Fairness After The Charter: A Rose By Any Other Name?" *Queen's Law Journal,* 10 (1985), 297.

31. Donald L. Horowitz, "Decreeing Organizational Change: Judicial Supervision of Public Institutions," *Duke Law Journal* (1983), 1289.

32. Weinrib, "The Supreme Court of Canada and Section One of the Charter," 486.

33. Canada, Office of the Auditor General, *Report of the Auditor General of Canada: Fiscal Year Ended 31 March 1990* (Ottawa: Supply and Services Canada, 1990), 343, 348, 351.

34. Horowitz, *The Courts and Social Policy,* 45. See also Barry Strayer, *The Canadian Constitution and the Courts: The Function and Scope of Judicial Review* (Toronto: Butterworths, 1983), 56-57.

35. *Reference re Anti-Inflation Act,* [1976] 2 S.C.R. 373 at 424-25. Laskin discusses the general question of extrinsic evidence at 422-27.

36. Wolf, *Trial and Error,* 259-60. See also Elliott, *Litigating Intelligence.*

37. On the information-gathering weaknesses of appellate courts, see Thomas Marvell, *Appellate Courts and Lawyers: Information Gathering in the Adversary System* (Westport, Conn.: Greenwood Press, 1978), 184. See also Jethro K. Lieberman, ed., *The Role of Courts in American Society: Final Report of the Council on the Role of Courts* (St. Paul, Minn.: West Publishing, 1984), 148. On the axiomatic treatment of hypotheses by courts, see Ralph A. Rossum, "The Problem of Prison Crowding: On The Limits of Prison Capacity and Judicial Capacity," *Benchmark,* 1 (1984), 23.

38. See Peggy C. Davis, " 'There is a Book Out . . .': An Analysis of Judicial Absorption of Legislative Facts," *Harvard Law Review,* 100 (1987), 1539-1604.

39. [1985] 1 S.C.R. 441.

40. *Ibid.*, 454.

41. Canada, Committee on the Operation of the Abortion Law, *Report of the Committee on the Operation of the Abortion Law* (Ottawa: Supply and Services Canada, 1977), 3.

42. *Ibid.*, 146-47.

43. *Ibid.*, 310-11.

44. *Ibid.*, 93, 109, 139.

45. *Ibid.*, 141.

46. *Ibid.*, 17.

47. *Ibid.*, 66.

48. *Ibid.*, 57. The two exceptions were the Yukon Territory, where the rate dropped from 18.1 to 12.7 between 1973 and 1974, and Saskatchewan, where the rate went from 8.2 to 7.8 between the same two years.

49. *Ibid.*, 68. There were only eight such charges and convictions in 1971-72, according to the Report.

50. *Ibid.*, 93, 436.

51. *Ibid.*, 146-47.

52. *R. v. Askov* (1990), 74 D.L.R. (4th) 355.

53. See *R. v. Mills* (1986), 29 D.L.R. (4th) 161; *R. v. Rahey* (1987), 39 D.L.R. (4th) 481; *R. v. Conway*, [1989] 1 S.C.R. 1659; and *R. v. Smith*, [1989] 2 S.C.R. 1120.

54. The evidence contained in the Baar affidavit is discussed by Justice Cory at 74 D.L.R. (4th) 355 at 391-96.

55. *Askov v. The Queen*, Transcript of Appeal Proceedings, 23 March 1990, at 46, 49.

56. 74 D.L.R. (4th) at 398, 394.

57. Ronald Manzer, "Public Policy-Making as Practical Reasoning," *Canadian Journal of Political Science*, 17 (1984), 588.

58. Kenneth Kernaghan and David Siegal, *Public Administration in Canada*, 2nd ed. (Toronto: Nelson Canada, 1991), 118. Other disadvantages of incrementalism are discussed in Robert E. Goodin, *Political Theory and Public Policy* (Chicago: University of Chicago Press, 1982), 19-38.

59. Manzer, "Public Policy-Making as Practical Reasoning," 589.

60. Horowitz, *The Courts and Social Policy*, 36.

61. *Ibid.*, 38-45.

62. The attraction of litigation to these groups is the relative ease of access to the judicial process and the potentially significant spoils of victory. A favourable decision on constitutional grounds transforms the interest into a right, providing the group with a trump card in future policy deliberations. See William C. Louthan, *The Politics of Justice* (Port Washington, N.Y.: Kennikat Press, 1979).

63. See Stephen L. Wasby, "Civil Rights Litigation By Organizations: Constraints and Choices," *Judicature*, 68 (1985), 345-50.

64. F.L. Morton, "The Political Impact of the Canadian Charter of Rights and Freedoms," *Canadian Journal of Political Science*, 20 (1987), 40-41. Venue selection may be less important in Canada than in the United States because of our unitary court system. However, differing positions taken by provincial courts of appeal may influence where interest groups launch test cases. For insights into the American

experience, see Karen O'Connor and Lee Epstein, "Rebalancing the Scales of Justice: Assessment of Public Interest Law," *Harvard Journal of Law and Public Policy,* 7 (1984), 483-505; Edward V. Heck and Joseph Stewart, Jr., "Ensuring Access to Justice: The Role of Interest Group Lawyers in the 60s Campaign for Civil Rights," *Judicature,* 66 (1982), 84-95.

65. Miller and Barron, "The Supreme Court, the Adversary System, and the Flow of Information to the Justices," 1227.

66. Tom Cumming, "Fundamental Justice in the Charter," *Queen's Law Journal,* 11 (1986), 151.

67. This was especially apparent in *Edwards Books and Arts v. The Queen,* [1986] 2 S.C.R. 713. The other important decision in this area is *R. v. Big M Drug Mart Ltd.,* [1985] 1 S.C.R. 295.

68. Horowitz, *The Courts and Social Policy,* 51.

69. *Ibid.,* 52-53.

70. Jerome R. Corsi, *Judicial Politics: An Introduction* (Englewood Cliffs, N.J.: Prentice-Hall, 1984), 302. The U.S. Supreme Court, for example, found it exceedingly difficult to design a plan for implementing school desegregation after *Brown.* The best it could do was to exhort states to proceed with "all deliberate speed" toward desegregation. See *Brown v. Board of Education (II),* 349 U.S. 294, 301 (1955). See also Lino A. Graglia, "When Honesty is 'Simply . . . Impractical' for the Supreme Court: How the Constitution Came to Require Busing for School Racial Balance," *Michigan Law Review,* 85 (1987), 1156.

71. Donald L. Horowitz, "The Judiciary: Umpire or Empire?" *Law and Human Behavior,* 6 (1982), 137.

72. Miller and Barron, "The Supreme Court, the Adversary System, and the Flow of Information to the Justices," 1222.

73. *R. v. Askov* (1990), 74 D.L.R. (4th) 355, 389-90.

74. *Ibid.,* 396.

75. *Globe and Mail,* July 17, 1991, A5.

76. *Ibid.,* March 27, 1992, A1-2. In this decision (*Morin*), the Court emphasized the flexibility inherent in the *Askov* guidelines by accepting a trial delay of almost fifteen months. Interestingly, Justice Cory was not a member of the panel hearing this case.

77. These data are taken from the affidavit submitted to the Supreme Court in *Askov* by Ontario Deputy Attorney-General Richard F. Chaloner.

78. 74 D.L.R. (4th) at 401.

79. Tinsley E. Yarborough, "The Political World of Federal Judges as Managers," *Public Administration Review,* 45 (1985), 660.

80. *Ruiz v. Estelle,* 503 F. Supp. 1265, 1387-89 (S.D. Tex. 1980).

81. *Jenkins v. Missouri,* 672 F. Supp. 400, 410-15 (W.D. Mo. 1987).

82. Phillip J. Cooper, *Hard Judicial Choices: Federal District Court Judges and State and Local Officials* (New York: Oxford University Press, 1988), 16-24.

83. On standing, see Dale Gibson and Scott Gibson, "Enforcement of the Canadian Charter of Rights and Freedoms," in Gérald-A. Beaudoin and Ed Ratushny, eds., *The Canadian Charter of Rights and Freedoms,* 2nd ed. (Toronto: Carswell, 1989),

786-94. On intervener status, see Jillian Welch, "No Room at the Top: Interest Group Intervenors and Charter Litigation in the Supreme Court of Canada," *University of Toronto Faculty of Law Review,* 43 (1985), 204-31.

84. Michael S. Wald, "Thinking About Public Policy Toward Abuse and Neglect of Children: A Review of *Before The Best Interests of the Child,*" *Michigan Law Review,* 78 (1980), 678-79.

85. Cooper, *Hard Judicial Choices,* 18.

86. *Milliken v. Bradley,* 418 U.S. 717 (1974). Ironically, these limits may lead federal courts to create even broader remedies, as the court did in *Jenkins.*

87. *Re Phillips and Lynch* (1986), 27 D.L.R. (4th) 156.

88. *Ibid.,* 159.

89. *Schacter v. The Queen* (1988), 52 D.L.R. (4th) 525, 548 (F.C.T.D.).

90. *Schacter v. The Queen* (1990), 66 D.L.R. (4th) 635, 652 (F.C.A.). The Supreme Court reversed this decision on July 9, 1992.

91. See André Braen, "Les droits scolaires des minorités de langue officielle au Canada et l'interprétation judiciare," *Revue générale de droit,* 19 (1988), 335-36; Daniel Proulx, "La précarité des droits linguistiques scolaires ou les singulières difficultés de mise en oeuvre de l'article 23 de la Charte canadienne des droits et libertés," *Revue générale de droit,* 14 (1983), 366.

92. *Marchand v. Simcoe Board of Education* (1986), 29 D.L.R. (4th) 596, 621 (Ont. H.C.J.).

93. *Lavoie v. Nova Scotia* (1988), 47 D.L.R. (4th) 586, 593 (N.S.S.C.T.D.).

94. *Mahé v. Alberta* (1990), 68 D.L.R. (4th) 69.

95. *Ibid.,* 85.

96. *Ibid.*

97. *Ibid.,* 86.

98. *Reference re Electoral Boundaries Commission Act* (1991), 81 D.L.R. (4th) 16.

99. *Re Lavigne and Ontario Public Service Employees Union* (1986), 29 D.L.R. (4th) 321 (Ont. H.C.J.); *Re Lavigne and Ontario Public Service Employees Union (No. 2)* (1987), 41 D.L.R. (4th) 86 (Ont. H.C.J.); *Re Lavigne and Ontario Public Service Employees Union* (1989), 56 D.L.R. (4th) 474 (Ont. C.A.); *Lavigne v. Ontario Public Service Employees Union* (1991), 81 D.L.R. (4th) 545.

100. *National Citizens' Coalition v. A.-G. Canada* (1984), 11 D.L.R. (4th) 481 at 487-96 (Alta. Q.B.).

101. *Re Baldwin and B.C. Government Employees' Union* (1986), 28 D.L.R. (4th) 301 (B.C.S.C.).

102. 29 D.L.R. (4th) at 352.

103. *Ibid.,* 360.

104. *Ibid.,* 331-37.

105. *Ibid.,* 340. See *Abood v. Detroit School Board,* 431 U.S. 209 (1977).

106. 29 D.L.R. (4th) at 343.

107. *Ibid.,* 366.

108. *Ibid.,* 367.

109. *Ibid.,* 380.

110. *Ibid.,* 385.

111. *Ibid.*, 385-87.
112. For a critical analysis of the original *Lavigne* decision, see Brian Etherington, "Freedom of Association and Compulsory Union Dues," *Ottawa Law Review*, 19 (1987), 1-48.
113. 41 D.L.R. (4th) at 92-97.
114. *Ibid.*, 101.
115. *Ibid.*, 98.
116. *Ibid.*, 105-06.
117. 56 D.L.R. (4th) at 494-95 (Ont. C.A.).
118. The fact that the Court ordered Lavigne and the National Citizens' Coalition to pay all costs of the litigation deserves special mention, since it may have been intended by the Court to act as a deterrent to future litigation of this sort.
119. *A.-G. Quebec v. Irwin Toy*, [1989] 1 S.C.R. 927.
120. Indeed, in the case of the dividing line between vulnerable children and others, common-law principles would support an age as low as seven and as high as fourteen.

Chapter Seven

1. The description of courts as "oracles" of the constitution is taken from Rainer Knopff and F.L. Morton, *Charter Politics* (Toronto: Nelson Canada, 1992), 169-96.
2. David Beatty, *Talking Heads and the Supremes: The Canadian Production of Constitutional Review* (Toronto: Carswell, 1990), 261.
3. *Ibid.*, 265-66.
4. Technically, of course, the President is not directly elected by popular vote. In fact, the President is chosen by the electors in the electoral college of each state, who are selected by popular election in those states.
5. Philip M. Blair, *Federalism and Judicial Review in West Germany* (Oxford: Clarendon Press, 1981), 12-13.
6. Beatty, *Talking Heads and the Supremes*, 265.
7. One response to this argument is that membership in constitutional courts does not remain static, allowing sufficient opportunities for continuously changing legislative bodies to make appointments and thereby renew the democratic legitimacy of these courts. However, despite the rapid turnover in personnel on the Canadian Supreme Court since the Charter's entrenchment (eight of nine justices having been appointed since 1984), courts are relatively more stable institutions than legislatures. Consequently, membership in these bodies becomes increasingly unrepresentative of changing political forces. If it is unreasonable and illegitimate for contemporary citizens to be ruled by the anachronistic constitutional language of the document's framers and ratifiers (hence the need for "broad" and "purposive" constitutional interpretation), then it is equally illegitimate to expect contemporary political majorities to be ruled by the judicial appointments made by previous majorities.
8. Alexander Hamilton, James Madison, and John Jay, *The Federalist Papers*, ed. Clinton Rossiter (New York: New American Library, 1961), No. 81, 485.
9. The justices sitting on the Supreme Court at the end of 1991 had between nine and twenty-seven years left in their terms before reaching mandatory retirement.

10. Beatty, *Talking Heads and the Supremes,* 271. Beatty also discusses the Spanish and Italian cases, where appointment to the highest court is for nine years. European exceptions to this rule of fixed-term appointments are Austria, which follows Canada in imposing a mandatory retirement age, and Switzerland, which has renewable six-year terms.

11. *Ibid.,* 269.

12. *Ibid.,* 272-75.

13. This was the case, for example, in *A.-G. Quebec v. Association of Quebec Protestant School Boards,* [1984] 2 S.C.R. 66 and *Ford v. A.-G. Quebec* (1988), 54 D.L.R. (4th) 577.

14. Andrew Heard, "The Charter in the Supreme Court of Canada: The Importance of Which Judges Hear an Appeal," *Canadian Journal of Political Science,* 24 (1991), 304-07.

15. These reforms are also discussed in Peter H. Russell, *The Judiciary in Canada: The Third Branch of Government* (Toronto: McGraw-Hill Ryerson, 1987), 349-54.

16. Arthur Selwyn Miller and Jerome A. Barron, "The Supreme Court, the Adversary System, and the Flow of Information to the Justices: A Preliminary Inquiry," *Virginia Law Review,* 61 (1975), 1233-44.

17. Donald L. Horowitz, "Decreeing Organizational Change: Judicial Supervision of Public Institutions," *Duke Law Journal* (1983), 1297-1302.

18. Bertha Wilson, "Decision-Making in the Supreme Court," *University of Toronto Law Journal,* 36 (1986), 242-44.

19. Dale Gibson, "Judges As Legislators: Not Whether But How," *Alberta Law Review,* 25 (1987), 261-63. The last of these proposals is no longer available, since the government eliminated the Law Reform Commission in its 1992 budget.

20. This point is made by Donald Horowitz, *The Courts and Social Policy* (Washington, D.C.: Brookings, 1977), 298.

21. John Agresto, *The Supreme Court and Constitutional Democracy* (Ithaca, N.Y.: Cornell University Press, 1984), 107. Daniel Patrick Moynihan, "What Do You Do When the Supreme Court Is Wrong?" *Public Interest,* No. 57 (Fall, 1979), 3-24.

22. In 1940, Parliament acquired the constitutional power under section 91(2A) to enact unemployment insurance, overturning a 1937 decision of the Judicial Committee. In 1982, the provinces gained constitutional control over aspects of non-renewable natural resources under section 92A. This amendment reversed decisions rendered by the Supreme Court in 1978 and 1979.

23. Agresto, *The Supreme Court and Constitutional Democracy,* 107-11.

24. Constitution Act, 1982, s.38.

25. *Chisholm v. Georgia,* 2 U.S. 419 (1793); *Dred Scott v. Sandford,* 60 U.S. 393 (1857); *Pollock v. Farmers' Loan and Trust Company,* 157 U.S. 429 (1895); *Oregon v. Mitchell,* 400 U.S. 112 (1970). See David M. O'Brien, *Storm Center: The Supreme Court in American Politics,* 2nd ed. (New York: W.W. Norton, 1990), 362-63.

26. This episode is recounted effectively in O'Brien, *Storm Center,* 87-88. Shortly thereafter, the recalcitrant justices began to retire, and Roosevelt made eight appointments to the Court over the next six years.

27. *The Civil Rights Cases,* 109 U.S. 3 (1883). The Court upheld the 1964 Civil Rights Act in *Heart of Atlanta Motel v. United States,* 379 U.S. 241 (1964).

28. Agresto, *The Supreme Court and Constitutional Democracy,* 29.

29. *Swain v. The Queen,* [1991] 1 S.C.R. 933.

30. The alleged constitutional deficiencies of the new immigration procedures are canvassed in Beatty, *Talking Heads and the Supremes,* 222-45. The sexual assault provisions are considered below.

31. For a general discussion of this option, see Ralph A. Rossum, "Congress, the Constitution, and the Appellate Jurisdiction of the Supreme Court: The Letter and Spirit of the Exceptions Clause," *William and Mary Law Review,* 24 (1983), 385-428.

32. *Ex parte McCardle,* 74 U.S. (7 Wallace) 506 (1869).

33. Leonard G. Ratner, "Congressional Power Over the Appellate Jurisdiction of the Supreme Court," *University of Pennsylvania Law Review,* 109 (1960), 157.

34. Ralph A. Rossum and G. Alan Tarr, *American Constitutional Law: Cases and Interpretation,* 2nd. ed. (New York: St. Martin's, 1987), 49. This position was articulated by Justice William Douglas in his dissenting opinion in *Glidden Co. v. Zdanok,* 370 U.S. 530 (1962).

35. Rossum and Tarr, *American Constitutional Law,* 50.

36. Agresto, *The Supreme Court and Constitutional Democracy,* 121.

37. *Ibid.,* 134.

38. *Ibid.*

39. James Madison, "Observations on Jefferson's Draft of a Constitution for Virginia" (1788), in *The Writings of James Madison,* ed. G. Hunt, 9 vols. (New York: Putnam, 1900-1910), 5:294. Madison would not have allowed the executive to veto congressional overrides of judicial decisions.

40. For an early argument against entrenching a charter of rights, see Donald V. Smiley, "The Case Against the Canadian Charter of Human Rights," *Canadian Journal of Political Science,* 2 (1969), 277-91.

41. The details of these negotiations are set out in Roy Romanow, John Whyte, and Howard Leeson, *Canada Notwithstanding: The Making of the Constitution, 1976-1982* (Toronto: Carswell/Methuen, 1984), 193-215.

42. *Ibid.,* 211.

43. *House of Commons Debates,* 20 November 1981, 13042-43 (Jean Chrétien).

44. The legislation was Bill 62, An Act Respecting the Constitution Act, 1982. See Daniel J. Arbess, "Limitations on Legislative Override Under the Charter of Rights and Freedoms: A Matter of Balancing Values," *Osgoode Hall Law Journal,* 21 (1983), 117-19; Donna Greschner and Ken Norman, "The Courts and Section 33," *Queen's Law Journal,* 12 (1987), 161-62.

45. Greschner and Norman, "The Courts and Section 33," 155-59.

46. Stephen A. Scott, "Entrenchment By Executive Action: A Partial Solution to 'Legislative Override'," *Supreme Court Law Review,* 4 (1982), 287-303.

47. Arbess, "Limitations on Legislative Override Under the Charter of Rights and Freedoms," 140.

48. Greschner and Norman, "The Courts and Section 33," 166.

49. Peter Hogg, *Constitutional Law of Canada,* 2nd ed. (Toronto: Carswell, 1985), 690-92.

50. *Alliance des Professeurs de Montréal v. A.-G. Quebec* (1985), 21 D.L.R. (4th) 354.

51. *Ford v. A.-G. Quebec,* [1988] 2 S.C.R. 712 at 741.

52. *Ibid.,* 743.

53. See, generally, Arbess, "Limitations on Legislative Override Under the Canadian Charter of Rights and Freedoms"; Greschner and Norman, "The Courts and Section 33"; Brian Slattery, *"Canadian Charter of Rights and Freedoms* – Override Clause Under Section 33 – Whether Subject to Judicial Review Under Section 1," *Canadian Bar Review,* 61 (1983), 391-97.

54. Arbess, "Limitations on Legislative Override Under the Canadian Charter of Rights and Freedoms," 129.

55. Patrick Monahan, *Meech Lake: The Inside Story* (Toronto: University of Toronto Press, 1991), 165.

56. *House of Commons Debates,* 6 April 1989, 153 (Brian Mulroney).

57. Patrick Monahan, *Politics and the Constitution: The Charter, Federalism and the Supreme Court of Canada* (Toronto: Carswell/Methuen, 1987), 118-19.

58. Monahan, *Meech Lake,* 169.

59. Andrew Heard, *Canadian Constitutional Conventions: The Marriage of Law and Politics* (Toronto: Oxford University Press, 1991), 147.

60. See, e.g., *Forsythe v. The Queen,* [1980] 2 S.C.R. 268.

61. Bill C-49, 3d Session, 34th Parliament, 40 Elizabeth II, 1991.

62. Roger Tassé, "Application of the Canadian Charter of Rights and Freedoms," in Gérald-A. Beaudoin and Ed Ratushny, eds., *The Canadian Charter of Rights and Freedoms,* 2nd ed. (Toronto: Carswell, 1989), 103; Hogg, *Constitutional Law of Canada,* 692.

63. Samuel V. LaSelva, "Only in Canada: Reflections on the Charter's Notwithstanding Clause," *Dalhousie Review,* 63 (1983), 387.

64. A similar point is made in Knopff and Morton, *Charter Politics,* 189.

65. These discussions are found primarily in *Federalist* 78 and 81. See Alexander Hamilton, James Madison, and John Jay, *The Federalist Papers,* ed. Clinton Rossiter (New York: New American Library, 1961), 464-72, 481-91.

66. There is one statement in *Federalist* 78 that appears to contradict the assertion that legislatures possess an independent power of constitutional interpretation. According to Hamilton, it cannot be presumed that "the legislative body are themselves the constitutional judges of their own powers and that the construction they put upon them is conclusive upon the other departments" *unless* this presumption can be deduced from "particular provisions in the Constitution." There are at least two points that might be made about this statement. First, the term *conclusive* implies that what Hamilton wished to avoid was a situation in which the courts would have absolutely no role in judging legislation. As I shall argue later, this suggests that pre-emptive uses of section 33 may be inconsistent with liberal constitutional theory. The second point is that Hamilton appears to recognize that there is no inherent contradiction between liberal constitutional theory and particular constitutional provisions that might give the legislature the last word in defining its own powers. This is further

evidence that a legislative override does not necessarily contradict liberal constitutionalism. See *The Federalist Papers,* 467.

67. The actual history of the *Edwards* case is more complicated than this, of course. Indeed, despite commitments made by prime ministers and legislation conferring the status of "persons" on women in other contexts, the federal government actually defended a narrow and legalistic definition of section 24 before the Judicial Committee of the Privy Council. This somewhat contradictory behaviour may have been motivated by the government's desire to avoid the long-term implications of the "living tree" approach to constitutional interpretation. See A. Anne McLellan, "Legal Implications of the Persons Case," *Constitutional Forum,* 1 (1989), 11-14.

68. Michael Mandel, *The Charter of Rights and the Legalization of Politics in Canada* (Toronto: Wall & Thompson, 1989), 79.

69. Peter H. Russell, "Standing Up For Notwithstanding," *Alberta Law Review,* 29 (1991), 301-02.

70. Canada, *Shaping Canada's Future Together: Proposals* (Ottawa: Supply and Services, 1991), 4.

71. It should be noted that one change *not* suggested here is to extend the legislative override to the entire Charter. In principle, the argument advanced in this chapter would support such an extension, and the absence of an amendment to effect this expansion is primarily pragmatic: preserving section 33 is difficult enough without advocating its expansion. Nevertheless, the consistent application of the constitutional principles advocated here does not justify exempting any exercise of judicial review from legislative review. The only possible exception might be the basic rules governing the political process (e.g., right to vote, length of parliamentary sessions, etc.). However, one can say about these constitutional provisions what has been said about others: a political regime that allowed these basic rules to be fundamentally broken would cease to be a liberal democracy.

72. *Reference re British Columbia Motor Vehicle Act* (1985), 24 D.L.R. (4th) at 554.

73. See, generally, Heard, *Canadian Constitutional Conventions.*

74. According to this analytical approach, the decisions and actions of governments are best conceptualized as the result of political bargaining among a number of independent bureaucratic players. See Graham T. Allison, *Essence of Decision: Explaining the Cuban Missile Crisis* (Boston: Little, Brown, 1971), 162-81. The applicability of this approach to Canadian politics has been discussed in Kim Richard Nossal, "Allison Through the (Ottawa) Looking Glass: Bureaucratic Politics and Foreign Policy in a Parliamentary System," *Canadian Public Administration,* 22 (1979), 610-26; and Richard J. Schultz, *Federalism, Bureaucracy and Public Policy* (Montreal: McGill-Queen's University Press, 1980).

75. Agresto, *The Supreme Court and Constitutional Democracy,* 134.

Conclusion

1. This is the subtitle of Robert Bork's book, *The Tempting of America: The Political Seduction of the Law* (New York: Simon and Schuster, 1990). The phrase "legal

seduction of politics" is inspired by Michael Mandel, *The Charter of Rights and the Legalization of Politics in Canada* (Toronto: Wall & Thompson, 1989).

2. The original understanding of this problem in liberal democratic theory is best expressed by James Madison. See Alexander Hamilton, James Madison, and John Jay, *The Federalist Papers,* ed. Clinton Rossiter (New York: New American Library, 1961), No. 10, 78.

3. For a series of important essays on the question of technology in modern society, see George Grant, *Technology and Empire: Perspectives on North America* (Toronto: Anansi, 1969). Grant has also written of the modern tendency to debase the public in favour of the private. See Grant, *English-Speaking Justice* (South Bend, Indiana: University of Notre Dame Press, 1985), 11. This may in part explain the enthusiasm for solving public policy disputes in the private realm of litigation.

4. *Casagrande v. Hinton Roman Catholic Separate School District,* [1987] 4 W.W.R. 167 (Alta. Q.B.).

5. Section 29 provides that "[n]othing in this Charter abrogates or derogates from any rights or privileges guaranteed by or under the Constitution of Canada in respect of denominational, separate or dissentient schools."

6. Jane J. Mansbridge, *Why We Lost The ERA* (Chicago: University of Chicago Press, 1986), 29. The amendment repealing prohibition passed in 1933. What made the proposed Equal Rights Amendment so controversial that it failed was that its unique substantive implications were highly uncertain, especially given the presence of another "equality rights" provision (the Fourteenth Amendment) in the constitution. The ERA thus lacked the specificity that would clarify its future meaning, and therefore remained controversial.

7. Alan C. Cairns, "Constitutional Minoritarianism in Canada," in Ronald L. Watts and Douglas M. Brown, eds., *Canada: The State of the Federation, 1990* (Kingston, Ont.: Queen's University Institute of Intergovernmental Relations, 1990), 71-96.

8. Canada, *Shaping Canada's Future Together: Proposals* (Ottawa: Supply and Services, 1991).

9. *Ibid.,* 3.

10. Will Kymlicka and Wayne J. Norman, "The Social Charter Debate: Should Social Justice Be Constitutionalized?" *Network Analyses,* No. 2 (January, 1992), 2.

11. Ontario, *A Canadian Social Charter: Making Our Shared Values Stronger* (Ministry of Intergovernmental Affairs, September, 1991), 1.

12. Kymlicka and Norman, "The Social Charter Debate," 7-8.

Bibliography

Agresto, John. *The Supreme Court and Constitutional Democracy.* Ithaca, N.Y.: Cornell University Press, 1984.

Aleinikoff, T. Alexander. "Constitutional Law in the Age of Balancing," *Yale Law Journal,* 96 (1987): 943-1005.

Allison, Graham T. *Essence of Decision: Explaining the Cuban Missile Crisis.* Boston: Little, Brown, 1971.

Alvaro, Alexander. "Why Property Rights Were Excluded From the Canadian Charter of Rights and Freedoms," *Canadian Journal of Political Science,* 24 (1991): 309-29.

Arbess, Daniel J. "Limitations on Legislative Override Under the Charter of Rights and Freedoms: A Matter of Balancing Values," *Osgoode Hall Law Journal,* 21 (1983): 115-41.

Atcheson, M. Elizabeth, Mary Eberts, and Beth Symes. *Women and Legal Action: Precedents, Resources and Strategies for the Future.* Ottawa: Canadian Advisory Council on the Status of Women, 1984.

Baker, David. "The Changing Norms of Equality in the Supreme Court of Canada," *Supreme Court Law Review,* 9 (1987): 497-555.

Beatty, David M. *Talking Heads and the Supremes: The Canadian Production of Constitutional Review.* Toronto: Carswell, 1990.

Beaudoin, Gérald-A., and Ed Ratushny, eds. *The Canadian Charter of Rights and Freedoms,* 2nd ed. Toronto: Carswell, 1989.

Beckton, Clare F. "Section 15 of the *Charter* – Statute Audits and the Search For Equality," *Saskatchewan Law Review,* 50 (1986): 111-20.

Bender, Paul. "The Canadian Charter of Rights and Freedoms and the United States Bill of Rights: A Comparison," *McGill Law Journal,* 28 (1983): 811-66.

Berger, Mark. *Taking The Fifth: The Supreme Court and the Privilege Against Self-Incrimination.* Lexington, Mass.: Lexington Books, 1980.

269

Berger, Raoul. *Congress v. The Supreme Court.* Cambridge, Mass.: Harvard University Press, 1969.

Berger, Raoul. *Government By Judiciary: The Transformation of the Fourteenth Amendment.* Cambridge, Mass.: Harvard University Press, 1977.

Berger, Thomas R. *Fragile Freedoms: Human Rights and Dissent in Canada.* Toronto: Clarke, Irwin & Company, 1981.

Bickel, Alexander M. *The Supreme Court and the Idea of Progress.* New York: Harper and Row, 1970.

Blair, Philip M. *Federalism and Judicial Review in West Germany.* Oxford: Clarendon Press, 1981.

Bonner, Ethan. *Battle For Justice: How The Bork Nomination Shook America.* New York: W.W. Norton, 1989.

Bork, Robert H. *The Tempting of America: The Political Seduction of the Law.* New York: Simon & Schuster, 1990.

Braen, André. "Les droits scolaires des minorités de langue officielle au Canada et l'interpretation judiciare," *Revue générale de droit,* 19 (1988): 307-37.

Brest, Paul. "The Misconceived Quest For The Original Understanding," *Boston University Law Review,* 60 (1980): 204-54.

Brodsky, Gwen, and Shelagh Day. *Canadian Charter Equality Rights For Women: One Step Forward or Two Steps Back?* Ottawa: Canadian Advisory Council on the Status of Women, 1989.

Brooks, Roger. "*Garcia,* The Seventeenth Amendment, and the Role of the Supreme Court in Defending Federalism," *Harvard Journal of Law and Public Policy,* 10 (1987): 189-211.

Bushnell, S.I. "The Use of American Cases," *University of New Brunswick Law Journal,* 35 (1986): 157-81.

Cairns, Alan C. "Constitutional Minoritarianism in Canada," in Ronald L. Watts and Douglas M. Brown, eds., *Canada: The State of the Federation, 1990* (Kingston: Queen's University Institute of Intergovernmental Relations, 1990): 71-96.

Cairns, Alan C. "The Judicial Committee and Its Critics," *Canadian Journal of Political Science,* 4 (1971): 301-45.

Carter, Leif H. "When Courts Should Make Policy: An Institutional Approach," in John Gardner, ed., *Public Law and Public Policy* (New York: Praeger, 1977): 141-57.

Cavanagh, Ralph, and Austin Sarat. "Thinking About Courts: Toward and Beyond a Jurisprudence of Judicial Competence," *Law and Society Review,* 14 (1980): 371-420.

Chapman, Bruce. "Criminal Law Liability and Fundamental Justice: Toward A Theory of Substantive Judicial Review," *University of Toronto Faculty of Law Review,* 44 (1986): 153-78.

Chayes, Abram. "The Role of the Judge in Public Law Litigation," *Harvard Law Review,* 89 (1976): 1281-1316.

Christian, Timothy J. "Section 7 of the *Charter of Rights and Freedoms*: Constraints on State Action," *Alberta Law Review,* 22 (1984): 222-46.

Commager, Henry Steele. "Judicial Review and Democracy," in Leonard Levy, ed., *Judicial Review and the Supreme Court* (New York: Harper and Row, 1967).

Commager, Henry Steele. *Majority Rule and Minority Rights.* New York: Oxford University Press, 1943.

Cooper, Phillip J. *Hard Judicial Choices: Federal District Court Judges and State and Local Officials.* New York: Oxford University Press, 1988.

Corsi, Jerome R. *Judicial Politics: An Introduction.* Englewood Cliffs, N.J.: Prentice-Hall, 1984.

Cover, Robert M. "The Origins of Judicial Activism in the Protection of Minorities," *Yale Law Journal,* 91 (1982): 1287-1316.

Cumming, Tom. "Fundamental Justice in the Charter," *Queen's Law Journal,* 11 (1986): 134-65.

Davis, Peggy C. " 'There is a Book Out . . .': An Analysis of Judicial Absorption of Legislative Facts," *Harvard Law Review,* 100 (1987): 1539-1604.

Days, Drew S., III. "Civil Rights in Canada: An American Perspective," *American Journal of Comparative Law,* 32 (1984): 328-38.

de Tocqueville, Alexis. *Democracy in America,* 2 vols. tr. George Lawrence, ed. J.P. Mayer. New York: Doubleday, 1969.

Dicey, A.V. *Introduction to the Study of the Law of the Constitution,* 8th ed. London: Macmillan, 1915.

Diver, Colin S. "The Judge as Political Powerbroker: Superintending Structural Change in Public Institutions," *Virginia Law Review,* 65 (1979): 43-106.

Dworkin, Ronald. *Taking Rights Seriously.* Cambridge, Mass.: Harvard University Press, 1978.

Elkins, David J. "Facing Our Destiny: Rights and Canadian Distinctiveness," *Canadian Journal of Political Science,* 22 (1989): 699-716.

Elliott, Rogers. *Litigating Intelligence: IQ Tests, Special Education, and Social Science in the Courtroom.* Dover, Mass.: Auburn House, 1987.

Ely, John Hart. "The Wages of Crying Wolf: A Comment on *Roe v. Wade,*" *Yale Law Journal,* 82 (1973): 920-44.

Ely, John Hart. *Democracy and Distrust: A Theory of Judicial Review.* Cambridge, Mass.: Harvard University Press, 1980.

Epstein, Richard A. "Substantive Due Process By Any Other Name: The Abortion Cases," *Supreme Court Review* (1973): 159-85.

Epstein, Richard A. *Takings: Property and the Power of Eminent Domain.* Cambridge, Mass.: Harvard University Press, 1985.

Etherington, Brian. "Freedom of Association and Compulsory Union Dues," *Ottawa Law Review,* 19 (1987): 1-48.

Fairley, H. Scott. "Enforcing The Charter: Some Thoughts on an Appropriate and Just Standard for Judicial Review," *Supreme Court Law Review,* 4 (Special Issue, 1982): 217-54.

Farrand, Max, ed. *The Records of the Federal Convention of 1787,* 4 vols. New Haven: Yale University Press, 1966.

Forsey, E.A. "Disallowance of Provincial Acts, Reservation of Provincial Bills, and Refusal of Assent by Lieutenant-Governors since 1867," *Canadian Journal of Economics and Political Science,* 4 (1938): 47-59.

Freeman, Jody. "Justifying Exclusion: A Feminist Analysis of the Conflict Between

Equality and Association Rights," *University of Toronto Faculty of Law Review,* 47 (1989): 269-316.

Gibson, Dale. "Distinguishing the Governors from the Governed: The Meaning of 'Government' under Section 32(1) of the Charter," *Manitoba Law Journal,* 13 (1983): 505-22.

Gibson, Dale. "Judges As Legislators: Not Whether But How," *Alberta Law Review,* 25 (1987): 249-63.

Gibson, Dale. "The Charter of Rights and the Private Sector," *Manitoba Law Journal,* 12 (1982): 213-19.

Gibson, Dale. *The Law of the Charter: Equality Rights.* Toronto: Carswell, 1990.

Gold, Alan D. "The Legal Rights Provisions – A New Vision or Déjà Vu," *Supreme Court Law Review,* 4 (1982): 107-30.

Goodin, Robert E. *Political Theory and Public Policy.* Chicago: University of Chicago Press, 1982.

Government of Canada. *A Time For Action: Toward The Renewal of the Canadian Federation.* Ottawa: Supply and Services Canada, 1978.

Government of Canada, Committee on the Operation of the Abortion Law. *Report of the Committee on the Operation of the Abortion Law.* Ottawa: Supply and Services Canada, 1977.

Government of Canada, Office of the Auditor General. *Report of the Auditor General of Canada: Fiscal Year Ended 31 March 1990.* Ottawa: Supply and Services Canada, 1990.

Government of Canada, Royal Commission on Equality in Employment. *Report of the Commission on Equality in Employment.* Ottawa: Supply and Services Canada, 1984.

Government of Canada. *Shaping Canada's Future Together: Proposals.* Ottawa: Supply and Services Canada, 1991.

Government of Canada, Standing Committee on Justice and Legal Affairs, Sub-Committee on Equality Rights. *Equality For All: Report of the Parliamentary Committee on Equality Rights.* Ottawa: Supply and Services Canada, 1985.

Government of Canada. *Minutes of Proceedings and Evidence of the Special Joint Committee of the Senate and House of Commons on the Constitution of Canada,* 32nd Parliament, 1st Session (1980-81).

Government of Ontario. *A Canadian Social Charter: Making Our Shared Values Stronger.* Toronto: Ministry of Intergovernmental Affairs, 1991.

Graham, Fred P. *The Due Process Revolution: The Warren Court's Impact on Criminal Law.* New York: Hayden Book Co., 1970.

Graglia, Lino A. "When Honesty Is 'Simply . . . Impractical' for the Supreme Court: How the Constitution Came To Require Busing for School Racial Balance," *Michigan Law Review,* 85 (1987), 1153-82.

Grant, George. *English-Speaking Justice.* South Bend, Indiana: University of Notre Dame Press, 1985.

Grant, George. *Technology and Empire: Perspectives on North America.* Toronto: Anansi, 1969.

Greene, Ian. *The Charter of Rights.* Toronto: Lorimer, 1989.

Greschner, Donna, and Ken Norman. "The Courts and Section 33," *Queen's Law Journal,* 12 (1987): 155-98.

Gunther, Gerald, ed. *John Marshall's Defense of McCulloch v. Maryland.* Palo Alto, Calif.: Stanford University Press, 1969.

Gutmann, Amy. "Communitarian Critics of Liberalism," *Philosophy and Public Affairs,* 14 (1985): 308-22.

Hafen, Bruce C. "Exploring Test Cases in Child Advocacy," *Harvard Law Review,* 100 (1986): 435-49.

Hamilton, Alexander, James Madison, and John Jay. *The Federalist Papers,* ed. Clinton Rossiter. New York: New American Library, 1961.

Harmer, Lily. "The Right To Strike: Charter Implications and Interpretations," *University of Toronto Faculty of Law Review,* 47 (1989): 420-64.

Harvie, Robert, and Hamar Foster. "Ties That Bind? The Supreme Court of Canada, American Jurisprudence, and the Revision of Canadian Criminal Law Under The Charter," *Osgoode Hall Law Journal,* 28 (1990): 729-87.

Heard, Andrew. "The Charter in the Supreme Court of Canada: The Importance of Which Judges Hear an Appeal," *Canadian Journal of Political Science,* 24 (1991): 289-307.

Heard, Andrew. *Canadian Constitutional Conventions: The Marriage of Law and Politics.* Toronto: Oxford, 1991.

Heck, Edward V., and Joseph Stewart, Jr. "Ensuring Access to Justice: The Role of Interest Group Lawyers in the 60s Campaign for Civil Rights," *Judicature,* 66 (1982): 84-95.

Hogg, Peter W. "Is The Supreme Court Biased in Constitutional Cases?" *Canadian Bar Review,* 57 (1979): 721-39.

Hogg, Peter W. "The Charter of Rights and American Theories of Interpretation," *Osgoode Hall Law Journal,* 25 (1987): 87-113.

Hogg, Peter W. *Constitutional Law of Canada,* 2nd ed. Toronto: Carswell, 1985.

Holland, Kenneth M., ed. *Judicial Activism in Comparative Perspective.* New York: St. Martin's Press, 1991.

Holmes, Stephen. "The Permanent Structure of Antiliberal Thought," in Nancy L. Rosenblum, ed., *Liberalism and the Moral Life* (Cambridge, Mass.: Harvard University Press, 1989): 227-53.

Horowitz, Donald L. "Decreeing Organizational Change: Judicial Supervision of Public Institutions," *Duke Law Journal* (1983): 1265-1307.

Horowitz, Donald L. "The Judiciary: Umpire or Empire?" *Law and Human Behavior,* 6 (1982): 129-43.

Horowitz, Donald L. *The Courts and Social Policy.* Washington, D.C.: Brookings Institute, 1977.

Horowitz, Gad. "Conservatism, Liberalism and Socialism in Canada: An Interpretation," *Canadian Journal of Economics and Political Science,* 32 (1966): 143-71.

Hutchinson, Allan C., and Andrew Petter. "Private Rights/Public Wrongs: The Liberal Lie of the Charter," *University of Toronto Law Journal,* 38 (1988): 278-97.

Jaffa, Harry V. "What Were the 'Original Intentions' of the Framers of the Constitution of the United States?" *University of Puget Sound Law Review,* 10 (1987): 343-448.

Jaffa, Harry V. *Crisis of the House Divided: An Interpretation of the Issues in the Lincoln-Douglas Debates,* Phoenix edition reprint. Chicago: University of Chicago Press, 1982.

Jaffa, Harry V. *The Conditions of Freedom: Essays in Political Philosophy.* Baltimore: Johns Hopkins University Press, 1975.

Johnstone, Ian. "Section 7 of the *Charter* and Constitutionally Protected Welfare," *University of Toronto Faculty of Law Review,* 46 (1988): 1-47.

Kernaghan, Kenneth, and David Siegal. *Public Administration in Canada,* 2nd ed. Toronto: Nelson Canada, 1991.

Kesler, Charles R. "The Founders and the Classics," in James W. Muller, *The Revival of Constitutionalism* (Lincoln, Neb.: University of Nebraska Press, 1988): 43-68.

Knopff, Rainer. "What Do Constitutional Equality Rights Protect Canadians Against?" *Canadian Journal of Political Science,* 20 (1987): 265-86.

Knopff, Rainer. *Human Rights and Social Technology: The New War on Discrimination.* Ottawa: Carleton University Press, 1989.

Knopff, Rainer, and F.L. Morton. *Charter Politics.* Toronto: Nelson Canada, 1992.

Kome, Penney. *The Taking of Twenty-Eight: Women Challenge the Constitution.* Toronto: Women's Press, 1983.

Kymlicka, Will. *Liberalism, Community and Culture.* Oxford: Clarendon Press, 1991.

Kymlicka, Will, and Wayne J. Norman. "The Social Charter Debate: Should Social Justice Be Constitutionalized?" *Network Analyses,* No. 2 (January, 1992).

Lapsley, Arthur Brooks, ed. *The Writings of Abraham Lincoln,* 8 vols. New York: Lamb Publishing Co., 1906.

LaSelva, Samuel V. "Only in Canada: Reflections on the Charter's Notwithstanding Clause," *Dalhousie Review,* 63 (1983): 383-98.

Laskin, Bora. "'Peace, Order and Good Government' Re-Examined," *Canadian Bar Review,* 25 (1947): 1054-87.

Lee, Tanya. "Section 7 of the *Charter*: An Overview," *University of Toronto Law Review,* 43 (1985): 1-15.

Levy, Leonard W. *Original Intent and the Framers' Constitution.* New York: Macmillan, 1988.

Lieberman, Jethro K., ed. *The Role of Courts in American Society: Final Report of the Council on the Role of Courts.* St. Paul, Minn.: West Publishing, 1984.

Locke, John. *Two Treatises on Government,* ed. Peter Laslett. New York: New American Library, 1960.

Louthan, William C. *The Politics of Justice.* Port Washington, N.Y.: Kennikat Press, 1979.

MacIntyre, Alasdair. *After Virtue.* South Bend, Indiana: University of Notre Dame Press, 1981.

MacKay, A. Wayne. "Fairness After The Charter: A Rose By Any Other Name?" *Queen's Law Journal,* 10 (1985): 263-335.

Madison, James. "Observations on Jefferson's Draft of a Constitution for Virginia" (1788), in *The Writings of James Madison,* ed. G. Hunt, 9 vols. (New York: Putnam, 1900-1910).

Mallory, J.R. "Beyond 'Manner and Form': Reading Between the Lines in *Operation Dismantle Inc. v. R.*," *McGill Law Journal,* 31 (1986): 480-95.

Mallory, J.R. *Social Credit and the Federal Power in Canada.* Toronto: University of Toronto Press, 1954.

Mandel, Michael. *The Charter of Rights and the Legalization of Politics in Canada.* Toronto: Wall & Thompson, 1989.

Manfredi, Christopher P. "Human Dignity and the Psychology of Interrogation in *Miranda v. Arizona,*" *Canadian Journal of Law and Society,* 1 (1986): 109-24.

Manfredi, Christopher P. "Adjudication, Policy-Making and the Supreme Court of Canada: Lessons From the Experience of the United States," *Canadian Journal of Political Science,* 22 (1989): 313-35.

Manfredi, Christopher P. "The Use of United States Decisions By The Supreme Court of Canada Under The Charter of Rights and Freedoms," *Canadian Journal of Political Science,* 23 (1990): 499-518.

Manfredi, Christopher P. "*Re Lavigne and Ontario Public Service Employees Union*: Public Administration and Remedial Decree Litigation Under The Charter of Rights and Freedoms," *Canadian Public Administration,* 34 (1991): 395-416.

Manning, Morris. *Rights, Freedoms, and the Courts: A Practical Analysis of the Constitution Act, 1982.* Toronto: Emond-Montgomery, 1983.

Mansbridge, Jane J. *Why We Lost The ERA.* Chicago: University of Chicago Press, 1986.

Manzer, Ronald. "Public Policy-Making as Practical Reasoning," *Canadian Journal of Political Science,* 17 (1984): 577-94.

Marvell, Thomas. *Appellate Courts and Lawyers: Information Gathering in the Adversary System.* Westport, Conn.: Greenwood Press, 1978.

Massey, Calvin R. "The Locus of Sovereignty: Judicial Review, Legislative Supremacy, and Federalism in the Constitutional Traditions of Canada and the United States," *Duke Law Journal* (1990): 1229-1310.

McBean, Jean. "The Implications of Entrenching Property Rights in Section 7 of the *Charter of Rights,*" *Alberta Law Review,* 26 (1988): 548-83.

McCloskey, Robert G. *The American Supreme Court.* Chicago: University of Chicago Press, 1960.

McDonald, David C. *Legal Rights in the Canadian Charter of Rights and Freedoms,* 2nd ed. Toronto: Carswell, 1989.

McKeon, Richard, ed. *The Basic Works of Aristotle.* New York: Random House, 1941.

McLellan, Anne, and Bruce P. Elman. "To Whom Does the Charter Apply?: Some Recent Cases on s.32," *Alberta Law Review,* 24 (1986): 205-50.

McWhinney, Edward. *Judicial Review in the English-Speaking World,* 2nd ed. Toronto: University of Toronto Press, 1960.

Miller, Arthur Selwyn, and Jerome A. Barron. "The Supreme Court, the Adversary System, and the Flow of Information to the Justices: A Preliminary Inquiry," *Virginia Law Review,* 61 (1975): 1187-1245.

Miller, Arthur Selwyn. *Toward Increased Judicial Activism.* Westport, Conn.: Greenwood Press, 1982.

Monahan, Patrick. *Meech Lake: The Inside Story.* Toronto: University of Toronto Press, 1991.

Monahan, Patrick. *Politics and the Constitution: The Charter, Federalism and the Supreme Court of Canada.* Toronto: Carswell/Methuen, 1987.

Monahan, Patrick, and Andrew Petter. "Developments in Constitutional Law: 1986-1987," *Supreme Court Law Review,* 10 (1988): 61-145.

Monahan, Patrick, and Andrew Petter. "Developments in Constitutional Law: The 1985-86 Term," *Supreme Court Law Review,* 9 (1987): 69-180.

Moran, Rachel F. "Reflections on the Enigma of Indeterminacy in Child Advocacy Cases," *California Law Review,* 74 (1986): 603-48.

Morano, Anthony A. "A Reexamination of the Development of the Reasonable Doubt Rule," *Boston University Law Review,* 55 (1975): 507-28.

Morgan, Richard E. *Disabling America: The "Rights Industry" in Our Time.* New York: Basic Books, 1984.

Morton, F.L. "The Political Impact of the Canadian Charter of Rights and Freedoms," *Canadian Journal of Political Science,* 20 (1987): 31-55.

Morton, F.L. "The Politics of Rights: What Canadians Should Know About the American Bill of Rights," *Windsor Review of Legal and Social Issues,* 1 (1989): 61-96.

Morton, F.L., and Rainer Knopff. "Permanence and Change in a Written Constitution: The 'Living Tree' Doctrine and the Charter of Rights," 2 *Supreme Court Law Review,* 1 (1990): 533-46.

Morton, F.L., and Peter H. Russell. "The Supreme Court of Canada's First 100 Charter of Rights Decisions: A Quantitative Analysis," paper presented to the annual meeting of the Canadian Political Science Association, May 27-29, 1990.

Moynihan, Daniel Patrick. "What Do You Do When the Supreme Court is Wrong?" *Public Interest,* No. 57 (Fall, 1979): 3-24.

Mullan, David J. "Natural Justice and Fairness – Substantive as well as Procedural Standards for the Review of Administrative Decision-Making," *McGill Law Journal,* 27 (1982): 250-98.

Neal, Patrick, and David Paris. "Liberalism and the Communitarian Critique: A Guide for the Perplexed," *Canadian Journal of Political Science,* 23 (1990): 419-39.

Neier, Aryeh. *Only Judgment: The Limits of Litigation in Social Change.* Middletown, Conn.: Wesleyan University Press, 1982.

Nossal, Kim Richard. "Allison Through the (Ottawa) Looking Glass: Bureaucratic Politics and Foreign Policy in a Parliamentary System," *Canadian Public Administration,* 22 (1979): 610-26.

O'Brien, David M. *Constitutional Law and Politics: Civil Rights and Liberties.* New York: W.W. Norton, 1991.

O'Brien, David M. *Storm Center: The Supreme Court in American Politics,* 2nd ed. New York: W.W. Norton, 1990.

O'Connor, Karen, and Lee Epstein. "Rebalancing the Scales of Justice: Assessment of Public Interest Law," *Harvard Journal of Law and Public Policy,* 7 (1984): 483-505.

Packer, Herbert L. *The Limits of the Criminal Sanction.* Palo Alto, Calif.: Stanford University Press, 1968.

Perry, Michael J. *The Constitution, The Courts, and Human Rights.* New Haven: Yale University Press, 1982.

Powell, H. Jefferson. "The Original Understanding of Original Intent," *Harvard Law Review,* 98 (1985): 885-948.

Proulx, Daniel. "La précarité des droits linguistiques scolaires ou les singulières difficultés de mise en oeuvre de l'article 23 de la Charte canadienne des droits et libertés," *Revue générale de droit,* 14 (1983): 335-70.

Rabkin, Jeremy. *Judicial Compulsions: How Public Law Distorts Public Policy.* New York: Basic Books, 1989.

Ratner, Leonard G. "Congressional Power Over the Appellate Jurisdiction of the Supreme Court," *University of Pennsylvania Law Review,* 109 (1960): 157-202.

Rawls, John. *A Theory of Justice.* Cambridge, Mass.: Harvard University Press, 1971.

Romanow, Roy, John Whyte, and Howard Leeson. *Canada Notwithstanding: The Making of the Constitution, 1976-1982.* Toronto: Carswell/Methuen, 1984.

Rossum, Ralph A. *The Politics of the Criminal Justice System.* New York: Marcel Dekker, 1978.

Rossum, Ralph A. "Congress, the Constitution, and the Appellate Jurisdiction of the Supreme Court: The Letter and Spirit of the Exceptions Clause," *William and Mary Law Review,* 24 (1983): 385-428.

Rossum, Ralph A. "The Problem of Prison Crowding: On The Limits of Prison Capacity and Judicial Capacity," *Benchmark,* 1 (1984): 22-30.

Rossum, Ralph A. "The Courts and the Judicial Power," in Leonard W. Levy and Dennis J. Mahoney, eds., *The Framing and Ratification of the Constitution* (New York: Macmillan, 1987): 222-41.

Rossum, Ralph A., and G. Alan Tarr. *American Constitutional Law: Cases and Interpretation,* 2nd ed. New York: St. Martin's, 1987.

Russell, Peter H. "Standing Up For Notwithstanding," *Alberta Law Review,* 29 (1991): 293-309.

Russell, Peter H. "The Effect of a Charter of Rights on the Policy-Making Role of Canadian Courts," *Canadian Public Administration,* 25 (1982): 3-33.

Russell, Peter H. "The Political Purposes of the Canadian Charter of Rights and Freedoms," *Canadian Bar Review,* 61 (1983): 1-33.

Russell, Peter H. *The Judiciary in Canada: The Third Branch of Government.* Toronto: McGraw-Hill Ryerson, 1987.

Russell, Peter H., Rainer Knopff, and F.L. Morton, eds. *Federalism and the Charter: Leading Constitutional Decisions,* new ed. Ottawa: Carleton University Press, 1989.

Sandel, Michael. *Liberalism and the Limits of Justice.* Cambridge: Cambridge University Press, 1982.

Schlesinger, Stephen R. "Criminal Procedure in the Courtroom," in James Q. Wilson, ed., *Crime and Public Policy* (San Francisco: Institute for Contemporary Studies, 1983): 183-206.

Schultz, Richard. *Federalism, Bureaucracy and Public Policy.* Montreal: McGill-Queen's University Press, 1980.

Scott, Frank R. *Essays on the Constitution.* Toronto: University of Toronto Press, 1977.

Scott, Stephen A. "Entrenchment By Executive Action: A Partial Solution to 'Legislative Override'," *Supreme Court Law Review,* 4 (1982): 303-20.

Sharpe, Robert J. "Commercial Expression and the Charter," *University of Toronto Law Journal*, 37 (1987): 229-59.

Shugarman, David P., and Reg Whitaker, eds. *Federalism and Political Community*. Peterborough, Ont.: Broadview Press, 1989.

Siegan, Bernard H. *Economic Liberties and the Constitution*. Chicago: University of Chicago Press, 1980.

Slattery, Brian. *"Canadian Charter of Rights and Freedoms* – Override Clause Under Section 33 – Whether Subject to Judicial Review Under Section 1," *Canadian Bar Review*, 61 (1983): 391-97.

Slattery, Brian. "The *Charter*'s Relevance To Private Litigation: Does *Dolphin* Deliver?" *McGill Law Journal*, 32 (1987): 905-23.

Smiley, Donald. *Constitutional Adaptation and Canadian Federalism Since 1945*. Ottawa: Royal Commission on Bilingualism and Biculturalism, 1970.

Smith, Jennifer. "The Origins of Judicial Review in Canada," *Canadian Journal of Political Science*, 16 (1983): 115-34.

Smith, M.H. *The Writs of Assistance Case*. Berkeley: University of California Press, 1978.

Smith, Rogers M. *Liberalism and American Constitutional Law*. Cambridge, Mass.: Harvard University Press, 1985.

Snell, James G., and Frederick Vaughan. *The Supreme Court of Canada: History of the Institution*. Toronto: University of Toronto Press, 1985.

Stone, Dennis, and F. Kim Walpole. "The Canadian Constitution Act and the Constitution of the United States: A Comparative Analysis," *Canadian-American Law Journal*, 2 (1983): 1-36.

Storing, Herbert J. *What The Anti-Federalists Were For*. Chicago: University of Chicago Press, 1981.

Strayer, B.L. *Judicial Review of Legislation in Canada*. Toronto: University of Toronto Press, 1968.

Strayer, Barry. *The Canadian Constitution and the Courts: The Function and Scope of Judicial Review*. Toronto: Butterworths, 1983.

Swinton, Katherine E. *The Supreme Court and Canadian Federalism: The Laskin-Dickson Years*. Toronto: Carswell, 1990.

Tarnopolsky, Walter, and Gérald-A. Beaudoin. *The Canadian Charter of Rights and Freedoms: Commentary*. Toronto: Carswell, 1982.

Tarnopolsky, Walter S. "The New Canadian Charter of Rights and Freedoms as Compared and Contrasted with the American Bill of Rights," *Human Rights Quarterly*, 5 (1983): 227-74.

Tarnopolsky, Walter S. *Discrimination and the Law in Canada*. Toronto: Richard De Boo, 1982.

Tarnopolsky, Walter S. *The Canadian Bill of Rights*, 2nd rev. ed. Toronto: Macmillan of Canada, 1978.

Taylor, Charles. "Alternative Futures: Legitimacy, Identity and Alienation in Late Twentieth Century Canada," in Alan Cairns and Cynthia Williams, eds., *Constitutionalism, Citizenship and Society in Canada* (Toronto: University of Toronto Press, 1985).

The Federalist Society. *The Great Debate: Interpreting Our Written Constitution.* Washington, D.C., 1986.

Thigpen, Robert, and Lyle Downing. "Liberalism and the Communitarian Critique," *American Journal of Political Science,* 31 (1987): 637-55.

Tremblay, Luc. "Section 7 of the Charter: Substantive Due Process," *University of British Columbia Law Review,* 18 (1984): 201-53.

Tribe, Laurence. *American Constitutional Law.* Mineola, N.Y.: Foundation Press, 1978.

Tushnet, Mark. *Red, White, and Blue: A Critical Analysis of Constitutional Law.* Cambridge, Mass.: Harvard University Press, 1988.

Van Alstyne, William W. "A Critical Guide to *Marbury v. Madison*," *Duke Law Journal* (1969): 1-47.

Vaughan, Frederick. "Critics of the Judicial Committee of the Privy Council: The New Orthodoxy and an Alternative Explanation," *Canadian Journal of Political Science,* 19 (1986): 495-519.

Vipond, Robert C. "Constitutional Politics and the Legacy of the Provincial Rights Movement in Canada," *Canadian Journal of Political Science,* 18 (1985): 267-94.

Vipond, Robert C. *Liberty and Community: Canadian Federalism and the Failure of the Constitution.* Albany: State University of New York Press, 1991.

Wald, Michael S. "Thinking About Public Policy Toward Abuse and Neglect of Children: A Review of *Before the Best Interests of the Child*," *Michigan Law Review,* 78 (1980): 645-93.

Waltman, Jerold L., and Kenneth M. Holland, eds. *The Political Role of Law Courts in Modern Democracies.* New York: St. Martin's Press, 1988.

Wasby, Stephen L. "Civil Rights Litigation By Organizations: Constraints and Choices," *Judicature,* 68 (1985): 337-52.

Weiler, J.M., and R.M. Elliot, eds. *Litigating the Values of a Nation: The Canadian Charter of Rights and Freedoms.* Toronto: Carswell, 1986.

Weiler, Paul. *In the Last Resort.* Toronto: Carswell, 1974.

Weinrib, Lorraine Eisenstat. "The Supreme Court of Canada and Section One of the Charter," *Supreme Court Law Review,* 10 (1988): 469-513.

Welch, Jillian. "No Room at the Top: Interest Group Intervenors and Charter Litigation in the Supreme Court of Canada," *University of Toronto Faculty of Law Review,* 43 (1985): 204-31.

White, Welsh S. "Police Trickery in Inducing Confessions," *University of Pennsylvania Law Review,* 127 (1979): 581-629.

Whyte, John D. "Fundamental Justice: The Scope and Application of Section 7 of the Charter," *Manitoba Law Journal,* 13 (1983): 455-75

Wilson, Bertha. "Decision-Making in the Supreme Court," *University of Toronto Law Journal,* 36 (1986): 227-48.

Wolf, Eleanor. *Trial and Error: The Detroit School Segregation Case.* Detroit: Wayne State University Press, 1981.

Wolfe, Christopher. "A Theory of U.S. Constitutional History," *Journal of Politics,* 43 (1981): 292-316.

Yarborough, Tinsley E. "The Political World of Federal Judges as Managers," *Public Administration Review,* 45 (1985): 660-66.

INDEX OF CASES CITED

SUBJECT INDEX

Abbott, Douglas, 31
Aboriginal peoples, 130
Abortion, 19-21, 27, 34, 114, 204; absence of
national policy, 197; and balancing test,
161; and communitarianism, 214; and
community diversity, 163; and extrinsic
evidence, 167-69; and fundamental justice,
114-19; and legal rights, 93; public funding
in U.S., 197
Absolute liability, 57, 60, 93, 98, 100
Adams, John, 22, 24
Adjudication, 118, 164, 171-73
Adjudicative (historical) facts, 166
Administration of justice: and limited
resources, 111
Affirmative action, 47; and employment
discrimination, 133; and human rights
legislation, 126; and *section 15*, 120-21,
144, 153; and systemic discrimination,
135; *see also* Discrimination, Equality,
Human rights legislation
Agresto, John, 9, 198, 203
Alberta, 89, 147; and education, 71-72, 102;
and human rights legislation, 133; and
minority-language educational rights, 178;
and Social Credit legislation, 49-50; and
Victoria Charter, 13; labour legislation,
84-86
American civil rights jurisprudence, 14-15
Anti-Federalists, 12, 23
Aristotle, 121
Attributes of adjudication: adjudicative vs.
legislative facts, 166-70; and judicial
policy-making, 158; focus on rights,
165-66; incrementalism, 170-71; judicial
passivity, 171; policy review, 172
Auditor General, 166

Baar, Carl, 169
Badgley Report, 116-17, 119; as extrinsic
evidence, 167-69
Balancing test: and constitutional
interpretation, 61, 161; and judicial review,

71; and *Oakes* test, 161-62; and *section 1*,
81, 90; and *section 2*, 66, 83; *see also*
Oakes test, Reasonable limits
Barron, Jerome, 194
Beatty, David, 162-63, 190
Berger, Raoul, 22-23
Bickel, Alexander, 165
Blackmun, Harry, 191
Blakeney, Allan, 199
Bork, Robert, 42
Bourassa, Robert, 13, 79, 202
Brennan, William, 42, 56, 70, 109
British Columbia, 57, 142
Bureaucratic politics, 210
Burger, Warren, 55

Cairns, Alan, 120, 216, 217
Canada Elections Act, 180
Canadian Advisory Council on the Status of
Women, 139
Canadian Bill of Rights, 32-34; and abortion,
114; and Charter adjudication, 65, 100; and
equality, 45, 128-32; and frozen rights
theory, 89, 128; and principles of
fundamental justice, 58, 60; and refugee
proceedings, 95-96; and religious freedom,
66; interpretation by Supreme Court, 52,
60, 132; origin and structure, 32;
recognition of existing rights, 85; *see also*
Indian Act, Discrimination, Judicial power,
Judicial review
Canadian Civil Liberties Association, 171
Canadian Human Rights Act, 125, 135-36; *see
also* Human rights legislation
Canadian Labour Congress, 180
Canadian women's movement, 10
Cartwright, John, 129
Charter adjudication, 47, 76, 85; and
fundamental rights, 210; and judicial
power, 91; and living tree doctrine, 53; and
procedural rights, 92; and substantive
judicial review, 59; and traditional
decision-making, 20, 173; enforcement of